Ultimate Deno for Web Development

Build Lightning-Fast, Secure Web Applications with Deno Using TypeScript, React, Rust, and Cloud-Ready Tools like Docker, Azure, and Chocolatey

Prof. Veerendra Kumar Jain

www.orangeava.com

First Published: May 2025

Published By: Orange Education Pvt Ltd, AVA®

Address: 9, Daryaganj, Delhi, 110002, India

275 New North Road Islington Suite 1314 London,

N1 7AA, United Kingdom

ISBN (PBK): 978-93-49888-21-0

ISBN (E-BOOK): 978-93-49888-79-1

Scan the QR code to explore our entire catalogue

www.orangeava.com

Dedicated To

My Wife, Heera Rani Jain and My Grandsons, Aahan and Aryan Jain

For Their Unwavering, Boundless Support and Encouragement

About the Author

Prof. Veerendra Kumar Jain, BE (E), M.Tech (Applied Electronics), FIETE, FIE, and Life Member ISHRAE, is a versatile professional with a distinguished career spanning engineering, academia, and authorship. A retired CPWD engineer, he has authored over 150 technical books on diverse subjects, including computer science, IT, management, engineering, and architecture, with over 130 focused on computer science and IT. His expertise in computing covers a wide range of languages and technologies, from early languages such as COBOL and Fortran IV to modern tools such as Python, R, and Deno. He also holds a certificate in PC Awareness from NIIT, New Delhi and received training in Big Data and Hadoop from HCL Noida.

As of 2025, Prof. Jain imparts his knowledge in building services at prominent architecture and town planning institutions such as Amity University, Jamia Millia Islamia, Indraprastha University, Sunderdeep Group of Institutions, Vastukala Academy, Accurate Institute (Greater Noida), APG School of Planning and Architecture (Greater Noida), and TMU Moradabad. A renowned MEP consultant engineer and designated ME expert for the AICTE in India, he has contributed to numerous projects across the country.

Beyond his professional pursuits, Prof. Jain is a seasoned traveler, having explored over 30 major cities worldwide. His travels have taken him to iconic destinations across Europe, Asia, North America, and the Middle East, including London, Paris, New York, and Dubai.

Acknowledgements

I would like to express my gratitude to a few people for their continued and unwavering support throughout the writing of this book. First and foremost, I would like to thank my wife and grandsons for continuously encouraging me to write the book. I could have never completed this book without their support.

I also extend my sincere thanks for all the behind-the-scenes support provided by Sourabh Dwivedi, CEO of Orange Education Pvt Ltd.

My gratitude also goes to the entire AVA team–Priyanka, the project coordinator, Kriti Goel, Sonali and many others–for being supportive enough to improve my manuscript and for publishing my work in a very short time, providing a lot of facilities and guidance in editing and improving the content.

Preface

Deno is primarily used universally for building websites or applications. It is an open source runtime for JavaScript, TypeScript, and Web Assembly projects that is built on V8 and Rust. It is modern, fast, flexible, and secure by default. Deno is an alternative JavaScript runtime that uses V8 and Rust.

Deno is a modern runtime for JavaScript and TypeScript that aims to address some of Node.js's shortcomings, offering a more secure and efficient development experience. Deno is built to be safe. It keeps your code safe by making sure it cannot access data such as your files or the internet unless you authorize it.

Deno prioritizes security as its core principle. By default, it adopts a least-privilege approach, denying access to files, networks, child processes, and the environment unless explicitly granted. Every access request must be explicitly approved, ensuring a high level of control and security. For example, file access can be restricted to specific directories or files using permissions, limiting reading and writing capabilities. Similarly, network access can be controlled to specific IPs, domains, and more. Environmental interactions are also governed by permissions, ensuring a granular level of control.

Many applications need to manipulate file paths in one way or another; the Deno Standard Library provides simple utilities for this.

Downloading the code bundles and colored images

Please follow the links or scan the QR codes to download the ***Code Bundles and Images*** of the book:

https://github.com/ava-orange-education/Ultimate-Deno-for-Web-Development

The code bundles and images of the book are also hosted on ***https://rebrand.ly/5oq2b3w***

In case there's an update to the code, it will be updated on the existing GitHub repository.

Errata

We take immense pride in our work at **Orange Education Pvt Ltd,** and follow best practices to ensure the accuracy of our content to provide an indulging reading experience to our subscribers. Our readers are our mirrors, and we use their inputs to reflect and improve upon human errors, if any, that may have occurred during the publishing processes involved. To let us maintain the quality and help us reach out to any readers who might be having difficulties due to any unforeseen errors, please write to us at :

errata@orangeava.com

Your support, suggestions, and feedback are highly appreciated.

DID YOU KNOW

Did you know that Orange Education Pvt Ltd offers eBook versions of every book published, with PDF and ePub files available? You can upgrade to the eBook version at **www.orangeava.com** and as a print book customer, you are entitled to a discount on the eBook copy. Get in touch with us at: **info@orangeava.com** for more details.

At **www.orangeava.com**, you can also read a collection of free technical articles, sign up for a range of free newsletters, and receive exclusive discounts and offers on Print Books and eBooks.

PIRACY

If you come across any illegal copies of our works in any form on the internet, we would be grateful if you would provide us with the location address or website name. Please contact us at **info@orangeava.com** with a link to the material.

ARE YOU INTERESTED IN AUTHORING WITH US?

If there is a topic that you have expertise in, and you are interested in either writing or contributing to a book, please write to us at **business@orangeava.com**. We are on a journey to help developers and tech professionals to gain insights on the present technological advancements and innovations happening across the globe and build a community that believes Knowledge is best acquired by sharing and learning with others. Please reach out to us to learn what our audience demands and how you can be part of this educational reform. We also welcome ideas from tech experts and help them build learning and development content for their domains.

REVIEWS

Please leave a review. Once you have read and used this book, why not leave a review on the site that you purchased it from? Potential readers can then see and use your unbiased opinion to make purchase decisions. We at Orange Education would love to know what you think about our products, and our authors can learn from your feedback. Thank you!

For more information about Orange Education, please visit **www.orangeava.com**.

Table of Contents

CHAPTER 1
Introduction to Deno-Based Web Development

Introduction

Deno is a contemporary JavaScript/TypeScript runtime built on V8, Rust, and Tokio that is intended for web development. It improves security and lowers vulnerabilities by providing secure defaults and requiring explicit permissions for file, network, and environment access. Deno makes it simple to create applications without requiring a lot of configuration because it supports TypeScript natively and comes with an integrated toolchain. Deno is positioned as a Node substitute as well as .js, offering an experience that is more developer-friendly. There are resources available for those who want to learn more, including books that discuss Deno's ideas and real-world applications.

Structure

In this chapter, we will cover the following topics:

- Introduction to Deno
- V8 Version of Deno
- ES6 or the ECMAScript 2015
- Deno Web Development
- React/Next

Introduction to Deno

Deno is a safe Java runtime. It is a safe JavaScript and TypeScript runtime. The environment in which your code runs is called a runtime. It handles tasks such as memory management, I/O operations, and communication with external resources, providing the infrastructure your applications need to function. Your high-level code (TypeScript or JavaScript) must be converted into machine instructions that the computer can comprehend by the runtime.

A browser runtime is used when JavaScript is executed in a web browser, such as Chrome, Firefox, or Edge.

The browser and its runtimes are closely related. They include APIs for managing events, submitting network requests, modifying the Document Object Model (DOM), and more. These runtimes function within the security model of the browser and are sandboxed. They are unable to access resources such as the file system or environment variables that are not within the browser.

Deno offers a smooth JavaScript and TypeScript code execution experience. You might favor TypeScript's type safety or JavaScript's dynamic nature.

To use Deno, you do not need any additional software other than Deno itself:

Deno: A runtime for JavaScript, TypeScript, and WebAssembly that includes a built-in module manager and a standard library.

Project initializer: A built-in tool that creates a new Deno project with a basic file structure and configuration.

XCode Command Line Tools: Required for Mac users who want to build Deno from source.

CMake: Required for Mac users who want to build Deno from source.

Unique Features of DENO

The following are the some of the unique features of DENO:

Sandboxing

Sandboxing is a security practice in which you use an isolated environment, or a "sandbox," for testing. Within the sandbox, you run code and analyze the code in a safe, isolated environment without affecting the application, system, or platform.

Sandboxing is thus the practice of isolating a piece of software so that it can access only certain resources, programs, and files within a computer system, so as to reduce the risk of errors or malware affecting the rest of the system. "in theory sandboxing is a great idea–it allows for the execution of partially trusted code in a secure manner"

Security is Deno's top priority and guiding concept. It uses a least-privilege strategy by default, preventing access to networks, files, child processes, and the environment unless specifically authorized. High levels of control and security are ensured by the explicit approval of each access request. For instance, permissions can be used to limit reading and writing capabilities by restricting file access to particular directories or files. In a similar manner, network access can be restricted to particular IP addresses, domains, and more. Permissions also regulate environmental interactions, guaranteeing a fine degree of control.

A new security feature dubbed "deny," which was added to Deno in recent releases, enables the complete barring of several kinds of access. This denial list serves as an additional security measure, completing the allow list and offering a two-pronged defense strategy. Deno's security posture is greatly improved by its strict sandboxing methodology. Access privileges can be set generally or granularly, and a Deno process does not inherit the user's permissions when it is started. Without requiring actual container technology, this method produces an extremely secure environment for Deno's operation, much like operating inside a container.

Typescript Support

Because Deno has built-in support for TypeScript, installing other libraries is not necessary. TypeScript compilation is handled by Deno's built-in TSC/SWC compiler, which then transforms it into JavaScript for the V8 engine to run. Keep in mind that TypeScript is not yet directly supported by V8, therefore this modification is necessary.

With the exception of dynamic imports, the compiler converts TypeScript code to JavaScript when Deno is started. For TypeScript projects, this smooth integration guarantees a smooth experience and streamlines the setup procedure. In this process, the TSC/SWC compiler is essential since it allows Deno to manage the conversion in the background. Deno is a runtime that puts developer productivity and usability first by letting developers concentrate on writing code rather than worrying about technical details.

This subject is discussed in detail in *Chapter 3, Using TypeScript, JavaScript, and Rust with Deno* of this book.

Single Executable

Deno comes with a full range of development tools and is provided as a standalone executable. Several crucial elements are included in this single executable, including:

- **Core Engine:** Provides the framework for the runtime environment by executing TypeScript (TS) and JavaScript (JS) code.
- **Upgrade Manager:** Provides smooth upgrades so that users may take advantage of the newest features and improvements.
- **Format**: Code is automatically formatted for readability and uniformity.

- **Debugger/Inspector**: Enables effective code exploration and debugging.
- **Test Framework**: Enables thorough and trustworthy testing.
- **Lintern**: Examines code, pointing out possible mistakes and departures from best practices.
- **Bundler:** For easier deployment, bundle and package code and dependencies.
- **Code Coverage**: Offers information on the efficacy of testing.
- **Extra Tools and Utilities**: To accommodate a wide range of developers, Deno's executable comes with a number of additional basic tools.

Notably, Deno is self-contained, therefore no extra package managers or tool installations are required. There are no distinct dependencies to fetch and install; instead, the entire environment is configured as a single executable upon installation. Throughout the software development lifecycle, this simplified method promotes efficiency and simplicity, improving the development experience.

Third-Party Packages

Deno takes a different approach than Node.js, which mostly depends on its private package manager, NPM. Third-party packages can be hosted by Deno without the need for a package manager. Rather, it facilitates the use of standard ES modules, which can be accessed locally or over HTTP (we will learn more about these in a moment). This method provides a variety of hosting options, such as the local file system, GitHub, business web servers, and personal web servers. Before using these packages, Deno caches them. The rules that control file transfers across the World Wide Web (WWW) are known as HTTP or Hypertext Transfer Protocol. Images, movies, webpages, and other multimedia items are loaded via HTTP. It serves as the WWW's basis.

HTTPS stands for Hypertext Transfer Protocol Secure, a protocol that encrypts communication between a web browser and a website. Hypertext Transfer Protocol Secure (HTTPS) is the secure variant of HTTP, the main protocol that a web browser uses to communicate with a website. To improve data transfer security, HTTPS is encrypted. In order to emulate the Go programming language's strategy of obtaining packages from a variety of sources, Deno's developers were initially reluctant to embrace Node Package Manager (NPM). But as a replacement for Node.js, Deno had to deal with the loss of the enormous collection of 1.4 million NPM packages. This was a major barrier to uptake by businesses and developers. Since then, Deno has added support for NPM in response to user demand, balancing the original design principles with the requirement for package management. As of this writing, Deno is in complete support of NPM.

Top-Level Await

The top-level await function in Deno gives programmers a useful tool for handling asynchronous programming. This feature enables the await keyword to be used outside of conventional async functions, hence generating a broad async scope that affects how importing modules behave. These modules will wait for the Promise to be resolved before executing their main code.

This feature has a big impact on development even though it might not seem novel at first. It is no longer necessary to encapsulate code in async Immediately Invoked Function Expressions (IIFEs) just to use await because the await keyword may now be used across the codebase.

It is crucial to remember that this feature is not exclusive to Deno; rather, it is enabled by the V8 engine that underpins Deno. As a result, Deno can offer this feature, and its convenience has even extended beyond Deno to other runtime environments such as Node.js, which has also incorporated support for top-level await in its ES modules.

Standard Library

Deno distinguishes itself from Node.js by offering a comprehensive standard library, similar to Go's impressive standard library. A variety of peer-reviewed tools for everyday tasks are available in this vast library, including:

- File handling
- Hash generation
- HTTP request management
- Input/output management
- MIME type handling
- WebSocket connections
- Logging
- Date and time management
- UUID generation
- Cryptographic operations
- Stream handling

This library is actively maintained by the Deno team, guaranteeing its quality and relevance going forward. Interestingly, Deno's standard library APIs do not require antiquated callback methods because they only employ promises. With consistent and predictable techniques for handling asynchronous activities, this modern solution brings Deno into line with current asynchronous programming conventions and streamlines the development experience. Because of its improved usability and its extensive and inclusive standard library, Deno is a desirable option for developers looking to create dependable and effective applications.

Deno History

An important turning point in Deno's growth was marked on March 29, 2021, when the Deno team announced the founding of Deno Company. A group of investors, including Dan Scholnick from Four Rivers Ventures, Guillermo from Rauch Capital, Lee Jacobs from Long Journey Ventures, the Mozilla Corporation, Shasta Ventures, and Ben Noordhuis, gave the startup a $4.3 million seed investment, which was eventually raised to $4.9 million.

In the technical environment, Deno stands out as a rejuvenating force that gives the current ecology new life. Its goal is to provide a modern, effective programming framework that is nevertheless compatible with browser APIs. Instead of being a single, cohesive system, Deno is a collection of technologies that can be easily tailored to meet a variety of needs.

Understanding that not all serverside JavaScript scenarios require file system interaction, the underlying framework permits unnecessary connections to be removed.

Consider Electron-style graphical user interfaces, Cloudflare Workerstyle Serverless Functions, or even embedded scripts specifically designed for databases, since this clever method enables developers to create customized runtimes for a variety of applications.

V8 Version of Deno

Both Google's browser and V8 were initially made available in 2008. Google created the V8 JavaScript and WebAssembly engine for their Chrome web browser. V8 is open-source and free software that is used independently in non-browser contexts, such as the Node.js runtime system, and as part of the Chromium project.

V8 can be integrated into stand-alone projects or used in a browser. The following program makes use of V8:

- Chromium-based web browsers: Google Chrome, Brave, Opera, Vivaldi and Microsoft Edge
- Couchbase database server
- Deno runtime environment [1]
- Electron desktop application framework, used by the Atom and Visual Studio Code text editors
- MarkLogic database server
- NativeScript mobile application framework
- Node.js runtime environment

Here is a tabular representation of the evolution of modern operating systems:

Chrome 51	Edge 14	Firefox 52	Safari 10	Opera 38
May 2016	Aug-16	Mar-17	Sep-16	Jun-16

Table 1.1: *Date of Evolution of Modern Operating Systems*

ES6 or the ECMAScript 2015

The sixth major edition of the ECMAScript language specification standard is called ES6, or ECMAScript 2015. Compared to the previous edition, ES5, it has gained a lot of popularity and established the standard for JavaScript implementation.

The JavaScript language has undergone significant changes with ES6. To make JavaScript programming simpler and more enjoyable, it introduced a number of new features, including the let and const keywords, rest and spread operators, template literals, classes, modules, and many more. Some of the greatest and most well-liked ES6 capabilities that you can utilize in your regular JavaScript coding will be covered later. ES6 was a great success as well.

By March 2017, it was completely compatible with all major browsers, having been launched in 2015.

- Keywords for let and const
- Functions of Arrows
- Strings with multiple lines
- The default settings
- Literal templates
- The destructuring task improved object literals
- Enhanced object lLiterals
- Promises
- Classes
- Modules comprehending these features [2]

- **let and const Keywords**

  While the keyword "`const`" allows users to define constants, the keyword "`let`" allows users to define variables. Previously, "`var`" was used to declare variables, which were elevated to the top and had function scope. It indicates that using a variable prior to declaration is possible. However, the "`let`" variables and constants cannot be used before declaration since they have block scope, which is encircled by curly brackets "`{}`."

```
let i = 10;
console.log(i);   //Output 10

const PI = 3.14;
console.log(PI);  //Output 3.14
```

- **Arrow Functions**

  ES6 provides a feature known as Arrow Functions. It provides a more concise syntax for writing function expressions by removing the "**`function`**" and "**`return`**" keywords.

  Arrow functions are defined using the fat arrow (**`=>`**) notation.

```
// Arrow function
let sumOfTwoNumbers = (a, b) => a + b;
console.log(sum(10, 20)); // Output 30
```

It is clear that the arrow function declaration lacks the "**`return`**" and "**`function`**" keywords. When there is just one argument, we can also omit the parenthesis; but, when there are zero or more parameters, it must always be used. However, curly brackets ("**`{}`**") must be used to enclose the function body if it contains more than one expression. To return the necessary value, we must also utilize the "return" statement.

- **Multi-Line Strings**

  ES6 also provides Multi-line Strings. Users can create multi-line strings by using back-ticks(`).

  It can be done as follows:

```
let greeting = `Hello World,
       Greetings to all,
       Keep Learning and Practicing!`
```

- **Default Parameters**

  In ES6, users can provide the default values right in the signature of the functions. But, in ES5, the OR operator had to be used.

```
//ES6
let calculateArea = function(height = 100, width = 50) {
    // logic
}

//ES5
var calculateArea = function(height, width) {
   height =  height || 50;
   width = width || 80;
   // logic
}
```

- **Template Literals**

  ES6 introduces very simple string templates along with placeholders for the variables. The syntax for using the string template is **`${PARAMETER}`** and is used inside the back-ticked string.

  ```
  let name = `My name is ${firstName} ${lastName}`
  ```

- **Destructuring Assignment**

  One of ES6's most well-liked features is destructuring. Values from arrays or properties from objects can be easily extracted into separate variables using the destructuring assignment statement.

  Array destructuring and object destructuring are the two categories of destructuring assignment expressions. It can be applied in the ways listed as follows:

  ```
  //Array Destructuring
  let fruits = ["Apple", "Banana"];
  let [a, b] = fruits; // Array destructuring assignment
  console.log(a, b);

  //Object Destructuring
  let person = {name: "Peter", age: 28};
  let {name, age} = person; // Object destructuring assignment
  console.log(name, age);
  ```

- **Enhanced Object Literals**

  Enhanced object literals in ES6 facilitate the rapid creation of objects with properties enclosed in curly braces.

  ```
  function getMobile(manufacturer, model, year) {
     return {
        manufacturer,
        model,
        year
     }
  }
  getMobile("Samsung", "Galaxy", "2020");
  ```

- **Promises**

  In ES6, Promises are used for asynchronous execution. We can use promise with the arrow function as demonstrated here.

  ```
  var asyncCall =  new Promise((resolve, reject) => {
     // do something
     resolve();
  ```

```
}).then(()=> {
   console.log('DON!');
})
```

- **Classes**

  Classes were nonexistent in JavaScript before. Classes, which resemble classes in other object-oriented languages such as C++, Java, PHP, and so on are introduced in ES6. They do not, however, operate in precisely the same manner. Using the "**`extends`**" keyword to define inheritance, creating objects, and economically reusing code are all made easier by ES6 classes. A class can be declared in ES6 by utilizing the new "**`class`**" keyword and the class name.

```
class UserProfile {
   constructor(firstName, lastName) {
      this.firstName = firstName;
      this.lastName = lastName;
   }

   getName() {
     console.log(`The Full-Name is ${this.firstName} ${this.
lastName}`);
   }
}
let obj = new UserProfile('John', 'Smith');
obj.getName(); // output: The Full-Name is John Smith
```

- **Modules** [2]

  Previously, there was no native support for modules in JavaScript. ES6 introduced a new feature called modules, in which each module is represented by a separate ".js" file." We can use the "import" or "export" statement in a module to import or export variables, functions, classes or any other component from/to different files and modules.

```
export var num = 50;
export function getName(fullName) {
   //data
};
import {num, getName} from 'module';
console.log(num); // 50
```

Deno Web Development

Deno offers a secure and developer-friendly environment for building web applications, making your web development a delightful experience.

Deno has secure defaults, meaning it requires explicit permission for file, network, and environment access, reducing the risk of security vulnerabilities.

Deno has built-in TypeScript support, allowing you to write TypeScript code without additional configuration or tooling.

Deno comes with a standard library that includes modules for common tasks such as HTTP servers, file system operations, and more.

Most likely, if you are building a more complex application, you will be interacting with Deno through a web framework.

Deno Basics

Deno is a modern runtime for JavaScript and TypeScript that aims to address some of Node.js's shortcomings, offering a more secure and efficient development experience.

Here is what you need to know about Deno [3]:

- **Designed for Security**: Deno runs your code in a sandbox ensuring scripts cannot access your files or the network without permission.
- **Supports TypeScript Out of the Box**: You can run TypeScript code natively without additional tooling.
- **Includes a Standard Library**: Comes packed with a useful standard library for common tasks.
- **Simplifies Module Management:** Uses URLs for importing modules, eliminating the need for a package manager.
- **Easy to Install and Use**: You can quickly install Deno with a single command and start building applications.

Key Features and Benefits

Deno has some cool features that make coding better:

- **TypeScript Support** - You can use TypeScript right away without setting anything up. This makes coding faster.
- **Secure Defaults** - Your scripts cannot access your files or the internet unless you allow it. This keeps things safe.
- **Promise-Based APIs** - Deno uses promises, which are a modern way to handle tasks that take time, such as downloading files.

  API stands for Application Programming Interface. A Web API is an application programming interface for the Web. A Browser API can extend the functionality of a web browser. A Server API can extend the functionality of a web server.
- **Standard Library** - Deno comes with useful tools and web features such as fetch for getting data from the internet.

- **Single Executable** - Everything you need is in one file, making it easy to share and use your code.

These features help you write web apps more easily and safely, using the latest JavaScript tech without needing extra stuff.

Installation and Setup

To put Deno on your computer, follow these steps in your terminal:

MacOS/Linux:

```
curl -fsSL https://deno.land/x/install/install.sh | sh
```

Windows (PowerShell):

```
iwr https://deno.land/x/install/install.ps1 -useb | iex
This step grabs the latest Deno setup file and puts it in your
home directory under ~/.deno.
```

You can find other ways to install it, such as using different folders or package managers, on the Deno website.

Verify Installation

To make sure Deno is ready to go, type this in your terminal:

```
deno -version
```

If you see a version number, you are all set.

For instance:

```
deno 1.29.1
```

Upgrade Deno

To switch to the newest version:

```
deno upgrade
```

If you want a specific version:

```
deno upgrade --version 1.29.1
```

Deno will get the new version and update your current one.

It is a good idea to update Deno now and then to get the latest tools, security improvements, and fixes.

Your First Deno Program: Hello World

Starting with Deno is usually done with the simple "`Hello World`" program. This basic program shows a message to check that Deno is working and can run code.

The following line will cause to display the following message on the deno console:

```
console.log("Hello, World!");
```

You can alternatively write the greeting program in Indian style as shown here, **`console.log("Namaste, India!");`** to display output in the following figure:

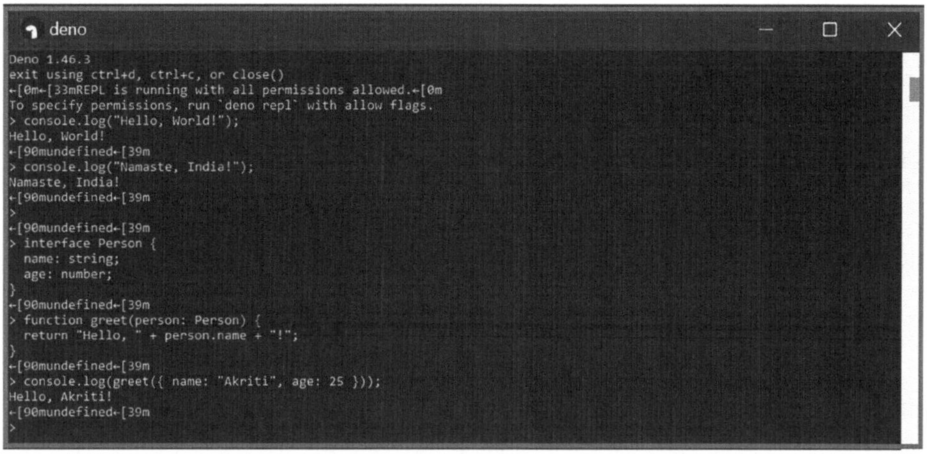

Figure 1.1: *Output of First Deno Program: Hello World*

Deno Program may be written in TypeScript (preferably) or Javascript.

Run this example locally using the Deno CLI:

```
deno run https://docs.deno.com/examples/hello-world.ts
```

Built-In TypeScript Support

Deno natively understands TypeScript code with no compiler to configure. Start writing code in **`.ts`** files, and the runtime will work with them just fine.

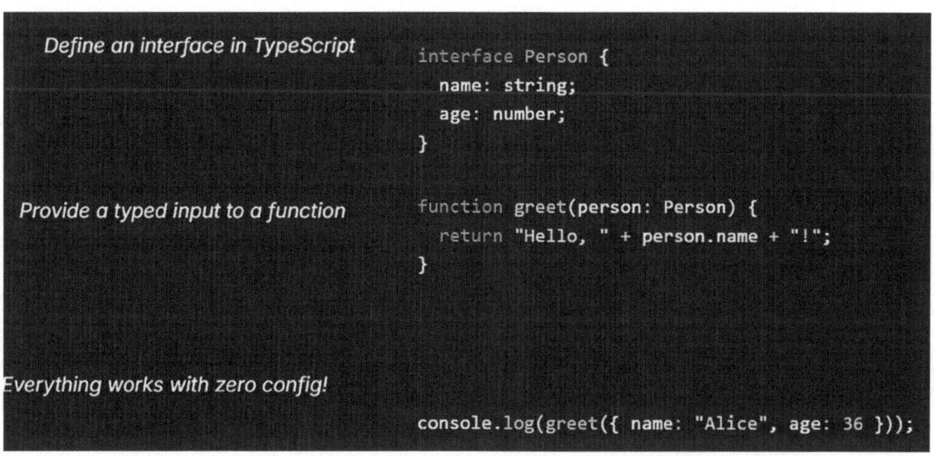

Figure 1.2: *The Explanation of Different Parts of the First Program*

Similarly, we can write,

```
interface Person {
  name: string;
  age: number;
}
function greet(person: Person) {
  return "Hello, " + person.name + "!";
}
console.log(greet({ name: "Akriti", age: 25 }));
```

Here is how to do a Hello World program in Deno:

```
console.log("Hello World");
```

To run this, put the code in a file like **`main.js`**.

Next, open your terminal, go to where the file is, and type:

```
deno run main.js
```

If Deno is working right, you will see **`"Hello World"`** on your terminal screen.

The deno run command lets you run the JavaScript file, just like how node works in Node.js.

Input Prompts

Prompts are used to ask the user for input or feedback on actions.

```
alert("Please acknowledge the message.");
console.log("The message has been acknowledged.");
const shouldProceed = confirm("Do you want to proceed?");
console.log("Should proceed?", shouldProceed);
const name = prompt("Please enter your name:");
console.log("Name:", name);
const age = prompt("Please enter your age:", "18");
console.log("Age:", age);
```

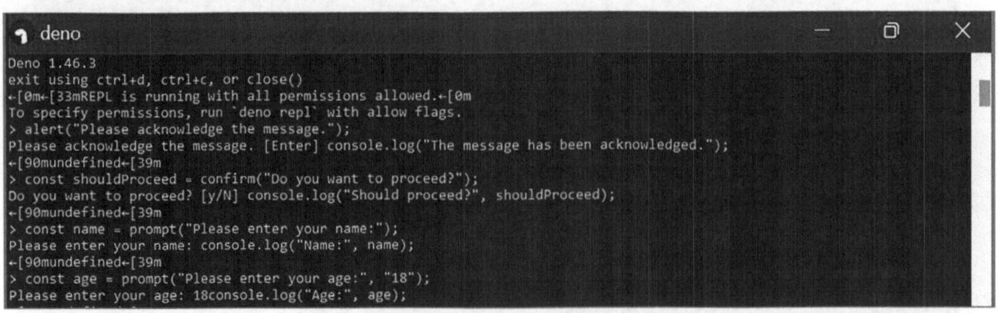

Figure 1.3: *Interactive Console*

Command Line Arguments

Command line arguments are often used to pass configuration options to a program.

You can get the list of command line arguments from `**Deno.args**`.

```
const name = Deno.args[0];
const food = Deno.args[1];
console.log(`Hello ${name}, I like ${food}!`);
```

Often you want to parse command line arguments such as **--foo=bar**` into structured data. This can be done using **std/cli**.

```
import { parseArgs } from "jsr:@std/cli/parse-args";
```

The **parseArgs** function takes the argument list and a list of options. In these options, you specify the types of the accepted arguments and possibly default values. An object is returned with the parsed arguments.

Note: *This function is based on [`minimist`](https://github.com/minimistjs/minimist), not compatible with the **parseArgs()** function in **node:util**.*

```
const flags = parseArgs(Deno.args, {
  boolean: ["help", "color"],
  string: ["version"],
  default: { color: true },
  negatable: ["color"],
});
console.log("Wants help?", flags.help);
console.log("Version:", flags.version);
console.log("Wants color?:", flags.color);
The `_` field of the returned object contains all arguments that
were not recognized as flags.
console.log("Other:", flags._);
```

HTTP Server: WebSockets

An example of an HTTP server that handles websocket requests.

To start the server on the default port, call `**Deno.serve**` with the handler.

```
Deno.serve((req) => {
```

First, we verify if the client is negotiating to upgrade to websockets. If not, we can give a status of 501 to specify we do not support plain http requests.

```
  if (req.headers.get("upgrade") != "websocket") {
    return new Response(null, { status: 501 });
  }
```

We can then upgrade the request to a websocket.

```
const { socket, response } = Deno.upgradeWebSocket(req);
```

We now have access to a standard websocket object. Let us handle the "**open**" event.

```
socket.addEventListener("open", () => {
        console.log("a client connected!");
});
```

We can also handle messages in a similar way. Here we set up a simple ping/pong example.

```
socket.addEventListener("message", (event) => {
  if (event.data === "ping") {
    socket.send("pong");
  }
});
```

Lastly, we return the response created from upgradeWebSocket.

```
  return response;
});
```

HTTP Server: Streaming

An example HTTP server that streams a response back to the client.

```
function handler(_req: Request): Response {
```

Set up a variable to store a timer ID and the ReadableStream.

```
let timer: number | undefined = undefined;
const body = new ReadableStream({
```

When the stream is first created, start an interval that will emit a chunk every second containing the current time.

```
start(controller) {
  timer = setInterval(() => {
    const message = `It is ${new Date().toISOString()}\n`;
    controller.enqueue(new TextEncoder().encode(message));
  }, 1000);
},
```

If the stream is closed (the client disconnects), cancel the interval.

```
cancel() {
  if (timer !== undefined) {
    clearInterval(timer);
  }
```

```
    },
  });
```

Return a response with the stream as the body.

```
  return new Response(body, {
    headers: {
      "content-type": "text/plain",
      "x-content-type-options": "nosniff",
    },
  });
}
```

To start the server on the default port, call **`Deno.serve`** with the handler.

```
Deno.serve(handler);
```

Figure 1.4: *Calling `Deno Server*

Path Operations

A lot of programs require some sort of file path manipulation. For this, the Deno Standard Library offers basic utilities. The Deno Standard Library module will be imported first.

```
import * as path from "jsr:@std/path";
import * as posix from "jsr:@std/path/posix";
import * as windows from "jsr:@std/path/windows";
```

Converting from a file url to a directory can be done simply by the `from **FileUrl**` method from the appropriate implementation.

```
const p1 = posix.fromFileUrl("file:///home/foo");
const p2 = windows.fromFileUrl("file:///home/foo");
console.log(`Path 1: ${p1} Path 2: ${p2}`);
```

We can also choose to not specify the platform and automatically use whatever Deno is running on.

```
const p3 = path.fromFileUrl("file:///home/foo");
console.log(`Path on current OS: ${p3}`);
```

We can get the last part of a file path using the basename method.

```
const p = path.basename("./deno/is/awesome/mod.ts");
console.log(p); // mod.ts
```

We can get the directory of a file path using the dirname method.

```
const base = path.dirname("./deno/is/awesome/mod.ts");
console.log(base); // ./deno/is/awesome
```

We can get the extension of a file path using the extname method.

```
const ext = path.extname("./deno/is/awesome/mod.ts");
console.log(ext); // .ts
```

We can format a path using a **FormatInputPathObject**.

```
const formatPath = path.format({
  root: "/",
  dir: "/home/user/dir",
  ext: ".html",
  name: "index",
});
console.log(formatPath); // "/home/user/dir/index.html"
```

When we want to make our code cross-platform, we can use the join method. This joins any number of strings by the OS-specific file separator. On Mac OS this would be **foo/bar**. On Windows, this would be **foo\bar**.

```
const joinPath = path.join("foo", "bar");
console.log(joinPath);
```

We can get the current working directory using the built-in **cwd** method.

```
const current = Deno.cwd();
console.log(current);
```

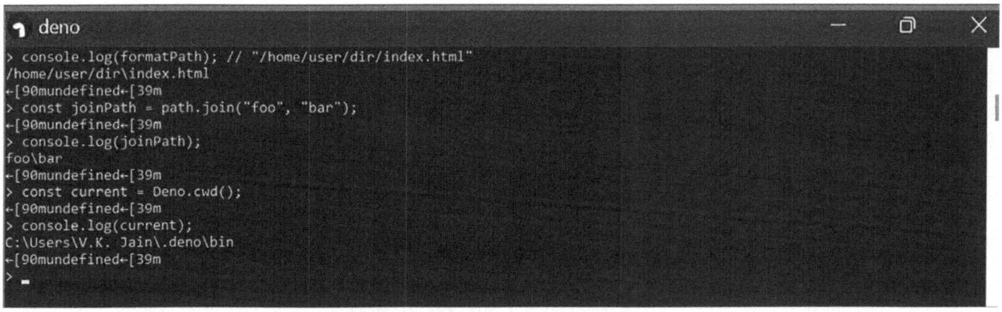

Figure 1.5: *Getting the Current Working Directory Using the Built-In cwd Method*

Reading Files

Numerous programs must read files from the disk. Deno offers a straightforward file-reading interface. Reading a file's whole contents as bytes into memory is the simplest method.

```
const bytes = await Deno.readFile("hello.txt");
```

This function allows you to read the file as a string rather than as bytes.

```
Const text = await Deno.readTextFile("hello.txt");
```

Frequently, you require additional control over which file sections are read at what times. To begin, open a file to obtain a **`Deno.FsFile`** object.

```
awaiting Deno.open("hello.txt") const file = read a few bytes from
the file's start.
```

Let up to five be read, but make a note of how many were read.

```
const buffer = new Uint8Array(5);
const bytesRead = await file.read(buffer);
console.log(`Read ${bytesRead} bytes`);
```

You can also seek to a known location in the file and read from there.

```
const pos = await file.seek(6, Deno.SeekMode.Start);
console.log(`Sought to position ${pos}`);
const buffer2 = new Uint8Array(2);
const bytesRead2 = await file.read(buffer2);
console.log(`Read ${bytesRead2} bytes`);
```

You can rewind back to the start using seek as well.

```
await file.seek(0, Deno.SeekMode.Start);
```

Make sure to close the file when you are done.

```
file.close();
```

Synchronous reading is also supported.

```
Deno.readFileSync("hello.txt");
Deno.readTextFileSync("hello.txt");
const f = Deno.openSync("hello.txt");
f.seekSync(6, Deno.SeekMode.Start);
const buf = new Uint8Array(5);
f.readSync(buf);
f.close();
```

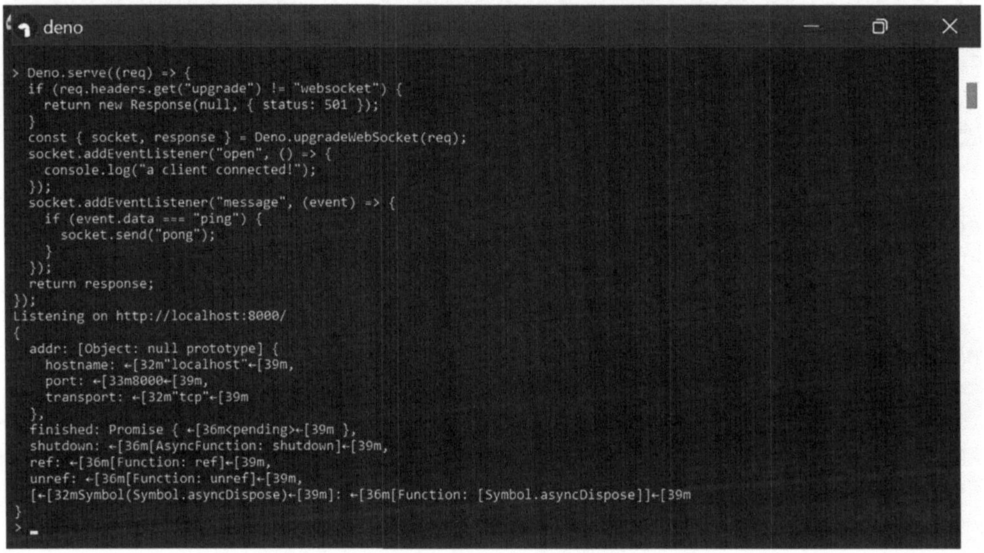

Figure 1.6: *Synchronous Reading*

Granting File Access

Because Deno is designed to be secure, it will not allow scripts to access your files or the internet unless you explicitly provide permission.

For example, if you attempt to read a local file in this way without authorization:

```
Deno.readTextFileSync("readme.md") const text =

Additionally, use:

deno run main.js
```

Due to Deno's default blocking of file system access, you will receive an error stating that permission is refused.

Add the **`--allow-read`** flag as follows to enable it to read the file:

```
Run deno with --allow-read main.js.
```

This flag makes it easy for the script to read readme.md and insert its contents into the text variable.

These permission flags allow you to limit the capabilities of each script, which helps to keep things safe. Do not offer more permissions than you actually need.

Core Concepts

Security Model:

Deno's Security Model protects your code by preventing it from accessing resources such as your files or the internet unless you grant permission. It is similar to granting permission to apps on your phone.

You can let your scripts do more by using special commands when you run them:

- **`--allow-read`**: Lets the script read files
- **`--allow-write`**: Lets the script write to files
- **`--allow-net`**: Lets the script access the internet
- **`--allow-env`**: Lets the script access environment info

For example:

```
deno run --allow-net main.js
```

This setup means you are in control of what your code can and cannot do, making things safer.

TypeScript Integration

You can use TypeScript directly with Deno. This implies that there are no additional processes required to write and execute.ts files.

For example:

```
function add(a: number, b: number) {
  return a + b;
}

console.log(add(1, 2)); // Shows 3
```

By ensuring that your code receives the appropriate type of data, TypeScript helps you avoid errors.

System Module

Instead of using a package manager, Deno manages code segments (modules) using web links. It is similar to bookmarking a page.

For instance:

```
"https://deno.land/std@0.114.0/http/server.ts" import { serve };
```

Because you only utilize URLs, this method of handling code makes it easier to share and manage.

React/Next

A well-liked JavaScript package for creating user interfaces is called React. You can utilize the well-known web framework Next.js to integrate React with Deno. *Chapter* 8, *'Using React with Deno and Next.js'* of this book goes into great length on this. You may start using Next.js in Deno by making a new Next app and launching it right away:

```
deno run -A npm:create-next-app@latest my-next-app
cd my-next-app
deno task dev
```

Node Projects

This will use TypeScript to construct a new Next.js application and use Deno to run it. After that, you can view your new application by opening your browser to http://localhost:3000. You can then begin editing page.tsx to observe your changes as they happen.

Out of the box, Deno will run your Node.js projects. For more on moving your Node.js project to Deno, see our guide. Windows PowerShell can be opened by:

1. Launch the **`Start`** menu.
2. Open the search box and type **`Windows PowerShell`**.
3. Choose PowerShell for Windows.
4. Choose **`Open`**.

You can also open an elevated PowerShell prompt by:

1. Opening the **`Start`** menu.
2. Typing **`PowerShell`** in the search bar.
3. Right-clicking **`Windows PowerShell`** in the search results.
4. Selecting **`Run as administrator`**.
5. Clicking **`Yes`** in the **`User Account Control (UAC)`** dialog.

You can also start a Windows PowerShell session in a Command Prompt window by typing PowerShell.

PowerShell is a command shell that can accept and return .NET objects, unlike most shells that only accept and return text.

Starting Windows PowerShell - Microsoft Learn

Download and Install

`deno_install` provides convenience scripts to download and install the binary.

- macOS
- Windows
- Linux

Using PowerShell (Windows)

`irm https://deno.land/install.ps1 | iex`

Method 1: Using the **`Start`** Menu

1. You have to Open the **`Start`** menu
2. Type **`Windows PowerShell`** in the search bar
3. Select **`Windows PowerShell`**
4. Select **`Open`**

Method 2 and Onward:

Deno is a single binary executable. It has no external dependencies. Deno works on macOS, Linux, and Windows. On macOS, both M1 (arm64) and Intel (x64) executables are provided. On Linux and Windows, only x64 is supported. Apart fom the PowerShell method, it can be used to install by using npm, Homebrew, and several other methods.

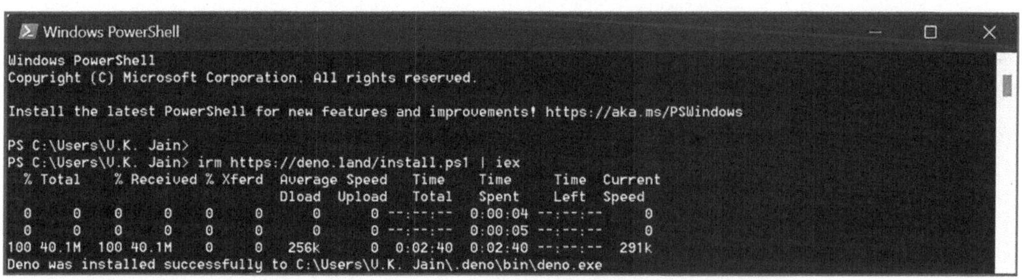

Figure 1.7: *Installing Window's PowerShell and Deno*

Figure 1.8: *Exiting Deno*

Conclusion

In this chapter, we first studied about various features of Deno and Sandboxing.

Then V8 version of Deno was described and also ES6 or the ECMAScript 2015.

We further learned about the basics of Deno and how Web Development can be achieved.

Then we learned about installation and setup and learned to make first Deno program: Hello World. At last, we learned about React/Next frameworks.

In the next chapter, we shall explore the Deno Toolchain Ecosystem, Components, and Architecture.

References

1. **“A secure JavaScript/TypeScript runtime built with V8, Rust, and Toki**o: denoland/deno”. 8 July 2019 – via GitHub

2. **Features introduced in ES6, by Shubham Gupta, Sep 11**: 2023,https://medium.com/@shubham3480/features-introduced-in-es6

3. **Deno Basics for Beginners, Mar 28, 2024**: https://daily.dev/blog/deno-basics-for-beginners#

CHAPTER 2
The Deno Toolchain Ecosystem, Components, and Architecture

Introduction

Deno's toolchain is a collection of built-in utilities that help you build, test, and deploy applications. The Deno ecosystem includes tools, services, and a growing community that supports the Deno JavaScript runtime. The main components of Deno are - Ext Cli, runtime, core, graph, NPN, and cache. The main components that makeup Deno's native architecture are a rundown of the primary elements created and maintained by the Deno team.

Structure

We shall learn about the following in this chapter:

- Deno's Toolchain
- Ecosystem
- Overall Architecture of Deno
- Deno 2.0
- Components of Deno
- Cache
- Deno's Overall Architecture
- Rusty_v8

- Web Scripting
- Other JS Engines
- Tokio: Asynchronous Programming

Deno's Toolchain

In software, a toolchain is a set of programming tools that are used to perform a complex software development task or to create a software product, which is typically another computer program or a set of related programs.

Deno's toolchain is a collection of built-in utilities that help you build, test, and deploy applications:

- **Deno fmt**: A formatter
- **Deno lint**: A linter
- **Deno compile**: Creates a standalone binary from JavaScript or TypeScript source code

A linter is a developer tool that analyzes source code for errors, vulnerabilities, suspicious constructs, and stylistic issues to improve code quality. The term originates from a Unix utility that examined C language source code. A program that performs this function is also known as a "*linter.*"

Deno's toolchain includes everything you need to get started, so you do not need to configure your toolchain, project, or TypeScript.

Ecosystem

Ecosystem is a rich and evolving landscape that offers a wide range of tools and libraries to streamline your development process, enhance your application's performance, and unlock new possibilities.

The Deno ecosystem includes tools, services, and a growing community that supports the Deno JavaScript runtime:

- Comes with built-in Node modules such as **`node:fs`** and **`node: child_process`**. Npm packages are also supported by Deno.
- **Deno Standard Library:** An assortment of TypeScript packages that have been verified to be compatible with Deno by the Deno team. The JavaScript Registry, or JSR, now offers the Deno Standard Library.
- **The Runtime Code for Deno:** The runtime, which is written in JavaScript, implements low-level Rust processes and offers user programs a Deno API.
- **Workers:** Workers, which resemble Node.js workers, are a part of Deno's

runtime environment. If more web worker threads are required, Deno can generate them.

- **Long-Term Support (LTS) Release Channel:** Important bug fixes are backported for six months to LTS releases.
- **Deno for Enterprise**: This initiative provides priority assistance. This program offers priority support, direct access to Deno engineers, and guaranteed response times.
- **Community:** Deno has a vibrant community that supports the runtime.

Deno is a JavaScript runtime that was developed by Node.js founder Ryan Dahl. It is considered a more secure alternative to Node.js.

Overall Architecture of Deno

Deno is a runtime environment that functions as a small monolith inside a single process, similar to Node.js, Bun, Go, and Python. Major runtime environments frequently use this design strategy, which makes use of multi-threading capabilities to effectively manage computationally demanding activities. Notably, Go sets itself apart by offering strong support for green threads, which improves performance in some situations. Rust, TypeScript, and JavaScript were used to build the basic components of Deno's foundation, which is unique in that it spans numerous programming languages. Remarkably, Deno's main runtime–which was originally developed in TypeScript–has been recreated entirely in JavaScript, excluding ES modules, demonstrating Deno's flexibility and agile development methodology.

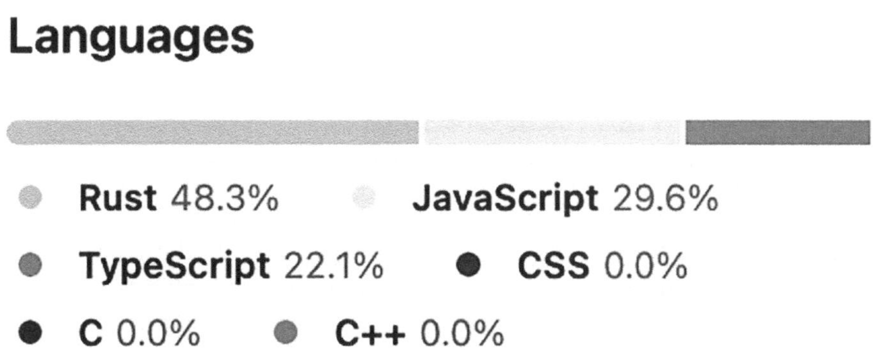

Figure 2.1: *Use Percentage of Denos Components*

Seven essential elements underpin Deno's complex operations, working together to carry out a variety of activities. In addition to these fundamental elements, the ecosystem is enhanced by three crucial third-party libraries that allow JavaScript programs to run while preserving asynchronous internal mechanisms. This harmony of third-party and native components allows Deno to maintain the asynchronous character of JavaScript while running programs with ease.

Deno's architecture is made up of roughly ten parts, divided into three third-party blocks and seven core components. These components highlight Deno's strong and flexible design and serve as the fundamental building blocks of its features and functioning.

Architecture Diagram

Key building blocks that constitute Deno's architecture are shown in *Figure* 2.2.

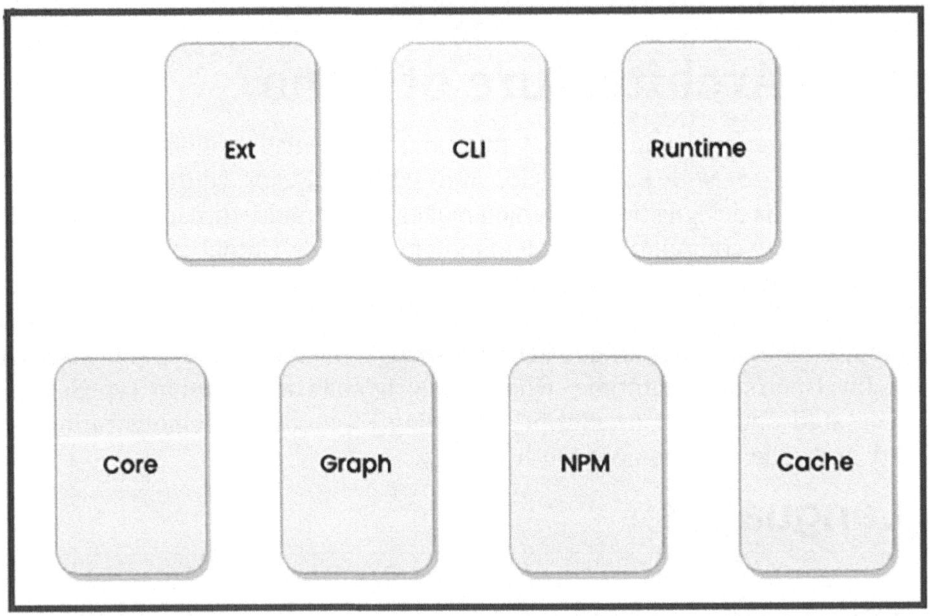

Figure 2.2: *Main Components of Deno's Architecture*

This diagram shown in *Figure* 2.2 offers a thorough rundown of the primary elements created and maintained by the Deno team. Please be aware that there are no elements from outside sources included in this diagram; it only highlights Deno's native components. This distinction is significant because it draws attention to the essential elements that, independent of external libraries and dependencies, make up Deno's runtime environment.

Deno 2.0

Developers may benefit from Deno's advancements in JS while continuing to utilize the libraries and frameworks they have been using for the previous 15 years thanks to Deno 2.0's direct compatibility with Node.js and npm. [1]

Deno 2: Stability and Scale

The migration guide for Deno 1.x to 2.x states this:

The next major release of Deno is centered on using Deno at scale, even though we have made great progress with Deno 1.x. In addition to enabling a greater variety of projects and development teams, this entails smooth interaction with Node.js and npm JavaScript infrastructure—all without compromising the "*batteries included*," simplicity, and security that developers adore.

The main idea behind Deno 2.0 is to preserve what functions while enabling developers to scale Deno more effectively. At its essence, that means two things.

- In Deno 1.28, Deno stabilized npm support via the npm [1]: specifier. Since then, they have progressively enhanced the runtime's support for Node.js and npm. Backward compatibility with Node.js and npm is offered by Deno 2.0:
    - **The majority of Node.js built-in modules are** now supported by Deno and may be imported by using the node: prefix. Take import * as os from "**node:os**"; as an example.
    - **Support for CommonJS**: Deno 2.0 enhances support for CommonJS, enabling developers to run CommonJS files directly using the .cjs extension. Developers can use **require()** to import ES modules (as long as they do not use top-level await) or import CommonJS modules in ES modules using import statements.
    - **npm Packages**: By employing the npm: specifier, developers can utilize npm packages directly in Deno, taking advantage of the extensive npm ecosystem.
    - **package.json and node_modules:** Deno 2.0 understands **package.json** files and can work with **node_modules** directories, facilitating easier migration of existing Node.js projects.
    - **Global Variables:** Deno 2.0 introduces the process of global variables widely used in Node.js applications and frameworks.
- We can convert our Node.js example to Deno if we go back to our earlier examples. Actually, all we need to do to do that is:
    1. To read the package, run deno install in the **directory.JSON**.
    2. Since the code contains a **CommonJS** module, change the file extension to **.cjs**.
    3. To enable Deno to read the **node_modules**, execute **deno run --allow-net --allow-env --allow-read node_index.cjs** with the extra **--allow-read flag**.

An alternative is to modify the Deno code to utilize the Postgres library's npm version. We modify our import to:

```
import pg from "npm:pg";
const { Client } = pg;
```

Then, we also have to change the query call itself as the **pg** library does not support **queryObject**:

```
const result = await client.query(
    "SELECT name, value FROM playing_with_neon LIMIT 5"
  );
```

You can already see how Deno and Node work together with these simple examples. However, for serious developers who must expand their projects, this is truly all about improving the developer experience. The Node.js frameworks that practically all developers today use, such as Next.js, SvelteKit, Remix, and Nuxt, are now supported by Deno 2.0 thanks to these enhancements in compatibility. For the same outcome, you ought to be able to use deno task dev rather than npm run dev.

All of this enables developers to use well-known Node.js tools and modules in Deno projects while facilitating the progressive transfer of current Node.js projects to Deno. Crucially, the opposite is also true: Node developers can still use the npm ecosystem while utilizing Deno's security measures, tooling, DX, and contemporary JavaScript compatibility.

Since the web is the biggest software platform in existence, developing it may potentially reach more than 5 billion people. However, the increased acceleration of web development has also resulted in an unmanageable increase in complexity. Developers would much prefer to concentrate on creating products and providing value to users than deal with laborious configuration and sifting through superfluous boilerplate before writing a single line of code.

Notwithstanding these complications, JavaScript–the language of the web–has maintained its position as the most widely used language for the past ten years, with TypeScript swiftly taking third place. This indicates that JavaScript is here to stay and is proof of its widespread use and value in web development.

To make web programming easier, we developed Deno: a contemporary, all-in-one, zero-config toolchain for JavaScript and TypeScript development.

Support for TypeScript Natively Based on Web Standards:

Modules for ES, fetch, and promises Built-in formatter, linter, type checker, test framework, compile to executable, and more batteries are supplied. By default, secure, like popular browsers such as Chrome, Firefox and Mozilla. The Deno repository has grown to be one of the most starred Rust projects on GitHub, second only to the Rust language itself, and hundreds of thousands of developers now adore using it.

Apart from a ton of accomplishment in Deno 1, the next major version is focused on using *Deno at scale*. This means seamless interoperability with legacy JavaScript infrastructure and support for a wider range of projects and development teams. All without sacrificing the simplicity, security, and "batteries included" nature that Deno users love.

Deno 2 consists of:

- Backward compatibility with npm and Node.js, which enables you to easily run pre-existing Node apps.
- Native support for **`node_modules`** and **`package.json`**.
- Using the new Deno install, Deno add, and Deno uninstall commands for package management.
- A standardized, stable library.
- Assistance with private npm registries.
- Support for monorepo and workspaces.
- Releases of Long-Term Support (LTS).
- JSR: A contemporary registry enabling cross-runtime sharing of JavaScript libraries.

Numerous current Deno features are being continuously improved by the Deno team:

- Deno FMT is now capable of formatting YAML, CSS, and HTML.
- Quick fixes and Node-specific rules are now included in Deno Lint.
- Deno test may now execute tests created with **`node:test`**.
- **`Package.json`** scripts can now be executed by deno tasks.
- The HTML output from Deno Docs offers better search and design.
- Windows icons and code signing are now supported by deno compile.
- Deno Serve may concurrently launch HTTP servers on several cores.
- Now, **`deno init`** can scaffold servers or libraries.
- Deno Jupyter can now generate HTML, graphs, and photos.
- Deno Bench has essential elements for more accurate measurements.
- Deno Coverage can now produce HTML reports.

Compatibility backwards with npm and Node.js

Deno 2 is cross-platform using npm and Node.js. In addition to using Deno in your existing Node.js projects, this enables you to gradually integrate components of Deno's comprehensive toolkit.

For instance, you may use deno lint to check for common hazards instead of using ESLint, use **`deno fmt`** to format code without the requirement for Prettier, or use deno install to install dependencies on a Node.js project.

Deno 2 can easily migrate your existing projects using ESM because it understands package.json, the **`node_modules`** directory, and even npm workspaces.

LTS Deno

Long-term support is another essential component of Deno 2.0 that is important for making Deno a workable option for huge builds. Deno will offer an LTS channel six months of support for bug fixes and significant performance enhancements beginning with v2.1.0.

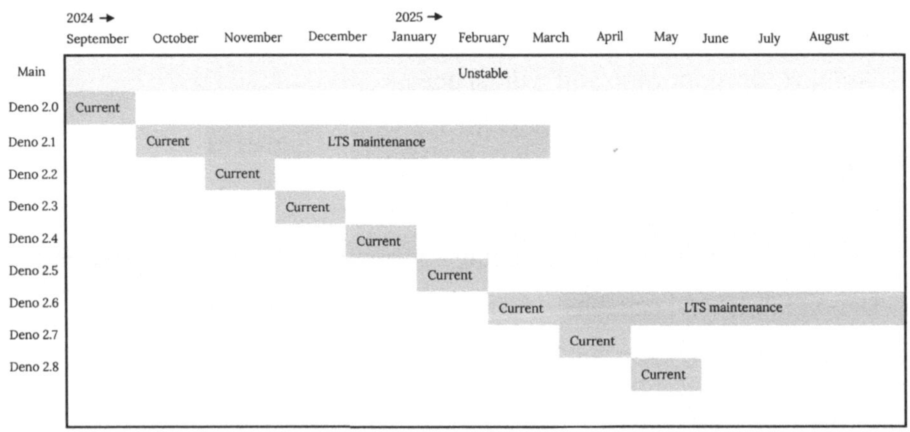

Figure 2.3: *Proposed Evolution of Various Versions of Deno 2*

For large-scale projects and businesses, LTS channels are crucial because they offer consistency and predictability. By lowering the possibility of unforeseen behavior changes that could disrupt their applications, organizations can depend on these versions to stay consistent across time. A defined support duration helps organizations better manage their update cycles. For large projects where upgrades need to be meticulously planned and tested, LTS is especially crucial.

Many businesses need LTS versions for their production settings because of corporate regulations or regulatory needs. Deno is a better choice for these enterprises because it offers LTS.

This implies the following for the Deno ecosystem:

- Greater uptake in production settings.
- Greater assurance that companies will invest in Deno-based projects.

- A more straightforward route for businesses switching from Node.js to Deno.
- The possibility of additional outside resources and services to formally help Deno.
- All things considered, Deno 2.0's addition of LTS is a big step toward developing Deno into a sophisticated, scalable JavaScript runtime. It resolves a major issue that larger projects and organizations may have had with Deno adoption, which could hasten its use in production settings either in addition to or instead of Node.js.

Scaly Denos

Were scales present in dinosaurs? Deno has scalability now, however, it cannot be said for sure if feathers or scales are the current trend.

Inside the same **`src/index.test.ts`** file, create a new test for the login functionality:

Get hands-on with 1200+ tech skills courses.

All of this could appear to be a submission to the Node universe and the package's delivery. For Deno lovers, seeing json and **`node_modules`** in a project that is supposed to be Deno may be a dinosaur tear. However, this is only about reality and, more crucially, creating what developers require or desire.

The community has told the Deno team that they still live and breathe Node; therefore, they require the crossover even though they adore Deno's simplicity, security, and performance. That is exactly what Deno 2 offers, enabling any developer to continue creating in Node and begin fully utilizing the Deno environment while gradually switching over previous testing, but we will utilize the client this time. Let us begin:

Deno will provide a Long-Term Support (LTS) channel beginning with Deno v2.1.0, which is scheduled for release in November 2024.

Before a new version is upgraded to LTS, an LTS version is supported for six months, during which time it receives bug fixes and important performance improvements. Controlling dependencies with features like these, Deno 2 significantly enhances dependency management for npm and JSR projects.

- **`deno install`**
- **`deno add`**
- **`deno remove`**

You should anticipate a smooth experience with projects that are Deno-first (using **`deno.json`**), Node.js-first (using **`package.json`**), and hybrid (using both **`deno.json`** and **`package.json`** to facilitate an easy migration path).

Assistance with the Framework

With enhanced compatibility for Node.js and npm, Deno 2 supports numerous user-favorite frameworks, such as:

- Next.js
- SvelteKit
- Remix
- Nuxt
- TanStack

Why would you want to switch if you are content with Node? Imagine working on a project without having to deal with **`tsconfig.json`**, **`webpack.config.js`**, **`babel.config.js`**, or any other annoying files. Secure-by-default execution, built-in TypeScript compatibility, and a robust standard library that is closely linked with the runtime are all features of Deno. Do you need to import a package from NPM? **`Node_modules`** and **`package.json`** are not required–unless you want them, of course–just use the npm, and Deno will take care of the rest.

You may progressively migrate your current Node.js projects using Deno 2. Do you want to continue utilizing your preferred Node.js or SvelteKit tools? No issue! You can mix and match as you like because Deno fully supports npm.

Reason to Choose Deno 2

And if you are a member of a bigger group? Deno 2 is ideal for handling complicated projects because of its workspaces and monorepo support. Regardless of whether they are Node-based or Deno-based, each workspace can have its own linter, formatter, and dependency configuration. In a single environment, Deno 2 combines the best aspects of both worlds.

Other noteworthy characteristics are:

- Deno fmt now formats HTML, CSS, and YAML in addition to TypeScript and JavaScript.
- New Node-specific rules are included in deno lint.
- Node:test-written tests are supported by the deno test.
- Your package can be executed by a deno **`task.scripts`** in JSON.
- Beautiful HTML reports are produced by deno coverage.
- Deno Serve now operates HTTP servers in parallel across several cores for increased speed.

We covered both core and third-party components in the preceding section's high-level discussion of Deno's overall structure. Let us now concentrate on Deno's essential features, omitting third-party components for the moment.[2]

The basic elements of Deno itself, excluding third-party libraries, are referred to as Deno components. Deno's main purpose is simple: it runs JavaScript and TypeScript apps.

Deno manages a number of duties, such as:

- Offering the primary program framework
- Overseeing subcommands
- Setting up the event loop
- Providing an inspector for debugging
- Participating in a linter
- File retrieval
- Module resolution
- Offering a common library
- Outlining the main APIs

Components of Deno

When we refer to Deno components in this section, we mean the essential parts of Deno itself, excluding third-party libraries. Deno's primary function is straightforward: it executes TypeScript and JavaScript programs.

Deno handles various tasks, including:

- Providing the main program structure
- Managing sub-commands
- Orchestrating the event loop
- Offering a debugger inspector
- Acting as a linter
- Fetching files
- Resolving modules
- Providing a standard library
- Presenting core APIs

Everything outside of Tokio and v8's duties–especially v8–is handled by Deno. Although v8 effectively executes JavaScript in a sandbox, it depends on Deno for a number of functions, including networking, file management, input-output, timers, and more. Deno and v8 work together to provide a complete runtime environment for program execution. We gave a high-level summary of Deno's components before. Using the same diagram as a guide, we will now examine them in more detail:

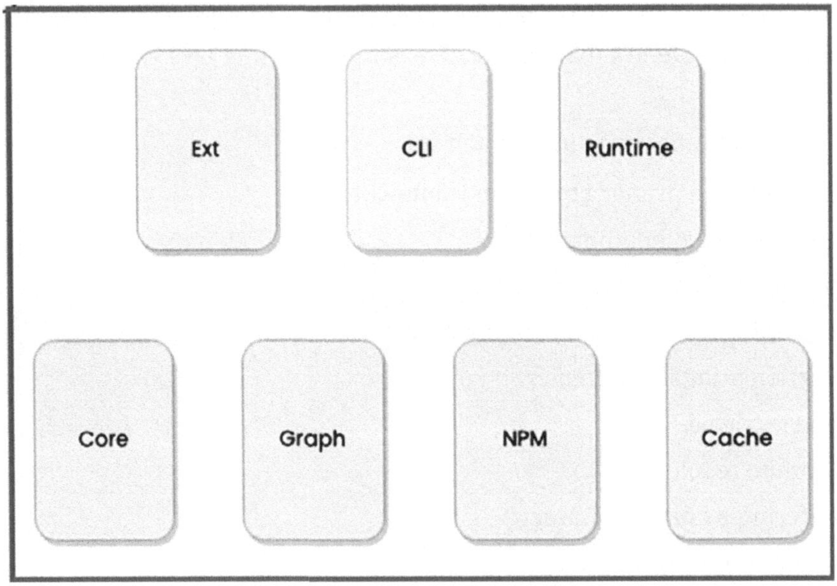

Figure 2.4: *Components of Deno*

Command Line Interface (CLI)

As was previously said, the CLI component is essential to Deno. But it is crucial to remember that V8 is the largest component, surpassing CLI in size with its vast codebase of about a million lines. The CLI is essential to the Deno ecosystem because it fulfills two crucial functions: orchestration and service provision.

Essential services such as ext, runtime, graph, cache, file fetching, core functionality, ops, tokio, and the V8 engine are all coordinated by the CLI, which acts as an orchestrator. The CLI guarantees seamless operation and effective cooperation amongst Deno's components by coordinating their interactions.

Other Deno components also receive critical services from the CLI. Its significance in the Deno system is highlighted by its dual function as an orchestrator and service provider, which permits appropriate communication, seamless execution, and robust performance among Deno's components.

The Deno executable, which includes the core (or main) program that implements a number of subcommands and user-oriented APIs, is also made available by the CLI. Although not all APIs are covered by the CLI, a sizable percentage are. In essence, the CLI acts as the entry point to Deno's capabilities, offering resources for carrying out Deno-powered operations and engaging with its features.

The following list outlines the capabilities of the CLI.

- **The Main Program:** In Deno, the primary program is where all operations start. The use of the "`deno`" command initiates the execution process. Note that the program's functionality does not start at this moment, even though Deno's activities occur.

  A few necessary actions must be finished before the application may be executed. A thorough grasp of the procedures that take place prior to the program's real running can be obtained. This knowledge will offer important new perspectives on the basic mechanisms behind Deno's operation.

- **Subcommands:** Although Deno appears as a single executable, its sub-commands provide a variety of development tools. The most popular and often used sub-commands among developers are '`run`' and '`test`.' While '`test`' starts unit tests to guarantee code integrity, '`run`' runs JavaScript or TypeScript programs.

  Deno offers a number of sub-commands for distinct areas of growth, such as:

  - `run`: Runs TypeScript or JavaScript applications.
  - `Bench`: Performs benchmarking standard comparisons.
  - `bundle`: Consolidates dependencies and modules into a single file.
  - `cache`: Caches dependencies to improve efficiency.
  - `check`: Verifies the dependencies' types.
  - `compile`: Creates self-contained executables (UNSTABLE) from scripts.
  - `Finalizations`: Creates scripts for shell completion.
  - `coverage`: Generates code analysis coverage reports.
  - `Doc`: Shows the documentation for the module.
  - `eval`: Runs scripts for real-time assessment.
  - `fmt`: Formats source files automatically to ensure uniform code styles
  - `init`: Starts new initiatives.
  - `info`: Offers details about cache or source files.
  - `Install`: Installs executable scripts.
  - `Uninstall`: Deletes scripts that are installed.
  - `lsp`: Launches the language server to enable more comfortable code editing.
  - `Lint`: Enhances quality by performing source code linting.
  - `Repl`: Configures an environment for interactive scripting using the Read-Eval-Print Loop.

- `task`: Does out operations specified in configuration files.
- `test`: Starts code validation tests.
- `Types`: Runtime TypeScript declarations are output.
- `update`: Brings the Deno executable up to date with designated versions.
- `Vendor`: Adds distant modules to local folders.
- `Help`: Offers direction and details about subcommands.

- **The File Retrieval:** An essential component of the Deno ecosystem is the file fetcher. Deno adopts a flexible strategy in contrast to systems that have specialized package managers. It makes it possible to access modules via NPM repositories, local sources, or HTTP. Finding module files, no matter where they are, is the primary duty of the file fetcher.
- **Flags:** Deno's sandboxing feature is largely dependent on flags. Enforcing permissions that preserve Deno's reliable sandboxing scheme depends on these flags.

  As a cybersecurity technique, sandboxing involves running code, observing, and analyzing it in a secure, separated network environment that closely resembles end-user operating environments. Sandboxing is commonly used to examine untested or untrusted code and is intended to keep risks off the network.

  Command-line arguments are used to build the flags. A key element of Deno's security architecture is sandboxing, which restricts and manages the operations that a Deno script is capable of carrying out. By permitting or prohibiting particular actions and interactions within the script's runtime environment, the flags serve as gatekeepers.
- **Module Loader:** In Deno, the module loader is essential for managing ES modules. It offers a number of features to load, resolve, and get modules ready for use. This comprises:
  - Modules are retrieved from their sources.
  - Gathering them as required.
  - Using a cache to maximize efficiency.

  The module loader oversees the entire procedure, guaranteeing that ES modules are handled effectively and efficiently.
- **Watcher of Files:** When it notices changes, the file watcher restarts the Deno process. It keeps an eye on the primary source code and its dependencies. This guarantees that the Deno runtime remains up to date with the most recent changes, enabling a more seamless and rapid development process.

The file watcher tracks your code changes while working on a Deno project and notifies the system if it notices changes to the dependent files or main code. The Deno process is automatically restarted in response to this notice, guaranteeing that the most recent code is used.

Execution Time

The runtime, which includes all of Deno's fundamental functions, is its central component. It provides dependable and effective performance by fusing the main JavaScript-written features of Deno with Rust-coded underlying operations.

Deno's multitasking capabilities are improved by the runtime framework's use of "workers"–specialized components that manage particular activities in parallel. Whether they are managing I/O operations, coordinating jobs, or running scripts, workers are essential to maximizing Deno's capabilities.

The runtime is located in the main Deno repository due to its significance. The runtime is made up of several interrelated services that fall into the following categories:

- **Workers:** Improve performance and efficiency by using distinct execution contexts for concurrent code execution.
- **Permissions**: By limiting access to code execution to specific permissions, this feature ensures security and control.
- **Metrics:** Gathers and offers behavior and performance data to help developers optimize.
- **Operations**: Enables system-level operations by facilitating communication with the underlying operating system.
- **JavaScript Runtime**: The fundamental component that runs JavaScript code, facilitating the functionality and execution of programs.

Combining various services, Deno's runtime offers a safe, effective, and developer-friendly environment for running TypeScript and JavaScript code. This combination guarantees that Deno functions properly, enabling a range of applications and contemporary development techniques.

The Deno API can be accessed through the runtime in TypeScript and JavaScript environments. It has every essential functionality required to run applications in Deno. The runtime implements these services in both JavaScript and Rust, however, Deno's CLI and core services are mostly implemented in Rust. Deno does not use ECMAScript modules; all of its runtime code is written in JavaScript. The runtime is an essential component of the Deno ecosystem since it implements low-level Rust processes and offers a thorough Deno API for user programs.

Employees

Like Node.js, workers are essential to Deno's runtime environment. Deno can establish more web worker threads if necessary, but it runs the main program in the principal thread. Every worker, including the main worker, has a unique event loop and runtime.

Two different categories of workers exist:

- **Principal Employee**: The principal program must be run by the main worker, as the name suggests. It does not need a separate thread to execute; it works inside the main thread itself. This primary employee is created automatically.
- **Web Worker**: Another kind of worker that an application can start is the web worker.

These extra workers are typically used to complete activities that need a lot of CPU power, which may result in the main event loop being stuck. Because Deno efficiently handles asynchronous I/O activities within the primary thread, a separate worker is not required for tasks that involve intense input/output operations. These web workers adhere to the standard web worker specification used by web browsers. In conclusion, workers are essential to Deno's runtime environment's operation. They give the software a way to delegate resource-intensive tasks from the main thread so that it can continue to function properly. Web workers are a useful tool while the primary worker manages the main program execution.

While the main worker handles the main program execution, web workers are an advantageous tool to tackle heavy computational tasks without hampering the overall responsiveness of the application. This enables developers to build robust and scalable applications without compromising performance.

Permissions

In Deno, permissions are essential to establishing a safe sandbox environment. Reading and writing files, connecting to the network, controlling the environment, starting processes, using plugins, and many other activities are covered by these rights. Permissions are especially important in Deno, which sets it apart from other platforms such as Node.js.

One significant distinction is the way Deno handles permissions. It improves security by enabling users to provide or refuse their program's particular capabilities. This strategy differs from traditional systems, where scripts frequently have unfettered access to resources, which could result in security flaws.

Node.js has recently acknowledged the significance of permissions as well. In recognition of the security advantages it offers, it has been implementing a permission-like structure in its releases over time. This change reflects the increasing understanding of how crucial permissions are to maintaining safe sandbox settings.

Features of the JS Runtime

Deno's JS Runtime is a set of programs that run in the user's JavaScript environment. Written entirely in JavaScript, this essential component serves as the cornerstone of Deno's capabilities.

- JavaScript-written Deno's runtime code
- Basic lower-level operations
- An inspector for troubleshooting
- Performance indicators

Essential features, such as:

- The primary employee
- A web worker
- Security of permissions

This component is essential to the operation of Deno's key features, including process management, security authorization enforcement, and the provision of vital debugging and performance evaluation tools.

With the help of the JS Runtime API's many features, developers can create applications that are reliable and packed with features. Notably, the JS runtime streamlines the development process and offers a flawless user experience by automating a number of intricate tasks, including controlling interactions with Deno. Building apps is made simpler by this automation, which removes the requirement for developers to possess an in-depth understanding of low-level activities. By abstracting away underlying difficulties, the JS Runtime API helps developers concentrate on creating apps rather than worrying about minute details.

The JavaScript runtime offers the following features:

- **Build Information:** This includes specifics such as the operating system, architecture, target platform, vendor, and environment. Deno's behavior can be optimized for various setups with the use of this information.
- **Colors:** You can deal with colorization in Deno's runtime, which improves the output's visual appeal in the terminal.
- **Non-ECMAScript Errors:** Although not included in the official ECMAScript specification, Deno's runtime adds its own error-handling features to make programs more resilient.

- **Version Information**: Users can stay informed about the latest Deno version and its features by accessing information about it.
- **Console Utilities:** To facilitate debugging and logging, the runtime offers tools for effective console interaction.
- **Dispatch:** This entails efficiently processing the responses after submitting operations to Rust, the computer language that underpins Deno.
- **Timers:** The runtime facilitates scheduling and synchronization in applications by supporting a number of timer capabilities, including timeout and interval.
- **Workers:** Deno's runtime enables communication between parent and child workers and understands the complexities of the web worker lifecycle.
- **I/O Operations**: Copying, reading, and writing files are examples of input and output operations that are handled seamlessly.

Effective handling and manipulation of buffers, which are utilized for a variety of data operations, is known as buffer management.

- **Websockets**: Bidirectional, real-time communication between clients and servers is made possible by support for websockets.
- **File Operations:** Standard I/O streams, such as stdout and stdin, as well as file creation, opening, seeking, and manipulation are handled by Deno's runtime.
- **File System Operations**: A wide range of file system operations, including reading directories, altering permissions and ownership, copying files, and more, are included in the runtime.
- **Metrics:** Resources for collecting different metrics in order to track and improve Deno's performance.
- **Networking (Net):** Connecting, listening, and interacting with datagrams are all made easier by Deno's runtime.
- **Operating System Information**: Obtaining vital details about the operating system, such as averages for CPU, memory, release, and load.
- **TypeScript Compiler:** To facilitate smooth TypeScript development, a TypeScript compiler is accessible within the user space.
- **File Watcher**: A file watcher is a feature of Deno's runtime that can track file changes and initiate the necessary actions.

Permissions management is the process of asking, rescinding, and querying the permissions needed for particular tasks.

- **Process Control**: The runtime manages the execution and termination of processes.

Facilities for initiating, listening, and establishing secure Transport Layer Security (TLS) connections.

- **User Prompts:** Alerts, confirmations, and input questions are examples of prompts that help with user interaction.

  Functionalities that go beyond the ECMAScript definition are referred to as Operations (OPs). The V8 engine rigorously complies with ECMAScript rules while running in a limited environment. However, other services such as file input/output, networking, timers, and more are managed by the runtime environment.

  Examining the world of OPs is an important subject that deserves its own section.

  In the next segment, we will thoroughly examine OPs, illuminating their intricacies and importance within Deno's functionality. This upcoming section will provide a detailed understanding of OPs, their role in Deno, and their impact on the runtime environment.

EXT

"**Ext**" stands for external APIs, which are essential to Deno's operation. Each of the modules that make up these external APIs has a distinct function. These modules consist of two essential parts:

User-space accessible JS APIs: These JavaScript APIs are made to be used straight out of your code. They act as a link between Deno's capabilities and the logic of your application. These JS APIs make it easier to integrate Deno's capabilities into your apps by allowing you to communicate with its many functionalities.

JS API-Supporting Operations (OPs)

OPs provide support for the JS APIs by carrying out the actions that are requested via the JS APIs. They are the unseen employees who do duties that are initiated by your code. In conclusion, Deno's "Ext" modules integrate underlying OPs and accessible JS APIs to offer a smooth and efficient means of interacting with external capabilities while upholding a distinct separation of duties for improved code structure and execution. Building reliable applications is made simpler by this combination, which permits effective and structured connections with external capabilities.

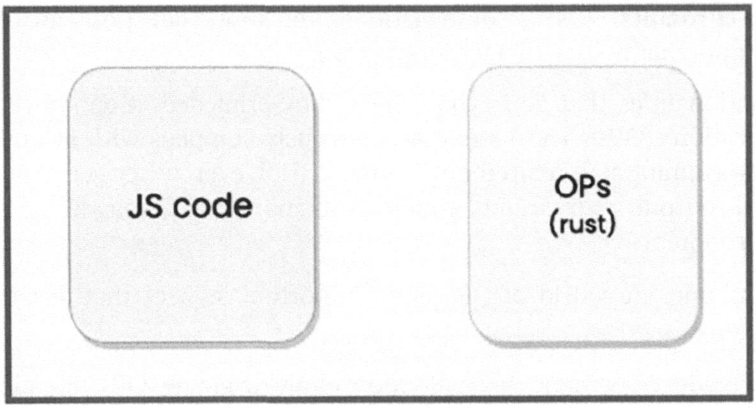

Figure 2.5: *JS API-Supporting Operations*

Each of the modules that make up Deno's "**ext**" component has a specific function. These modules include "**broadcast_channel**", "**cache**", "**console**", "**crypto**", "**fetch**", "**ffi**", "**fs**", "**http**", "**io**", "**kv**", "**napi**", "**net**", "**node**", "**tls**", "**url**", "**web**", "**webidl**", "**websocket**", and "**webstorage**." Each module offers different features for a certain web API and correlates to a particular set of web APIs.

The extensibility of the "**ext**" component, which enables developers to add new modules without changing the current codebase, is one of its noteworthy features. Because of its adaptability, developers can add custom modules to Deno that are suited to their own requirements, increasing its capability.

The "**ext**" component essentially acts as a complete toolkit, offering easy access to a range of web-related features. As new web APIs and technological advancements occur, Deno's "**ext**" component's extensibility ensures adaptability and accommodation, fostering a platform for continuous growth and innovation. This modular approach makes sure that new web APIs do not touch the core Deno code.

Core Framework

An essential part of the Deno architecture, the Deno core component is vital to its functionality. Interestingly, this crucial element is housed in a separate repository that is separate from Deno's main repository. This distinct repository contains the code that drives this essential functionality, underscoring the significance of the Deno core component as an independent unit.

Like the heart of a living thing, the core component serves as the Deno runtime's essential center. Essential features that allow Deno's runtime code to function smoothly are provided by this foundational framework. Managing JavaScript APIs, running JavaScript code segments, coordinating an event loop for asynchronous tasks, communicating with the V8 engine for effective code execution, enabling a number of actions (referred to as ops), and more.

Interestingly, when Deno initializes its runtime environment, the core component loads first. It serves as the foundation of the Deno ecosystem and establishes the framework for the functionality of the entire runtime. Furthermore, external modules that increase Deno's functionality beyond its core functions are loaded by the core component. By adding additional features and tools that meet a variety of programming requirements, these modules increase Deno's adaptability.

The following list focuses on the main features that Deno's basic framework offers:

- **V8 Interfacing**: Facilitating communication with the V8 engine to ensure effective code execution.
- **Data Interchange**: Enabling data interchange across JavaScript, Rust, and V8.
- **Performing Operations**: Using JavaScript with Rust to carry out synchronous and asynchronous operations and return the outcomes.
- **Console Logging**: Offering the ability to log console capabilities for debugging and monitoring purposes.
- **Preserving OPs Metrics**: Monitoring and controlling OPs metrics.
- **Event Loop**: Setting up an event loop to provide seamless asynchronous processes.
- **Low-Level APIs for Reading and Writing Data:** Providing low-level APIs.

Graph

As the name implies, the graph component gives the Deno CLI the necessary services to construct a module graph. This graph illustrates the interdependencies between different modules.

In accordance with the module resolution logic of the Deno CLI, the graph component is a Rust crate that contains the basic code for building the module graph. Furthermore, it provides a web assembly interface for the code that is generated, enabling the built logic to be accessed and used from environments that use TypeScript or JavaScript.

This feature allows the module graph to be used in a variety of scenarios by extending its capability outside the Deno CLI. The graph component loads all dependencies recursively using a basic graph data structure, beginning with the main file or main module. By tracking visited modules, this structure prevents the need for frequent reloads and recompilations. We will learn more about the inner workings of the graph component as we work through a basic program with dependencies. We will have a comprehensive grasp of its operation and significance thanks to our investigation.

Module Graphs

Module graphs play a significant role in Deno's underlying system. In a nutshell, a module graph connects several sections to cover all the necessary parts, beginning with the primary module, much like a building block puzzle. This module graph is created step-by-step, much like when you follow a cake recipe. To truly understand how everything fits together, let us examine each of these steps in more detail. A module graph is just a map that illustrates the interdependencies between several modules. Consider that you are organizing a journey and that you must determine which cities you will travel through in order to get to your destination. Likewise, Deno's module graph aids in the system's comprehension of the trip.

Similarly, Deno's module graph helps the system understand the journey of dependencies from the starting point, which is the root module.

In Deno, every module utilized within the application follows a process governed by module graphs. These graphs serve to retrieve, interpret, and uphold modules.

The idea is simple: modules are added to the graph according to their own specifiers, and then the nodes of the graph, which stand in for modules, are walked through.

The standard graph data structure can be used to gain a deeper understanding of these graphs. We are working with a primary module in this example, which does not require any further imports. It is therefore expected that our graph will consist of only one node. However, the next chapter delves into programs that involve numerous modules, so our investigation of modules does not end here.

There are two main stages to this graph-building process:

- Introduction of the main module:
    - Retrieval of the module
    - Integration into the graph
    - Addition to the list of modules pending processing
- Iteration through pending modules:
    - Examination of the pending module
    - Parsing of the module
    - Iteration through its dependencies

Retrieval of these Dependencies:

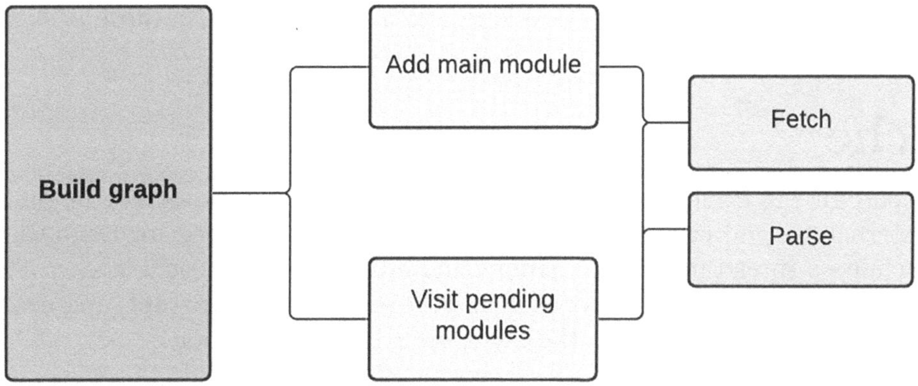

Figure 2.6: *Two Main Stages of this Graph-Building Process*

Node Package Manager (NPM): A Software Package Manager

The name Node Package Manager (npm) stems from when npm was first created as a package manager for Node.js. All npm packages are defined in files called package.json.

The content of package.json must be written in JSON. At least two fields must be present in the definition file: name and version.

As the name implies, the NPM component is in charge of handling packages that are acquired from NPM. This includes locating and assembling the required packages, making sure they are installed correctly, and providing ongoing maintenance. Deno's NPM component acts as a guide for browsing the extensive NPM repository, comprehending package metadata, and other tasks. However, when talking about Deno's internal workings, we will not delve into the specifics of NPM packages in order to keep this book short.

In 2020, GitHub purchased npm, Inc., a business that was established in 2014. One of the most important components of the JavaScript community, npm supports one of the biggest developer ecosystems globally.

npm is Capable of Several Things:

The package manager for Node.js is called npm. It was developed in 2009 as an open-source initiative to facilitate the sharing of packed code modules among JavaScript developers.

A public collection of open-source code packages for Node.js, front-end web apps, mobile apps, robots, routers, and a myriad of other JavaScript-related requirements may be found in the npm Registry.

The command-line tool used by developers to install and publish those packages is called npm.

Cache

The code for the cache component is found in two locations: in a different crate for external use and inside Deno's CLI code. It was first created for Deno CLI, but its usefulness spread to other situations and enabled reliable cache access. Similar to Deno CLI, additional elements such as **deno_graph**, **deno_doc**, **dnt**, and **emit** can communicate with and populate the cache using the same methods.

The cache system serves as a storage area on your computer's drive, where downloaded modules and packages are kept. The **DENO_DIR/cache** folder serves as the primary storage place.

This is how it operates:

- Deno looks for a required module in the cache.
- Deno uses the cached version rather than downloading it again if it is located.
- Deno downloads the module and saves a copy in the cache for later usage if it cannot be located.

To put it simply, JavaScript modules are conveniently stored in the cache system, which prevents repeated downloads and allows for instant access. As we examine a program with dependencies, we will go more into the cache idea.

The parts that are native to Deno and do not depend on outside sources have now been covered. We shall then look at the elements that originate from outside sources. To further comprehend the Operations (OPs') function in Deno's architecture, we shall first examine them in greater detail.

Deno's Overall Architecture

Deno is a runtime environment that functions as a small monolith inside a single process, similar to *Node.js, Bun, Go, and Python*. Major runtime environments frequently use this design strategy, which makes use of multi-threading capabilities to effectively manage computationally demanding activities. Notably, Go sets itself apart by offering strong support for green threads, which improves performance in some situations.

Rust, TypeScript, and JavaScript were used to build the basic components of Deno's foundation, which is unique in that it spans numerous programming languages. Remarkably, Deno's main runtime–which was originally developed in TypeScript–has been recreated entirely in JavaScript, excluding ES modules, demonstrating Deno's flexibility and agile development methodology.

Seven essential elements underpin Deno's complex operations, working together to carry out a variety of activities. In addition to these fundamental elements, the ecosystem is enhanced by three crucial third-party libraries that allow JavaScript programs to run while preserving asynchronous internal mechanisms. This harmony of third-party and native components allows Deno to maintain the asynchronous character of JavaScript while running programs with ease.

Deno's architecture is made up of roughly ten parts, divided into three third-party blocks and seven core components. These components highlight Deno's strong and flexible design and serve as the fundamental building blocks of its features and functioning.

Diagram of the Architecture

The main components that makeup Deno's native architecture are depicted in the block in *Figure* 2.7. This diagram offers a thorough rundown of the primary elements created and maintained by the Deno team. Please be aware that there are no elements from outside sources included in this diagram; it only highlights Deno's native components. This distinction is significant because it draws attention to the essential elements that, independent of external libraries and dependencies, make up Deno's runtime environment.

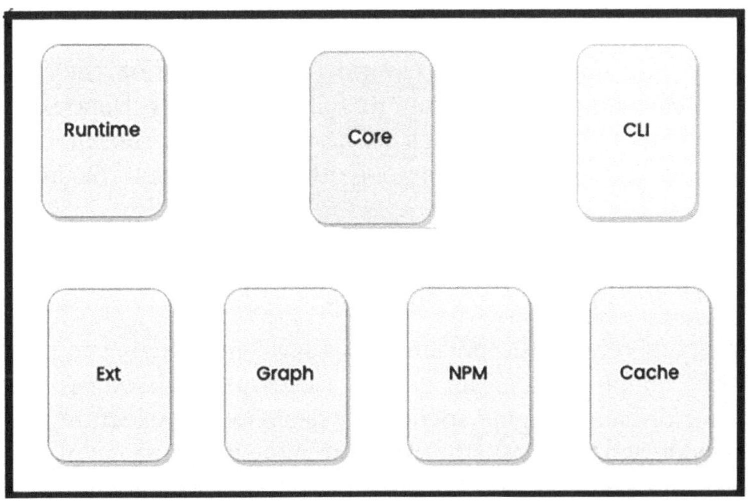

***Figure* 2.7**: *Main Components of Deno Architecture*

Let us first quickly review the main elements that make up this runtime environment before moving on to a more thorough analysis of Deno's design. This first overview will provide you with a basic grasp of Deno's functionality and the part each component plays in its broader framework, even though we will go into more detail about each of these elements in later parts. The context for a more thorough examination of Deno's internal operations will be established by this introduction.

Rusty_v8

As the following diagram illustrates, the Rusty_v8 component is an essential part of the Deno project. It acts as a bridge between the Rust programming language and V8's essential features by offering top-notch Rust bindings to the C++ API. Rusty_v8 facilitates smooth communication between Rust and V8 by providing a dependable and effective interface, making it easier to combine Rust's memory safety assurances with V8's potent engine.

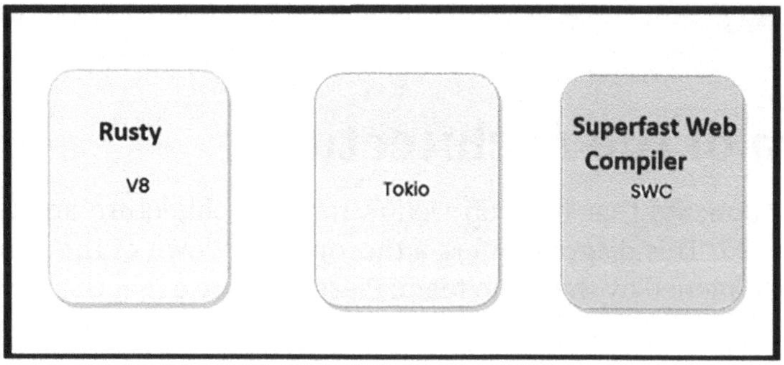

Figure 2.8: *Rusty_v8 Component. SWC Denotes Super-Fast Web Compiler*

Third-Party Components

Although Deno's core components are essential for its operation, they are insufficient on their own to execute tasks. To attain its full functionality, Deno relies on critical external components that act as the backbone of the Deno runtime. These external components, including Tokio and V8, among others, play a vital role in enabling Deno to run JS code.

V8

JavaScript programs rely on the presence of a JavaScript engine to execute, and V8 is a prominent example of such an engine. Developed by Google, V8 is an open-source, high-performance engine specifically designed for executing JavaScript and WebAssembly code. Built using the C++ programming language, V8 plays a vital role in powering JavaScript execution, enabling the runtime environment.

Super-Fast Web Compiler (SWC) for Typescript

The TypeScript compiler is a crucial third-party component in Deno, though not depicted in the diagram. As previously mentioned, V8 solely processes JavaScript code. However, Deno supports both TypeScript (TS) and JavaScript (JS). To allow TypeScript, Deno uses the TypeScript compiler to transform TypeScript code into

JavaScript before presenting it to V8 for execution. This process enables Deno to have bTSC/SWC.

Google's V8 engine is exclusively designed to run JavaScript code and does not support TypeScript, a superset of JavaScript that includes additional type information. To address this, TypeScript code must be translated into JavaScript through a transformation process, enabling the V8 engine to execute it.

Deno, however, utilizes a combination of tools - the TypeScript Compiler (TSC) and the Super-fast Web Compiler (SWC) - to handle both TypeScript and JavaScript files. When type-checking is required, Deno employs Microsoft's TSC compiler, which converts TypeScript to JavaScript and performs type error checking. Otherwise, Deno leverages the high-performance SWC compiler for rapid transpilation. This preference is due to TSC's slower performance, being implemented in JavaScript, compared to SWC's speed and efficiency.

SWC, built with Rust, is a fast TypeScript/JavaScript compiler that takes in modern files featuring async-await and generates browser-compatible JavaScript code. This transformation ensures code compatibility across various browsers with different levels of support for newer language features. Deno utilizes SWC to convert TypeScript files to JavaScript seamlessly. With its compatibility with the latest ECMAScript specifications, Deno eliminates the need to convert JavaScript files for compatibility reasons. By default, SWC selectively processes TypeScript files, leaving JavaScript files untouched unless explicitly requested to modify them.

- Built-in support for TypeScript applications.
- Rust-based platform for the Web.
- Speedy Web Compiler (SWC) is a super-fast JavaScript compiler.

SWC is an extensible Rust-based platform for the next generation of fast developer tools. It is used by tools such as Next.js, Parcel, and Deno, as well as companies such as Vercel, ByteDance, Tencent, Shopify, and more. SWC can be used for both compilation and bundling. For compilation, it takes JavaScript/TypeScript files using modern JavaScript features and outputs valid code that is supported by all major browsers.

SWC is designed to be extensible. Currently, there is support for:

- Compilation
- Bundling (swcpack, under development)
- Minification
- Transforming with WebAssembly
- Usage inside webpack (swc-loader)
- Improving Jest performance (@swc/jest)
- Custom Plugins

V8 is Google's open-source high-performance JavaScript and WebAssembly engine, written in C++. It is used in Chrome and Node.js, among others. It implements ECMAScript and WebAssembly and runs on Windows, macOS, and Linux systems that use x64, IA-32, or ARM processors. V8 can be embedded into any C++ application.

V8 is a JavaScript and WebAssembly engine developed by Google for its Chrome browser. V8 is free and open-source software that is part of the Chromium project and also used separately in non-browser contexts, notably the Node.js runtime system.

ECMAScript is an object-oriented programming language for performing computations and manipulating computational objects within a host environment. ECMAScript as defined here is not intended to be computationally self-sufficient; indeed, there are no provisions in this specification for input of external data or output of computed results. Instead, it is expected that the computational environment of an ECMAScript program will provide not only the objects and other facilities described in this specification but also certain environment-specific objects, whose description and behavior are beyond the scope of this specification except to indicate that they may provide certain properties that can be accessed and certain functions that can be called from an ECMAScript program.

ECMAScript was originally designed to be used as a scripting language but has become widely used as a general-purpose programming language. A scripting language is a programming language that is used to manipulate, customize, and automate the facilities of an existing system. In such systems, useful functionality is already available through a user interface, and the scripting language is a mechanism for exposing that functionality to program control. In this way, the existing system is said to provide a host environment of objects and facilities, which completes the capabilities of the scripting language. A scripting language is intended for use by both professional and non-professional programmers.

ECMAScript was originally designed to be a Web scripting language, providing a mechanism to enliven Web pages in browsers and to perform server computation as part of a Web-based client-server architecture. ECMAScript is now used to provide core scripting capabilities for a variety of host environments. Therefore the core language is specified in this document apart from any particular host environment.

ECMAScript usage has moved beyond simple scripting and it is now used for the full spectrum of programming tasks in many different environments and scales. As the usage of ECMAScript has expanded, so have the features and facilities it provides. ECMAScript is now a fully featured general-purpose programming language.

V8 compiles and executes JavaScript source code, handles memory allocation for objects, and garbage collects objects it no longer needs. V8's stop-the-world, generational, accurate garbage collector is one of the keys to V8's performance.

JavaScript is commonly used for client-side scripting in a browser, being used to manipulate Document Object Model (DOM) objects for example. The DOM is not, however, typically provided by the JavaScript engine but instead by a browser. The same is true of V8 – Google Chrome provides the DOM. V8 does however provide all the data types, operators, objects, and functions specified in the ECMA standard.

V8 enables any C++ application to expose its own objects and functions to JavaScript code. It is up to you to decide on the objects and functions you would like to expose to JavaScript.

Web Scripting

A web browser provides an ECMAScript host environment for client-side computation including, for instance, objects that represent windows, menus, pop-ups, dialog boxes, text areas, anchors, frames, history, cookies, and input/output. Further, the host environment provides a means to attach scripting code to events such as change of focus, page and image loading, unloading, error and abort, selection, form submission, and mouse actions. Scripting code appears within the HTML and the displayed page is a combination of user interface elements and fixed and computed text and images. The scripting code is reactive to user interaction, and there is no need for a main program.

A web server provides a different host environment for server-side computation including objects representing requests, clients, and files; and mechanisms to lock and share data. By using browser-side and server-side scripting together, it is possible to distribute computation between the client and server while providing a customized user interface for a Web-based application.

Each Web browser and server that supports ECMAScript supplies its own host environment, completing the ECMAScript execution environment.

Hosts and Implementations

To aid in integrating ECMAScript into host environments, this specification defers the definition of certain facilities (for example, abstract operations), either in whole or in part, to a source outside of this specification. Editorially, this specification distinguishes the following kinds of deferrals.

An implementation is an external source that further defines facilities enumerated in Annex D or those that are marked as implementation-defined or implementation-approximated. In informal use, an implementation refers to a concrete artifact, such as a particular web browser.

An implementation-defined facility is one that defers its definition to an external source without further qualification. This specification does not make any recommendations for particular behaviors, and conforming implementations are free to choose any behavior within the constraints put forth by this specification.

An implementation-approximated facility is one that defers its definition to an external source while recommending an ideal behavior. While conforming implementations are free to choose any behavior within the constraints put forth by this specification, they are encouraged to strive to approximate the ideal. Some mathematical operations, such as Math.exp are implementation-approximated.

A host is an external source that further defines facilities listed in Annex D but does not further define other implementation-defined or implementation-approximated facilities. In informal use, a host refers to the set of all implementations, such as the set of all web browsers, that interface with this specification in the same way via Annex D. A host is often an external specification, such as WHATWG HTML (https://html.spec.whatwg.org/). In other words, facilities that are host-defined are often further defined in external specifications.

A host hook is an abstract operation that is defined in whole or in part by an external source. All host hooks must be listed in Annex D. A host hook must conform to at least the following requirements:

It must return either a normal completion or a throw completion.

A host-defined facility is one that defers its definition to an external source without further qualification and is listed in Annex D. Implementations that are not hosts may also provide definitions for host-defined facilities.

A host environment is a particular choice of definition for all host-defined facilities. A host environment typically includes objects or functions which allow obtaining input and providing output as host-defined properties of the global object.

This specification follows the editorial convention of always using the most specific term. For example, if a facility is host-defined, it should not be referred to as implementation-defined.

Both hosts and implementations may interface with this specification via the language types, specification types, abstract operations, grammar productions, intrinsic objects, and intrinsic symbols defined herein.

ECMAScript Overview

The following is an informal overview of ECMAScript – not all parts of the language are described. This overview is not part of the standard proper.

ECMAScript is Object-Based: Basic language and host facilities are provided by objects, and an ECMAScript program is a cluster of communicating objects. In ECMAScript, an object is a collection of zero or more properties each with attributes that determine how each property can be used–for example, when the Writable attribute for a property is set to false, any attempt by executed ECMAScript code to assign a different value to the property fails. Properties are containers that hold other objects, primitive values, or functions.

A primitive value is a member of one of the following built-in types: Undefined, Null, Boolean, Number, BigInt, String, and Symbol; an object is a member of the built-in type Object; and a function is a callable object. A function that is associated with an object via a property is called a method.

ECMAScript defines a collection of built-in objects that round out the definition of ECMAScript entities. These built-in objects include the global object; objects that are fundamental to the runtime semantics of the language including Object, Function, Boolean, Symbol, and various Error objects; objects that represent and manipulate numeric values including Math, Number, and Date; the text processing objects String and RegExp; objects that are indexed collections of values including Array and nine different kinds of Typed Arrays whose elements all have a specific numeric data representation; keyed collections including Map and Set objects; objects supporting structured data including the JSON object, ArrayBuffer, SharedArrayBuffer, and DataView; objects supporting control abstractions including generator functions and Promise objects; and reflection objects including Proxy and Reflect.

ECMAScript also defines a set of built-in operators. ECMAScript operators include various unary operations, multiplicative operators, additive operators, bitwise shift operators, relational operators, equality operators, binary bitwise operators, binary logical operators, assignment operators, and the comma operator.

Large ECMAScript programs are supported by modules which allow a program to be divided into multiple sequences of statements and declarations. Each module explicitly identifies declarations it uses that need to be provided by other modules and which of its declarations are available for use by other modules.

ECMAScript syntax intentionally resembles Java syntax. ECMAScript syntax is relaxed to enable it to serve as an easy-to-use scripting language. For example, a variable is not required to have its type declared nor are types associated with properties, and defined functions are not required to have their declarations appear textually before calls to them.

Objects

Even though ECMAScript includes syntax for class definitions, ECMAScript objects are not fundamentally class-based such as those in C++, Smalltalk, or Java. Instead, objects may be created in various ways including via a literal notation or via constructors which create objects and then execute code that initializes all or part of them by assigning initial values to their properties. Each constructor is a function that has a property named “prototype” that is used to implement prototype-based inheritance and shared properties. Objects are created by using constructors in new expressions; for example, new Date(2009, 11) creates a new Date object. Invoking a constructor without using new has consequences that depend on the constructor. For example, Date() produces a string representation of the current date and time rather than an object.

Every object created by a constructor has an implicit reference (called the object’s prototype) to the value of its constructor’s `"prototype"` property. Furthermore, a prototype may have a non-null implicit reference to its prototype, and so on; this is called the prototype chain. When a reference is made to a property in an object, that reference is to the property of that name in the first object in the prototype chain that contains a property of that name. In other words, first, the object mentioned directly is examined for such a property; if that object contains the named property, that is the property to which the reference refers; if that object does not contain the named property, the prototype for that object is examined next; and so on.

- V8 is the name of the JavaScript engine that powers Google Chrome. It is the thing that takes our JavaScript and executes it while browsing with Chrome.
- V8 is the JavaScript engine that is it parses and executes JavaScript code. The DOM and the other Web Platform APIs (they all makeup runtime environments) are provided by the browser.

The cool thing is that the JavaScript engine is independent of the browser in which it is hosted. This key feature enabled the rise of Node.js. V8 was chosen to be the engine that powered Node.js back in 2009, and as the popularity of Node.js exploded, V8 became the engine that now powers an incredible amount of server-side code written in JavaScript.

The Node.js ecosystem is huge and thanks to V8 which also powers desktop apps, with projects such as Electron.

Other JS Engines

Other browsers have their own JavaScript engine:

- Firefox has SpiderMonkey.
- Safari has JavaScriptCore (also called Nitro).
- Edge was originally based on Chakra but has recently been rebuilt using Chromium and the V8 engine.
- And many others exist as well.

All those engines implement the ECMA ES-262 standard, also called ECMAScript, the standard used by JavaScript.

JavaScript is generally considered an interpreted language, but modern JavaScript engines no longer just interpret JavaScript, they compile it.

This has been happening since 2009 when the SpiderMonkey JavaScript compiler was added to Firefox 3.5, and everyone followed this idea.

JavaScript is internally compiled by V8 with Just-In-Time (JIT) compilation to speed up the execution.

This might seem counter-intuitive, but since the introduction of Google Maps in 2004, JavaScript has evolved from a language that was generally executing a few dozen lines of code to complete applications with thousands to hundreds of thousands of lines running in the browser.

Our applications can now run for hours inside a browser, rather than being just a few form validation rules or simple scripts.

In this new world, compiling JavaScript makes perfect sense because while it might take a little bit more to have the JavaScript ready, once done it is going to be much more performant than purely interpreted code.

npm Package Manager for Node.js

npm is the standard package manager for Node.js.

In September 2022, over 2.1 million packages were reported to be listed in the npm registry, making it the biggest single language code repository on Earth, and you can be sure there is a package for (almost!) everything.

It started as a way to download and manage dependencies of Node.js packages, but it has since become a tool used also in frontend JavaScript.

Tokio: Asynchronous Programming

Tokio, a crucial third-party component, plays a central role in Deno's architecture, serving as the foundation upon which Deno's asynchronous capabilities are built. The harmonious integration of Tokio empowers Deno to unlock its full asynchronous potential, enabling the efficient execution of concurrent tasks.

It interprets and executes JavaScript code efficiently.

Tokio, a vital third-party library, plays a central role in Deno's framework. Deno relies heavily on asynchronous programming to minimize callbacks. To achieve this, Deno utilizes Tokio, which converts synchronous functions into asynchronous ones.

Tokio is a runtime environment for building reliable, efficient, and asynchronous applications in Rust. Tokio is the foundation of Deno's asynchronous functionality, enabling Deno to run entirely asynchronously. While this book focuses on Deno, it is important to recognize Tokio's significance in the Deno ecosystem.

It provides an event-driven, non-blocking platform for creating asynchronous applications in Rust. Deno benefits from Tokio's non-blocking nature, aligning with its internal architecture.

As an asynchronous runtime, Tokio provides developers with the essential tools to build network-oriented applications. Its design enables developers to target a wide range of systems, from large servers with multiple cores to compact embedded devices.

Tokio's Usage in Deno

Deno utilizes Tokio in two main ways:

Creating Green Threads for Asynchronous Operations: Deno uses Tokio to create green threads, specialized threads that handle asynchronous operations efficiently. These threads enable concurrent task execution without the complexities of traditional multithreading, enhancing Deno's ability to manage multiple asynchronous tasks smoothly.

Extending Tokio's Async Capabilities to User Space: Deno provides users with access to Tokio's asynchronous functions, allowing developers to leverage Tokio's asynchronous runtime capabilities, such as efficient event handling and I/O operations, in their applications.

Deno also integrates with the Tokio runtime and other asynchronous modules. The following code snippet from Deno's codebase illustrates this integration:

The highlighted op_connect function demonstrates how Deno utilizes Tokio's capabilities to manage asynchronous operations efficiently, particularly in establishing TCP connections. This integration enables Deno to provide a robust and performant environment for handling various network-related tasks.

The functionality provided by Tokio is extensive and versatile. Here are some of the notable features it offers:

Tokio's core functionality is built around asynchronicity, a unifying theme that runs throughout its features. It provides asynchronous versions of traditional synchronous functions, ensuring non-blocking operations. For instance, Tokio wraps OS system calls in asynchronous functions, adhering to its *asynchronous programming approach*. This integration harmonizes Deno's async-oriented design with Tokio's non-blocking capabilities, leading to a synergistic relationship that enhances overall performance.

Tokio Functionalities

FS: This Tokio module provides essential tools and flexible structures for handling input/output operations with files and standard streams such as Stdin, Stdout, and Stderr. It also helps manage the filesystem. These tools are designed for use within the Tokio runtime environment. `fs` module encompasses utility methods and adapter types tailored for input/output operations involving files and standard streams (such as Stdin, Stdout, and Stderr). It also facilitates filesystem manipulation. The async `fs` module provides various asynchronous functions, including:

- Buffer copying
- Standard error (stderr) management
- Standard output (stdout) handling
- Standard input (stdin) handling
- And others

The async fs module offers a collection of asynchronous functions that efficiently handle various filesystem tasks. These functions are designed for asynchronous programming, ensuring non-blocking execution and preventing thread halting. The following asynchronous functions are available:

- **Copy File**: This function facilitates the copying of a file from one location to another.
- **Create Directory**: This function allows you to create a new directory, aiding in organizing your filesystem.
- **Read Directory**: With this function, you can access the contents of a directory, enabling you to gather information about the files it contains.
- **Remove Directory**: When you need to delete a directory and its contents, this function comes to your rescue.
- **Read File:** Utilize this function to read the contents of a file asynchronously, avoiding any disruption to the program's flow.
- **Write File:** If you wish to write data to a file, this function ensures that the process occurs smoothly within the async environment.
- **Remove File:** This function handles the deletion of a specific file in an asynchronous manner.
- **Rename File**: When the need arises to rename a file, this function provides a seamless solution.
- **Set Permissions**: With this function, you can set the permissions for a file or directory according to your requirements.

- **Net Module**: The 'net' module contains three sub-modules, each focused on a specific networking aspect.
- **TCP:** Ensures reliable, ordered, and error-checked data delivery between devices, making it a fundamental building block of internet communication.
- **UDP:** Offers faster but less reliable communication, suitable for tasks where speed is crucial and occasional data loss is acceptable.
- **Unix Domain Sockets**: Enables local Inter-Process Communication (IPC) on the same machine, providing a means for processes to communicate locally.

These sub-modules provide developers with tools to create and manage connections, establish communication channels, and design applications that prioritize speed, efficiency, and reliability.

These types, similar to those present in the standard library, enable the implementation of diverse networking protocols.

- **Process**: This module presents asynchronous versions of functions responsible for creating processes. The Tokio module introduces a Command structure, inspired by the std::process::Command type in the standard library, but with enhanced asynchronous capabilities for process creation. The module offers asynchronous variations of spawn, status, output, and related functions, which yield types compatible with futures and seamlessly integrate with Tokio's features.

  This module provides a range of asynchronous features, including:

- **Child Process Creation**: Asynchronous spawning of child processes for efficient multitasking.
- **Communication with Child Processes**: Asynchronous interaction with child processes, managing inputs and outputs (stdin, stdout, stderr) with ease.

The Command structure proves valuable for executing commands in various scenarios, such as:

- **Runtime:** The core of Tokio involves an I/O event loop, aptly referred to as the driver. This component manages I/O resources and distributes corresponding I/O events to tasks reliant on them. Furthermore, Tokio includes a scheduler designed to execute tasks that harness these I/O resources, along with a timer mechanism for scheduling tasks to commence after specific time intervals.

The Tokio runtime is a vital component in the Deno ecosystem, providing essential services for asynchronous program execution. Unlike typical Rust programs, asynchronous applications require runtime support for efficient operation.

The Tokio runtime offers the following vital services:

- **I/O Event Loop (Driver):** A dynamic loop managing I/O resources and dispatching events to dependent tasks for seamless execution.
- **Scheduler (Task Executor):** A dedicated scheduler efficiently orchestrates tasks relying on I/O resources, ensuring organized execution and optimal performance.
- **Timer (Temporal Precision):** A time-sensitive component enabling precise task scheduling at predefined intervals.

Tokio's comprehensive Runtime integrates these services into a unified entity, allowing for initiation, conclusion, and customization as a cohesive whole. Notably, manual runtime creation is not always necessary, as the **`tokio::main`** attribute macro automatically generates a Runtime, simplifying the process. This convenience feature eliminates the need for manual configuration, making it easier to utilize the Tokio runtime.

In Deno, the Tokio runtime is easily accessible via the **`tokio::main`** attribute, streamlining asynchronous operations. While understanding the Tokio runtime may seem complex initially, its core concept is to provide unwavering support for asynchronous tasks, serving as the backbone for efficient operation and outcome management. By leveraging the Tokio runtime, developers can create scalable and efficient asynchronous applications with ease.

Task: Encompassing asynchronous green threads, this module aids in managing concurrent tasks. Tokio tasks are asynchronous green threads, representing a lightweight and non-obstructive unit of execution. Similar to operating system threads, tasks execute independently, but unlike OS threads, they are managed by the Tokio runtime instead of the OS scheduler. This concept is commonly known as green threads, a term that highlights their resource-efficient and eco-friendly nature.

The realm of tasks offers a range of essential functionalities, including:

- **Task Spawning**: Initiating a new task's lifecycle.
- **Non-Blocking Tasks**: Tasks that execute without causing obstructions.
- **Blocking Mode Task Spawning:** Creating tasks in a mode that allows for potential blocks.
- **Selective Blocking Mode:** Instances where utilizing a blocking mode is warranted.
- **Block-In-Place:** Temporarily halting the ongoing operations of the present thread at a specific juncture.

The underpinning of tasks rests upon their exceptional efficiency, attributable to several factors:

- **Lightweight Nature:** Tasks are notably gentle on system resources.
- **Cooperative Scheduling**: Task scheduling is orchestrated in a cooperative manner.
- **Non-Blocking Essence**: The inherent design of tasks ensures they operate without inducing blocks.
- **IO**: Serving as the asynchronous counterpart to **`std::io`**, this module handles input/output tasks asynchronously. This Tokio module serves as an asynchronous version of **`std::io`**, introducing two key traits: AsyncRead and AsyncWrite. These traits are the asynchronous equivalents of the Read and Write traits in the standard library.
- **And Many More**: Tokio's offerings extend beyond the aforementioned modules, encompassing a diverse array of functionalities.

The aforementioned functions are asynchronous, meaning they are designed to operate without interrupting the program's execution. This allows other tasks to continue running concurrently without being blocked.

To help illustrate their usage, here is a simple code example that demonstrates how to use these async filesystem functions within a Tokio runtime:

Example: To Use `tokio fs`

Code Snippet

```
use tokio::fs;

#[tokio::main]
async fn main() -> Result<(), Box<dyn std::error::Error>> {
    // Example usage of async filesystem functions
    let content = fs::read_to_string("input.txt").await?;
    println!("Content of the file: {}", content);

    fs::write("output.txt", "Hello, Tokio!").await?;

    Ok(())
}
```

Example : Using `fs` and `io` in `tokio`

Code Snippet

```
use tokio::fs;
use std::io;

#[tokio::main]
```

```
async fn main() -> io::Result<()> {
    fs::create_dir("/some/dir").await?;
    Ok(())
}
```

The main thread is not blocked when the code snippet accesses the "**/some/dir**" directory asynchronously. '**create_dir'** is an asynchronous operation, as shown by the usage of 'await' at the conclusion.

You can enhance your comprehension of the capabilities and advantages of async filesystem functions in the Tokio ecosystem by studying and experimenting with code such as this.

Example of an async `fs` Operations:

Code Snippet

```
use tokio::fs;

fs::write("foo.txt", b"Hello world!").await?;
```

The code writes "**Hello world**" to a file named **foo.txt** asynchronously.

To show how these ideas are used in practice, let us look at an example of writing content to standard output (stdout):

Code Snippet

```
use tokio::io::{self, AsyncWriteExt};

#[tokio::main]
async fn main() -> io::Result<()> {
    let mut stdout = io::stdout();
    stdout.write_all(b"Hello world!").await?;
    Ok(())
}
```

The **write_all** function enables asynchronous writing of "**Hello World**" to the standard output (**stdout**), without blocking the main thread.

Example of Buffer Usage

Code Snippet

```
use tokio::io;

let mut reader: &[u8] = b"hello";
let mut writer: Vec<u8> = vec![];
```

```
io::copy_buf(&mut reader, &mut writer).await?;

assert_eq!(b"hello", &writer[..]);
```

Asynchronous copying from a reader to a writer is possible with the **copy_buf** interface.

Example of Illustration: Net Important networking elements including TCP, UDP, and Unix networking types are included in this Tokio module. These elements are essential for creating a variety of networking protocols, such as those for local networks and internet communication, among others. The efficient establishment of a TCP connection using Tokio's tools, which allow non-blocking communication between the client and server and improve overall responsiveness and scalability in networking interactions, is illustrated with an example of an asynchronous TCP client.

Code Snippet

```
use tokio::net::TcpSocket;
use std::io;

#[tokio::main]
async fn main() -> io::Result<()> {
    let addr = "127.0.0.1:8080".parse().unwrap();

    let socket = TcpSocket::new_v4()?;
    let stream = socket.connect(addr).await?;

    Ok(())
}
```

Example of the UdpSocket Connect System Call

The connect system call impedes the completion of other activities by blocking other processes until its work is finished. On the other hand, Tokio's **connect()** function employs a non-blocking methodology, allowing for effective and simultaneous processing. As soon as a connection is made, **connect()** quickly ends and returns a result without causing any delays to your main program thread. This enhances overall performance and responsiveness by guaranteeing that your software keeps running other activities without interruption. The advantages of Tokio's non-blocking **connect()** function are demonstrated in the following UDP server example to further clarify this idea:

Code Snippet

```
use tokio::net::UdpSocket;
use std::io;
```

```
#[tokio::main]
async fn main() -> io::Result<()> {
    let sock = UdpSocket::bind("0.0.0.0:8080").await?;
    let mut buf = [0; 1024];
    loop {
        let (len, addr) = sock.recv_from(&mut buf).await?;
        println!("{:?} bytes received from {:?}", len, addr);

        let len = sock.send_to(&buf[..len], addr).await?;
        println!("{:?} bytes sent", len);
    }
}
```

In this context, three essential system calls are **utilized: bind**, **recv_from**, and **send_to**. It is important to recognize that all three of these system calls function in a non-blocking mode, enabling efficient and concurrent processing. This means that these system calls will not obstruct other processes, allowing for seamless execution and improved performance.

Example of Process

Code Snippet

```
let mut cmd = Command::new("example_command");
cmd.arg("arg1").arg("arg2");

// Asynchronously spawn the child process
let child = cmd.spawn().await.expect("Failed to spawn the
process");

// Communicate with the child process's stdin, stdout, and stderr
asynchronously
let child_stdin = child.stdin().expect("Failed to open stdin");
let child_stdout = child.stdout().expect("Failed to open stdout");
let child_stderr = child.stderr().expect("Failed to open stderr");

// ... Further interactions with the child process ...
```

The Command module in Tokio provides a robust asynchronous foundation for efficiently managing child processes and their communication. This enables effective process management and seamless interaction with child processes.

Consider the following example, which demonstrates the module's capabilities:

Code Snippet

```
use tokio::process::Command;

#[tokio::main]
```

```
async fn main() -> Result<(), Box<dyn std::error::Error>> {
    // The usage is similar as with the standard library's
`Command` type
    let mut child = Command::new("echo")
        .arg("hello")
        .arg("world")
        .spawn()
        .expect("failed to spawn");

    // Await until the command completes
    let status = child.wait().await?;
    println!("the command exited with: {}", status);
    Ok(())
}
```

Example of Using Tokio Task

Let us look at some examples of task spawning in both blocking and non-blocking modes, together with an illustration of the block-in-place idea, to help you better understand task concepts. You will learn more about the versatility and power of Tokio tasks in Deno applications by going over these examples.

Code Snippet

```
use tokio::task;

// NON-BLOCKING

let join = task::spawn(async {
    // ...
    "hello world!"
});

// ...

// Await the result of the spawned task.
let result = join.await?;
assert_eq!(result, "hello world!");

// BLOCKING

let join = task::spawn_blocking(|| {
    // do some compute-heavy work or call synchronous code
    "blocking completed"
});

let result = join.await?;
assert_eq!(result, "blocking completed");
```

```
// BLOCK IN PLACE

let result = task::block_in_place(|| {
    // do some compute-heavy work or call synchronous code
    "blocking completed"
});

assert_eq!(result, "blocking completed");
```

Example of `TcpStreamResource`

Code Snippet

```
pub async fn op_net_connect_tcp<NP>(
  state: Rc<RefCell<OpState>>,
  addr: IpAddr,
) -> Result<(ResourceId, IpAddr, IpAddr), AnyError>
where
  NP: NetPermissions + 'static,
{
  {
    let mut state_ = state.borrow_mut();
    state_
      .borrow_mut::<NP>()
      .check_net(&(&addr.hostname, Some(addr.port)),
"Deno.connect()")?;
  }

  let addr = resolve_addr(&addr.hostname, addr.port)
    .await?
    .next()
    .ok_or_else(|| generic_error("No resolved address found"))?;
  let tcp_stream = TcpStream::connect(&addr).await?;
  let local_addr = tcp_stream.local_addr()?;
  let remote_addr = tcp_stream.peer_addr()?;

  let mut state_ = state.borrow_mut();
  let rid = state_
    .resource_table
    .add(TcpStreamResource::new(tcp_stream.into_split()));

  Ok((rid, IpAddr::from(local_addr), IpAddr::from(remote_addr)))
}
```

Conclusion

We learned in this chapter about, Deno's toolchain, ecosystem, and overall architecture of Deno. We also come to know the incoming version of Deno as Deno 2.0.

We learned about various components of Deno including cache and Deno's overall architecture. In the end, we learned about Rusty_v8, Web Scripting, other JS engines, and Tokio: asynchronous programming.

In the next chapter, we are going to learn about support on scripting TypeScript (Deno's exclusive) and JavaScript and Rust that makes Deno so safe.

References

1. **Deno 2.0 Is Here, and It's Scaly**: https://neon.tech/blog/deno-2-0-is-here-and-its-scaly
2. **Deno components**: https://choubey.gitbook.io/internals-of-deno/architecture/core

CHAPTER 3
TypeScript, JavaScript, and Rust

Introduction

Although Deno uses JavaScript, its specialty is due to its own scripting language, TypeScript which makes it very secure. Deno is a modern, zero-config JavaScript runtime written in Rust. At its core is Rusty V8, a library that has provided high-quality, zero-overhead Rust bindings to V8's C++ API over the past five years.

Structure

In this chapter, we are going to learn the following topics:

- Computer Programming Languages
- Scripting Languages
- JavaScript
- The Code Runner
- TypeScript
- Rust
- Application of Rust in Field

Computer Programming Languages

The three types of programming languages are:

- Machine language
- Assembly language
- High (or higher) level language

Machine language consists of simply digital bits, as computer machine understands only binary bit level 0 or 1.

Assembly language understands commands in short mnemonics. High-level languages are very easy to understand by human subjects, such as cobol, basic, C, C++, c.net, R, and Python. High-level means easy to understand by a programmer.

Higher-level languages convert a program into machine language by getting compiled through a compiler or interpreted by an interpreter. Both are software.

Machine Language and Assembly Language are both low-level (of understanding) programming languages that interact closely with a computer's hardware. The primary distinction between the two is that assembly language is a human-readable version of machine language, but machine language is a binary code that computers directly comprehend and run.

Machine Language

A sequence of bits that directly controls a processor. Machine language is made up of only two symbols, 0 and 1, which represent **on** for true states, and **off** for false states, respectively. Machine language is used to write detailed instructions for the processor, such as addition, comparison, data movement, and so on.

Machine Language Machine language is a low-level (level of ease of understanding) programming language that primarily uses 1s and 0s. In the early days of computing, using binary digits to draw an image or display data was a complex task. For instance, representing the number 120 in binary translates to 1111000, which is not exactly user-friendly. This complexity led to the development of assembly language.

Machine languages utilize a series of bits to issue commands. The 1s signify the 'on' or 'true' states, while 0s represent the 'off' or 'false' states. The conversion of a high-level language into machine language is CPU-dependent. However, machine language does not require mnemonics. It is nearly impossible for humans to memorize machine language's binary codes, making it a hard language to learn.

Machine languages do not require translators as they are already in a form that machines can understand. They execute commands quickly because their data is already in binary format. Machine language is the most basic of all programming languages and runs instructions directly through the system's CPU.

Assembly Language

Assembly language is a step up from low-level language but still lower than high-level language, positioning it as an intermediary language. It uses abbreviations, symbols, and numbers instead of binary digits (1s and 0s). For example, it uses symbols such as Mul, Sub, and Add to represent multiplication, subtraction, and addition respectively.

Assembly languages use mnemonics symbols and names instead of raw bit sequences. This makes assembly language codes more readable than machine language codes and easier for humans to convert into machine codes. The easier readability and conversion make assembly languages learnable.

Assembly languages require translators, also known as assemblers, to convert the mnemonics into a form that machines can understand. These languages have slower execution speeds than machine languages. Assembly language is a low-level programming language that requires an assembler to convert its instructions into executable machine code.

A human-readable representation of machine language that uses mnemonic codes to represent machine language instructions. Assembly language is used to directly manipulate hardware, access specialized processor instructions, or evaluate critical performance issues.

Conversion Among Low-Level Languages

An **assembler** is a program that converts assembly language code into machine language.

While programming directly in machine language can provide a deeper understanding of how a computer works, it can also be time-consuming, prone to errors, and difficult to debug and maintain.

Difference between Machine Language and Assembly Language

Machine languages are *first-generation languages*. Assembly languages are *second-generation languages*. Machine languages represent data and information using

Binary (Two digits1s and 0s), used in CPU (exactly in ALU),

Octadecimal or Octaganal (8 digits-1,2,3,4,5,6,7,8), used for computer punching, and **Hexadecimal (also base-16 or simply hex)** (deploys 16 digits- 0,1,2,3,4,5,6,7,8,9, A, B, C, D, E, and F). For example, the decimal value 711 would be expressed in hexadecimal as 2C716. Hex codes are a hexadecimal format for identifying colors. This is a system used in HTML, CSS, and SVG.

For example, color values and MAC addresses are often represented in hex. Additionally, hex is easier to understand than binary. Hex is often used in computer science and cryptography because it is a convenient way to represent binary data. The hexadecimal value for red in HTML is #FF0000, and the hexadecimal value for black is #000000.

Remember that Machine language does not recognize our decimal system of 10 digits.

Main Differences between Machine Language and Assembly Language:

The main differences between Machine Language and Assembly Language include their syntax, ease of comprehension, speed of execution, use of mnemonics, and more. For instance, while Machine Language uses binary digits, Assembly Language uses English-like syntax. Also, Machine Language executes faster than Assembly Language but is harder for humans to understand.

Parameters	Machine Language	Assembly Language
Syntax Nature	Machine languages are composed of binary digits (1s and 0s).	Assembly languages use a syntax similar to English, making it more understandable to non-programmers.
Comprehension Ease	Machine languages are only comprehensible to computers. It's nearly impossible for humans to decipher it.	Assembly language is easy for humans to understand and use. However, machines cannot directly interpret them.
Language Level	Machine language is the most basic programming language. It runs instructions directly through the system's CPU.	Assembly language is a low-level programming language. It requires an assembler to convert its instructions into executable machine code.
Dependency	Machine languages are platform-dependent, with features varying accordingly.	Assembly languages use a standard set of instructions.
Application Areas	Machine languages are primarily used for machine coding.	Assembly languages can be used in microprocessor-based applications and real-time systems.
Language Generation	Machine languages are first-generation languages.	Assembly languages are second-generation languages.
Code Representation	Machine languages represent data and information using binary (1s and 0s), octadecimal, and hexadecimal formats.	Assembly languages use mnemonics like End, Sub, Ass, Mov, Mul, etc., to represent data and information.

Mnemonics Usage	Machine languages issue commands using a series of bits. They do not require mnemonics.	Assembly languages use mnemonics symbols and names instead of raw bit sequences. This makes the codes more readable and easier for humans to convert into machine codes.
Execution Speed	Machine languages execute commands quickly because their data is already in binary format.	Assembly languages have slower execution speeds than machine languages.
Translator Requirement	Machine languages do not require translators as they are already in a form that machines can understand.	Assembly languages require translators, also known as assemblers, to convert the mnemonics into a form that machines can understand.
Dependency	Machine languages are hardware-dependent.	Assembly languages are machine-dependent, making them non-portable.
Modifications	Machine languages do not support modifications, alterations, or error fixing.	Assembly programming languages can be easily modified.
Memorization	It's nearly impossible for humans to memorize machine language's binary codes.	Humans can easily memorize the codes/commands used in assembly languages.
Error Risk	Machine languages generally have a higher risk of syntax errors.	Assembly languages have a comparatively lower risk of syntax errors.
Compiler Requirement	Machine languages do not require a compiler for command execution.	Assembly languages require an assembler (commonly referred to as a compiler) for proper command execution.

***Figure 3.1**: Distinguishing between Machine Language and Assembly Language*

Compiler

A compiler is a translator that produces an output of low-level language (such as an assembly or machine language) by taking an input of high-level language. It is basically a computer program used to transform codes written in a programming language into machine code (human-readable code to a binary 0 and 1 bit language for a computer processor to understand). The computer then processes the machine code for performing the corresponding tasks.

Compilers check all types of *errors, limits, and ranges*. Thus, it is more intelligent. The run time of its program is longer, and it occupies more memory. C, C++, C#, Java, and Scala use Compilers.

Interpreter

It is a program that functions for the translation of a programming language into a comprehensible one. It is a computer program used for converting high-level program statements into machine codes. It includes pre-compiled code, source code (written with the help of high-level language), and scripts. *Perl, Ruby, and* PHP use Interpreters.

An interpreter translates only one statement at a time in the program.

Scripting Languages [1]

Scripting languages are a type of programming language. They are **interpreted** rather than requiring **compilation**. These are languages designed for specific runtime environments to provide additional functions, integrate complex systems, and communicate with other programming languages.

Scripting languages can fall into two broad categories:

- **Client-Side:** Client-side scripting languages focus on the parts of a website or web application that the end user (or client) interacts with directly.
- **Server-Side:** Server-side scripting languages interact directly with and run on the server. These scripts are typically invisible to the end user.

Here is a list of the twelve most famous scripting languages:

1. JavaScript
2. PHP
3. Python
4. Perl
5. Ruby
6. Bash which is a Unix command language.
7. R (popular in statistics and data analysis)
8. Lua is an embeddable scripting language.

9. Groovy (syntax similar to Java)
10. PowerShell is a command-line scripting language that can work with many platforms.
11. VBA is a domain-specific scripting language Visual Basic for Applications.
12. Type Script (famous for Deno Web Applications)

JavaScript

JavaScript is a powerful programming language that can add interactivity to a website. It was invented by Brendan Eich.

JavaScript is versatile and beginner-friendly. With more experience, you will be able to create games, animated 2D and 3D graphics, comprehensive database-driven apps, and much more! JavaScript is a programming language that adds interactivity to your website. This happens in games, in the behavior of responses when buttons are pressed or with data entry on forms, with dynamic styling, with animation, and so on. JavaScript is easy to learn. It is the world's most popular programming language.

JavaScript itself is relatively compact, yet very flexible. Developers have written a variety of tools on top of the core JavaScript language, unlocking a vast amount of functionality with minimum effort. These include:

Browser Application Programming Interfaces (APIs) built into web browsers, providing functionality such as dynamically creating HTML and setting CSS styles, collecting and manipulating a video stream from a user's webcam, or generating 3D graphics and audio samples.

Third-party APIs allow developers to incorporate functionality in sites from other content providers, such as Disqus or Facebook.

Third-Party Frameworks and Libraries that you can apply to HTML to accelerate the work of building sites and applications. JavaScript frameworks on Windows *include Node.js, React.js, Vue.js, Next.js, Nuxt.js, and Gatsby.*

JavaScript is a versatile and powerful programming language that is commonly used for web development. Running JavaScript on Windows 10 is easy with the right tools and setup. In this guide, we will walk you through the steps to set up your Windows 10 environment for running JavaScript programs.[2]

Step 1: Install Node.js

You need to install Node.js for JavaScript development when you want to run JavaScript code outside of a web browser.

Downloading Node.js

1. Open your web browser and navigate to the official Node.js website at nodejs.org.
2. On the homepage, you will see the "`LTS`" tab, which stands for Long-Term Support. Click on this tab to download the recommended version of Node.js for most users.
3. Once the download is complete, run the installer. Follow the on-screen instructions to install Node.js on your Windows 10 machine.

Installing Node.js

1. Run the Node.js installer that you downloaded in the previous step.
2. Click "`Next`" on the initial screen to begin the installation process. Accept the license agreement and click "`Next`."
3. Choose the destination folder where Node.js will be installed or leave the default setting. Click "`Next`."
4. Click "`Install`" to begin the installation process. Once the installation is complete, click "`Finish`" to exit the installer.

Figure 3.2: *Setup Wizard for node.js*

Checking if Node.js is Installed on Windows 10

Open the Command Prompt and type **`node -v`** and press *Enter*. This command will display the installed version of Node.js.

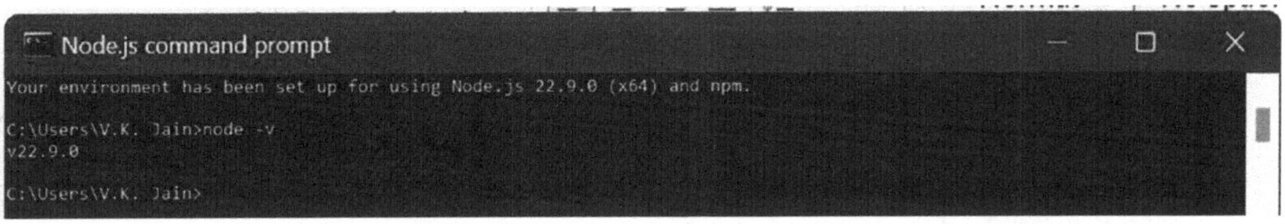

Figure 3.3: *Version Number Displayed*

Additionally, you can check if Node Package Manager (npm) is installed by typing **`npm -v`** and press *Enter*. This command will display the installed version of npm. You can see that we have installed the v22.9.0 version on our machine.

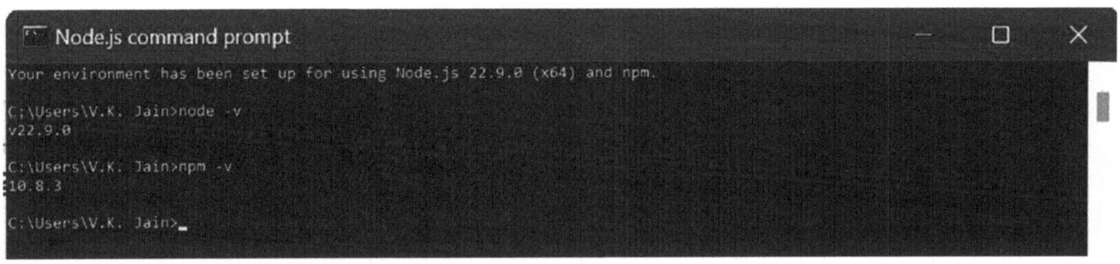

Figure 3.4: *Version Number of npn Displayed*

You can see that we have installed the 10.8.3 version of **npm** on our machine.

Step 2: Installing Visual Studio Code on Windows 10

Download the Visual Studio Code installer from the official website at code.visualstudio.com.

Run the installer and follow the on-screen instructions to install Visual Studio Code on your Windows 11 machine.

Figure 3.5: *Finishing of Setup Wizard*

User Interface

At its heart, Visual Studio Code is a code editor. Like many other code editors, VS Code adopts a common user interface and layout of an explorer on the left, showing all of the files and folders you have access to, and an editor on the right showing the content of the files you have opened.

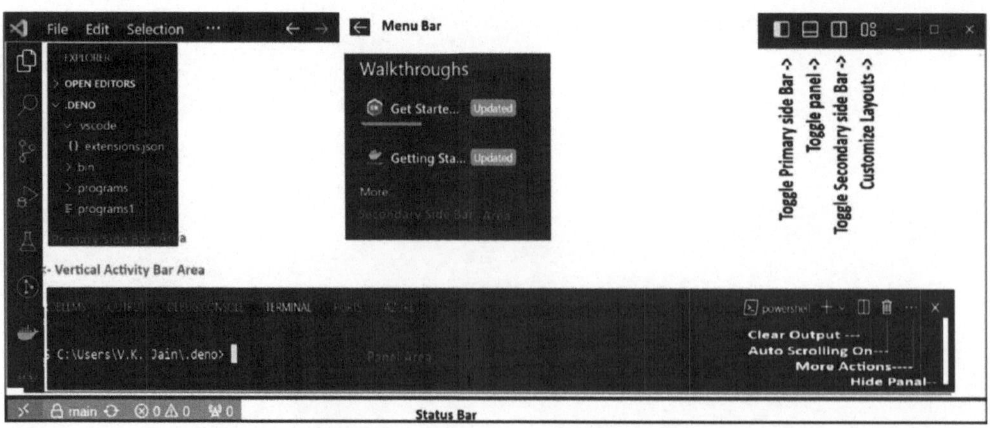

Figure 3.6: *User Interface of Visual Studio Code*

VS Code comes with a simple and intuitive layout that maximizes the space provided for the editor while leaving ample room to browse and access the full context of your folder or project. The user interface is divided into five main areas:[3]

1. **Editor** - The main area to edit your files. You can open as many editors as you like side by side vertically and horizontally.
2. **Primary Side Bar** - Contains different views like the Explorer to assist you while working on your project.
3. **Status Bar** - Information about the opened project and the files you edit.
4. **Activity Bar** – Located vertically on the far left-hand side. It Lets you switch between:
    a. Search
    b. Source Control
    c. Run and debug
    d. Testing and other options. (Vide *Figure* 3.5 and *Figure* 3.6)

    You can change the position of the Activity Bar.
5. **Panel** - An additional space for views below the editor region. By default, it contains output, debug information, errors and warnings, and an integrated terminal. The Panel can also be moved to the left or right for more vertical space.

Tip: A *Secondary Side Bar is also available to display views opposite the Primary Side Bar. You can show it with Ctrl+*Alt+B *and drag a view from the Primary Side Bar to the Secondary Side Bar.*

Each time you start VS Code, it opens up in the same state it was in when you last closed it. The folder, layout, and opened files are preserved.

Open files in each editor are displayed with tabbed headers (Tabs) at the top of the editor region. To learn more about tabbed headers, see the Tabs section.

Tip: *You can move the Primary Side Bar to the right-hand side by right-clicking the Activity Bar and selecting Move Primary Side Bar Right or toggle its visibility* (Ctrl+B).

Side by Side Editing

You can open as many editors as you like side by side vertically and horizontally. If you already have an editor open, there are multiple ways of opening another editor to the side:

1. Alt and select a file in the Explorer view.

2. *Ctrl+* to split the active editor into two.
3. Open to the Side (*Ctrl+Enter*) from the Explorer context menu on a file.
4. Select the **Split Editor** button in the upper right of an editor.
5. Drag and drop a file to any side of the editor region.
6. Press *Ctrl+Enter* in the Quick Open (*Ctrl+P*) file list.

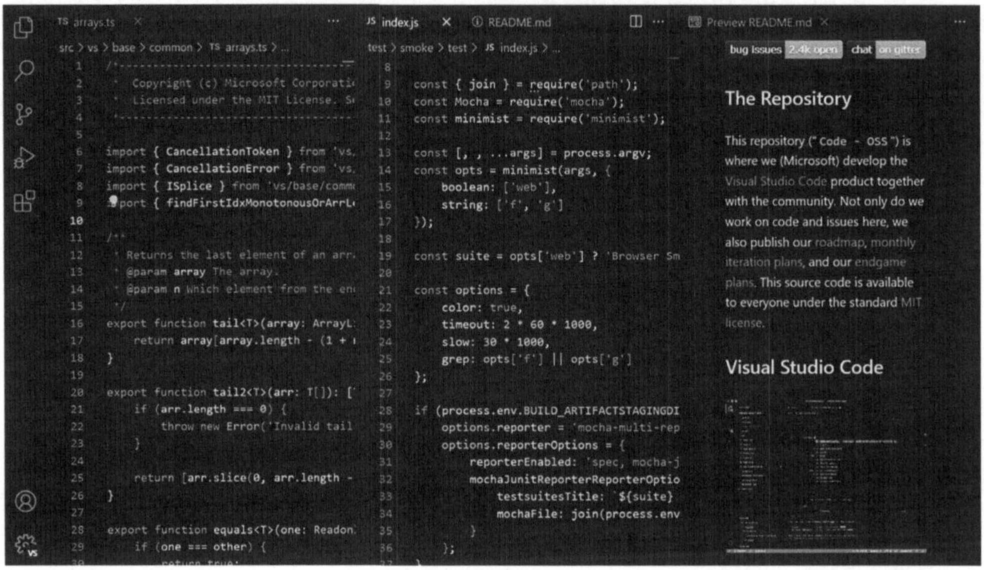

***Figure 3.7:** Different Types of Code Editors are Displayed*

The content of the active editor will be shown when you open another file. To open the file "**foo.cs**" into the right-hand editor while using two editors side by side, make sure the right-hand editor is active (by clicking inside it) before opening the file.

When you open another file, the contents of the active editor will be displayed. When utilizing two editors side by side, open the "**foo.cs**" file in the right-hand editor. To do this, click inside the right-hand editor to ensure it is active.

By default, editors open to the right of the one that is now active. This behavior can be changed using the workbench editor. Instead, use the **openSideBySideDirection** argument to open new editors to the bottom of the active one.

When you have multiple editors open, you can swiftly switch between them by pressing 1, 2, or 3 while holding down the *Ctrl* key (or Cmd on macOS).

Editors can be resized and rearranged. To move or resize the editor, drag and drop the editor title area.

Groups of Editors in VS

A new editor zone, known as an edit group, is produced when you divide an editor using the divide Editor or Open to the Side commands. This region can include a collection of things. As many editing groups as you like can be opened side by side in both vertical and horizontal orientations. These are easily seen in the Explorer view's **`Open Editors`** section (**`toggle...`** > **`Open Editors`** in the Explorer view).

When you open another file, the editor that is active will display the content of that file. If you have two editors side by side and you want to open file **`'foo.cs'`** into the right-hand editor, make sure that this editor is active (by clicking inside it) before opening file **`'foo.cs`**.'

By default, editors open to the right-hand side of the active one. You can change this behavior with the **`workbench.editor.openSideBySideDirection`** setting to open new editors to the bottom of the active one instead.

When you have more than one editor open, you can switch between them quickly by holding the *Ctrl* key (Cmd on macOS) and pressing 1, 2, or 3.

Tip: *You can resize editors and reorder them. Drag and drop the editor title area to reposition or resize the editor.*

When you split an editor (using the **`Split Editor`** or **`Open to the Side`** commands), a new editor region (edit group) is created which can hold a group of items. You can open as many editor groups as you like side by side vertically and horizontally.

You can see these clearly in the **`Open Editors`** section at the top of the Explorer view (toggle ... > **`Open Editors`** in the Explorer view).

Main Menu

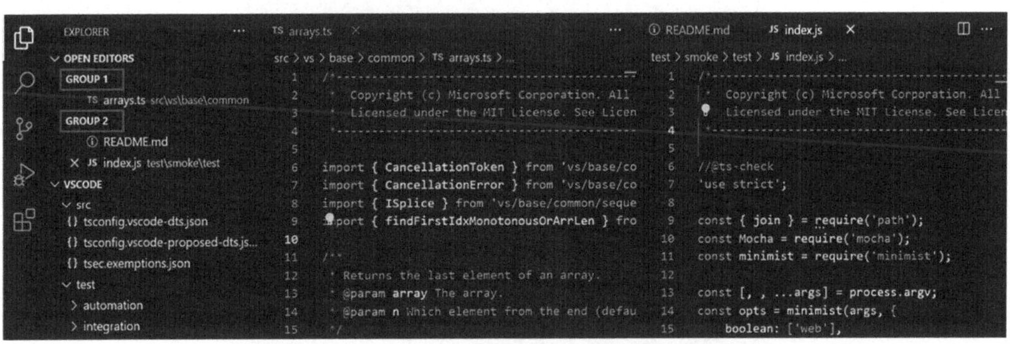

Figure 3.8: Main Menu

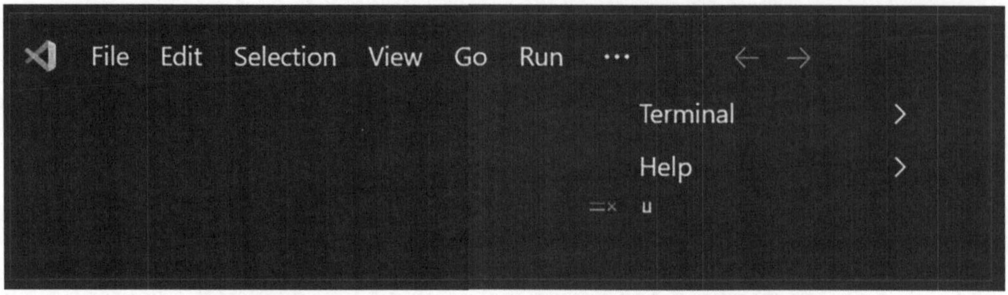

Figure 3.9: *Options Displayed After Pressing ... of Main Menu*

The menu is always on the top of the VS screen on the left side in the shape of a horizontal bar containing the following options as shown in *Figure* 3.8.

`File, Edit, Selection, Views, Go, Run, and` ... This last item has two options: The first option provides the terminal (VS Code) and the other option is **`Help`**.

The views option of the menu provides many facilities as depicted in *Figure* 3.9.

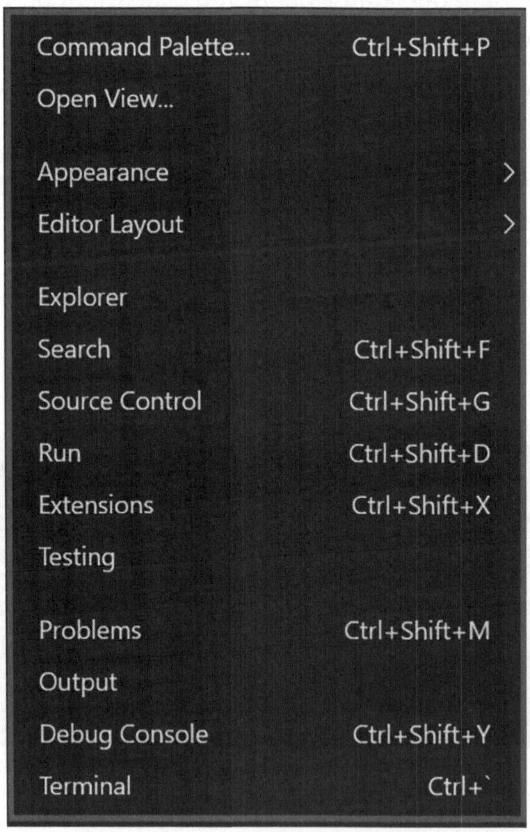

Figure 3.10: *The Views Option of Menu Provides Many Facilities*

Configuring Visual Studio Code to Execute JavaScript Applications

1. Click the Extensions icon in the window's Activity Bar or hit *Ctrl* + *Shift* + X to launch Visual Studio Code.
2. Look for the "**`Debugger for Chrome`**" and "**`JavaScript (ES6) code snippets`**" extensions in the Extensions view.
3. To install each extension, click the "**`Install`**" button.
4. Either hit *Ctrl* + *Shift* + X or click the **`Extensions`** icon in the window's Activity Bar.

Using Visual Studio Code to Create Your First JavaScript Program

1. To create a new file, click "**`File`**" in the menu bar and choose "**`New File`**."
2. In the editor, type your JavaScript code. You may write a straightforward "**`Hello, World!`**" program, for instance.
3. Use **`a.js`** extension to save the file, such as **`hello.js.console.log("Hello, World!")`**;
4. Look for the "**`Code Runner`**" extension in the Extensions view.
5. To install the extension, click the "**`Install`**" button.

The Code Runner

Launching the Visual Studio Code JavaScript Program

In Visual Studio Code, open the **`hello.js`** JavaScript file you produced.

Choose "**`Run Code`**" from the context menu by performing a right-click anywhere in the editor.

As an alternative, you can execute the code by pressing *Ctrl* + *Alt* + N.

TypeScript

Static typing is added by TypeScript, a syntactic superset of JavaScript. In essence, TypeScript enables developers to create types by superimposing syntax on top of JavaScript. The fact that TypeScript is a "Syntactic Superset" indicates that it adds something to JavaScript's underlying syntax.

Requirement of TypeScript in Deno

JavaScript is a language with relaxed typing. Understanding the kinds of data that JavaScript is passing around can be challenging. Variables and function arguments in JavaScript are informationless! Developers must therefore consult the documentation or make educated guesses based on the implementation.

The types of data that are passed around within the code can be specified using TypeScript, which also has the capability to report errors when the types of data do not match.

When a string is passed into a function that expects a number, for instance, TypeScript will raise an error; whereas, JavaScript will not.

Compile time type checking is used by TypeScript. In other words, it verifies that the types supplied match before executing the code rather than during execution.

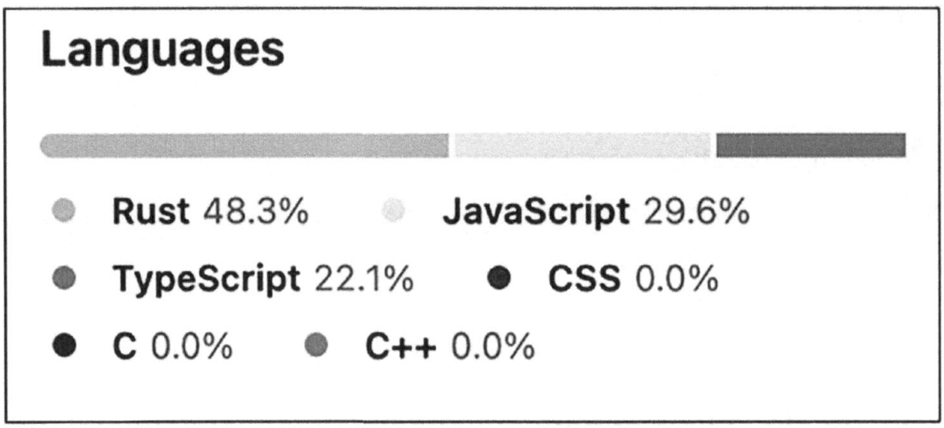

Figure 3.11: *Percentewise Deployment of Deno Progrogramming Packages*

Rust

In this section, we shall acquire general knowledge about Rust as applicable to Deno Web programming rather than learning the Rust programming language.

The Mozilla Corporation is the developer of the contemporary systems programming language Rust. It is designed to be a language for extremely secure and concurrent systems. It is as fast as C and C++ since it compiles to native code. Rust is a programming language for systems that is statically and tightly typed. Strongly indicates that certain kinds are intended to make it more difficult to build wrong programs, whereas statically indicates that all types are known at compile time. Compared to a cowboy language such as C, a successful compilation implies you have a far higher guarantee of correctness. Systems entail creating optimal machine code while maintaining complete control of memory usage. Thus, the applications are rather basic and include embedded systems, device drivers, and operating systems that may not even have an operating system. However, it is actually a very pleasant language to write normal application code in as well.

The primary difference between Rust and C and C++ is that all memory accesses are validated in Rust, making it safe by default. It is impossible for memory corruption to happen by accident. Rust is a systems-level programming language developed by Graydon Hoare. Later, Mozilla Labs acquired the application. Rust is not an object-oriented or functional programming language. It lacks classes and does not directly support object-oriented patterns. Despite the wide variety of programming languages, Rust is rapidly becoming the most talked-about topic in the computing business. Even though HTML and JavaScript are still the most widely used programming languages, Rust is growing in popularity among developers due to its simplicity, efficiency, and security.

Programming Languages for Applications versus Systems

Software and software platforms are created using systems programming languages such as C/C++. They can be used to create compilers, game engines, operating systems, and more. A significant amount of hardware interaction is necessary for these programming languages.

Software that directly serves users is created using application programming languages such as Java and C#. They assist us in creating business applications such as word processors, spreadsheets, web apps, and mobile apps.

There are two main issues with systems and application programming languages:

- Writing secure code is challenging.
- It is difficult to write multi-threaded code.

Design Goals of Creating a New Language:

The language was created to make it easy to create software that is incredibly dependable and quick. High-level programs as well as hardware-specific programs can be written in Rust. Rust prioritizes three objectives: Safety, speed, and concurrency Rust is based on the following guiding principles:

- Rigorously requiring safe data borrowing.
- Data operations using functions, methods, and closures.
- Using tuples, structs, and enums to compile information pattern matching to select and destructure data traits to define behavior on data.

Features of Rust Programming

Although there is a rapidly expanding ecosystem of libraries accessible through Cargo, we will focus on the fundamentals of the language by learning how to use the standard library. Writing many little programs is advisable, so mastering the use of rustc directly is essential. Here is a small script called rrun to perform a compilation and execute the outcome while working on the examples in this tutorial:

Rust is designed for high performance, speed, and safety. It has been voted one of the most loved programming languages for more than five years in StackOverflow's survey.

Rust is an open-source systems programming language that is syntactically similar to C++.

It is a general-purpose programming language that is extensively used to build:

- Kernels for operating systems.
- Game engines for video games.
- Browser engines for web browsers such as Chrome, Firefox, and so on.
- Command-line tools, and so on.

Here are some of the major features of Rust that make it one of the most popular programming languages in recent times.

- **Performance**: Just like C programming, Rust is fast and requires less memory. So, we are not compromising on performance with Rust. Rust programming language does not have a Garbage Collector (GC) by design. This improves the performance at runtime. Rust is extremely fast when it comes to compilation and execution time.
- **Zero-Cost Abstractions:** All Rust code is compiled into Assembly using the LLVM back-end (also used by C). Programming features such as Generics and Collections do not come with runtime costs; it will only be slower to compile. (Source: stackoverflow).
- **Memory Safety at Compile Time**: Rust prevents the crashing of programs by ensuring memory safety. Without memory safety, programs can crash unexpectedly.
- Software built using Rust is safe from memory issues such as dangling pointers, buffer overruns, and memory leaks.
- **Safe Concurrency:** Rust allows multiple parts of the program to run simultaneously. However, they cannot modify the same value at the same time. This ensures different parts of the program can safely run concurrently.

- **Platform Independent:** You can compile a Rust program on one platform, then take it to another platform and run it.
- **Multi-Threaded Applications:** Concurrency without data races is provided by Rust's ownership and memory safety requirements.
- **Support for Web Assembly (WASM):** Web Assembly facilitates the execution of complex algorithms on embedded devices, browsers, and other locations. It operates at native code speed. Web Assembly can be used to build Rust for dependable and quick execution.
- **Ownership System**: Rust's ownership model removes problems such as resource leaks and dangling pointers while guaranteeing memory safety.
- **Borrowing and Lifetimes**: To avoid common programming errors, the borrow checker imposes stringent guidelines for both mutable and immutable references. By imposing stringent limitations on the duration of valid references, the lifetime notion aids in the prevention of hanging references.
- **Pattern Matching**: The robust pattern matching feature in Rust makes it easier to write clear, expressive code that handles a variety of data structures and control flow. This feature makes code more understandable and maintainable by allowing for the handling of various circumstances in a concise and expressive manner.
- **Genetics and Traits:** Through trait-based polymorphism and generic programming, Rust's trait system facilitates code reuse. Generics improve code efficiency and reusability by giving programmers the freedom to write code that can function with a variety of data types.
- **Fearless Concurrency**: Safe and effective concurrent code free of data races is ensured by Rust's concurrency architecture, which is based on ownership and traits. Because of this, developers may design concurrent code with confidence and steer clear of frequent parallel programming mistakes.
- **Cargo Package Manager:** Cargo, a built-in package manager in Rust, makes building, testing, documentation creation, and dependency management easier.
- **Builds Optimized Code for Generics:** If you have generic code, Rust's compiler can smartly identify the code for, say, Lists and Sets, and optimize it differently for both.
- **Rust Compilation Errors:** Rust's compiler gives the most helpful error messages if you mess up your code. In some cases, the compiler will give you code that you can copy/paste in order for it to work.
- **Documentation:** Rust has an amazing Documentation, and a tutorial guide called The Rust Book. The Rust Book is your best friend on this journey.

Advantages of Deploying Rust

Some benefits are enumerated as follows:

- **Memory Safety**: By implementing stringent compile-time checks, Rust guards against the most prevalent memory-related errors. Data races, buffer overflows, and null pointer dereferences are a few of the issues.
- **Fast Testing and Debugging**: Rust is a very fast language that facilitates efficient debugging.
- **Integration Ease:** C and numerous other well-known programming languages are easily compatible with Rust.
- **Concurrency:** Writing concurrent and parallel code without compromising security is made simple by Rust's ownership system and lightweight threads, or "async."

Disadvantages of Rust

Some demerits are enumerated as follows:

- **High Learning Curve**: Beginners may find Rust's distinct syntax and ideas difficult to understand. It takes a learning investment to comprehend and apply ideas such as ownership, borrowing, and lifetimes appropriately.
- **Compilation Time:** Compared to other languages, Rust may take longer to compile due to its strong emphasis on performance and safety.
- **Smaller Ecology**: Despite its quick growth, the Rust ecosystem can still be smaller than that of more well-known languages such as Python or JavaScript. It may take more work to locate particular libraries or tools for specialized use cases.
- Learning Rust may take longer due to its handling complexity characteristic.
- Code written in Rust may be less effective and take longer to compile.
- Because Rust apps are more complicated, they could take longer to finish.
- **The Difficulty of Learning a New Programming Language:** Since Rust is a new language, it will take longer to gain traction, and employment opportunities may be less plentiful than for other well-known programming languages.
- **Potential Memory Leakage:** Rust may occasionally become slower than a well-known programming language due to memory leakage.
- Software maintenance is challenging because of the size of its code base.

Application of Rust in Field

The Rust programming language has several applications, ranging from creating backend systems for data research to creating games. It is highly dynamic because of its successful blend of speed, ease of use, and safety. The following are five of the most popular applications for the Rust programming language:

- **Development of Web Pages**

  It is no surprise that so many people choose Rust for web development as it is an all-purpose language known for its excellent performance and security. It is not only designed to be error-free, but it can also achieve lower latency and faster runs. The fact that Rust does not depend on a garbage collector, a memory management tool that might slow down development, is another factor driving developers to use it. However, some well-known languages such as JavaScript and Python are more closely associated with web development, Rust has the potential to become the go-to programming language for developers in the future.

- **Programming Networks**

  Rust is the perfect programming language for network development because of its concurrency and memory safety characteristics. The features that Rust offers will undoubtedly amaze those who want to create network applications that combine speed and security. Developers can use a variety of helpful features in the language's Tokio software library to create network applications that are safe, effective, and scalable. Numerous tasks pertaining to network programming, such as asynchronous networking, HTTP client and server development, and network protocol creation, can be accomplished with Rust.

- **Programming the System**

  Rust has gained popularity for system programming, especially in the building of operating systems, because of its successful blend of low-level control, high performance, and safety. Operating systems must be as secure as feasible in a time when cyberattacks are growing more frequent. This is why the remarkable degree of memory safety of the Rust programming language attracts a lot of system programmers. System programmers are also impressed by Rust's backward compatibility and comparatively fast execution times.

- **Development of Games**

  Rust is quickly taking over as the preferred programming language, even though many game developers still use C# and C++.

  It is ideal for creating games using game engines such as Piston and Amethyst Engine because of its quick runtimes and efficiency. Because of the many similarities between Rust and C++, developers who want to broaden their skill set should not have too much trouble picking it up. Rust can be utilized in game development for a variety of purposes, including cross-platform development, game logic implementation, and game engine creation.

- **Backend for Data Science**

  The Rust programming language is also useful for creating data science backend systems. For data science, programmers usually use R and Python, but Rust's great efficiency and security make it an ideal choice for developing secure and quick data analytics solutions. When developers use Rust for data science, they will be able to implement performance-critical algorithms, build data processing pipelines, and develop web-based data visualization tools with outstanding results.

Businesses Using the Rust Programming Language

After learning everything there is to know about Rust, you are undoubtedly curious about how your development team might use this programming language within your company. Here are some noteworthy instances of businesses that have made the most of Rust to give you an idea of how you can utilize the language:

- **Facebook**

  Python was the first programming language used by Facebook to create its source control backend; Rust has since been adopted. Rust caught the attention of Facebook's (now Meta) engineering team, who were searching for a programming language with robust security features because of the volume of sensitive data they handle.

  In 2016, the social media behemoth began using Rust, and by 2019, they had more than 100 Rust engineers working for them. Facebook is so dedicated to the growth of Rust that it is a member of the Rust Foundation, a nonprofit dedicated to supporting and advancing the language.

- **Microsoft**

  Microsoft uses the Rust programming language for their Windows operating system and is a big supporter of it. They are founder members of the Rust Foundation and have produced a Rust for Windows software. Their dedication to Rust stems from the language's focus on memory security. They discovered that memory-related issues account for 70% of security updates, and they think Rust could have identified these issues during the development stage. Microsoft's engineers are in the process of creating a standard Windows library for Rust, and one of their goals is to develop their own programming language inspired by Rust's features.

- **Amazon**

  Amazon is a global technology corporation that sells a wide range of products, including electronics, home goods, music, and more. Rust is used by Amazon Web Services, an IT service management business, and Amazon subsidiary, to maintain its quick and safe software. Amazon's 2018 introduction of Firecracker, their first Rust-based product, is evidence of how much they appreciate Rust. Amazon Web Services, one of the first proponents of the language, is especially pleased with its outstanding memory safety and its ability to fix memory-related issues that are prevalent in other languages, such as C and C++.

In many instances, their software engineers discovered that Rust was superior to other languages, including Python. They employ Rust for essential components that are necessary for their services, such as load balancing and block storage.

- **Dropbox**

  The cloud storage and file synchronization services provided by Dropbox, a file hosting platform, are dependent on Rust programming language for core parts of its file-syncing system.

- **Discord**

  Rust was chosen because, like Facebook, Discord is a platform that needs a stable and secure programming language. Their software engineers made the decision to go from Go to Rust for their Read States service, and both the client and server sides of its codebase are written in Rust. They were attracted to Rust because of its speed and memory efficiency, which are made possible by the absence of a garbage collector and runtime.

Rust Tools

- **Cargo** is a package manager and build system for Rust that makes building, testing, documentation creation, and dependency management easier.
- Rust compiler **rustc** is in charge of converting Rust code into executable binaries.
- **Rustfmt:** A Rust code formatter that guarantees legible and consistent code formatting.
- **Clippy** is a linting tool that offers recommendations for enhancing code quality and best practices compliance.
- **Rustdoc** is an integrated documentation generator that helps developers efficiently document their code.

Rust Libraries and Frameworks

- **Actix:** A strong and effective actor framework for creating scalable, effective, and concurrent applications.
- **Rocket:** A web framework that makes it easy to create reliable web applications by emphasizing speed, security, and simplicity.
- **Serde:** A library for serialization and deserialization that facilitates smooth data interchange and supports a variety of data formats.
- **Tokio**: A Rust asynchronous runtime that offers a framework for creating effective and scalable network applications.
- **Diesel:** An effective and secure Object-Relational Mapping (ORM) library for Rust database interaction.

Conclusion

In this chapter, we first learned about computer programming languages and scripting languages such as JavaScript and TypeScript. At last, we learned about Rust programming and the application of Rust in the field.

In the next chapter, we are getting introduced to Node.js and Deno V/s Node.js.

References

1. **What is a scripting language?**: https://www.indeed.com/career-advice/career-development/top-scripting- languages#:~:text
2. **Californium**: https://github.com/divyaGrvgithub/californium_javascript
3. **User interface**: https://code.visualstudio.com/docs/getstarted/userinterface#

CHAPTER 4
Introduction to Node.js and Deno versus Node.js

Introduction

Node.js can be used for a variety of tasks, including building APIs and server-side programming. JavaScript server-side programming is done with Node.js. Because of this, you can design both front-end and back-end applications using the same programming language (JavaScript). [1]

Node.js uses the async and await techniques to implement asynchronous task execution in a single thread. Because of this, Node.js apps are substantially faster than multi-threaded ones.

REST APIs, web apps, real-time chat apps, command-line apps, and more are all built with Node.js.

After learning this chapter fully, you will be able to learn about Node.js and Deno, the differences between CommonJS and ECMAScript modules, using TypeScript with Deno, and faster deployments with Deno Deploy.

Structure

In this chapter, we are going to learn the following topics:

- Introduction and History of Node.js
- How is Node.js Installed
- Node.js Package Manager (NPM)
- Application for the Console
- Different Parts of Node.js

- Features of Node.js
- Node.js Examples
- Package Manager for Node.js (NPM)
- `Node_modules`
- The Distinction between Node.js, CJS, and MJS files.J.S
- Node.js versus Deno

Introduction and History of Node.js

We learned in the previous chapter that Deno is a safe runtime environment, especially for TypeScript and JavaScript code execution. Building on the framework established by its predecessor, it was published about ten years after Node.js was first made available. Node.js, the name Deno comes from, is a popular JavaScript runtime that allows developers to use JavaScript on the server-side, which adds to its appeal. The most widely used programming language in the world is still JavaScript, which has a long history. With a thriving community and a vast array of powerful tools and frameworks, Node.js makes it easier to create online apps.

Its broad adoption has been facilitated by its community support, versatility, and ease of use.

Ryan Dahl, the man behind Node.js, created Deno, which is similar to its predecessor but has some unique features as well. Both are server-side runtimes that run JavaScript and TypeScript (TypeScript is supported by Node.js via NPM packages). Building on the expertise and understanding acquired from Node.js, Deno is frequently considered the next generation of runtime environments. Deno, which is still in its infancy (it will be four years old in August 2024, with 45 updates from version 1.0 to 1.45), has not yet reached maturity, whereas Node.js has made a name for itself in the industry. Deno seeks to provide developers with a contemporary and safe substitute for Node.js by addressing its drawbacks and difficulties.

Based on Google's V8 JS engine, Node.js is a popular server-side, open-source, cross-platform JavaScript runtime environment. Since 2009, it has dominated the field of web development.

Event-driven HTTP servers are the primary emphasis of Node. It uses a single-threaded event loop that is registered with the system to handle requests, and every incoming request initiates a JavaScript callback function. Requests can be handled by the callback functions through non-blocking I/O calls.

By launching threads from a pool to do blocking or CPU-intensive activities, it can also divide the load among CPU cores. Node's scaling mechanism, which is built on callback functions, can handle more requests with less memory use than the majority of competing frameworks that scale via threads.

Because of its asynchronous I/O and event-driven architecture, Node.js is lightweight and perfect for scalable, data-intensive, real-time web applications that can operate on dispersed devices.

Understanding Deno's history and the driving forces behind its development is crucial before delving into its internal workings. This entails looking at Node.js's shortcomings and how Deno overcomes them.

The historical background and sources of inspiration for Deno's creation are covered in this chapter, opening the door for a more thorough examination of its architecture in the following chapters.

We must first look at the conditions that led to the development of Deno, a novel server-side runtime, in order to comprehend its genesis. Node.js is a well-known server-side application runtime that has been around for more than 13 years and is well-known for its dependability and efficiency. Over time, its popularity has increased dramatically, and it has gained the trust of well-known companies that depend on Node.js to power quick and effective web apps, including PayPal, Netflix, Trello, NASA, Twitter, Walmart, and many more.

Despite the popularity of Node.js, a new runtime became necessary. We will investigate the rationale for this choice and look at the driving forces behind Deno's development. We can appreciate Deno's design more fully if we comprehend the background and reasoning behind its creation.

Node.js is a cross-platform, open-source JavaScript runtime environment. It is a widely used tool for nearly all types of projects!

Outside of the browser, Node.js powers Google Chrome's V8 JavaScript engine. This enables the high performance of Node.js.

Instead of starting a new thread for each request, a Node.js application operates in a single process. Because Node.js libraries are typically designed using non-blocking paradigms, blocking behavior is the exception rather than the rule. Additionally, Node.js's standard library includes a set of asynchronous I/O primitives that prevent JavaScript code from blocking. [1]

Node.js will not stall the thread and waste CPU cycles waiting while it executes an I/O operation, such as reading from the network, accessing a database, or the filesystem instead of blocking the thread and wasting CPU cycles waiting, Node.js will resume the operations when the response comes back.

This eliminates the need to manage thread concurrency, which might be a major source of errors, and enables Node.js to manage thousands of concurrent connections with a single server.

Millions of frontend developers who write JavaScript for the browser can now create server-side code in addition to client-side code without having to learn a new language, which is a unique feature of Node.js.

The new ECMAScript standards can be used in Node.js without any issues because you do not need to wait for all of your users to update their browsers. You can choose which version of ECMAScript to use by modifying the Node.js version, and you can also run Node.js with flags to enable specific experimental features.

Open Access Software

Google's V8 JavaScript engine is used by both Node.js and Deno to run JavaScript applications. Their stances on isolation and security, however, diverge.

We already learned about V8, which restricts JavaScript code execution and blocks direct access to important system resources by operating in a secure sandboxed environment similar to Chrome. Node.js, on the other hand, has historically adopted a more open strategy, enabling applications to access a variety of resources that are accessible to user-level processes. Before version 20, this was true for every version of Node.js.

Node.js started implementing sandboxing for apps with version v20, marking a change toward increased security and isolation. This feature represents a substantial shift in Node.js' methodology, despite the fact that it is still experimental. As this sandboxing functionality develops, it will likely require considerable time, as it undergoes refinement and enhancement.

Installation of Node.js

Please follow the instructions provided based on the operating system you are using to install Node.js. Different operating systems require different steps. [2]

You can install Node.js on Windows and Linux, specifically Ubuntu.

Windows Installation

1. Download the 64-bit installer for Windows from this link: https://nodejs.org/dist/v20.9.0/node-v20.9.0-x64.msi.
2. Double-click the downloaded file to begin the installation, assuming you are using a machine running Windows 10 or 11.

Figure 4.1: *The Setup Wizard for Installing Node.js*

You go through a few of the installation wizard's steps during the installation. Additionally, it adds the Node.js executable installation directory to the system path.

To check whether Node.js has been installed successfully, type node -v at the command prompt. The version of Node.js installed on your computer will be displayed, seen as follows if the installation was successful.

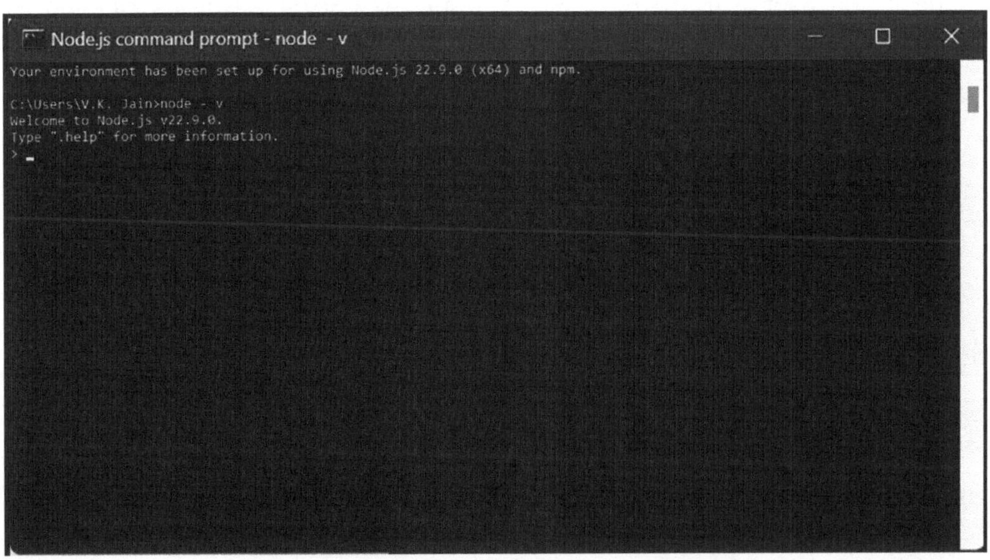

Figure 4.2: *Showing Installed Version of Node.js*

The window in *Figure* 4.2 intimates that the node version installed by the user V.K. Jain is Node.js v22.9.0.

Node.js Package Manager (NPM)

Since Node version 0.6.0, NPM has been a part of the Node.js binaries from its official website, thus you do not need to install it individually.

The Node.js script can be entered and saved using any text editor that comes with your operating system (notepad in Windows, vi, or nano in Ubuntu). It is advised that you utilize an appropriate IDE for this purpose, though, as it offers a number of advantages including syntax highlighting. The well-known source code editor Visual Studio Code comes with built-in support for JavaScript (and thus Node.js), which is strongly advised.

When learning a new language or framework, the first application to create is a Hello World program. This is a de facto norm in the computer industry.

This software shows the Hello World message. In addition to demonstrating the language's fundamental syntax, this checks to see if the language compiler installation was completed correctly. We will create a Hello World application using Node.js in this chapter.

Application for the Console

There is a command-line interface for Node.js. You can also run JavaScript code outside of a browser by using the Node.js runtime. As a result, any JavaScript code can be executed using the Node.js executable in a command terminal.

The single line of JavaScript that follows should be saved as a **`hello.js`** file.

```
log from console ("Hello World");
```

In the folder containing the **`hello.js`** file, open a powershell (or command prompt) terminal and type the following command:

```
The PS D: odejs> node hello.js
Hi there, world
```

The terminal displays the '**`Hi there world`**' greeting.

Learning by Examples

Our "**`Show Node.js`**" tool provided by W3Schools makes it easy to learn Node.js, it shows both the code and the result.

```
var http = require('http');
http.createServer(function (req, res) {
    res.writeHead(200, {'Content-Type': 'text/plain'});
    res.end('Hello World!');
}).listen(8080);
```

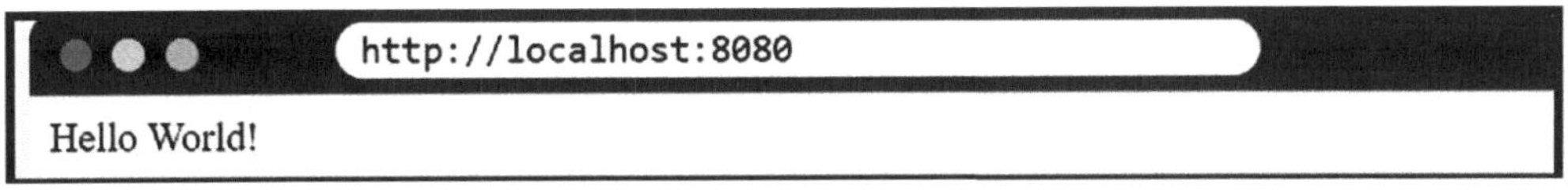

Figure 4.3: *The Message Hello World! Displayed Broadcasted on Local Host: 8080*

Different Parts of Node.js

The following diagram specifies some important parts of Node.js:

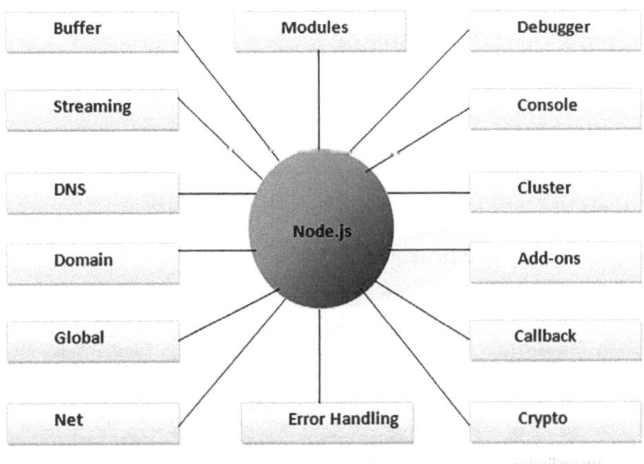

Figure 4.4: *Important Components of Node.js*

Features of Node.js

The list of key characteristics of Node.js that make it the top option for software architects is as follows:

- **Exceptionally Quick:** Node.js's library executes code incredibly quickly because it is based on Google Chrome's V8 JavaScript Engine.
- **I/O is Event Driven and Asynchronous**: Every Node.js library API is asynchronous, or non-blocking. Thus, a server built using Node.js never waits for data to be returned by an API. After accessing an API, the server advances to the next one, and a Node.js event notification system assists the server in receiving a response from the previous API request. It is also the cause of its high speed.

- **Single Threaded**: Node.js uses event looping in a single threaded paradigm.
- **Incredible Scalability**: Node.js is incredibly scalable because the event mechanism helps the server to respond in a non-blocking way.
- **No Buffering**: When uploading audio and video files, Node.js reduces processing time overall. Applications built with Node.js never buffer any data. The data is simply output in chunks by these apps.
- **Open Source:** The Node.js community is open source and has created a number of top-notch modules to give Node.js apps more functionality.
- **License**: The MIT license governs the release of Node.js.

Node.js Examples

First Example

Node.js apps can be web-based or console-based.

Console-Based Node.js: The file example is **`console_example1.js`**.

```
'Hello JavaTpoint' console.log;
```

Run the following code on the Node.js command prompt:

```
console_example1.js in node
```

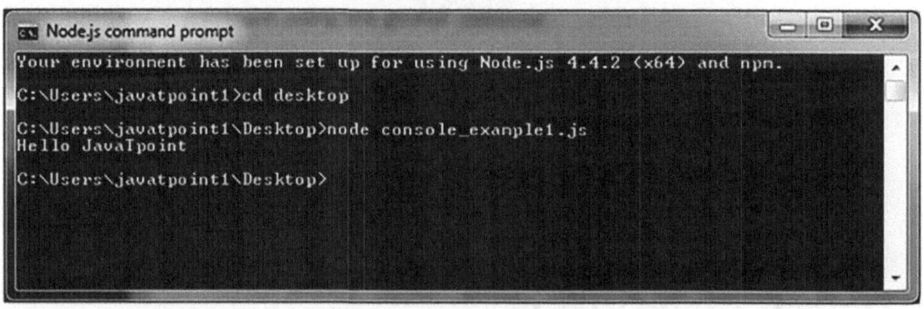

Figure 4.5: *Node.js Apps*

Here, **`console.log()`** function displays a message on the console.

Second Example

Node.js Web-Based: Hello World and setting Path

The three components of a node.js web application are as follows:

- **Bring in the Necessary Modules:** The Node.js module is loaded using the "**`require`**" directive.
- **Build a Server:** You must set up a server that can listen to client requests, much like the Apache HTTP Server.

- **Read the Request and Reply as Follows:** When a client, such as a browser or terminal, sends an HTTP request, the server built in the second step will read it and reply.

How to build web applications using Node.js?

Take these actions:

- **Import Necessary Module**: Use "**require**" as the initial step. Directive to store the returned HTTP instance in the http variable and load the http module. For instance:

  ```
  require("http"); var http
  ```

- **Construct Server**: In the second step, you must utilize the created http instance to construct a server instance by calling the **http.createServer()** function. Then, you must use the listen method linked to the server instance to bind it at port 8081. Write the sample implementation to return "Hello World" after passing it a function with request and response parameters.

For instance:

```
http.createServer(function (request, response) {
   // Send the HTTP header
   // HTTP Status: 200 : OK
   // Content Type: text/plain
   response.writeHead(200, {'Content-Type': 'text/plain'});
   // Send the response body as "Hello World"
   response.end('Hello World\n');
}).listen(8081);
// Console will print the message
console.log('Server running at http://127.0.0.1:8081/');
```

Combining step1 and step2 together in a file named "**main.js**."

```
File: main.js

var http = require("http");
http.createServer(function (request, response) {
 // Send the HTTP header
   // HTTP Status: 200 : OK
   // Content Type: text/plain
   response.writeHead(200, {'Content-Type': 'text/plain'});
   // Send the response body as "Hello World"
   response.end('Hello World\n');
}).listen(8081);
// Console will print the message
console.log('Server running at http://127.0.0.1:8081/');
```

How to Start Your Server:

Go to the start menu and click the `Node.js command prompt`.

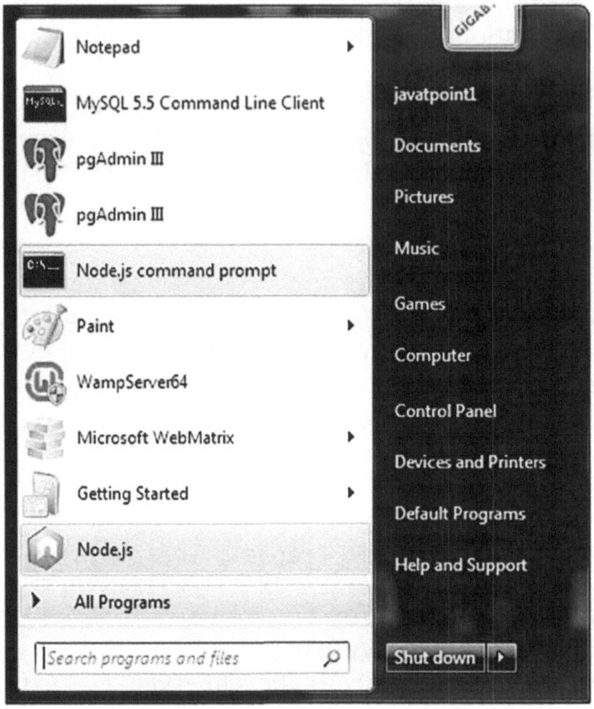

Figure 4.6: *Selecting Node.js Command*

Now the command prompt is open:

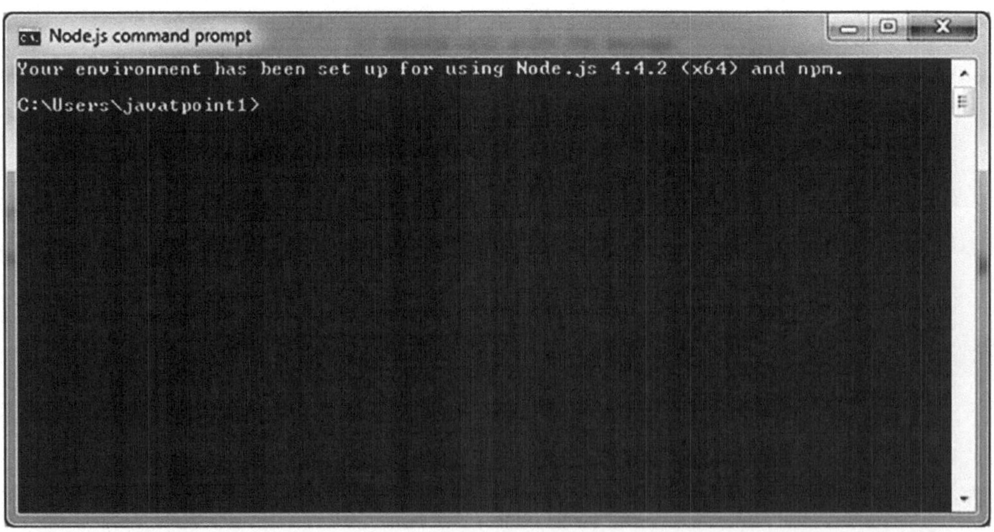

Figure 4.7: *Notification Regarding Environment being Set up as Node.js4.4.2*

Set Path: The "**`main.js`**" file is saved on the desktop here. In the command prompt, type **`cd desktop`**. Next, launch the server by running main.js as follows:

1. Main.js in Node.

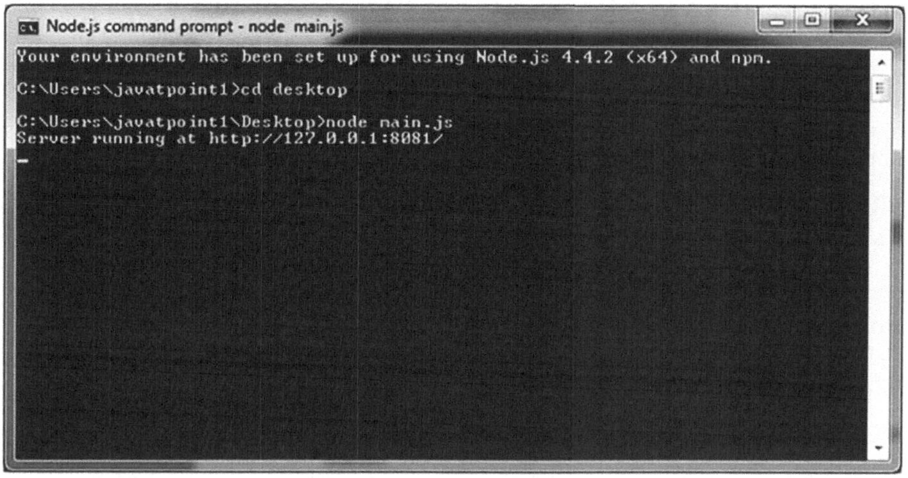

Figure 4.8: *Launching the Server*

2. The server has now started. Send a request to the server for Node.js.
3. Use any browser to access http://127.0.0.1:8081/.
4. The following outcome will be shown to you:

Figure 4.9: Hello World

You must now execute the "**`node main.js`**" command once more if you make any modifications to the "**`main.js`**" file.

Package Manager for Node.js (NPM)

Node Package Manager (**npm**), a popular package manager for Node.js, served as an inspiration for the concept of package.json. The use of package.json was first made possible by Node.js author Ryan Dahl, who enabled the need() function to reference the file for module resolution. Over time, NPM developed into the main repository for different Node.js modules and grew to become one of the biggest package managers for a variety of programming languages.

However, NPM's private ownership is a major disadvantage. **npm** was once a separate company, but it was later purchased by GitHub and then by Microsoft, which tightly linked NPM to Node.js. Ryan Dahl lamented that he could only source Node.js packages from one repository instead of multiple sources. As a result, a more decentralized method of package administration became desired.

Note: *In order to compete in the market, Deno must now fully support **npm**.*

Node Package Manager offers two primary features:

- It offers searchable online repositories for node.js packages and modules at search.nodejs.org.
- It also offers a commandline tool for installing Node.js packages and managing their versions and dependencies. In versions subsequent to v0.6.3, the npm is included with the Node.js installables. By opening the Node.js command prompt and using the following command, you may the version:

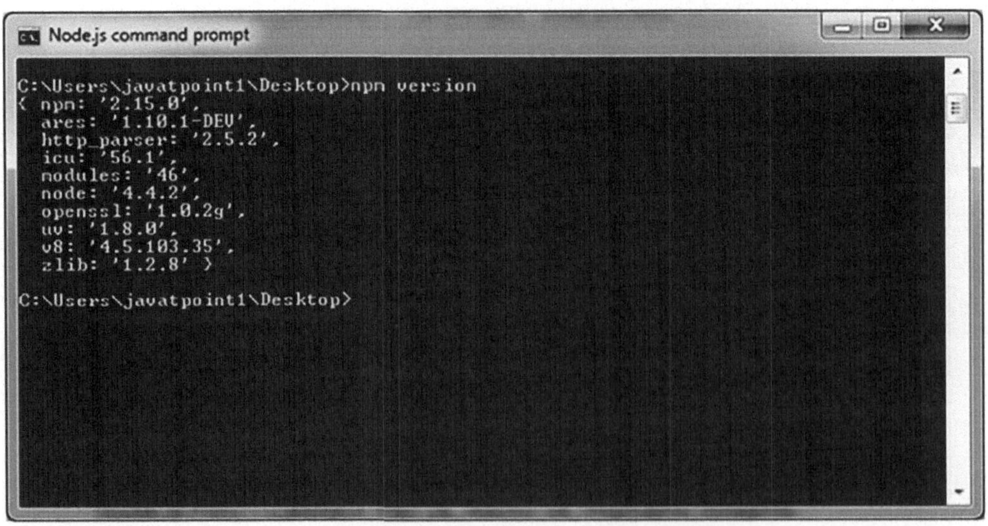

Figure 4.10: *Verifying the Version Number of npm*

Installing Modules Using npm

The syntax to install any Node.js module is as follows:

```
Install <Module Name> with npm
```

Let us install Express, a well-known Node.js web framework. Run the following command in the Node.js command prompt:

```
npm install express
```

After installing the "express" framework, the outcome is visible.

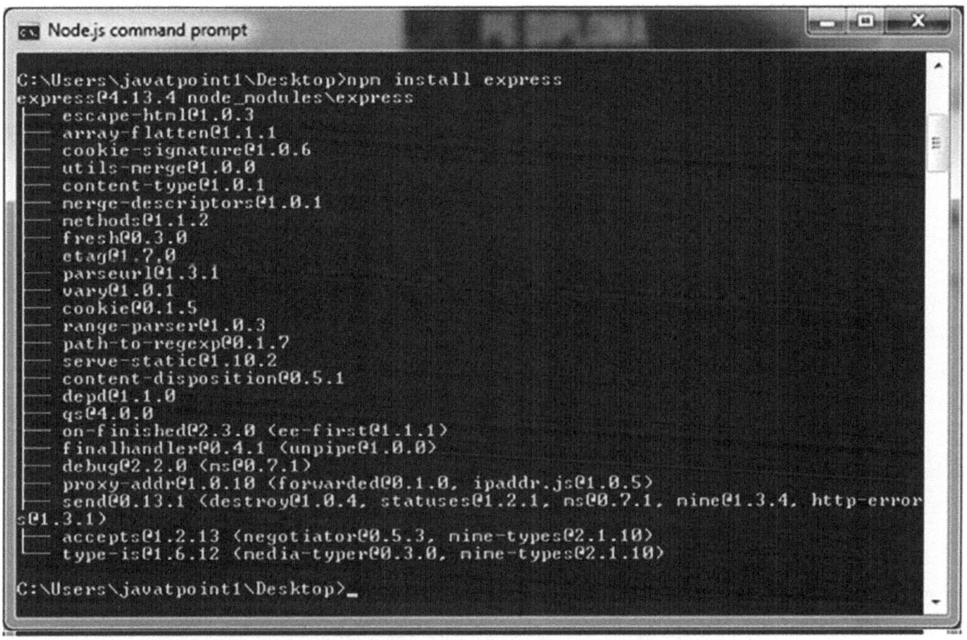

Figure 4.11: *Output after Installing the "Express" Framework*

Global versus Local Installation

npm installs dependencies in local mode by default. In this case, local mode indicates the folder containing the Node application. For instance, if you added the express module, the **`node_modules`** directory was created in the directory where the express module was already located.

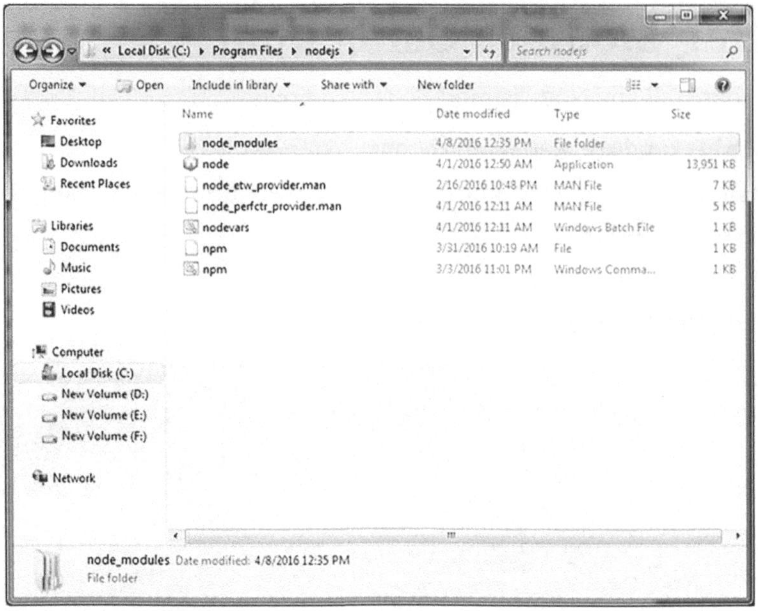

Figure 4.12: *Creation of node_module's Directory*

All of the locally installed modules can be listed using the npm ls command. Run "**npm ls**" in the Node.js command prompt:

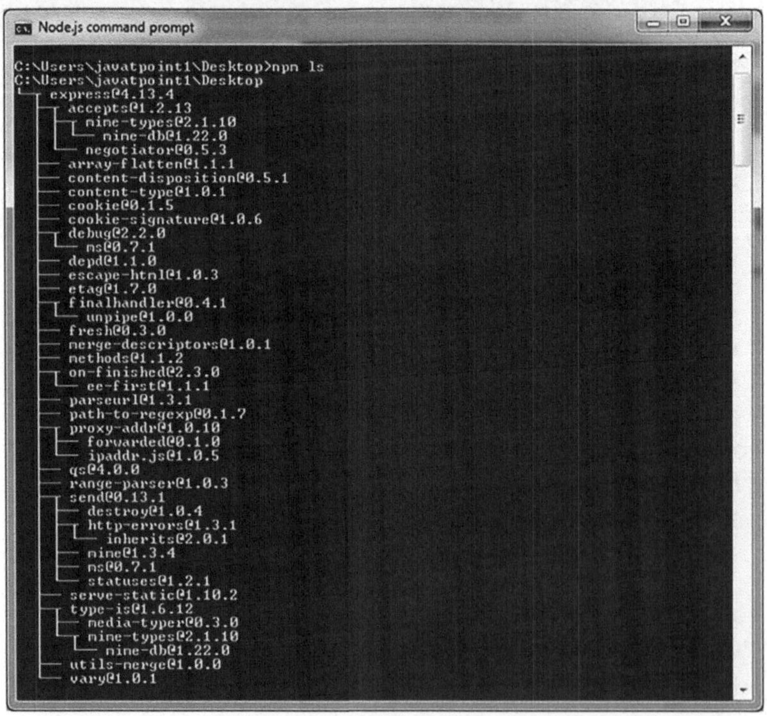

Figure 4.13: *Listing of Module Commands in Tree-like Structure*

Packages and dependencies that are installed globally are kept in the system directory. Let us use global installation to install the express module. Modules will be deployed worldwide, but the outcome will be the same. Launch the Node.js command prompt and run the code that follows:

```
Install express -g with npm.
```

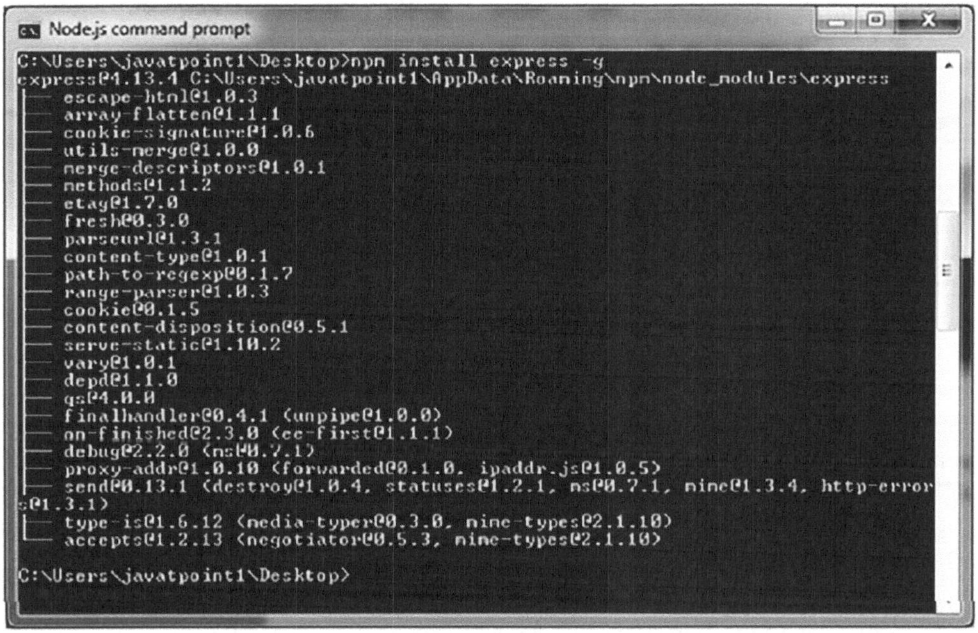

***Figure 4.14:** Listing in Case of Express -g with npm*

The module version and installation location are mentioned in the first line.

Node_modules

Over time, Node.js's module resolution method grew more intricate. The idea of vendor modules seemed promising at first, however using **$NODE_PATH** created problems. Moreover, this methodology diverged considerably from web browser norms. The Node.js framework failed to achieve Ryan Dahl's goal of bringing module resolution into compliance with accepted standards. As a result, Node.js's module resolution algorithm deviates from more general web standards while remaining specifically suited to its particular context.

- **Implicit Require:** One special feature created especially for the Node.js environment was the **required("module")** function, which was used without the "**.js**" extension. This method is not the same as how JavaScript functions in web browsers, though. It is invalid to leave out the "**.js**" extension from a script tag's src attribute in browser-based JavaScript. Rather, in order to determine the user's intended module reference, the module loader must go across many file system locations, which might result in confusion and mistakes.

- **Index.js:** The name "**`index.js`**" appealed to Ryan Dahl because of its resemblance to "**`index.html`**." However, the module loading system became needlessly complicated as a result of this naming approach. When the 'require' method started to support package.json files, this complexity increased even further and caused unanticipated difficulties with module loading.

The Distinction between Node.js, CJS, and MJS files.J.S

Most JavaScript files in Node.js projects come with a .js file extension by default. JavaScript files with the .mjs or.cjs extensions may also be visible to you. This page lists the distinctions and offers recommendations about which one to use. In conclusion, files ending in `.js` or`.cjs` are automatically handled by Node.js using the Common. js module system. Use a `.mjs` file extension if you wish to use ES modules, or set "**`type`**" to "**`module`**" in the package.json file if you prefer .js file extensions. [3] A file is regarded as a "**`module`**" in Node.js. Unless one module specifically exports functionality, JavaScript code in one module (file) cannot be viewed from another module (file) unless one module explicitly exports functionality and the other module explicitly imports that functionality. mjs means Module JS. cjs means CommonJS, which is an old javascript format. Example: In mjs, you can use new features like import and new array prototypes. In cjs, you can only use require.

A file with .mjs extension is a JavaScript source code file that is used as an ECMA Module (ECMAScript Module), js's native module system is CommonJS that is used to split the code into different files to keep the JS code organized.

JavaScript files that comply with the ECMAScript Modules (ESM) specification are extended with the MJS (ECMAScript Modules) extension. A more contemporary and uniform method of defining modules is offered by ECMAScript modules, which are a component of the JavaScript language standard.

Modules for Common.js

Common.js is the name of the older, default module system. This is the Common.js format if you see imports and exports that look like this:

```
// `require` for imports
const fs = require("fs");

function loadData(filename) {
  const content = fs.readFileSync(filename);
  return content.toString();
```

```
}

// `module.exports` for exports
module.exports = {
  loadData,
};
```

An Example CJS Type Node.js Application

The most common example, Hello World of Node.js is a web server:

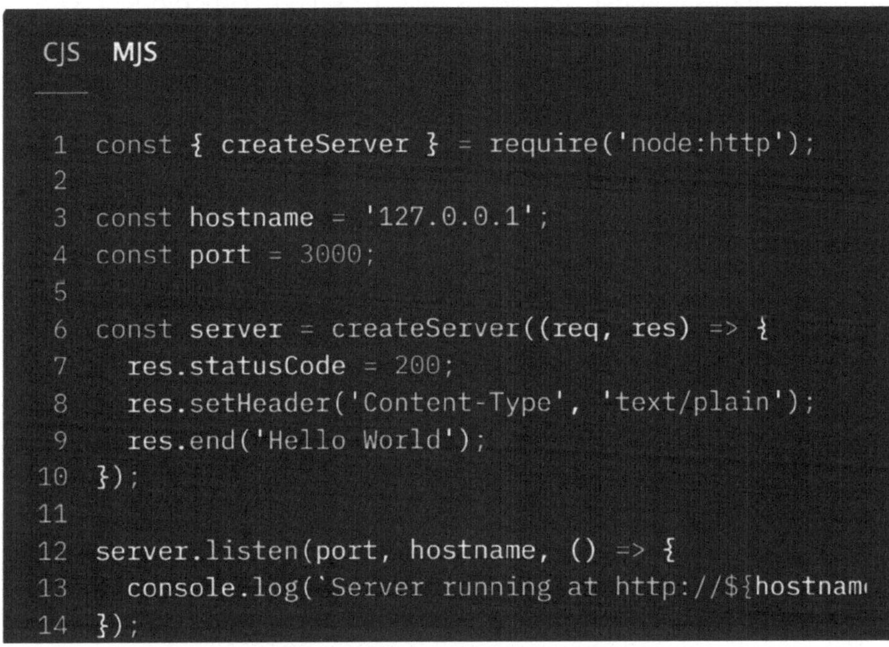

Figure 4.15: *CJS type Node.js Application*

```
const { createServer } = require('node:http');

const hostname = '127.0.0.1';
const port = 3000;

const server = createServer((req, res) => {
  res.statusCode = 200;
  res.setHeader('Content-Type', 'text/plain');
  res.end('Hello World');
});

server.listen(port, hostname, () => {
  console.log(`Server running at http://${hostname}:${port}/`);
});
```

Run node server.js in your terminal after saving this snippet into a server.js file. You should run node **`server.mjs`** in your terminal and save the code as a **`server.mjs`** file if you are using the mjs version.

The Node.js http module is included first in this code.

The excellent standard library of Node.js includes excellent networking capabilities.

A new HTTP server is created and returned by the **`createServer()`** function of http.

The hostname and port are configured for the server to listen on. The callback function, which in this example notifies us that the server is operating, is called when the server is ready.

The request event is invoked each time a new request is received, delivering two objects: a request (an **`http.IncomingMessage`** object) and a response (an **`http.ServerResponse`** object).

These two objects are essential to handle the HTTP call.

The request information is given in the first. Although this is not used in this straightforward example, you could still retrieve the request data and headers.

Data is returned to the caller using the second.

In this instance, with:

```
200 is res.statusCode;
```

To show a successful answer, we set the **`statusCode`** attribute to **`200`**.

`res.setHeader('Content-Type', 'text/plain')`; is how we set the Content-Type header.

We add the content as a parameter to `end()` to close the response:

```
"Hello World," res.end();
```

Node.js versus Deno

We hear from Ryan Dahl, the man behind Deno and Node.js, about his foray into software development and the development of Node.js. He gives an explanation of why he launched the new JavaScript runtime, Deno.

Both Deno and NodeJS are great technologies for web development. If you are looking for high performance, then the Deno framework would work better for you. However, if you want to build servers for your application quickly then NodeJS could be your best bet.[4]

Node.js is without a doubt the most well-known and extensively utilized JavaScript runtime environment in the world. However, there was a lot of excitement when

Deno arrived in 2018, and developers can now use a more secure framework with contemporary functionality. [2]

Ryan Dahl, the same author who introduced Node.js, also introduces Deno. Known as its successor, it aims to address some of the main Node.js architectural flaws. However, there was a lot of conjecture following Deno's announcement regarding whether or not Deno will replace Node.js. There have not been any notable modifications thus far. Node.js continues to satisfy the majority of developers.

Dahl, who developed both runtimes, claims that Node.js has three major shortcomings:

- A centralized distribution system with subpar module design.
- Legacy APIs that are unstable.
- Insufficient security.

Deno is said to improve the experience and resolve all three issues.

Unless specifically enabled, Deno, a JavaScript, TypeScript, and WebAssembly runtime, has secure defaults and no access to files, networks, or environments.

It features a number of standard modules that have been examined and inspected to make sure they operate correctly throughout the Deno runtime. Additionally, Deno allows native TypeScript file execution without requiring additional commands.

Deno versus Node: Main Differences

Let us now examine a head-to-head analysis of Node and Deno.

- **Management of Third-Party Packages**

  Instead of relying on a centralized registry like npm, developers can use Deno to install packages directly from URLs. Although downloading packages straight from a URL carries some danger – for instance, if the server hosting the package is hijacked, an attacker may alter the code to include malicious functionality – Deno provides a mechanism to reduce this risk by caching downloaded modules. It is possible to import packages as libraries straight into the script. With Deno, you can run scripts from any public URL; thus, you do not need package management to import the modules. Nevertheless, importing modules from a third party still carries some risk. The **`node_modules`** and package.json files are also deleted.

  In contrast, Node.js uses npm to handle all packages. It also has a vast ecosystem of libraries and packages.

  You may import code from any location, including GitHub and any CDN or registry you host, thanks to Deno's more adaptable module import system than

Node. This makes it possible for modules to be imported smoothly without requiring downloads or installations.

- **APIs**

  Node.js was developed prior to JavaScript's introduction of the Promises, or async/await paradigm. Because of this, the majority of APIs were made to support error-first callbacks. Often, this approach produced lengthy and intricate code. This async/await syntax is now available to Node developers, but they also need to handle backward compatibility because APIs are fragile and change often.

  This is quite different in Deno. Since it already makes use of await and supports the most recent JavaScript capabilities, there is no need to encapsulate in an callback-based APIs into JavaScript promises by simplifying this process for developer's function. Thus, Deno simplifies binding by adopting APIs based into JavaScript promises, making the process easier for developers.

  Additionally, Deno is designed to work with the web platform APIs that browsers' JavaScript code uses. Standards-compliant support is provided for several of the most widely used advanced web APIs, including Fetch, Web Storage, Web Workers, and Broadcast Channels.

- **Security**

  Ryan Dahl founded Deno primarily for security reasons All of the code is run by Deno in a safe sandbox environment that prevents file system access. Prior to gaining access to the file system, Deno requests authorization.

  You would need to use a command-line parameter to obtain permission, which would stop any file from being deleted without the developer's approval. Deno has a number of command-line options that can be used at runtime to activate specific features for specific scripts. You must specifically set a flag for any elements your script might need because these functions are deactivated by default.

  These flags include:

  - **`allow-env`**: Allow environment access for things like getting and setting environment variables.
  - **`allow-hrtime`**: Allow high-resolution time measurement.
  - **`allow-net`**: Allow network access.
  - **`allow-read`**: Allow file system read access.
  - **`allow-run`**: Allow running subprocesses.
  - **`allow-write`**: Allow file system write access.

It was never intended for Node.js to be an extremely secure framework. For instance, Node is not sandboxed and does not need permission to read or write to the file system. Therefore, a small amount of carelessness can lead to problems for any third-party library. Additionally, Node users benefit from conventional security protections that protect against attacks like Cross-Site Scripting (XSS) and Cross-Site Request Forgery (CSRF). Verifying user input, appropriately handling mistakes and exceptions, and reviewing the logs are all part of these procedures.

Therefore, Deno is the greatest choice for a more secure environment, even if you grow acclimated to the security module's strictness.

- **Support for TypeScript**

  A superset of JavaScript called TypeScript allows users to add optional static typing. Deno uses a TypeScript compiler with a caching mechanism to support TypeScript right out of the box. Consequently, Deno does not need to translate your code to JavaScript in order to compile, type-check, and run it.

  TypeScript is a popular and widely used language in the Node.js community because of the TypeScript package, even though Node.js does not have built-in TypeScript support like Deno does. Consequently, TypeScript and Node.js may work together with little effort. To install TypeScript globally on your computer, simply run **`npm install -g`** typescript if you already have Node.js and npm installed. The TypeScript configuration file is then created by running **`tsc --init`**. After that, the TypeScript compiler tsc can be used to compile your .ts files.

  If you enjoy TypeScript and would like to experiment with a new framework, Deno is the one for you. Moreover, no additional setups are needed while using TypeScript for development in Deno.

The Case of Node Being More Popular among Developers than Deno

It is clear from everything we have discussed so far that Deno offers developers some unique features, such as native TypeScript compatibility and a robust support system. The goal of the design strategies and other integrated tools is to provide developers with a positive and productive runtime environment.

Then why has Deno not taken Node's place already? As we can see, Deno is being adopted much more slowly than Node.js. Despite a new, contemporary framework that tackles many of its architectural flaws, there are still a number of reasons why developers favor Node.js.

Some of us started using Node.js and were using it in real-world applications when it was first introduced. Node has evolved significantly over time to satisfy the demands of the software development community. The most popular JavaScript runtime at the moment is this one. Due to its extensive use, you have access to a highly qualified development community. The Node.js package system, which is based on npm, is comprehensive and easy to use. Node.js is therefore the greatest choice if familiarity and flexibility are your top priorities.

But Node has not quite mastered it. Actually, much the opposite. Node is still lagging behind Deno in a number of critical areas, namely security and standard compliance. Deno is more portable than node due to its single binary pattern, and the open-ended module architecture may be established as the future norm for dependency imports.

Examining the Case of Developers Not Switching to Deno

Despite its activity, Deno's community is still quite small. The Node compatibility layer is not always dependable, and deno-specific packages are somewhat uncommon. This could disadvantage you if you need assistance or if you want to use a certain library.

The absence of third-party packages and the fact that Deno has not been used as extensively in the real world as Node due to its infancy are two obvious areas where it falls short. Conversely, Node.js is quite modular. The Node Package Manager (npm) makes it possible to locate numerous libraries in one place. Its ability to refresh your work by downloading an infinite number of packages is largely responsible for its popularity.

Furthermore, with the help of third-party libraries, many of Deno's capabilities may be implemented in Node.js. As a result, if you only like a few features of Deno, you can probably achieve the same goal using Node.js, albeit more slowly than with Deno.

Another important characteristic of Node is how easy it is to work with permissions. Without going through a number of authorizations, you can get feedback on the platform very rapidly. Because Node.js rarely asks for specific permissions, it needs little work for speedy coding. It is therefore perfect for a wide range of dynamic projects that require frequent updates and a sizable team of professionals.

In light of these considerations, we can conclude that the majority of developers are satisfied with the course that Node.js is pursuing and are unlikely to alter it very soon.

Deno is still 'learning how to walk' in comparison to the sizable and flourishing Node.js community, which is a community that merits more investigation. Developers are still getting used to this new runtime environment, and it has not been fully tested in production systems yet. Given that it addresses significant Node shortcomings like security, modules, callbacks, and the central distribution system, it undoubtedly holds great promise. As a novelty, Deno is currently primarily appealing to early adopters.

The Deno community should eventually be able to establish it as essential to web development.

Conclusion

In this chapter, we were introduced to Node.js and learned the history of Node.js. We learned to install Node.js and went through Node.js Package Manager (NPM), different parts of Node.js, and features of application for the console. Later on, we learned about Node_modules and the distinction between Node.js, CJS, and MJS files.J.S., and Node.js versus Deno.

In the next chapter, we will get involved in **Using Visual Studio Code.**

Visual Studio Code (VS Code) is a light weight (much lighter than Visual Studio software) code editor that helps developers *build, debug, and run* codes of most of the programming languages.

References

1. **Introduction to Node.js**: https://nodejs.org/en/learn/getting-started/introduction-to-nodejs
2. **Node.js Tutorial**: https://www.tutorialspoint.com/nodejs/index.htm
3. **The Difference Between MJS, CJS, and JS Files in Node.js, Updated on 28 May 2024**: https://codingforseo.com/blog/mjs-vs-cjs-files/
4. **Deno vs. Node: No One is Ready for the Move,Piumi Iyana**: https://cult.honeypot.io/reads/deno-vs-node-main-differences/

CHAPTER 5
Using Visual Studio Code

Introduction

Visual Studio Code (VS Code) is a lightweight (much lighter than Visual Studio software) code editor that helps developers *build, debug, and run* codes of most of the programming Languages.

It should be clear for this book purpose that VS code is not solely designed to meet *the requirement of Deno only but you can utilize the* VS *Code (that is, through its* IDE) *to serve most of the purposes of Deno.*

Structure

This chapter shall provide the study of Visual Studio (VS) code under the following topics:

- Features of Visual Studio Code
- Visual Studio (VS)
  Get Started with Visual Studio Code
- Use GitHub Copilot and AI to Improve Your Coding
- API Extension
- Code Extension for Deno and Visual Studio
- Bash

Features of Visual Studio Code

However, we will first explore the features provided in this code.

VS code features include built-in support for JavaScript, TypeScript, and Node.js, and extensions for other languages and runtimes. It also has features such as IntelliSense code completion, syntax highlighting, bracket-matching, and auto-indentation.

- **User Interface:** Has a common layout with an explorer on the left that shows files and folders, and an editor on the right that shows the content of open files.
- **Debugging:** Includes a Run and Debug view, Debug toolbar, Debug console, and Debug sidebar.
- **Availability:** Available for Windows, macOS, and Linux.
- **Extensible:** Has a rich ecosystem of extensions for other languages and runtimes.

VS Code is designed to provide developers with the tools they need for a quick code-build-debug cycle. It is lightweight and aims to get out of the way so developers can spend more time on their ideas.

Visual Studio (VS)

Visual Studio (VS) is an Integrated Development Environment (IDE) and is Microsoft's creative launching pad that developers can use *to build, edit, and debug* code, after which one can easily publish the app they are building.

Visual Studio's great editing and debugging capabilities distinguish it from its competitors. Visual Studio also includes code completion tools, compilers, graphic designers, and more, to ease a developer's process of building an app.

Visual Studio aims to be a feature-rich, robust, and comprehensive solution for building apps.

Visual Studio is used to develop computer programs including *websites, web apps, web services, and mobile apps*. Visual Studio uses Microsoft software development platforms including Windows API, Windows Forms, Windows Presentation Foundation (WPF), Microsoft Store, and Microsoft Silverlight. It can produce both native code and managed code.

If you are using Linux, you have to choose Visual Studio Code or some other IDE apart from Visual Studio. That is because Visual Studio does not run on Linux. If you are the kind of person who likes to customize your editor to your taste, just go for VS Code because it is highly customizable.

Difference between Visual Studio and Visual Studio Code (VS Code)

Visual Studio and Visual Studio Code (VS Code) are both Microsoft tools for code development, but they have different purposes:

- **Visual Studio:** An Integrated Development Environment (IDE) that is designed for large-scale software development. It is a one-stop solution for developers, with a full set of tools and functionalities. Visual Studio is a good choice for developers working with C#, .NET, C, C++, *Python, and web languages* such as HTML, CSS, *and JavaScript.*

- **Visual Studio Code:** A lightweight code editor that is more flexible and customizable than Visual Studio. It is a good choice for developers looking for a versatile coding environment for smaller-scale projects and front-end development. VS Code is compatible with Windows, macOS, and Linux devices. It supports many programming languages, including JavaScript, TypeScript, and Node JS. VS Code's real power lies in its extensibility, with a vast marketplace of extensions for other languages. Studio Code is free and available on your favorite platforms - Linux, macOS, and Windows. Download Visual Studio Code to experience a redefined code:

The main difference between Visual Studio and Visual Studio Code is that the first one is a comprehensive Integrated Development Environment (IDE) tool for software development, while the second one is an Extension-based Code Editor.

This sets them apart, allowing each to serve different purposes. Other distinct features that differentiate the two include:

Attribute	**Visual Studio**	**Visual Studio Code**
Download and Disk Space	Heavy and requires 2.3 GB to 60 GB.	Lightweight and may work with less than 200 MB.
RAM	At least 16 GB is recommended.	It only needs a little space to run. It can run on a 300 MB RAM machine.
Performance	Resource-intensive, making it slower on most operating systems.	Lightweight, which makes it relatively quicker.
User Interface	Multiple panels and windows can appear cluttered.	Simplified, focuses on core coding and debugging tasks.
Testing tool	Comprehensive set in paid versions.	Unit testing is supported through extensions.
Collaboration and Teamwork	Connects with Azure DevOps and TFS.	Live share extension for real-time collaborative coding, integrates with GitHub.
Web Applications	ASP.NET Core and Blazor development.	Front-end web development supports modern web technologies.
Desktop Applications	Templates and designers for WPF, Winforms, and more.	Use Visual Studio Community edition for desktop app development.

Cloud Applications	Strong support for Azure, AWS, and Google Cloud.	Similar support for Desktop and Mobile applications.
Debugger	Rich and seamless debugging.	Lightweight and modular, it works with various languages through extensions.
Startup Time	Relatively long startup time.	Quick startup time.
Operating System	Windows	Windows, Mac, and Linux
Language Support	Built-in support for programming languages such as C++, C#, JavaScript, TypeScript, Python, .NET, and more.	JavaScript, Typescript, and Node JS. Can support other programming languages if extension(s) exist for that.

Table 5.1: *Distinct Features that Differentiate the Visual Studio and Visual Studio Code*

Downloading and Installing Visual Studio Code on Windows

Download the Visual Studio Code installer for Windows.

Once it is downloaded, run the installer (VSCodeUserSetup-{version}.exe). This will only take a minute. By default, VS Code is installed under C:\Users\{Username}\AppData \Local\Programs\Microsoft VS Code.

Installing Basic Layout of Visual Studio Code on Windows

VS Code comes with a simple and intuitive layout that maximizes the space provided for the editor while leaving ample room to browse and access the full context of your folder or project. The user interface is divided into five main areas:

- **Editor:** The main area to edit your files. You can open as many editors as you like side by side vertically and horizontally.
- **Primary Side Bar:** Contains different views such as the Explorer to assist you while working on your project.
- **Status Bar:** Information about the opened project and the files you edit.
- **Activity Bar:** Located on the far left-hand side. It lets you switch between views and gives you additional context-specific indicators, such as the number of outgoing changes when Git is enabled. You can change the position of the Activity Bar.
- **Panel:** An additional space for views below the editor region. By default, it contains output, debug information, errors and warnings, and an integrated

terminal. The Panel can also be moved to the left or right for more vertical space.

Tip: *A Secondary Side Bar is also available to display views opposite the Primary Side Bar. You can show it with* Ctrl+Alt+B *and drag a view from the Primary Side Bar to the Secondary Side Bar.*

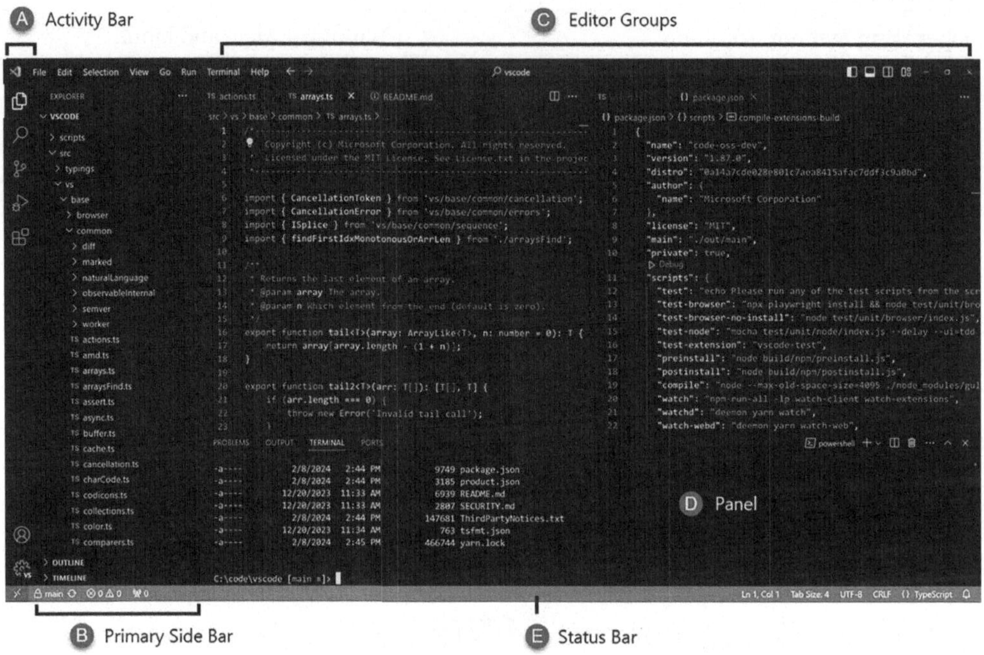

Figure 5.1: *Components of Visual Studio Code Displayed*

Each time you start VS Code, it opens up in the same state it was in when you last closed it. The folder, layout, and opened files are preserved.

Open files in each editor are displayed with tabbed headers (Tabs) at the top of the editor region. To learn more about tabbed headers, see the Tabs section.

Tip: *You can move the Primary Side Bar to the right-hand side by right-clicking the Activity Bar and selecting Move Primary Side Bar Right or toggle its visibility (Ctrl+B).*

Get Started with Visual Studio Code

Step 1: Open a Folder in VS Code

In VS Code, you can work with individual files seamlessly, for example, for quick edits or to view a file. Alternatively, by opening a folder, also known as a workspace, you unlock more features, such as folder-specific configuration settings, restoring the UI state for that folder, debug configurations, and more. Get more info about workspaces.

Let us start by creating a folder and opening it in VS Code. You will use this folder throughout the tutorial.

Create a new folder vscode101 on your computer.

Open Visual Studio Code

1. When you first open VS Code, you should see the Welcome page with different actions to get started.
2. On the **`Welcome`** page, select **`Open Folder...`**, and then select the folder you created.
3. The VS Code window reloads and you should see the folder name at the top of the Explorer view. You will use the Explorer view to view and manage the files and folders in your workspace.

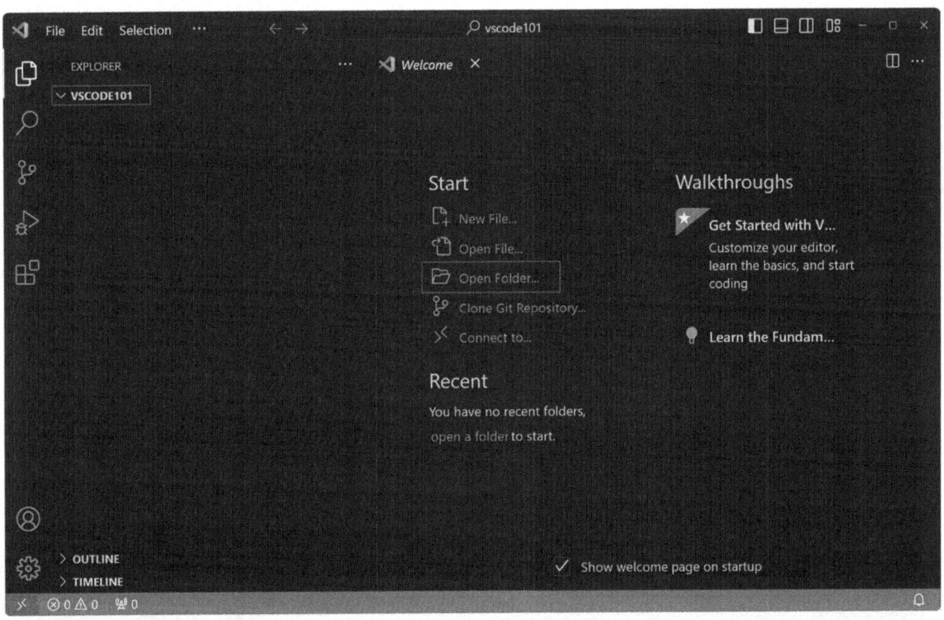

Figure 5.2: *Explorer View to View and Manage the Files and Folders in Your Workspace*

Alternatively, you can select **`Open Folder`**... from the **`File`** menu or press *Ctrl+K, then Ctrl+O* to open a folder.

Tip: *If you use the command line to work with VS Code, pass the folder name as a parameter to directly launch VS Code for that folder. For example, enter code, to open the current folder in VS Code.*

Step 2: Explore the User Interface

Now that you have a folder open in VS Code, let us take a quick tour of the user interface.

Switch between views with the Activity Bar.

The Activity Bar is located on the side of the window and gives you quick access to different views, such as the Explorer, Search, Source Control, and Run and Debug views.

Use the Activity Bar to Explore the Different Views

1. As you hover over the Activity Bar, you can see the name of each view and the keyboard shortcut to open each view. You will find that many of the features in VS Code have keyboard shortcuts already assigned to them, and you can also customize these shortcuts to your liking.

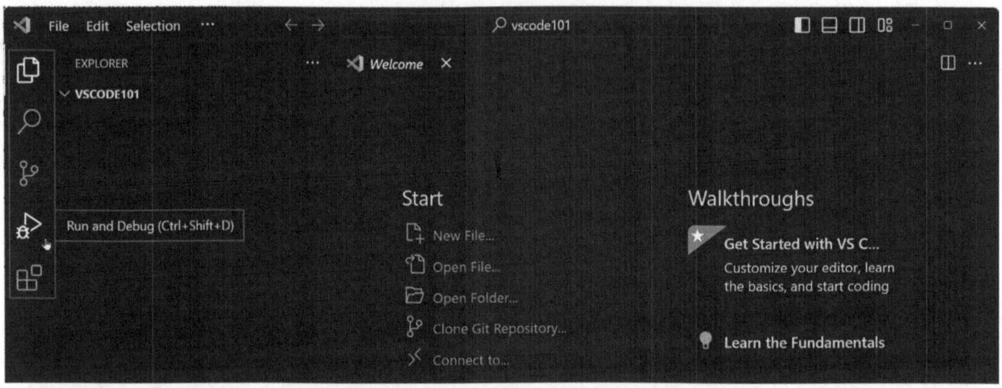

***Figure 5.3**: Selecting Run and Debug*

2. Notice the **`Primary Side Bar`** that opens when you select a view in the Activity Bar.

   The **`Primary Side Bar`** shows view-specific information. For example, the **`Source Control`** view shows the changes in your **`Git`** repository, and the **`Run`** and **`Debug`** view enables you to configure and start debugging sessions.

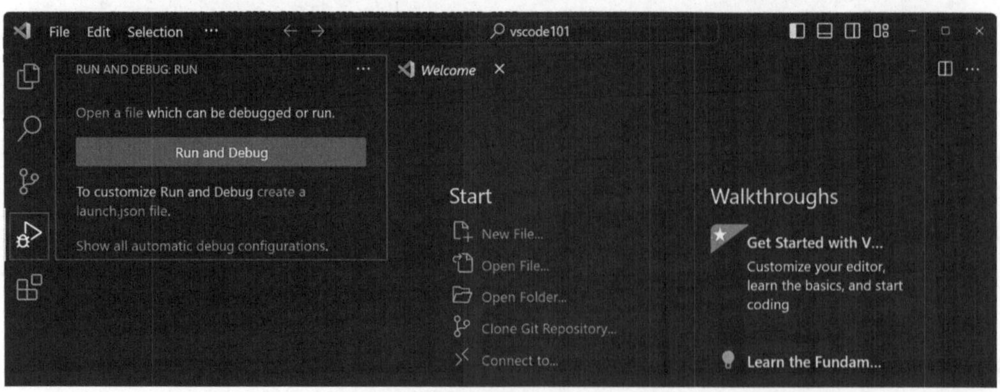

***Figure 5.4**: Primary Side Bar Shows View-Specific Information*

Tip: *Select the current view in the Activity Bar again to toggle the Primary Side Bar open and closed.*

View and Edit Files with the Editor (https://code.visualstudio.com/docs/getstarted/getting-started#_view-and-edit-files-with-the-editor)

The `Editor` is located in the main area of the window and is where you view and edit files in your workspace.

1. Select the Explorer view in the Activity Bar, and then select the `New File...` button to create a new file in your workspace.

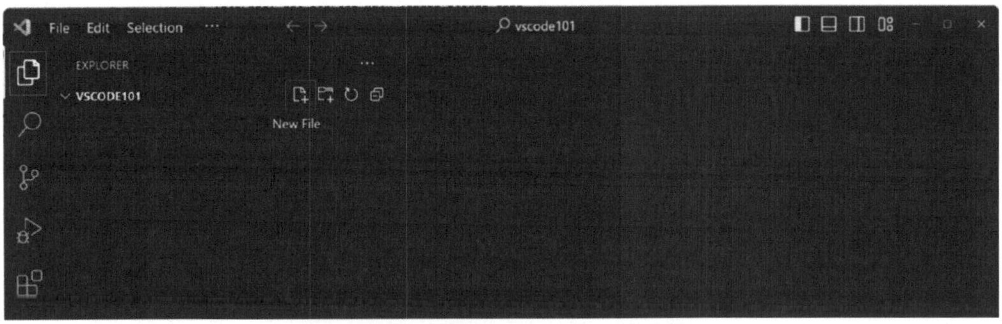

***Figure* 5.5**: *Selecting New File Option*

2. **Enter the Name index.html and Press *Enter***

   A file is added to your workspace and an Editor opens in the main area of the window, where you can start typing and editing the file.

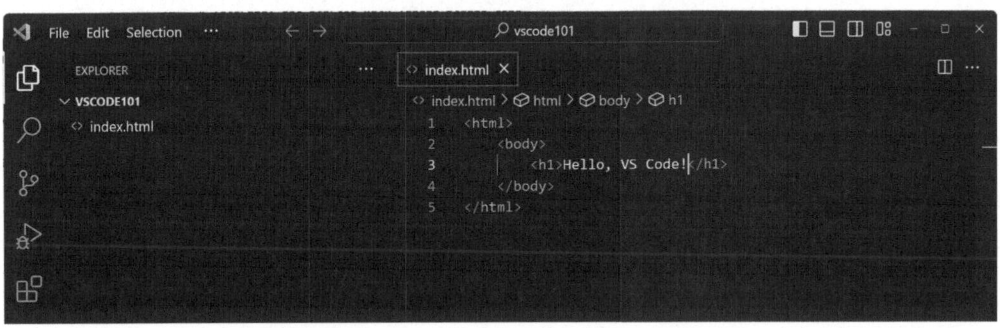

***Figure* 5.6**: *A File is Added to Your Workspace*

3. Add more files to your workspace and notice that each file opens in a new `Editor` tab.

   You can open as many editors as you like and view them side by side vertically or horizontally.

Figure 5.7: *Adding Another File*

Access the Terminal from the Panel Area (https://code.visualstudio.com/docs/getstarted/getting-started#_access-the-terminal-from-the-panel-area)

The **`Panel`** area is located below the **`Editor`** and contains different views, such as the output and debug information, and also gives you access to the integrated terminal.

1. Open the Panel area by selecting **`View`** > **`Appearance`** > **`Panel`** from the menu (or press *Ctrl+J*).

   Notice the different views in the Panel area. As you use different features in VS Code, such as debugging your code, you will use the information and functionality in these views.

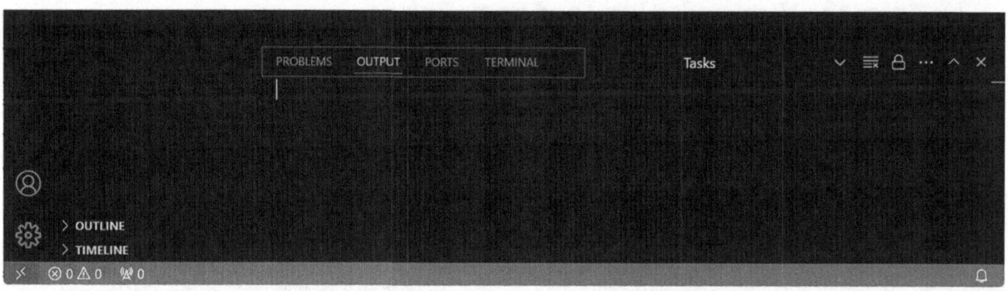

Figure 5.8: *Different Views in the Panel Area*

   Tip: *You can move the Panel area with the* ***`View`*** *>* ***`Appearance`*** *>* ***`Panel Position`*** *menu, for example, to the left or right for more vertical space.*

2. Open the integrated terminal by selecting **`Terminal`** in the **`Panel`** area > **`New Terminal`**, and try running some shell commands.

   The terminal enables you to run shell commands directly in VS Code, without switching to another terminal application. For example, you can use the terminal to install dependencies for your project or run a development server. Notice that the terminal working directory is the root of your workspace.

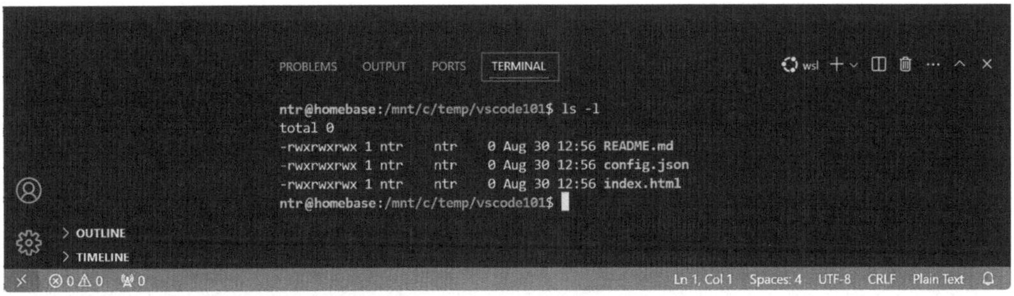

***Figure 5.9**: The Terminal Enables You to Run Shell Commands Directly in VS Code*

Depending on how your operating system is configured, you can select from a variety of shells, including PowerShell, Command Prompt, and Bash.

Use the Command Palette to Access Commands:

The **`Command Palette`** provides access to a large number of VS. For example, enter **`Create new file`** in the **`Command Palette`** to create a file in your workspace, or enter **`Git`** to view the list of Git actions you can trigger.

1. Select **`View`** > **`Command Palette`** or press *Ctrl+Shift+P* to open the **`Command Palette`**.

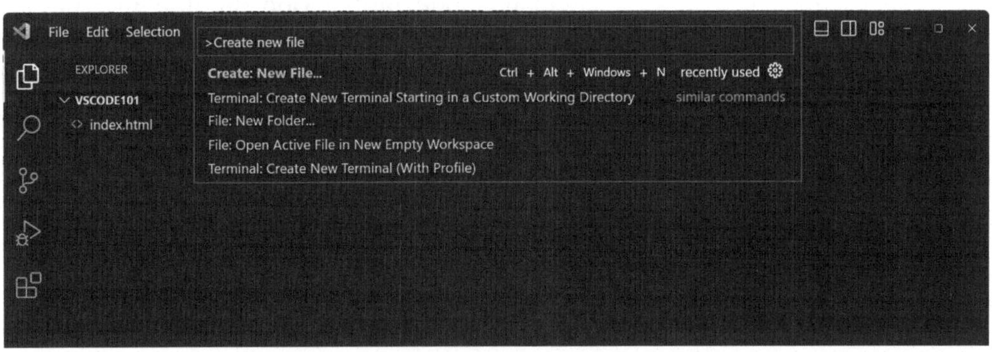

***Figure 5.10:** Opening of New Terminal*

Tip: *For commands that have a keyboard shortcut, note that the Command Palette displays the default shortcut. The command can be executed directly by using the keyboard shortcut.*

2. Press *Ctrl+P* to use the Command Palette to navigate to a file in your workspace. Start typing to filter the list.

   The **Quick Open** feature enables you to quickly open a file in your workspace, or search for symbols in files.

Figure 5.11: *Quick Open a File*

View Status Information with the Status Bar:

(https://code.visualstudio.com/docs/getstarted/getting-started#_view-status-information-with-the-status-bar)

The **Status Bar** is located at the bottom of the window and shows information about the file you are editing, and the workspace you have open. For example, if the folder you opened is a Git repository, the Status Bar shows the Git status and current branch.

1. Open a file by selecting it in the Explorer view.

   The Status Bar shows the language mode, indentation, and the line ending of the current editor.

Figure 5.12: *Status Bar Showing the Language Mode, Indentation, and More*

2. Select the indentation field (shown as Spaces: 4 in the figure) in the Status Bar to modify the indentation of the current file. For example, use tabs instead of spaces.

   If you have opened a Git repository, you can select the branch name in the Status Bar to create a new branch.

Step 3: Customize the User Interface (https://code.visualstudio.com/docs/getstarted/getting-started#_step-3-customize-the-user-interface)

Each developer has their own preferences for how their coding environment should look. VS Code enables you to change the layout, colors, keyboard shortcuts, and nearly every other aspect of the editor through various settings.

Let us start by using **Color Themes** to customize the colors in VS Code. Both the editor's highlighting colors and the VS Code user interface elements are impacted by a color theme.

To choose an alternative color theme:

1. Select the **`Manage`** button (gear icon) in the Activity Bar, and then select **`Themes`** > **`Color Theme`** to display the Color Theme picker.

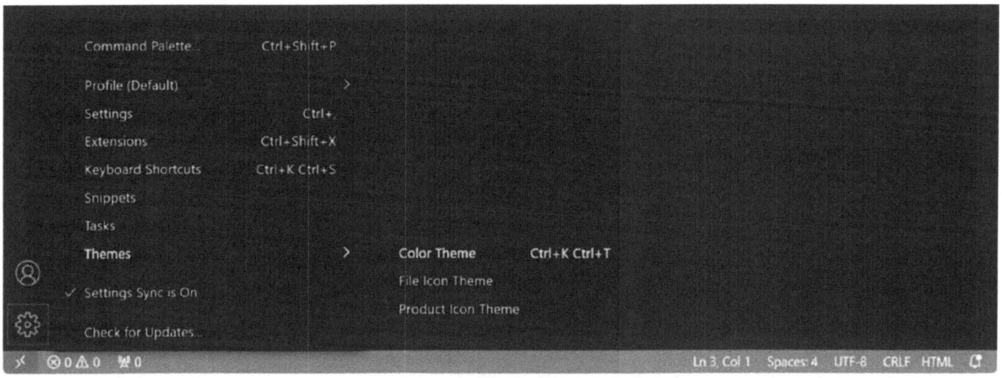

***Figure 5.13**: Selecting Color*

   Alternatively, you can enter **`Color Theme`** in the Command Palette or press *Ctrl+K Ctrl+T*.

2. Use the Up and Down keys to navigate through the list and preview the colors of the theme.

   VS Code comes with a list of built-in themes that you can choose from. As you move through the list, the active theme is previewed in VS Code.

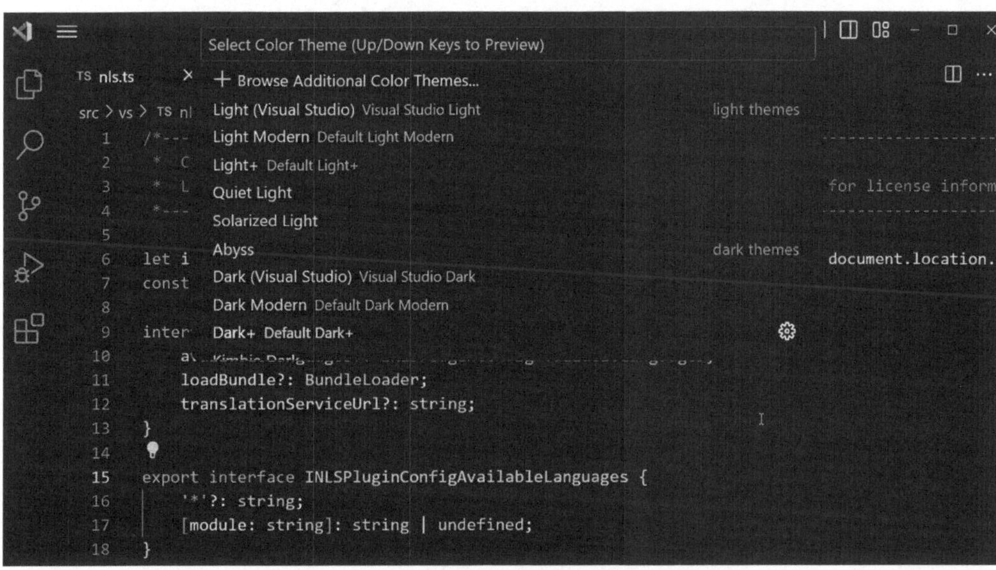

***Figure 5.14:** Choosing the Desired Color Theme*

By choosing **Browse Additional Color Themes...** from the **Color Theme** picker, you can also choose Color Themes straight from the VS Code Marketplace.

Beyond altering the UI's color scheme, VS Code's settings allow you to personalize nearly every aspect of the program. Perhaps you would want the editor to use a different font, change word wrapping, or enable floating editor windows (https://code.visualstudio.com/docs/configure/custom-layout#_floating-editor-windows).

Let us use the **Settings Editor** to modify the font size in the editor:

1. Select **File** > **Preferences** > **Settings** (or press Ctrl+,) to open the **Settings Editor**.

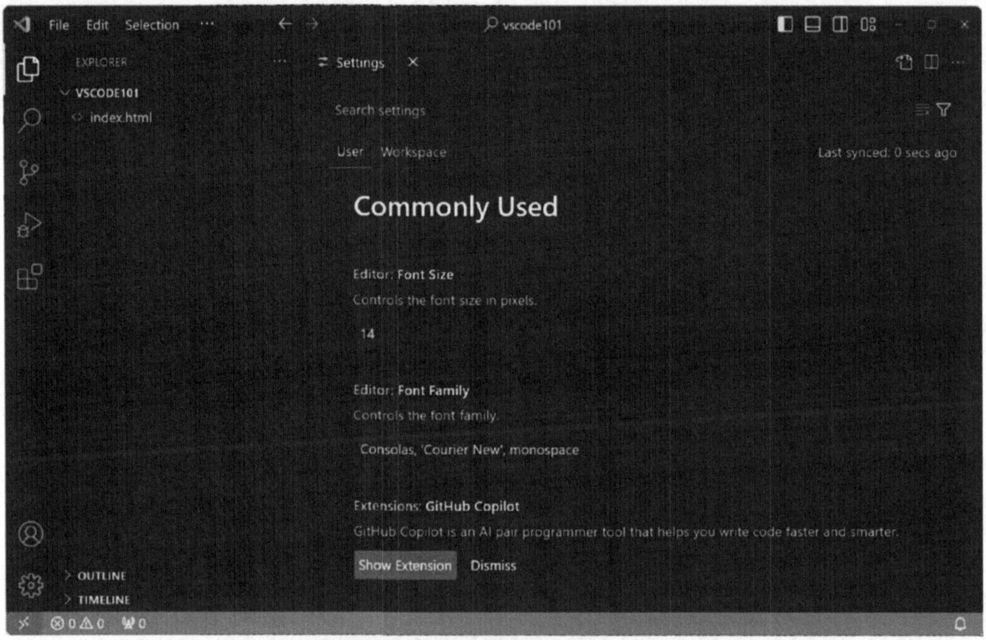

***Figure* 5.15**: *Setting Up the Commonly Used Attributes*

2. Modify the value of the **Editor: Font Size** setting to **36**.

   When you switch to the index.html editor tab, notice how the font size change is immediately applied in the editor. You can select the gear icon next to the setting and select **Reset Setting** to reset the value back to its default value.

   By default, when you change a setting, it applies to all your VS Code workspaces (**User Settings**). Switch to the **Workspace** tab to change a setting that only applies to the current workspace.

   Tip: *Use the search box in the Settings Editor to quickly find a setting.*

   There are many more ways to customize your VS Code experience, such as changing default keyboard shortcuts (https://code.visualstudio.com/docs/configure/keybindings), *adding code snippets* (https://code.visualstudio.com/docs/editing/userdefinedsnippets), *or adding extensions from the Visual Studio Marketplace* (https://code.visualstudio.com/docs/getstarted/getting-started#_step-5-install-a-language-extension).

Step 4: Write Some Code (https://code.visualstudio.com/docs/getstarted/getting-started#_step-4-write-some-code)

Since Visual Studio coding is mostly a coding editor, let us begin by creating some code! TypeScript, HTML, CSS, JavaScript, and more are all integrated into Visual Studio Code.

```
function sayHello(name) {
console.log('Hello, ' + name);
}

sayHello('VS Code');
```

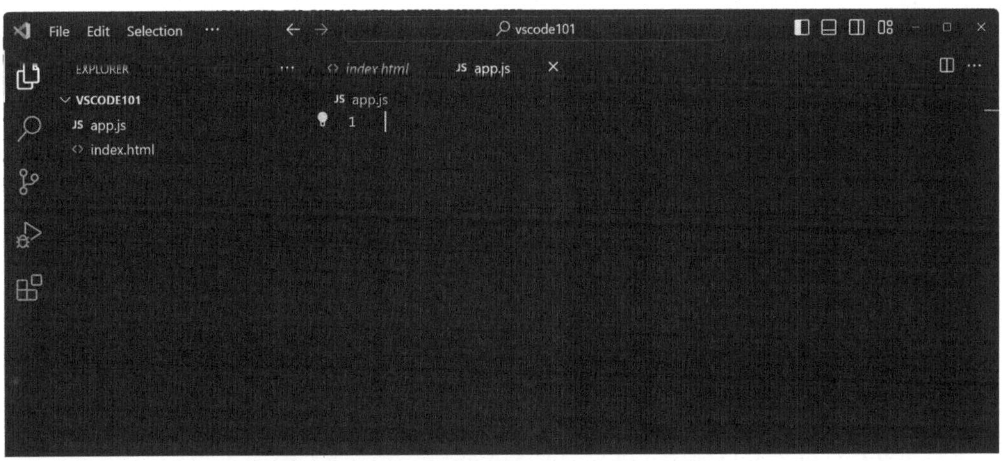

***Figure 5.16**: Dynamic View of Utilizing VS Code*

Select the lightbulb icon by moving the mouse over the "**`Hello`**" string, and then choose "**`Convert to template string`**."

The available Code Actions, which are recommendations that assist you in applying fast fixes to your code, are indicated by the lightbulb. The lightbulb menu can also be accessed by using the keyboard shortcut *Ctrl+Space*.

This Code Action uses a unique JavaScript technique to embed expressions in strings, transforming ""**`Hello`**, " + name" into a template string `` ` ``**`Hello, ${name}`**.

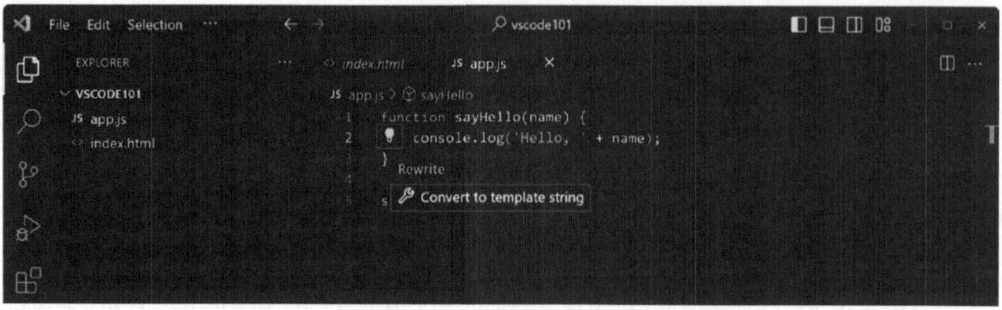

Figure 5.17: *Unique JavaScript Technique to Embed Expressions in Strings*

You can further experiment with IntelliSense in the different files in your workspace. For example, in the index.html file, start typing < to see suggestions for HTML tags.

Tip: *Toggle the* ***`File`*** *>* ***`Auto Save`*** *menu item to automatically save files whenever you make changes.*

Step 5: Use Source Control (https://code.visualstudio.com/docs/getstarted/getting-started#_step-5-use-source-control)

As you are writing code, you will want to save your work in a source control system to track changes or collaborate with others. Visual Studio Code has integrated Source Control Management (SCM) and includes Git (https://git-scm.com/) support out-of-the-box.

Let us use the built-in Git support to commit the changes you have made previously.

1. Make sure you have Git (https://git-scm.com/) installed on your computer. You can check if Git is installed by opening the terminal and entering the git --version.
2. Select the **`Source Control`** view in the Activity Bar, and select **`Initialize Repository`** to create a new Git repository for your workspace.

You also have the option to directly publish your changes to a GitHub repository (https://github.com/) by selecting **`Publish to GitHub`**.

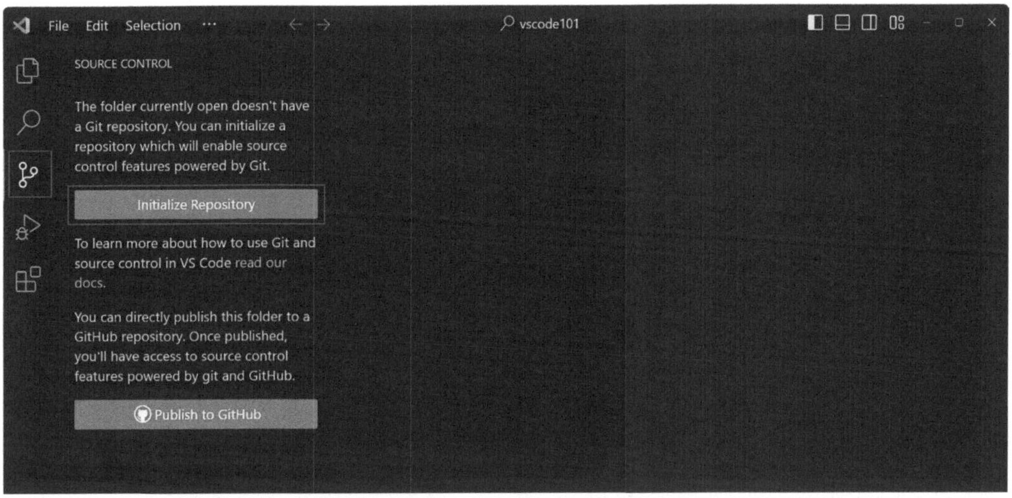

***Figure 5.18**: Directly Publish Your Changes to a GitHub Repository (https://github.com/)*

3. After you initialize a repository, the Source Control view shows the changes you have made in your workspace.

   Notice the letter indicating the type of change alongside each file. For example, U indicates an untracked/new file.

   When you hover over a change, you can choose to discard or stage the change. Staging a change means that you have marked it as ready to be committed.

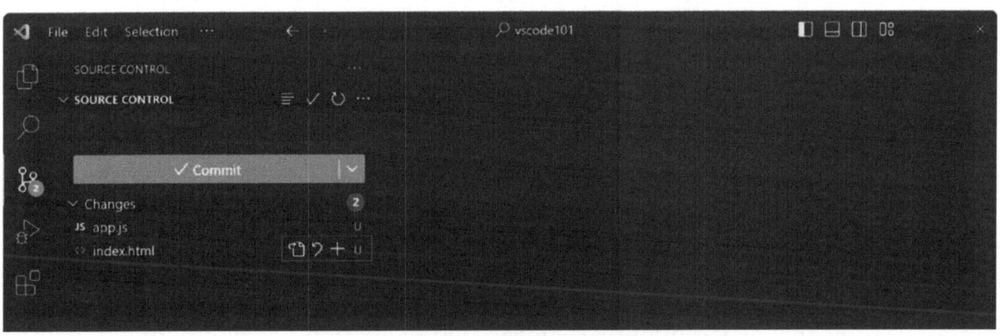

***Figure 5.19**: Using Commit Facility*

4. Select **+** next to **`Changes`** to stage all changes at once.
5. Enter a commit message, for example Add hello function, and then select **`Commit`** to commit the changes to your Git repository. A commit is the making of a set of tentative changes permanent, marking the end of a transaction used in computer science.

Source Control Graph shows a visual representation of the commit history of your Git repository. You can use the graph to explore the commit history, compare changes, and more.

Figure 5.20: *Source Control Graph Shows a Visual Representation of the Commit History of Your Git Repository*

Step 6: Installing a Language Extension (https://code.visualstudio.com/docs/getstarted/getting-started#_step-6-install-a-language-extension)

The capabilities that come pre-installed in Visual Studio Code are only the beginning. With the help of VS Code's robust ecosystem of extensions, you may enhance your installation with additional languages, debuggers, and tools to suit your unique development process. The Visual Studio Marketplace has thousands of extensions available.

Installing the Deno extension in Visual Studio Code is similar to installing other extensions. Either click the install button after searching for Deno in VS Code's extensions tab or click this link to bring up the extension page where you may select to install it.

Numerous tools that are frequently required for application development are included with Deno, such as a full language server (LSP) to support your preferred IDE. This page will assist you in configuring your surroundings so that you can get the most out of Deno while you are developing. In the Extensions tab, search for "**Deno**" and install the extension by Denoland. Next, press *Ctrl+Shift+P* to access the Command Palette, then type Deno: Initialize Workspace Configuration. In order to set up Deno for your workstation, choose this option.

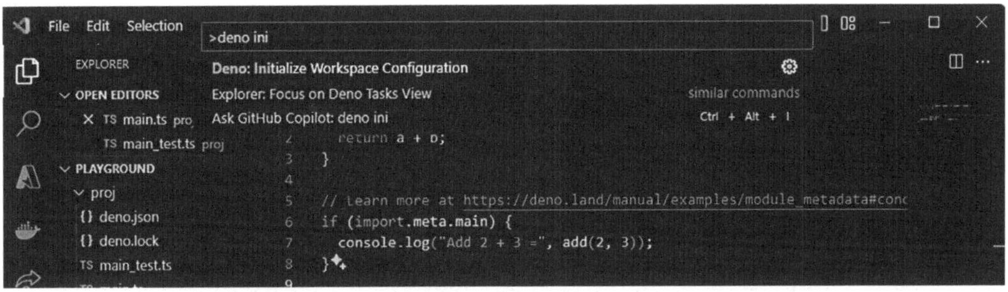

Figure 5.21: Installing the Extension by Denoland

A file called **`.vscode/settings.json`** will be created in your workspace with the following configuration:

```
{
  "deno.enable": true,
  "deno.lint": true,
  "deno.unstable": true
}
```

That is it! You have used VSCode to successfully set up your Deno development environment. All of Deno's LSP features, such as IntelliSense, code formatting, linting, and more, are now available to you. Remember that the Language Server Protocol (LSP) is an open, JSON-RPC-based protocol. It is for use between source code editors or Integrated Development Environments (IDEs) and servers that provide "language intelligence tools."

IDEs from JetBrains

Open your IDE and select **`File`** > **`Settings`** to install the Deno Plugin. Go to Plugins, then look for Deno. Get the official Deno plugin installed.

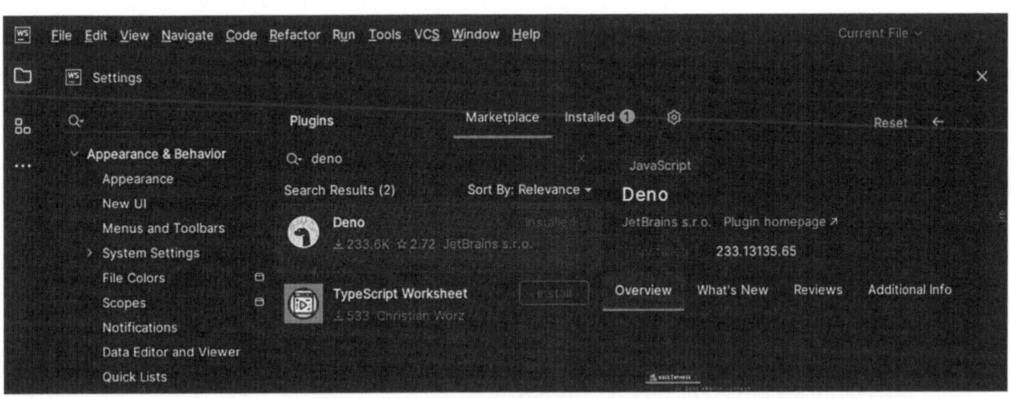

Figure 5.22: Installing the Deno Plugin

Return to **`File`** > **`Settings`** to configure the plugin. Go to **`Deno`** under **`Languages`** `and Frameworks`. Verify that Deno is enabled for your project and, if it has not been automatically detected, provide the path of the Deno executable.

Use GitHub Copilot and AI to Improve Your Coding:

You may improve your VS Code coding skills and even learn about previously unknown VS Code features and settings using GitHub Copilot. GitHub Copilot in Visual Studio Code may assist you with a variety of activities, including:

- **Code Completion**: Receive recommendations for entire functions or specific lines of code.
- **Explain Code**: To better grasp the functions of code snippets, get explanations.
- **Code Generation and Refactoring**: Produce artifacts such as documentation or tests and refactor your code.
- **Correct Errors:** Seek assistance with routine coding duties, such as identifying and resolving bugs or shell command problems.
- **Study Up on Visual Studio Code:** Inquire about commands, settings, or features in Visual Studio Code.

API Extension

The design of Visual Studio Code prioritizes extensibility. The Extension API allows for customization and enhancement of nearly every aspect of Visual Studio Code, from the user interface to the editing experience. Actually, a lot of VS Code's essential functions are extensions that make use of the same Extension API.

Using VS Code's extensive Extension API, building, running, debugging, testing, and publishing an extension, finding tutorials and code examples to get you started, and adhering to our UX guidelines for best practices are all covered in this reference.

It is possible to obtain code examples at Microsoft/vscode-extension-samples.

Visit the Visual Studio Code Extension Marketplace to find published extensions.

The Purpose of Making Extensions

Here are a few instances of what the Extension API may accomplish:

- Use a color or file icon theme to alter VS Code's appearance.
- Expand the Workbench by adding unique elements and views to the user interface.
- Using the Webview Guide, create a Webview to show a custom webpage constructed with HTML, CSS, and JS.
- Help debug a particular runtime - Debugger Extension Guide.
- Support a new programming language - Language Extensions Overview.

Check out the Extension Capabilities Overview page for a more thorough rundown of the Extension API. A series of code samples and tutorials that demonstrate different Extension API usage is also included in the Extension Guides Overview.

Constructing Extensions

It can take a lot of time and work to build a quality extension.

Here is what each section of the API docs can help you with:

- Get Started uses the Hello World sample to illustrate basic ideas for creating extensions.
- Extension Capabilities breaks down VS Code's extensive API into more manageable areas and directs you to more in-depth subjects.
- The Extension Guides section contains code samples and instructions that describe particular applications of the VS Code Extension API.
- The UX Guidelines highlight best practices for creating an extension that offers an excellent user experience.
- Language Extensions provides instructions and code samples to show how to add support for a programming language.
- Comprehensive instructions on a range of extension development subjects, including testing and publishing extensions, are included in Testing and Publishing.
- Advanced Topics describes more complex ideas including the proposed API, GitHub Codespaces, Extension Host, and Supporting Remote Development.
- References include comprehensive citations for Contribution Points, the VS Code API, and numerous other topics.

Code Extension for Deno and Visual Studio

The language server protocol is used by the Deno VS Code plugin to directly interface with the Deno CLI. By doing this, you can make sure that the details you receive about your code match how it will function when you run it using the Deno CLI. Installing the Deno extension in Visual Studio Code is similar to installing other extensions.

Setup

The language server protocol is used by the Deno VS Code plugin to directly interface with the Deno CLI. By doing this, you can make sure that the details you receive about your code match how it will function when you run it using the Deno CLI.

Integration of Language Servers: A built-in language server in the Deno CLI can offer an intelligent editing experience in addition to a way to easily access the other tools that come built-in with Deno. For most users, using the language server would be via an editor such as Visual Studio Code or other editors.

Installing the Deno extension in Visual Studio Code is similar to installing other extensions. Either click the install button after searching for Deno in VS Code's extensions tab or click this link to bring up the extension page where you may select to install it.

A splash page welcoming you to the extension should appear when you install it for the first time. (To view it again, press ⌘ ⇧ P to launch the command palette and execute the Deno: Welcome command.)

Activating Deno within a Visual Studio Code Environment

We understand that not every VS Code project you work on is a Deno project. When editing TypeScript, VS Code's built-in TypeScript/JavaScript language service is utilized.

You must enable Deno for the workspace in order to have support for Deno APIs and the same module resolution capabilities as the Deno CLI.

Using the Deno: Initialize Workspace Configuration command panel from Visual Studio Code is the simplest method for accomplishing this.

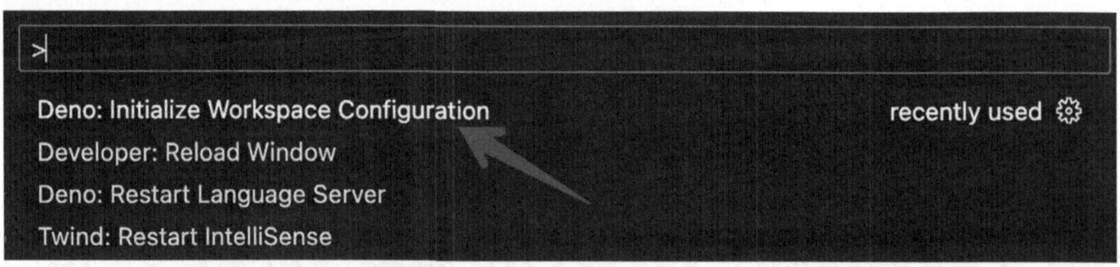

***Figure 5.23**: Screenshot of the Command Palette with Deno- Initialize Workspace*

Configuration

This will start a helper that will inquire if you wish to allow the project's Deno unstable APIs and linting. The workspace configuration (your workspace **`root.vscode/settings.json`**) is where VS Code will keep these settings if you run this command. You will be notified that Deno is ready for the project once the assistant is done.

Image of the workspace folder with the **`.vscode/setting.json`** configuration.

The VS Code settings window provides access to these and other parameters. Deno: Enable is the setting on the panel, and deno.enable is the setting when modifying the JSON by hand.

```
{
    "deno.enable": false,
    "deno.lint": true,
    "deno.unstable": false
}
```

Figure 5.24: *Modifying the JSON by Hand*

Note: *Workspace and user options are available in VS Code. Deno should ideally be activated in workspace settings rather than user settings, as this will make all workspaces Deno active by default.*

Configuration of Workspace Folders

These are the configuration options available in a workspace folder. At the moment, just the workspace is affected by the remaining settings:

- **`deno.enable`**: Determines if the Deno Language Server is turned on. When the extension is activated, the Deno language server will be used in place of the built-in VS Code JavaScript and TypeScript language services. False by default in a boolean.
- **`deno.enablePaths`**: Determines whether the Deno Language Server is activated for just particular workspace folder paths. A blank list is used by default.

The **`deno.codeLens.test. boolean`** controls the test code lens if it is activated, with a true default. The list of arguments provided to the deno test is named **`deno.codeLens.testArgs`**. string array ["**`--allow-all`**"] when a test code lens is activated. By default, after a project is activated, the extension will directly retrieve data from the installed Deno CLI. The extension will also muffle the built-in TypeScript/JavaScript extension.

For example, if your project is as follows: **`worker`** — **`front_end project`** ├── If you only want to make the worker route (and its subpaths) Deno enabled, you should **`add ./worker`** to the list of Deno paths: Enable pathways in the setting.

Projects Involving Mixed deno

A mixed Deno project, in which some workspace folders are Deno enabled and others are not, is made possible by this feature. This is helpful if you wish to utilize a separate configuration for the front-end code in a project that may contain a front-end component.

You would make a new workspace (or add a folder to an existing workspace) and adjust one of the folders' **`deno.enable`** properties to true and one to false in the settings to support this. The Deno language server only applies diagnostics to the enabled folders once you save the workspace setup; the other folder will use Visual Studio Code's built-in TypeScript compiler to provide diagnostics for TypeScript and JavaScript files.

Linting

When utilizing deno lint, you can utilize the same engine that provides the diagnostics thanks to the extension. If the Deno: Lint setting is activated in the settings panel (or deno.lint if changing settings in JSON), the editor will start displaying lint "warnings." Lint "warnings" in your code will begin to appear in the editor. To learn more about using the Deno linter, see the Linter section.

Making Use of a Configuration File

Although a configuration file is not necessary for a Deno project, there are a few situations in which it could be helpful. The Deno: Config option (or **`deno.config`** if editing by hand) can be used to apply the same settings as when using the --config option on the command line.

Additionally, by searching the workspace root for the configuration file and applying it, the Deno extension will automatically recognize and apply a **`deno.jsonc`** or **`deno.json`**. This automated behavior can be overridden by manually setting a Deno: Config option.

Organizing

The built-in formatter in the Deno CLI can be accessed with **`deno fmt`**, but it can also be set up to be utilized by Visual Studio Code.

Deno should be in the Editor: Default formatter setting drop-down list (or "**`editor.defaultFormatter`**": "**`denoland.vscode-deno`**" if you are manually editing settings).

Establishing a Connection to the Deno CLI

Sometimes that is not ideal, thus the Deno: Path (or **`deno.path`** if editing by hand) can be adjusted to point to the Deno executable instead of the extension searching for the Deno CLI executable in the host's PATH. It will be resolved in relation to the workspace root if the path supplied is relative.

Bring in Recommendations

The extension will make recommendations to finish the import when you try to import a module. The recommendations will contain any cached remote files in addition to local relative files.

The extension facilitates registry auto-completions, in which a client can find modules by using metadata that is optionally provided by a remote registry or module website. The extension will automatically scan hosts and origins to determine whether they support suggestions. If they do, it will ask you if you wish to enable it. Unchecking the box under **Deno** > **Suggest** > **Imports: Auto Discover** in **Settings** (or **deno.suggest.imports.autoDiscover** if editing manually) will alter this behavior.

By modifying the **Deno** > **Suggest** > **Imports: Hosts** setting - **deno.suggest.imports.hosts** in the relevant **settings.json** file, you can enable or disable specific hosts or origins.

Remote Module Caching

Deno is capable of retrieving and storing remote modules locally in a cache.

The Deno CLI will attempt to retrieve any remote modules and their dependencies and fill the cache when you type commands such as **deno run**, **deno test**, **deno info**, or **deno install**.

If the module is not in the cache when you are writing code in the editor, you will see a diagnostic that reads "**https://deno.land/example/mod.ts**" for any missing remote modules or "**Uncached or missing remote URL**." Unless the module is a completion of a registry import proposal (see aforementioned), Deno will not attempt to cache it automatically.

The plugin offers methods to cache dependencies inside the editor in addition to executing a command on the command line.

Deno will attempt to cache the dependency as a short fix for missing dependencies. Fixes can be accessible by hovering over the import specifier and choosing Quick Fix, hitting CTRL, or ⌘, while the editor is in the specifier. Additionally, the command palette contains the Deno: Cache Dependencies command, which aims to cache any dependencies of the module that are presently active in the editor. Code lenses provide actionable contextual information woven throughout the code. Several code lenses are currently supported by the language server, giving you a deeper understanding of the code. The majority are by default disabled; however, they are readily enabled.

Deno > Code Perspective: Actions deno.codeLens.implementations provide a lens listing any implementations of an object elsewhere in the code.

Deno > Code Viewpoint: References deno.codeLens.references provide a lens that will highlight any references to an item elsewhere in the code.

Deno > Code Viewpoint: References Each and Every Function Deno.code offers a lens that provides a list of all references to each function in the code.AllFunctions is referenced by Lens. All functions are not included in the previously mentioned References option.

Examining the Code Lens

A built-in testing API is accessible through **Deno.test** in the Deno CLI. The ability to run a test from within the editor is made possible by the code lens that is enabled by default on the extension and language server.

In the event that a section of code has a test:

```
------------------------------------------------------------------------------------------
import { assert } from "jsr:@std/assert@1";

Deno.test({
  name: "a test case",
  fn() {
    let someCondition = true;
    assert(someCondition);
  },
});
------------------------------------------------------------------------------------------
```

A code lens will be seen directly above the test:

Execute the Test

The extension will launch the Deno CLI to conduct the test and show you the results if you click on the code lens. The extension will attempt to run your test with the same configurations based on your existing settings. You can modify the **deno.codeLens.testArgs** parameter if you need to change the arguments supplied when performing the deno test.

Additionally, the extension will attempt to monitor whether the **Deno.test** function is destructured or assigned to a variable within the same module. In order to keep the code lens functioning, you can do something as follows:

```
---------------------------------------------------------------------------
const { test: denoTest } = Deno;

denoTest({
  name: "example test",
  fn() {},
});
---------------------------------------------------------------------------
```

By un-setting the **Deno** > **CodeLens: Test setting** - **deno.codeLens.test**, you can turn off this feature.

Tests can be executed using the command palette, the code lense decorations, or the

Test Explorer view. Additionally, you can omit specific tests from a test run by using the filter tool in the Text Explorer view.

Examining the test results in Visual Studio Code will provide the failure message, which includes the stack trace when a test fails.

Configuration for Testing

By default, tests are run similarly to how they would be if you used the command line option deno test --allow-all. You can modify these default settings by adjusting the Deno in your workspace or user settings, select the > **`Testing: Args`** option (or **`deno.testing.args`** if you are configuring manually). Enter the specific arguments you would have used with the deno test subcommand here.

Unless specifically specified in the **`Deno`** > **`Testing: Args`** setting, the "command line" used for running tests will automatically incorporate the parameters from other settings you have.

Making Use of the Debugger

Integration with the integrated Visual Studio Code debugger is made possible via the extension. You can produce a configuration by clicking create a **`launch.json`** filc in the Run and Debug tab, then choosing the Deno option from the list of debugger choices.

Activities

Sometimes you may want to use the CLI to execute Deno commands, even though the extension talks directly with the language server. Tasks can be defined in a **`deno.json`** file located in the tasks field at the workspace root.

Making Use of a Development Container

One excellent method to have a separate development environment without worrying about installing the Deno CLI on your local system is to use a development container with Visual Studio Code. The Deno extension is compatible with development containers, which Deno provides.

In the command panel, select **`Show All Definitions`**... and then search for **`Remote-Containers: Add Development Container Configuration Files`**... if you want to add dev container support to an existing Deno project.

The most recent version of the Deno CLI will be installed in the container as a result of setting up a **`baseline.devcontainer`** configuration.

VS Code will ask if you wish to open the project in a development container after it has been added. The Deno CLI and the **`vscode_deno`** extension will be installed in the development container when VS Code builds it and reopens the workspace using it if you want to.

Bash

The command-line shell and scripting language Bash, which stands for Bourne-Again Shell, is used to communicate with a computer's Operating System (OS).

Qualities

Using the Bash programming environment, users may automate processes, access the file system, and run commands. Most Linux distributions use it as their default shell, and it is also utilized on most Linux distributions and is also used on macOS and other Unix-like operating systems.

How it Works

Bash reads shell commands and interacts with the OS to execute them. Users can write Bash commands in a text editor and save them as an executable script file with a .sh extension.

Use Cases

Bash is essential for system administrators, programmers, and power users. Its applications include managing files and directories, verifying network configurations, altering configuration files, and showing the differences between two files.

An illustration of a bash:

```
> deno completions bash > /usr/local/etc/bash_completion.d/deno.bash
> source /usr/local/etc/bash_completion.d/deno.bash
```

Tips

Some things to keep in mind when using Bash include:

There are no spaces on either side of the equal (=) symbol in the strict syntax for variable assignment. Although Bash is capable of performing integer arithmetic computations, it is not appropriate for financial or scientific computing. The non-quoted backslash (' \ ') is the Bash escape character.

How it Operates

Bash reads shell commands and interacts with the OS to execute them. Users can write Bash commands in a text editor and save them as an executable script file with a .sh extension.

Use Cases

Power users, programmers, and system administrators all need Bash. File and directory administration, network configuration verification, configuration file editing, and displaying the differences between two files are among its uses.

Conclusion

In this chapter, we concentrated on learning various features of Visual Studio (VS) that provide ample facilities to design website design. We learned about the difference between Visual Studio and Visual Studio Code. We learned how to download and install Visual Studio Code on Windows. Then we get started with Visual Studio Code.

VS code can also be deployed using GitHub Copilot and AI to improve your coding. We have at last learned about API Extension and Code Extension for Deno and Visual Studio.

In the next chapter, we shall learn about Standard Library, Rust, and LSP.

Chapter 6
Standard Library, Rust, and LSP

Introduction

Deno provides a standard library written in TypeScript. It is a set of standard modules that can be reused by programs, allowing you to focus on your application logic rather than reinventing the wheel for common tasks.

Structure

In this chapter, we will cover the following topics:

- Standard Library
- Role of Library in Deno Web Development
    - ReactJS
    - Vue.js
    - Angular
    - Django (Using databases)
    - Ruby on Rails
    - Spring
    - ASP.NET Core

Standard Library

The standard library is a set of standard modules that can be reused by programmers, for common tasks. All of the modules in the Deno Standard Library are audited by the core team and are guaranteed to work with Deno, ensuring consistency and reliability.

Many packages in the Deno Standard Library are also compatible with Node.js, Cloudflare Workers, and other JavaScript environments. This allows you to write code that can be run in multiple environments without modification.

The standard library is hosted on JSR and is available at: https://jsr.io/@std. Packages are documented, and tested, and include usage examples. You can browse the full list of standard library packages on JSR, but here are a few examples:

- **`@std/path`**: Path manipulation utilities, akin to Node.js's path module.
- **`@std/jsonc`**: (De)serialization of JSON with comments.
- **`@std/encoding`**: Utilities for encoding and decoding common formats such as hex, base64, and variant.

Versioning and Stability

Each package of the standard library is independently versioned. Packages follow semantic versioning rules. You can use version pinning or version ranges to prevent major releases from affecting your code.

Importing Standard Library Modules

To install packages from the Deno Standard Library, you can use the deno add subcommand to add the package to your **`deno.json`** import map.

```
deno add @std/fs @std/path
```

The **`deno.json`** imports field will be updated to include those imports:

```
{
  "imports": {
    "@std/fs": "jsr:@std/fs@^1.0.2",
    "@std/path": "jsr:@std/path@^1.0.3"
  }
}
```

You can then import these packages in your source code:

```
import { copy } from "@std/fs";
import { join } from "@std/path";

await copy("foo.txt", join("dist", "foo.txt"));

Alternatively, you can import modules directly with the jsr:
specifier:

import { copy } from "jsr:@std/fs@^1.0.2";
import { join } from "jsr:@std/path@^1.0.3";

await copy("foo.txt", join("dist", "foo.txt"));
```

Node.js Compatibility

The Deno Standard Library is designed to be compatible with Node.js, Cloudflare Workers, and other JavaScript environments. The standard library is written in TypeScript and compiled into JavaScript, so it can be used in any JavaScript environment.

```
npx jsr add @std/fs @std/path
```

Running this command will add those packages to your package.json:

```
{
  "dependencies": {
    "@std/fs": "npm:@jsr/std__fs@^1.0.2",
    "@std/path": "npm:@jsr/std__path@^1.0.3"
  }
}
```

Then you can import them in your source code, just like you would with any other Node.js package. TypeScript will automatically find the type definitions for these packages.

```
import { copy } from "@std/fs";
import { join } from "@std/path";

await copy("foo.txt", join("dist", "foo.txt"));
```

Role of Library in Deno Web Development

Modules for typical activities like file system operations and HTTP servers are included in the standard library that comes with Deno.

If you are developing a more intricate application, you will probably use a web framework to communicate with Deno.

The Deno Standard Library is a collection of TypeScript modules that help with common tasks in web development, allowing developers to focus on their application's logic:

- **Reusability**

  The standard library includes modules that can be reused by programs, so developers do not have to reinvent the wheel for common tasks.

- **Consistency and Reliability**

  The core team audits all of the modules in the standard library to ensure they work with Deno.

- **Compatibility**

  Many packages in the standard library are compatible with other JavaScript environments, such as Node.js and Cloudflare Workers.

Range of Functionality

The standard library includes modules for a variety of tasks, such as:

- File system operations
- HTTP servers
- Data manipulation
- Web-related logic
- JavaScript-specific functionalities
- Advanced cryptographic functions

You can install packages from the standard library using the **`deno add`** command, and import them into your source code using the import statement. For example, to install the fs and path packages, you can use the command **`deno add @std/fs @std/path`**.

You can browse the full list of standard library packages on JSR.

Choosing the correct open-source library for web development might be overwhelming with so many options available. Here is a fast guide to help you pick, concentrating on elements such as simplicity of use, performance, community support, and real-world usage. We discuss well-liked options with their own advantages and disadvantages, including ReactJS, Vue.js, Angular, Django, Ruby on Rails, Laravel, Spring, and ASP.NET Core. This overview will assist you in selecting the most appropriate tool for your project, regardless of whether you are creating a straightforward website or a sophisticated web application.[1]

Library	Easy to Use	Performance	Community Support	Documentation Quality	Real-World Usage
ReactJS	Moderate	High	Very Strong	Excellent	Widely Used
Vue.js	Easy	High	Strong	Clear	Popular
Angular	Moderate	High	Strong	Detailed	Widely Used
Django	Easy	Moderate	Strong	Excellent	Popular
Ruby on Rails	Easy	Moderate	Very Strong	Excellent	Widely Used
Laravel	Easy	Moderate	Strong	Excellent	Popular

Spring	Moderate	High	Very Strong	Comprehensive	Widely Used
ASP.NET Core	Easy	High	Strong	Detailed	Widely Used

Table 6.1: *Comparing Various Library Stacks Based on Important Criteria*

Table 6.1 gives you a snapshot of how each library stacks up against important criteria, helping you make an informed decision based on your project needs and preferences.

Easy to Use

Is the library simple to install and start using? Does it come with clear instructions and examples?

Does it feel natural to use? Are things set up in a way that makes sense without needing a lot of time to learn?

Does it work right away with minimal setup, or do you need to tweak a lot of settings first?

Performance

Does using the library slow down your website, or does it keep things running smoothly?

Can you make the library smaller to speed up your website with special techniques such as only using parts you need (tree-shaking) or loading parts as they are needed (lazy-loading)?

How well does the library handle updating the page without making everything slow?

Community Support

How many people are using and helping improve the library? Is it a big group?

Do the creators fix problems and add new features quickly?

Are the guides and explanations for using the library kept up to date?

Documentation Quality

Is there a lot of good information on how to use the library? Is it easy for beginners?

Are there extra resources such as tutorials to help you learn?

Is it clear how to use the library's features with examples?

Real-World Usage

- Are people actually using the library for real websites? Is it being updated?
- Can you find examples of big websites that use it to see how well it works?

- Is there help for putting your website out there, making sure it works well, and fixing any issues?

Thinking about these points will help you choose the right tools for your web development projects. Finding the right balance between being easy to use, fast, and supported by a good community will make your work easier and your websites better.

ReactJS

ReactJS might take a bit of time to learn at first. It lets you write code that looks a lot like HTML, which is great because if you know how to make websites using HTML, CSS, and JavaScript, you will find React familiar. It is organized in a way that lets you break down big, complicated pages into smaller parts you can use again. But, you will need to spend some time understanding some of its special ideas, like how it updates what you see on the screen. Overall, React is pretty user-friendly once you get the hang of it.

- **Performance**: React makes websites fast. It has a smart way of making updates only where needed, which keeps things speedy. You can also use tricks to make your website even faster, such as loading only the parts that are needed right when they are needed. React is designed to be quick from the start.
- **Community Support:** React is supported by Facebook and used by lots of big companies, so it has a strong community. There are many people using it, which means lots of help, updates, and resources such as guides and tutorials. This makes learning and using React easier.
- **Documentation Quality:** The guides and info on how to use React are very clear and helpful. They start with the basics and also cover more advanced topics. Plus, there are extra resources such as blog posts to help you learn. React's instructions are top-notch.
- **Real-World Usage:** Big names such as Facebook, Netflix, Airbnb, and Uber use React for their websites. This shows it works well for making complicated and busy websites. There are also a lot of jobs for people who know how to use React. It is not just for websites; React Native can be used for making mobile apps too. React is a popular choice for real projects.

React is further discussed in *Chapter 8: React, HTML, and Next.js* of this book.

Vue.js

Vue.js is made to be easy for beginners but also works great for big projects. It mainly deals with what you see on the website, which helps make things less complicated when you are starting. Its setup lets you quickly make parts of a website that can change without a lot of code.

- **Performance:** Vue makes websites run fast. It does a good job of updating the website only where needed, thanks to smart ways of handling changes. Plus, it is built to load only the parts you need when you need them, which keeps things speedy.
- **Community Support**: Vue.js has a lot of fans and a big community, especially on GitHub. There is a lot of support out there, including forums and chat groups where you can ask questions.
- **Documentation Quality**: The guides and help for Vue.js are really clear and cover both basic and more tricky stuff. They are updated regularly, which is a big plus.
- **Real-World Usage**: Big names such as GitLab, Adobe, and BMW use Vue.js for their websites. It is versatile, so you can see it in action on everything from simple pages to more complex web applications. It also plays well with other web development tools, making it a good team player.

Angular

Angular helps you make complex web apps by breaking them down into smaller, reusable parts. It is true that it might take some time to get used to things like how it manages data and tasks, but Angular has a special tool that makes starting new projects faster by setting up the basics for you. It is all about setting you up to grow your app in a smart way.

- **Performance:** Angular is smart about updating your app only where and when it is needed, making sure it runs smoothly. It also has tricks such as loading only the parts of your app that are needed right when they are needed. This means even big apps with lots of information can work well without slowing down.
- **Community Support:** Google supports Angular, and more than 1.7 million developers use it. This means there is a lot of help out there, from how-to guides and tutorials to forums where you can ask questions. Angular stays up-to-date with the latest in web development.
- **Documentation Quality:** Angular's guides and information are really thorough and organized. They cover everything from the basics to more advanced stuff, and even special topics such as making your app accessible to everyone and managing data. There is a lot of support for learning how to use Angular well.
- **Real-World Usage:** Big websites such as Forbes and PayPal use Angular because it is strong and flexible. It is a good choice for all kinds of projects, from small websites to huge apps used by companies. It works well for things such as online stores, websites where you log in to access personal information, and apps that update in real time. Angular can also work with other tools, making even more things possible.

Django (Using Databases)

The database is set in the 'Database' dictionary. The aforementioned example is for the SQLite engine. As stated earlier, Django also supports:

- MySQL (**`django.db.backends.mysql`**)
- PostGreSQL (**`django.db.backends.postgresql_psycopg2`**)
- Oracle (**`django.db.backends.oracle`**) and NoSQL DB
- MongoDB (**`django_mongodb_engine`**)

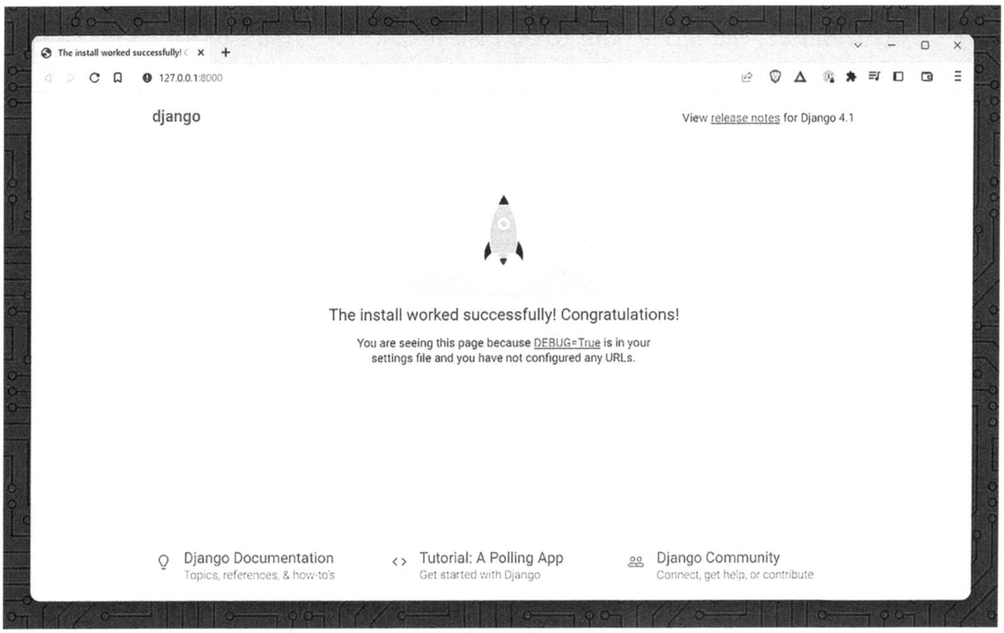

Figure 6.1: *Successful Installation of Django*

Django uses Python, making it fast to construct websites. It comes with a lot of features ready to use, which means less setup work. It also provides an admin interface that helps you manage your website without needing to write code. Django is all about making web creation simpler and more uncomplicated.

A few advantages of using Django are listed here:

- **Object-Relational Mapping (ORM) Support:** Django provides a bridge between the data model and the database engine, and supports a large set of database systems including MySQL, Oracle, Postgres, and more. Django also supports the NoSQL database through the Django-nonrel fork. For now, the only NoSQL databases supported are MongoDB and the Google app engine.

- **Multilingual Support:** Django supports multilingual websites through its built-in internationalization system. So, you can develop your website, which would support multiple languages.
- **Framework Support:** Django has built-in support for Ajax, RSS, Caching, and various other frameworks.
- **Administration GUI:** Django provides a nice ready-to-use user interface for administrative activities.
- **Development Environment:** Django comes with a lightweight web server to facilitate end-to-end application development and testing.
- **Performance:** Django is built to be fast. It talks to databases efficiently and its built-in tools are designed to load pages quickly. It can handle both small and big websites well.
- **Community Support:** Django is open-source and has a lot of people and companies supporting it. This means it is trusted and there are lots of extra tools you can use with it. It is also known for being secure.
- **Documentation Quality:** Django's guides and help documents are really detailed and kept up to date. They are great for both beginners and experts. Plus, because so many people use Django, there is a lot of extra help and tutorials out there.
- **Real-World Usage:** Big websites such as Instagram and Pinterest are built with Django. It is good for both small and large sites and works well with other tools. There are also lots of job opportunities if you know how to use Django.

Ruby on Rails

Ruby on Rails makes starting a new project pretty straightforward. It has rules that help you skip writing common, repetitive code. This framework is great for quickly creating and changing apps, although big projects might get a bit complex.

- **Performance:** While Ruby on Rails can be slow for big apps, there are tricks to make it run faster. Using caching, background tasks, and certain tools can help speed things up. However, large applications might need extra work to perform well.
- **Community Support:** Ruby on Rails has a supportive and worldwide community. You can find lots of help, from online tutorials and videos to books and conferences. Plus, there is a huge collection of free tools and add-ons made by other developers.
- **Documentation Quality:** The official Rails Guides are detailed and cover everything you need to know. There are also many great resources outside the official ones that can help you learn more.

- **Real-World Usage:** Big websites such as Airbnb, GitHub, Shopify, Basecamp, and Kickstarter are built with Ruby on Rails. It is good for complex websites that handle a lot of data.

Laravel

Laravel is a tool that helps you build web applications faster. It is designed to be easy to understand, which is great if you are just starting. It has built-in shortcuts for common tasks such as sending users to different parts of your app, logging them in, and managing data. Features such as HTML templates, database connectivity, user input validation, and authentication systems are frequently shared across web applications. These elements are made simpler by the developer-friendly and structured Laravel framework, which frees up programmers to focus on the artistic side of website development.

Laravel offers senior developers powerful capabilities for real-time events, queues, unit testing, dependency injection, and more. Laravel is optimized for creating high-end web applications and is prepared to manage heavy workloads. The PHP ecosystem's top packages are combined in Laravel to provide the most reliable and developer-friendly framework on the market. The framework has also been developed by thousands of skilled developers from around the globe.

Learning Laravel is not too hard if you are already familiar with how web apps are built.

- **Performance:** Laravel uses special tricks to work quickly, even when lots of people are using your app. It can do things in the background, such as sending emails, without slowing down the main parts of your app. While it might not be the fastest tool out there, it is good at handling big jobs without much trouble.
- **Community Support:** A lot of developers, over 7 million, use Laravel. This means there is a ton of help out there. You can find guides, tips, and tools made by other people. The people who made Laravel are also pretty active in helping out and adding new features.
- **Documentation Quality:** Laravel's guides are really detailed and easy for beginners. They cover everything you need to know and are updated regularly. Plus, there is a community that adds their own advice and solutions, which is super helpful.
- **Real-World Usage:** Big websites such as Business Insider and National Geographic use Laravel. It is also used for making all kinds of web apps, from small projects to big, complex systems. Laravel is good for creating secure and reliable apps for different needs.

Nevertheless, some factors contribute to a slow Laravel performance. Many developers have poor habits, such as uploading a large number of heavy images, using old PHP versions, compiling massive volumes of unneeded data, or neglecting to remove unnecessary files from their projects.

Performance: Laravel may not be the swiftest web framework, leading to comparatively slower web development when compared to other options.

Choose Django if you prioritize scalability, security, and rapid development, and if you are comfortable with Python or willing to learn it. Choose Laravel if you prefer PHP, value elegant and expressive syntax, and want to leverage Laravel's rich ecosystem and tools.

Spring

Spring is pretty straightforward when it comes to building web apps and services. It takes care of a lot of the routine work for you, allowing you to concentrate on what makes your app special. Getting started is easy, especially with its helpful guides for newcomers. Spring uses simple Java and special notes (annotations) to cut down on unnecessary code.

- **Performance:** Speed is a big deal for Spring. It is smart about using resources efficiently and can handle tasks without making you wait. It is also good at doing several things at once (asynchronous tasks), and it has features to make things run faster, such as caching and batch processing. For bigger apps, Spring Boot sets things up in a way that usually works well right from the start.
- **Community Support:** Spring has a huge community with over 5 million users worldwide. You can find lots of events, online forums, blog posts, and people willing to help. There is a wealth of knowledge and support available.
- **Documentation Quality:** The instructions and guides for Spring are very thorough and always kept current. They cover everything from the basics to more complex setups. Plus, there is a ton of extra learning materials such as tutorials, books, and courses from other sources.
- **Real-World Usage:** Big companies such as Netflix, Amazon, and Google rely on Spring for important parts of their services. It is versatile, fitting small projects as well as very large ones. Spring also works well with other popular tools such as Hibernate and React, making it a good choice for a wide range of projects.

ASP.NET Core

ASP.NET Core makes it straightforward to start building web apps. It has templates and tools that help you get going without much fuss. The language it uses, C#, is pretty straightforward to read and write. Plus, it works well with popular tools such as Angular and React, giving you more options. It is user-friendly for beginners and seasoned developers alike.

- **Performance:** ASP.NET Core is built to be fast and can handle a lot of work without slowing down. It lets you manage how your app runs very precisely. It is also good at doing many things at once, which means it can handle lots of users without a hitch. For big apps, it has ways to help reduce the load on databases.
- **Community Support:** ASP.NET Core has strong support thanks to Microsoft and its use in many businesses. There are lots of resources online, and if you have questions, you are likely to get answers quickly. The community also shares lots of helpful tools and libraries for free.
- **Documentation Quality:** Microsoft provides detailed and easy-to-understand documentation for ASP.NET Core. It is well-organized and updated regularly. There are also lots of free tutorials available online, making it easy to learn at your own pace.
- **Real-World Usage:** Big companies such as DHL, Samsung, and UPS use ASP.NET Core for their web apps because it is reliable and efficient. It strikes a good balance between being easy to use and giving developers control over how things work. Being able to use it on different types of computers and systems is a big plus for many organizations.

The various attributes of library components are compared in *Table 6.2*:

Library	Pros	Cons
ReactJS	Updates pages quickly and keeps them running smoothly, supported by Facebook and widely used, plenty of guides and help available and used by big websites.	Can be hard to learn at first Might need extra setup for the best speed.
Vue.js	Easy for beginners, quick and efficient, clear instructions for use, and plays nice with other web tools.	Not as many job opportunities as React.
Angular	Comes with tools for building complex websites, optimizes for fast loading, is backed by big companies, and has loads of detailed guides.	Has a bit of a learning curve, and may be too much for simple sites.
Django	Uses Python for quick website making, has many features ready out of the box, is secure and can grow with your site, and is well-documented.	The admin part is Python-based. Not the fastest with heavy lifting.
Ruby on Rails	Great for quickly making prototypes, strong support community, and running big websites.	Not great for very large apps. Not as many people know Ruby.

Laravel	Friendly for beginners using PHP, has features to make apps run smoothly, a large community for help, and good instructions for getting started.	PHP is slower than some languages. Not as flexible as other frameworks.
Spring	Simplifies Java web development, used by big tech companies, has features for faster operations, and comprehensive guides and help.	Java can be wordy. Initial setup can feel complicated.
ASP.NET Core	Beginner-friendly start to web apps, and handles lots of work quickly.	

Table 6.2: *Pros and Cons of Various Attributes of Library Components*

Conclusion

In this chapter, we learned about the Standard Library and the role of the Library in Deno Web Development. The various tools included in this library package are ReactJS, Vue.js, Angular, Django (using databases), Ruby on Rails, Spring, and ASP.NET Core.

In the next chapter, we are going to learn about Web frameworks that aim to automate the overhead associated with common activities performed in web development. For example, many web frameworks provide libraries for database access, templating frameworks, and session management, and they often promote code reuse.

Reference

1. **Top Open-Source Libraries for Web Development**: https://daily.dev/blog/top-open-source-libraries-for-web-development

CHAPTER 7
The Stateful of Web Frameworks on Deno

Introduction

Web frameworks provide a standard way to build and deploy web applications on the World Wide Web. A web development framework is a pre-established collection of software tools, libraries, and guidelines created to expedite and streamline the process of web application development.

Web framework architectures provide a standardized way of building web applications. They define the structure and organization of the application and how different components interact with each other. Most of the web frameworks depend on the Model-View-Controller (MVC) architecture.

Model-View-ViewModel (MVVM) architecture is a popular web development architecture that is similar to the Model-View-Controller (MVC) architecture but with some key differences.

Three-Tier Architecture, also known as Multi-Tier Architecture, is a popular web development architecture.

A stateful protocol is a communication protocol in which the receiver may retain the session state from previous requests.

Websites generated by Deno can be of two types: Static and dynamic sites.

Front-end frameworks are collections of pre-written, reusable code that provide a foundation for building the user interface of a website or web application.

Backend frameworks allow developers to build server-side applications and services that power websites and web applications.

We will discuss Node.js, an open-source, cross-platform JavaScript runtime environment that allows you to run JavaScript code outside a web browser.

Deno Deploy is a globally distributed platform for serverless JavaScript applications.

At the end, we shall learn about the linter tool. A linter serves as a valuable developer tool for improving and enhancing code quality. It achieves this by analyzing static source code to identify and flag issues that can lead to bugs, vulnerabilities, and code smells. A linter will scan source code looking for errors, defects, stylistic issues, and questionable constructs.

Structure

In this chapter, we will be covering the following topics:

- Web Frameworks in Deno
- Classification of Web Framework Architectures
- A Stateless and Stateful Protocol
- Static and Dynamic Sites on Deno
- Web Frameworks for Front-End Development
- Best Web Frameworks for Back-End Development
- Deno Deploy
- API Servers
- Playground
- Linter Developer Tool

Web Frameworks in Deno

A Web Framework (WF) or Web Application Framework (WAF) is a software framework that is designed to support the development of web applications including web services, web resources, and web APIs. Web frameworks provide a standard way to build and deploy web applications on the World Wide Web. Web frameworks aim to automate the overhead associated with common activities performed in web development. For example, many web frameworks provide libraries for database access, templating frameworks, and session management, and they often promote code reuse.[5] Although they often target the development of dynamic websites, they are also applicable to static websites.

Web Development Framework

A web development framework is a pre-established collection of software tools, libraries, and guidelines created to expedite and streamline the process of web application development. It offers a consistent framework and regulations for constructing web applications, simplifying developers' workloads by managing routine tasks such as routing, database interaction, session management, and authentication.

Web development frameworks are available for front-end and back-end development that support a wide range of features and functions, including UI components, data binding, server-side processing, and content management. They are accessible in several programming languages. Developers have a variety of web development frameworks to choose from depending on their project's particular needs. Using a web development framework can assist in ensuring that the finished product is scalable, reliable, and maintainable due to the standardized approach to development it offers.

Benefits of Using Web Development Frameworks

Using web development frameworks can bring many benefits to your development process, including:

- **Speed and Efficiency**: It allows developers to build applications faster and with less code.
- **Consistency and Modularity**: Easy to maintain and scale applications over time.
- **Security:** Includes built-in security features that help to protect against threats.
- **Community Support**: Supports large communities of developers who provide support and resources.
- **Scalability:** Allows scaling of applications as they grow in size and complexity.
- **Testing and Debugging**: Offers various tools and features to make testing and debugging easier.

As you work with different web development frameworks, testing becomes a crucial part of the development process to ensure the stability and reliability of your applications. This is where KaneAI by LambdaTest can make a significant impact.

Things to Check while Choosing a Web Development Framework

Choosing the right web development framework can have a significant impact on the success of your project. Here are some points to consider before choosing a web development framework:

- **Ease of Installation:** The ease of installation of a web development framework is important. The framework should have clear and concise installation instructions that are easy to follow. It should not require extensive configuration or installation of additional dependencies. A straightforward installation process can save time and effort for developers and prevent delays in project timelines.

- **Documentation and Support:** Good documentation and support are essential for any web development framework. The framework should have clear and concise documentation that covers all the features and functionality. It should also have an active community that supports and assists developers. This can help to resolve any issues quickly and efficiently and prevent roadblocks in the development process.
- **Licensing:** Licensing is an important factor to consider when choosing a web development framework. Some frameworks have strict licensing restrictions that may limit how the framework can be used or distributed. It is important to choose a framework that has a license that aligns with the project's goals and objectives.
- **Scalability and Flexibility:** A web development framework should be able to scale and adapt to changing requirements. The framework should be flexible enough to accommodate new features and functionality and allow for future growth. This can help to ensure that the framework is a long-term solution and can evolve with the project's needs.
- **Cost and Budget:** Cost and budget are important considerations when choosing a web development framework. Some frameworks may require expensive licenses or have ongoing maintenance costs. It is important to choose a framework that aligns with the project's budget and does not have hidden costs that may impact the overall project costs.
- **Learning Curve:** The learning curve of a web development framework is an important factor to consider. Some frameworks may have a steep learning curve requiring extensive training or specialized knowledge. It is important to choose a framework that has a manageable learning curve and can be easily adopted by the development team.
- **Customization and Extensibility:** Customization and extensibility are important factors to consider when choosing a web development framework. The framework should provide developers with the ability to customize and extend the framework's functionality to meet the project's unique needs. This can help to ensure that the framework is a good fit for the project and can be tailored to meet the project's specific requirements.

Once you have developed your application using the chosen web development framework, it is important to test your websites across different real browsers, devices, and OS for browser compatibility. AI-powered test orchestration and execution platforms such as LambdaTest let you perform cross browser testing of your websites developed using any of the aforementioned web development frameworks on an online browser farm of 3000+ real browser environments. This aspect is further explored in *Chapter 14, Deploying Deno Applications and Websites* of this book.

Limitations in Adopting Frameworks

While frameworks offer many advantages in IT development, they also have some disadvantages, including:

- **Limited Creativity:** Frameworks have strict rules and conventions that must be followed in order for the code to work properly. This can limit the developer's creativity and make it difficult to implement custom features.
- **Application Size:** They often include features and libraries that are not necessary for the application being developed, which can lead to an increase in the size of the application. This can slow down the time it takes to download and run the application.
- **Compatibility:** Some frameworks may not be compatible with all platforms and environments and this can potentially limit deployment options. In addition, various frameworks may also require specific versions of programming languages or third-party software, which can make installation and operation difficult.
- **Learning Curve:** Learning a new framework can take time and may require additional training for developers. It can also make the recruitment process more difficult, as it can often be challenging to find developers who have prior experience within a specific framework.

Types of Web Development Frameworks

Front-end and Back-end web development frameworks are designed to simplify the process of building web applications by providing tools and pre-written code for each specific layer of the application.

Front-end frameworks are focused on the presentation layer of a web application and are responsible for rendering the user interface. Some popular front-end frameworks include ***AngularJS, React, and Vue.js.***

On the other hand, back-end frameworks are focused on an application's server-side functionality. They provide the tools and structure necessary to build the application's backend, including database interaction, server-side rendering, and API development. Some popular back-end frameworks include Ruby on Rails, Django, and Express.

Both web development frameworks can significantly improve the development process by providing a set of conventions and tools to streamline the creation of complex applications. However, it is essential to choose the proper web development framework for the specific needs of a project, as some frameworks may be more suitable for certain types of applications or development teams.

Difference between Front-End Frameworks and Back-End Frameworks

Front-end frameworks and back-end frameworks are two types of web development frameworks that serve different purposes. The various features of both types are compared in *Table* 7.1.

Front-End Frameworks	Back-End Frameworks
Focus on the client-side components of a web application, including the user interface and user experience.	Focus on the server-side components of a web application, including handling requests, managing databases, and processing data.
Provide pre-written tools and libraries for building interactive and responsive user interfaces such as buttons, forms, and data visualization components.	Provide pre-written tools and libraries for building scalable and secure server-side applications, such as routing, authentication, and database integration.
Typically use a variety of programming languages, such as HTML, CSS, and JavaScript.	Typically use a variety of programming languages, such as Ruby, Python, and Java.
Handle tasks such as data binding, state management, and routing within the user's browser.	Handle tasks such as authentication, database interaction, and security within the server.
Examples of front-end frameworks include React, AngularJS, and Vue.js.	Examples of back-end frameworks include Ruby on Rails, Django, and Express.

Table 7.1: *Difference between Front-End Frameworks and Back-End Frameworks*

Overall, front-end and back-end frameworks serve different purposes and are designed to solve different types of problems in web development. These web development frameworks provide a comprehensive solution for building modern web applications.

Classification of Web Framework Architectures

Web framework architectures provide a standardized way of building web applications. They define the structure and organization of the application and how different components interact with each other. Here are some of the most common web framework architectures:

Model-View-Controller (MVC) Architecture

Most of the web frameworks depend on the Model-View-Controller (MVC) architecture. The reason why this pattern is preferred lies in its rational design that separates the app logic from the interface and forms the three essential parts that are represented in the architecture's name.

Model-View-Controller (MVC) architecture is a popular web development architecture that separates the application into three main components:

- Model
- View
- Controller

The model represents the data, the view represents the user interface, and the controller handles user input and business logic. This separation makes the application easier to develop, maintain, and test. Many web development frameworks are built using this architecture, and here are some popular examples: *Ruby on Rails, Laravel, Spring, Django, and* ASP.NET.

“As the design of the World Wide Web was not inherently dynamic, early hypertext consisted of hand-coded HTML text files that were published on web servers. Any modifications to published pages needed to be performed by the pages' author. In 1993, the Common Gateway Interface (CGI) standard was introduced for interfacing external applications with web servers, to provide a dynamic web page that reflected user inputs.” [2]

Original implementations of the CGI interface typically had adverse effects on the server load, however, because each request started a separate process. More recent implementations utilize persistent processes amongst other techniques to reduce the footprint in the server's resources and offer a general performance boost.

Most MVC frameworks follow a push-based architecture also called “action-based.” These frameworks use actions that do the required processing, and then “push” the data to the view layer to render the results.[3] An alternative to this is pull-based architecture, sometimes also called “component-based.” These frameworks start with the view layer, which can then “pull” results from multiple controllers as needed. In this architecture, multiple controllers can be involved with a single view. [3]

Model-View-ViewModel (MVVM) Architecture

Model-View-ViewModel (MVVM) architecture is a popular web development architecture similar to the Model-View-Controller (MVC) architecture but with some key differences. The MVVM architecture separates the application into three main components:

- Model
- View
- ViewModel

The model represents the data, the view represents the user interface, and the view model manages the communication between the model and the view. This separation makes the application easier to develop, maintain, and test. Many web development frameworks are built using this architecture, and here are some popular examples: AngularJS, Vue.js, Knockout.js, and React.

Three-Tier Architecture

Three-Tier Architecture, also known as Multi-Tier Architecture, is a popular web development architecture that separates the application into three main tiers:

- Presentation tier
- Application tier
- Database tier

The presentation tier handles the user interface, the application tier handles the business logic, and the database tier handles data storage and retrieval. This separation makes the application easier to develop, maintain, and test. Many web development frameworks are built using this architecture, and here are some popular examples: *CakePHP, Express.js, Ember.js, and Backbone.js.*

In a three-tier organization, applications are structured around three physical tiers: client, application, and database. The database is normally an RDBMS. The application contains the business logic, runs on a server, and communicates with the client using HTTP. The client on web applications is a web browser that runs HTML generated by the application layer. The term should not be confused with MVC, where, unlike in three-tier architecture, it is considered a good practice to keep business logic away from the controller, the "middle layer."

Web frameworks must function according to the architectural rules of browsers and protocols such as HTTP, which is stateless. Webpages are served up by a server and can then be modified by the browser using JavaScript. Either approach has its advantages and disadvantages.

A Stateless and Stateful Protocol

A stateless protocol is a communication protocol in which the receiver must not retain the session state from previous requests. The sender transfers the relevant session state to the receiver in such a way that every request can be understood in isolation, that is without reference to the session state from previous requests retained by the receiver.[4]

In contrast, a **stateful** protocol is a communication protocol in which the receiver may retain the session state from previous requests.

In computer networks, examples of stateless protocols include the **Internet Protocol (IP)**, which is the foundation for the Internet, and the **Hypertext Transfer Protocol**

(HTTP), which is the foundation of the World Wide Web. Examples of stateful protocols include the **Transmission Control Protocol (TCP) and the File Transfer Protocol (FTP)**.

Stateless protocols improve the properties of visibility, reliability, and scalability. Visibility is improved because a monitoring system does not have to look beyond a single request in order to determine its full nature. Reliability is improved because it eases the task of recovering from partial failures. Scalability is improved because not having to store session state between requests allows the server to quickly free resources and further simplifies implementation.

The disadvantage of stateless protocols is that they may decrease network performance by increasing the repetitive data sent in a series of requests since that data cannot be left on the server and reused.

Examples

An HTTP server can understand each request in isolation.

Contrast this with a traditional FTP server that conducts an interactive session with the user. During the session, a user is provided a means to be authenticated and set various variables (working directory, transfer mode), all stored on the server as part of the session state.

Server-side page changes typically require that the page be refreshed, but allow any language to be used and more computing power to be utilized. Client-side changes allow the page to be updated in small chunks which feel like a desktop application but are limited to JavaScript and run in the user's browser, which may have limited computing power. Some mix of the two is typically used. Applications which make heavy use of JavaScript and only refresh parts of the page, are called single-page applications and typically make use of a client-side JavaScript web framework to organize the code.

There can be complex interactions between stateful and stateless protocols among different protocol layers. For example, HTTP, a stateless protocol, is layered on top of TCP, a stateful protocol, which is layered on top of IP, another stateless protocol, which is routed on a network that employs BGP, another stateful protocol, to direct the IP packets riding on the network.

Static and Dynamic Sites on Deno

Websites generated by Deno can be of two types:

- Static sites
- Dynamic sites

Static Sites

For some time, it has been possible to host purely static sites on Deno Deploy. Using either an app server such as Hono or the static file server from the Deno standard library, you can quite happily serve up static files from Deploy.

Here are a few popular static site development options that are supported on Deno today :

- **Vanilla JS or Single-Page App (SPA) Frameworks**

  Vanilla JavaScript applications or Single-Page App (SPA) frameworks designed to run purely client-side (React, Angular, Vue.js, and so on) can be used with Deno-powered API servers.

  If your application does not require the use of frameworks (and it might not), you can use a Deno-based static file server or an application server such as Hono to serve up unprocessed HTML, CSS, and JavaScript, and incorporate backend API routes as needed.

  For web applications designed for long usage sessions and complex front-end interactions, a Single-Page Application (SPA) architecture might be the right choice. You would serve static assets through Deno, but you would develop more client-side code that uses front-end frameworks such as **React, Angular, or Vue.js.**

  Depending on your framework choice, there may be a compilation or pre-processing step required before your code can run in the browser. Some of those build processes can be run in Deno, but some may still require the use of Node.js.

  Here are a few templates for SPA development you can try with Deno and Deno Deploy today:

  - Vue.js template application
  - Angular template
  - React (with create-react-app)

- **Lume**

  Lume is a static site generator designed for Deno. It allows you to author web pages in markdown, JSX, or whatever format you deem appropriate and generates static HTML, CSS, and JavaScript as required. Because it is written for Deno, builds are especially fast with minimal dependencies to install. It supports a wide range of content types and can be extended to work with others.

- **Docusaurus**

  Docusaurus is a Static Site Generator (SSG) optimized for technical documentation. It has been adopted by a number of open-source and commercial projects because of its support for versioning, internationalization, and content features required by many documentation sites. In fact, Deno recently migrated much of our own documentation to a site powered by Hono and Docusaurus.

  For an optimal developer experience, we recommend using Docusaurus today alongside Node.js and an npm-compatible package manager. You can build your site with npm scripts, but then deploy and serve it through a Deno static file server or application server.

  This configuration allows you to take advantage of the tooling and ecosystem around Docusaurus, but still get the benefits of using Deno for any dynamic code your doc site might need.

- **Gatsby**

  Gatsby is a Static Site Generator (SSG) and an early pioneer of the "Jamstack" architecture, which favors static site generation from data fetched at build time. This React-based static site generator is still a great choice to build static sites that sit on top of data in a headless CMS, or across many different data sources. You can serve static assets exported from the Gatsby build process through a Deno static file server or application server.

- **Next.js (Static Export)**

  Next.js is a web framework based on React that uses a mixture of static site generation and dynamic rendering to serve websites. As of this writing, many Next.js dynamic rendering features are not yet supported on Deno or Deno Deploy.

  However, if you are using Next.js to generate static sites, that usage pattern works perfectly well with Deno and Deno Deploy. You can serve static assets exported from the Next.js build process through a Deno static file server or application server.

Dynamic Web Apps [5]

Deno Deploy really shines when you start building dynamic web applications. Minimal cold start times and low latency on our global network make Deploy a great option for building data-driven web applications of any kind.

Here are a number of dynamic web frameworks that work today on Deno Deploy:

- **Fresh**

  Fresh is a web framework designed for Deno that features dynamic rendering at the edge, interactive islands on the client, and super fast deploys with no build step by default. With a feature set similar to frameworks such as Next.js, SvelteKit, or Nuxt, we recommend checking it out for any green field projects you might want to try on Deno.

  If you are building a SaaS application, you might also want to check out SaaSKit, a Fresh application that has already implemented authentication, payments, and many other features you would need for a new SaaS project.

- **Hono**

  Hono is a lightweight web app framework in the tradition of Express and Sinatra. In just a few lines of code, you can set up an API server or a server for dynamic web pages. Hono provides a Deno-native installation path and works great with Deno's built-in TypeScript tooling.

- **Oak**

  Oak is a Deno-native middleware framework inspired by Koa. It provides a powerful and flexible way to write API servers in Deno and works great on Deno Deploy.

- **Astro**

  Astro is a web framework designed for content-focused websites. It is capable of server-side rendering in a number of runtime environments, including Deno Deploy. Beyond Astro components and pages, you can build interactive islands on the frontend using your favorite client-side frameworks.

  Astro runs in production in a number of different environments using adapters, with Deno Deploy among them. During local development, we recommend using npm to manage dependencies and run admin scripts, as Astro was designed around these workflows. However, you can still run your code on the Deno runtime, which gives you access to zero config TypeScript and built-in APIs such as Deno KV.

  If you would like to use Astro and Deno together, we strongly recommend starting with this template, which is preconfigured with a Deno SSR adapter and local development scripts.

- **SvelteKit**

  SvelteKit is a full-stack web framework that supports a mix of server rendering and client-side interactivity powered by Svelte. SvelteKit apps require a build step prior to running in production and work in a variety of JavaScript environments, including Deno Deploy, using this adapter.

Like other frameworks designed around npm, we recommend using npm for local development and dependency management. However, you can run the Svelte dev server using Deno, allowing you to take advantage of Deno runtime features.

- **Nuxt**

  Nuxt is a web framework that supports client and server rendering, built around Vue.js. Nuxt applications are deployed using the Nitro app server, using the Deno preset.

  As with the other Node-centric frameworks in this list, we recommend using npm to manage dependencies and run local development scripts. However, using the Deno preset for Nitro means your Nuxt runs great on Deno Deploy.

- **Remix**

  Remix is a full-stack web app framework built on React. It can run in a variety of JavaScript environments, including Deno and Deno Deploy.

  Your Remix project can be configured to output a production build using the deno server build target. The resulting project can then be run on Deno Deploy.

- **Qwik**

  Qwik is a new framework for creating dynamic web apps that are "resumable." It delays JavaScript execution in the browser to keep applications fast.

  Qwik supports Deno Deploy through a middleware component that takes advantage of the web standard Request and Response objects used by Deno. serve.

Web Frameworks for Front-End Development

Front-end frameworks are collections of pre-written, reusable code that provide a foundation for building the user interface of a website or web application. These frameworks can save time and improve the quality of the final product by providing a standardized set of tools and best practices for front-end development. Many front-end frameworks are available, each with its strengths and weaknesses. Let us discuss them one by one in detail.

React

Although it is more like a library, developers still consider React (https://react.dev/) one of the best and first web development frameworks developed by Facebook to adopt a component-based architecture. Let us take a look at what makes this framework popular among developers.

***Figure* 7.1:** *Starting Page of React, a JavaScript Library*

Benefits:

- Bringing HTML into your JavaScript helps developers write code quickly.
- Allows you to break down complex UI into smaller components and start developing the same.
- Virtual DOM helps React know when to re-render and ignore certain pieces of the DOM, thus increasing the page's performance.
- Due to the presence of many handy tools, when used as Chrome extensions, it allows developers to inspect and debug the DOM quickly.

Drawbacks:

- Although it is rapidly growing, community space is smaller than others.
- Continuous upgradation in technology has become troublesome for developers in terms of making proper documentation.

Learn more about testing React applications through this React testing tutorial (https://www.lambdatest.com/blog/react-testing-tutorial/).

Angular

Angular is a web development framework for building dynamic Single-Page Applications (SPAs) for mobile, desktop, and web. It is led by Google's Angular Team and supported by a large community of developers.

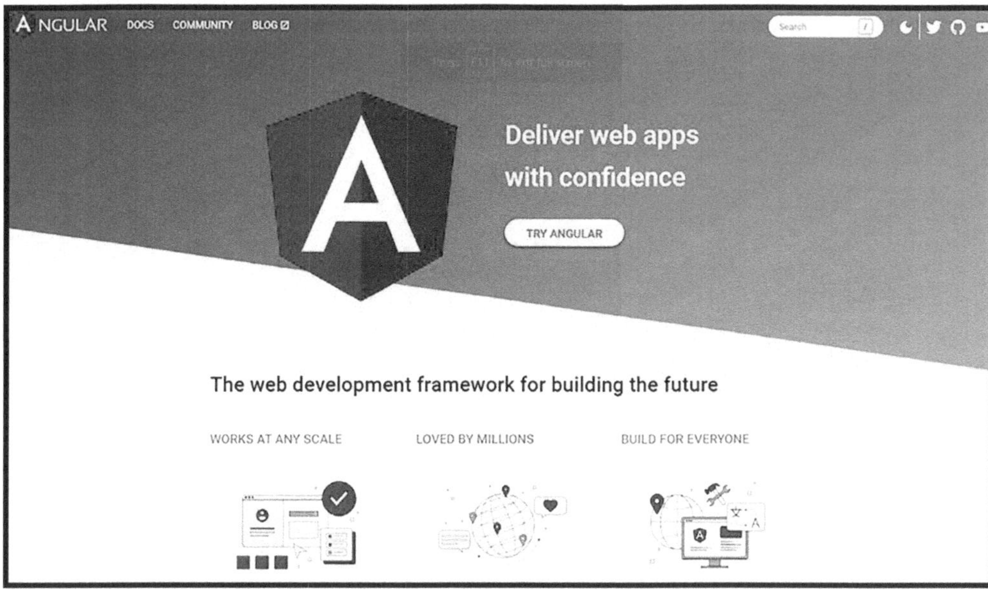

Figure 7.2: *Angular, a Web Development Framework*

Benefits:

- Well-detailed documentation that keeps updating in a timely manner by Google.
- Allows various third-party integrations that improve the overall functionality of websites.
- Allow dependency injection to execute several functions at a time.
- Provides faster loading time.

Drawbacks:

- Have a steep learning curve.
- Requires a lot of boilerplate code that makes it complex during installation.

Vue.js

Vue.js is one of the progressive JavaScript frameworks allowing developers to build desktop and mobile apps and web interfaces. Developed in 2013, Vue.js slowly ranked ahead of the other frameworks available in the market and is currently ranked among the third web development frameworks.

Figure 7.3: *Vue.js is One of the Progressive JavaScript Frameworks*

Benefits:

- With a minified jQuery library, the compressed Vue.js weighs around 29KB.
- Simple and easy to grasp.
- Offers extensive documentation, which makes it easier to learn.
- Can easily handle 2-way data binding, thus making the code reactive.

Drawbacks:

- Being flexible, but while working on large-scale projects with multiple developers, flexibility can lead to complexity.
- Smaller community and lacks widespread support.

Read our article on VueJS testing (https://www.lambdatest.com/blog/vuejs-testing/), an end-to-end guide to know how to perform testing with Vue.

Svelte

Svelte is a modern front-end web development framework for building web applications that allows developers to use its clear-to-read HTML templating and aesthetically pleasing appearance. Svelte approach to reactive programming is also unique, allowing for a more intuitive and efficient way of building reactive UI components. But is it an appropriate framework for your project? Let us find out the benefits and drawbacks.

SVELTE

Figure 7.4: *Svelte is a Modern Front-End Web Development Framework*

Benefits:

- The learning curve is relatively straightforward.
- Allows better performance due to the server-side rendering mode.
- Offers robust and good-looking APIs.
- Optimizes code during compilation; thus, overhead runtime reduces.

Drawbacks:

- The architecture of compilers moves complexity from source code and run time to tools and build time.
- Not suitable for large projects.

Comparing Svelte with React

Despite their individual strengths, Svelte and React have unique features and methodologies, unlike React. Svelte components are an extension of HTML, offering a more direct integration of data into the UI, whereas React uses JSX to combine UI templates with JavaScript logic. Svelte simplifies development with shortcut attributes for props and special blocks such as #await for handling asynchronous operations, contrasting with React's more explicit syntax.

Svelte's advantages over React include:

- Built-in reactivity that allows for reactive programming just by declaring variables.
- No need for hooks such as useState to create reactive data flows.
- No need for external state management libraries such as Redux.
- Two-way data binding that allows for more straightforward form and input management.
- These features make Svelte a powerful and efficient choice for building reactive web applications.

Choosing Svelte Over React

For certain projects, Svelte may be more suitable. Svelte apps usually load faster by default than React, due to their significantly smaller library size. In specific benchmarks, such as a simple counter application, Svelte's bundle size was found to be 1.26 KB, while React's was 8.28 KB, indicating that Svelte's smaller bundle size may enhance initial load times.

For projects prioritizing cleaner and less verbose code, Svelte's default reactive system can be a deciding factor in choosing it over React. React requires hooks or higher-order components to achieve reactivity, making Svelte a more direct and efficient option.

Sticking with React

In some cases, it is wiser to stick with React. It is especially suitable for applications requiring a highly interactive user interface. The virtual DOM in React ensures swift component updates and minimizes delays, making it an ideal framework for applications demanding quick responses to user interactions.

React's one-way data flow and reusable components foster code maintainability and simplify the management of large-scale applications. Coupled with React Native, React supports both web and mobile app development efficiently, addressing the needs of complex applications with frequent state updates.

Ongoing support and development from Facebook and extensive resources from a large community make React a reliable and safe choice for long-term enterprise projects.

Here is a guide on how to choose which framework is best for you:

Best Web Frameworks for Back-End Development

Backend frameworks allow developers to build server-side applications and services that power websites and web applications. These frameworks provide tools and best practices for handling server-side logic, managing data, and communicating with other services or APIs.

There are many backend frameworks available, each with its unique features and benefits. Some of the most popular backend frameworks include Node.js, Express.js, Next.js, Gatsby, Nuxt, and Django. Let us discuss one by one in detail a few back-end frameworks.

Node.js

Node.js is an open-source, cross-platform JavaScript runtime environment that allows you to run JavaScript code outside of a web browser. In simpler terms, it lets you use JavaScript to build server-side applications and tools. (See also *Chapter* 4 of this book).

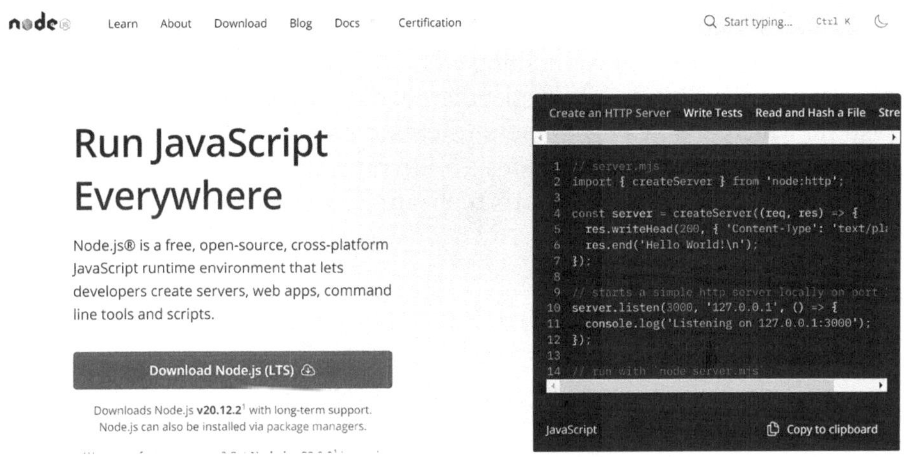

Figure 7.5: *Node.js, an Open-Source, Cross-Platform JavaScript Runtime Environment*

Benefits:

- JavaScript's familiarity and the availability of pre-built packages can speed up development compared to traditional server-side languages.
- Node.js excels at handling many concurrent connections due to its event-driven architecture. This makes it suitable for building scalable web applications.
- Node.js is well-suited for building real-time applications that require constant two-way communication between server and client, such as chat applications or collaborative editing tools.
- With the rise of JavaScript frameworks such as React or Angular, Node.js allows developers to use JavaScript for both front-end and back-end development, creating a more unified development experience.

Drawbacks:

- Not the best choice for applications that involve complex calculations or heavy data processing because Node.js is single-threaded. When a CPU-bound task comes in, Node.js can get bogged down, slowing down the entire event loop and impacting responsiveness.
- Compared to some mature back-end languages, the built-in Node.js standard library is relatively limited. However, this is mitigated by the vast ecosystem of third-party packages available through npm (Node Package Manager).

- While Node.js is under active development, there have been some changes to its API in the past. While not always dramatic, these changes can require developers to adapt their code to newer versions.

Express.js

Express.js is a lightweight and flexible web development framework for Node.js that allows developers to create server-side web applications and APIs easily. It provides a minimalist approach to building web applications, allowing developers to build applications according to their specific needs. Express.js includes a powerful routing system, which enables developers to create complex routes and define how web requests are handled. It also includes a wide range of middleware, which allows developers to easily add functionality to their applications, such as authentication, logging, and error handling.

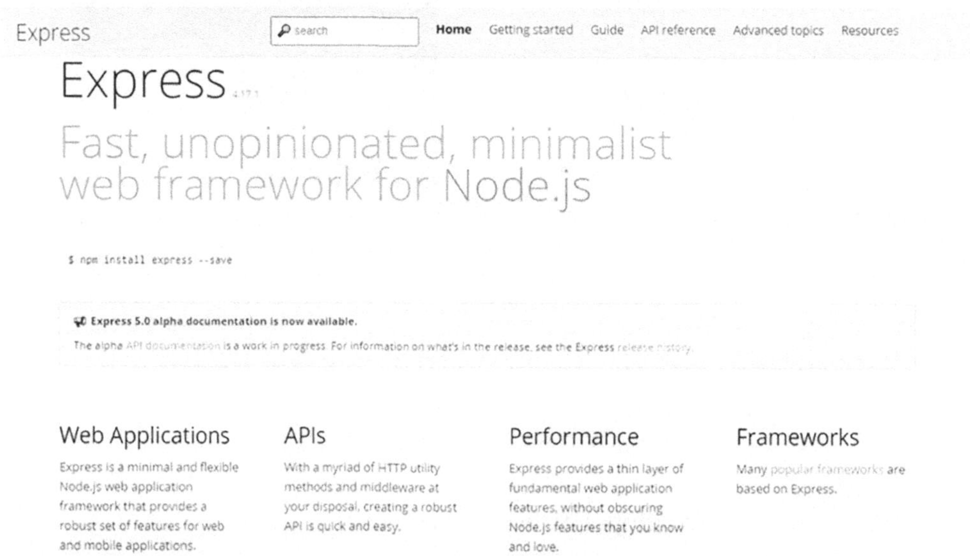

Figure 7.6: *Express.js, A Lightweight and Flexible Web Development Framework for Node.js*

Benefits:

- If a developer is comfortable with Node.js for the backend, they will become more comfortable with Express's improved and advanced process.
- You can define the routes of a preexisting app with the help of URL and HTTP.
- Static files and resources are easy to serve.
- A very advanced feature is creating a REST API server.
- You can connect with MongoDB, Redis as well as MySQL.

- You can easily customize and configure the framework as per user requirements.
- When used with Node.js, both frameworks can support multiple concurrent actions.
- With an open-sourced community, the code constantly gets reviewed and improved. And whenever you are stuck, you will get help from the other community users.

Drawbacks:

- When a developer is migrating from any different programming language, the event-driven nature of Express.js can be a little complex to comprehend.
- If you plan to develop a mobile app with Express.js, you must get familiar with the concept of middleware.
- The framework is perfect for medium and minor projects. If you aim to create a large project, a middleware framework such as Express.js should not be your choice.

To know more about Express.js, check out our complete tutorial on Express testing (https://www.lambdatest.com/blog/vuejs-testing/).

React and Next.js

Next.js is a React-based web development framework that simplifies building server-side rendered React applications. It was first released in 2016 and has since become popular among developers who want to build scalable and efficient web applications. One of the key features of Next.js is its server-side rendering capability, which provides fast initial load times and enhanced SEO capabilities. It also includes automatic code splitting, which allows developers to optimize their application's performance by only loading the necessary code for a particular page.

This subject is further explored in *Chapter* 8, *React*, HTML, *and* Next.*js* of this book.

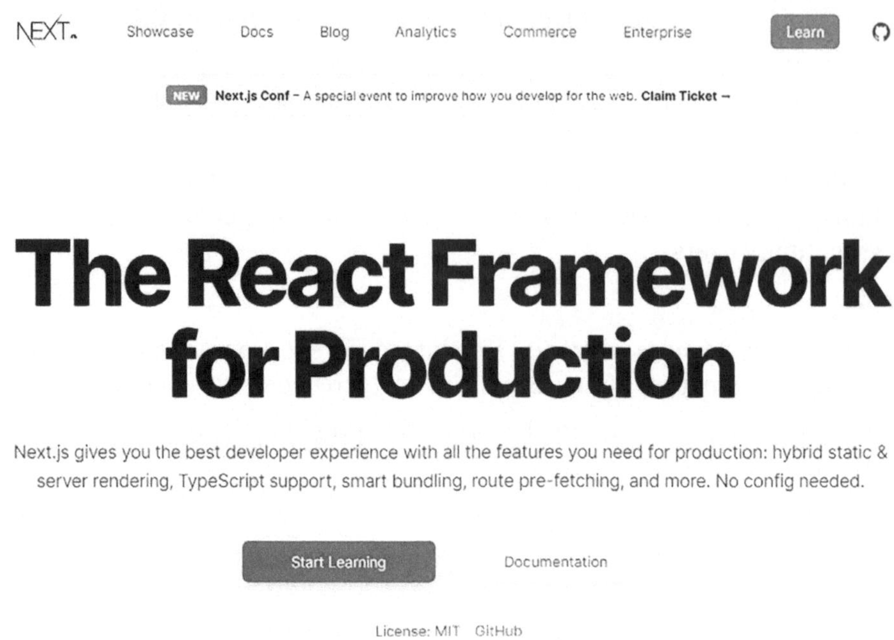

Figure 7.7: *Next.js, React-Based Web Development Framework that Simplifies Building Server-Side Rendered React Applications*

Benefits:

- It has built-in CSS support. Developers can easily import CSS files from JS.
- With the next/image component, developers can automatically optimize images.
- Because of its growing popularity, Next.js has several contributors. Thus, instead of solving an issue from scratch, you will get a solution from the community whenever you face any issue.
- Developers can update existing pages by re-rendering them in the background. Thus, static content gets converted to dynamic.
- Automatic TypeScript compilation makes AngularJS development easier.
- The main focus of Next.js is to focus on business logic. And since it provides an automatic bundling and compilation experience, projects are ready for production immediately.

Drawbacks:

- Since the framework is not front-end friendly, you must develop the entire UI layer from scratch.
- It does not have a built-in state manager. You must use Redux or a similar library if you need one.

- The usage is limited to its file-based router. To use dynamic routes, you must depend on a Node.js server.

Nuxt

Nuxt is an open-source, powerful Server-Side Rendering (SSR) web development framework for building Vue.js applications. It was first released in 2016 and has since become popular among developers who want to build fast and scalable web applications. One of the key features of Nuxt is its ability to generate static files from your Vue.js application, which allows for faster page load times and better SEO. Nuxt also includes a wide range of features and tools, such as a powerful routing system, automatic code splitting, and server middleware, which make it easy for developers to build complex and feature-rich web applications.

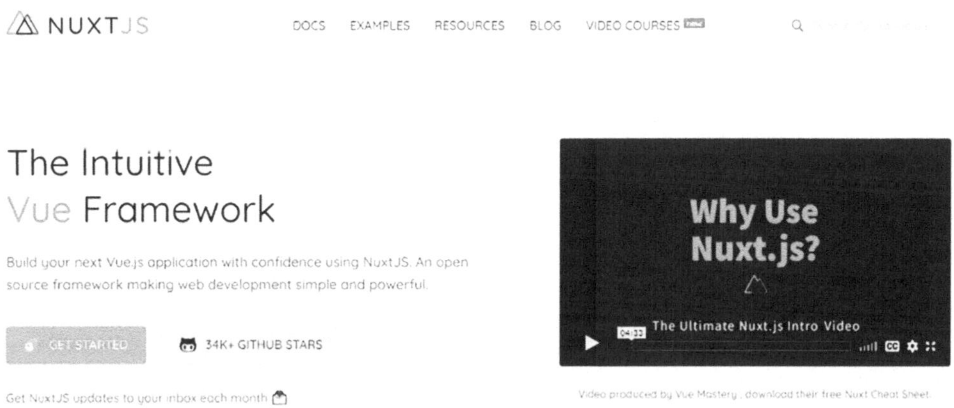

Figure 7.8: *Nuxt, an Open-Source, Powerful Server-Side Rendering (SSR) Web Development Framework for Building Vue.js Applications*

Benefits:

- It is well known for the friendly experience it provides to developers. The community is highly supportive and always ready to help if you have any queries or issues.
- The architecture of Nuxt is modular. You can choose from more than 50 modules to make your development faster and easier.
- Allows developers to build SSR applications, providing faster page load times and better SEO.
- Comes with pre-built features, such as automatic code splitting, hot module replacement, and dynamic imports, which can save developers time and effort.

Drawbacks:

- Using custom libraries can be challenging, especially if you have a short timeline.
- Heavy traffic can create a load on the server.
- Unlike other web development frameworks, Nuxt can be challenging to debug. Developers often do not know where to start to track the root cause of an issue.

Want to know how to perform testing applications using Nuxt, go and check out a complete tutorial on Nuxt testing https://www.lambdatest.com/blog/nuxt-testing/).

Fresh

Fresh is the most popular web framework for Deno. It uses a model where you send no JavaScript to clients by default.

To get started with a Fresh app, you can use the following command and follow the CLI prompts to create your app:

```
deno run -A -r https://fresh.deno.dev
cd my-fresh-app
deno task start
```

This will create a new Fresh app and run it with Deno. You can then open your browser to http://localhost:8000 to see your new app. Edit /routes/index.tsx to see your changes live.

Fresh does the majority of its rendering on the server, and the client is only responsible for re-rendering small islands of interactivity. This means the developer explicitly opts into client-side rendering for specific components.

Astro

Astro is a static site generator that allows developers to create fast and lightweight websites.

To get started with Astro, you can use the following command to create a new Astro site:

```
deno run -A npm:create-astro my-astro-site
cd my-astro-site
deno task dev
```

This will create a new Astro site and run it with Deno. You can then open your browser to http://localhost:4321 to see your new site. Edit /src/pages/index.astro to see your changes live.

Vite

Vite is a web dev build tool that serves your code via native ES modules, which can be run directly in the browser. Vite is a great choice for building modern web applications with Deno.

To get started with Vite, you can use the following command to create a new Vite app:

```
deno run -A npm:create-vite@latest
cd my-vite-app
deno install
deno task dev
```

Lume

Lume is a static site generator for Deno that is inspired by other static site generators such as Jekyll or Eleventy.

To get started with Lume, you can use the following command to create a new Lume site:

```
mkdir my-lume-site
cd my-lume-site
deno run -A https://lume.land/init.ts
deno task serve
```

Docusaurus

Docusaurus is a static site generator that is optimized for technical documentation websites.

To get started with Docusaurus, you can use the following command to create a new Docusaurus site:

```
deno run -A npm:create-docusaurus@latest my-website classic
cd my-website
deno task start
```

Hono

Hono is a lightweight web app framework in the tradition of Express and Sinatra.

To get started with Hono, you can use the following command to create a new Hono app:

```
deno run -A npm:create-hono@latest
cd my-hono-app
deno task start
```

This will create a new Hono app and run it with Deno. You can then open your browser to **http://localhost:8000** to see your new app.

Oak

Oak is a middleware framework for handling HTTP with Deno. Oak is the glue between your frontend application and a potential database or other data sources (for example, REST APIs and GraphQL APIs).

Oak offers additional functionality over the native Deno HTTP server, including a basic router, JSON parser, middlewares, plugins, and so on.

To get started with Oak, make a file called server.ts and add the following:

```
import { Application } from "jsr:@oak/oak/application";
import { Router } from "jsr:@oak/oak/router";

const router = new Router();
router.get("/", (ctx) => {
  ctx.response.body = `<!DOCTYPE html>
    <html>
      <head><title>Hello oak!</title><head>
      <body>
        <h1>Hello oak!</h1>
      </body>
    </html>
  `;
});

const app = new Application();
const port = 8080;

app.use(router.routes());
app.use(router.allowedMethods());
console.log(`Server running on http://localhost:${port}`);
app.listen({ port: port });
Run the server with the following command:
deno run --allow-net server.ts
```

Oak is further dealt with in *Chapter 11, Adding Users and Migrating to oak* of this book.

Deno Deploy

Deno Deploy is a globally distributed platform for serverless JavaScript applications. Your JavaScript, TypeScript, and WebAssembly code runs on managed servers geographically close to your users, enabling low latency and faster response times.

Deploy applications run on fast, lightweight V8 isolates rather than virtual machines, powered by the Deno runtime.

Let us deploy the first application - it should only take a few minutes.

Install Deno and **deployctl** Jump to heading#

If you have not already, you can install the Deno runtime using one of the following commands:

- macOS
- Windows
- Linux: irm https://deno.land/install.ps1 | iex

After Deno is installed, install the **deployctl** utility.

```
deno install -A jsr:@deno/deployctl
```

You can confirm **deployctl** has been installed correctly by running:

```
deployctl --help
```

Now, you are ready to deploy a Deno script from the command line!

Write and Test a Deno Program

First, create a directory for the project and create a file called **main.ts** in it, with the following "Hello World" web server:

main.ts

```
Deno.serve(() => new Response("Hello, world!"));
```

You can test that it works by running it with the following command:

```
deno run --allow-net main.ts
```

Your server should be viewable at localhost:8000. Now let us run this code on the edge with Deno Deploy!

Deploy Your Project

From the directory of the **main.ts** file you just created, run this command:

```
deployctl deploy
```

You will be asked to authorize Deno Deploy in GitHub to sign up to Deno Deploy and/ or to provision an access token for **deployctl**. A few moments after that, your Hello World server will be deployed in Deno Deploy infrastructure all around the world, ready to handle all the traffic you expect.

Next Steps

Now that you have created your first deployment, you can learn what kinds of apps you can run on Deno Deploy, check out what else you can do with **`deployctl`**, or keep reading to find out what other options you have to deploy your code to Deno Deploy. We are so excited to see what you will ship with Deno Deploy!

Deploy Your Existing Project

Import a project and run it on the edge with Deno Deploy. From the Deno Deploy dashboard click the "**`New Project`**" button. Connect to your GitHub account and select the repository you would like to deploy.

Follow the on-screen instructions to deploy your existing application.

If your project requires a build step, use the Project Configuration form to create a GitHub action to deploy your project. Give your project a name and select from the optional framework presets. If you are not using a framework, you can set up your build settings using the form.

Confirm that your build options are correct and click the "**`Deploy Project`**" button to kick off your new Github action and deploy your project.

In a few moments, your project will be deployed across ~12 data centers around the world, ready to handle large volumes of traffic.

Once your deployment is successful you can visit your newly deployed project at the url provided on the success page or manage it in your dashboard.

Start with a Playground

A playground is a browser-based editor that enables you to write and run JavaScript or TypeScript code right away This is a great choice for just kicking the tires on Deno and Deno Deploy!

From the Deno Deploy dashboard, click the "**`New Playground`**" button to create a playground. We also have a variety of ready-built tutorials for you to try out Deno Deploy try them out by clicking on "**`Learning Playground`**."

Deno Deploy Use Cases

Some popular use cases for Deno currently are:

- Middleware
- API servers
- Full websites

Middleware: Middleware refers to bits of code that execute before and after the request gets to the application server. You will be writing middleware if you want to execute some JavaScript or any other code very fast, early in the request. By deploying your middleware code at the edge, Deno Deploy ensures the best performance for your app.

Some examples include:

- Setting a cookie.
- Serving different versions of a site depending on geolocation.
- Path rewriting.
- Redirecting requests.
- Dynamically changing the HTML on its way back from the server before it gets to the user.

Deno Deploy is a good alternative to other platforms you might be using to host your middleware right now, for example:

- Cloudflare Workers
- AWS Lambda@Edge
- Traditional load balancers such as nginx
- Custom rules

API Servers

Deno is also a great fit for API servers. By deploying these servers "at the edge," closer to clients who are using them, Deno Deploy is able to offer lower latency, improved performance, and reduced bandwidth costs compared to traditional hosting platforms such as Heroku or even modern centralized hosting services such as DigitalOcean.

Full Websites

We foresee a future where you can actually write your entire website on edge functions. Some examples of sites that are already doing this include:

- blog
- chat
- calendly clone

Playgrounds

Playgrounds are an easy way to play around with Deno Deploy and create small projects. Using playgrounds you can write code, run it, and see the output fully inside the browser.

Playgrounds have the full power of Deno Deploy. They support all the same features as a normal project, including environment variables, custom domains, and logs.

Playgrounds are also just as performant as all other projects on Deno Deploy. They make full use of our global network to run your code as close to users as possible.

Creating a Playground

To create a new playground, press the New Playground button in the top right corner of the project overview page.

This will create a new playground with a randomly generated name. You can change this name in the project settings later.

Using the Playground Editor

The playground editor is opened automatically when you create a new playground. You can also open it by navigating to your project's overview page and clicking the Edit button.

The editor consists of two main areas: the editor on the left, and the preview panel on the right. The editor is where you write your code, and the preview panel is where you can see the output of your code through a browser window.

There is also a logs panel underneath the editor panel on the left side. This panel shows the console output of your code and is useful for debugging your code.

After editing your code, you need to save and deploy it so the preview on the right updates. You can do this by clicking the **`Save & Deploy`** button in the top right, by pressing *Ctrl* + S, or by opening the command palette with F1 and selecting **`Deploy: Save & Deploy`**.

In the toolbar in the top right of the editor, you can see the current deployment status of your project while saving. The preview panel on the right will refresh automatically every time you save and deploy your code.

The language dropdown in the top right of the editor allows you to switch between JavaScript, JSX, TypeScript, and TSX. The default selected language is TSX which will work for most cases.

Making a Playground Public

Playgrounds can be shared with other users by making them public. This means that anyone can view the playground and its preview. Public playgrounds cannot be edited by anyone: they can still only be edited by you. Logs are also only shown to you. Users have the option to fork a public playground to make a private copy of it that they can edit.

To make a playground public, press the Share button in the top toolbar in the editor. The URL to your playground will be copied to your clipboard automatically.

You can also change the playground visibility from the playground settings page in the Deno Deploy dashboard. This can be used to change the visibility of a playground from public to private again.

Exporting a Playground to GitHub

Playgrounds can be exported to GitHub. This is useful if your project is starting to outgrow the single file limit of the playground editor.

Doing this will create a new GitHub repository containing the playground code. This project will be automatically turned into a git project that is linked to this new GitHub repository. Environment variables and domains will be retained.

The new GitHub repository will be created in your personal account and will be set to private. You can change these settings later in the GitHub repository settings.

After exporting a playground, you can no longer use the Deno Deploy playground editor for this project. This is a one-way operation.

To export the playground, visit the playground settings page in the Deno Deploy dashboard or select **`Deploy: Export`** to GitHub from the command palette (press F1 in the editor).

Here you can enter a name for the new GitHub repository. This name will be used to create the repository on GitHub. The repository must not already exist.

Press **`Export`** to export the playground to GitHub.

Linter Developer Tool

In essence, a linter serves as a valuable developer tool for improving and enhancing code quality. It achieves this by analyzing static source code to identify and flag issues that can lead to bugs, vulnerabilities, and code smells. [6]

A linter will scan source code looking for errors, defects, stylistic issues, and questionable constructs. The term "linter" stems from the origins of a tool known as "lint," which was initially developed by Stephen C. Johnson in 1978 at Bell Labs. Originally designed to analyze C source code, this utility paved the way for the modern concept of linting.

Today modern linters are available for almost all programming languages and are used to improve code quality and maintainability.

Importance of Linter

A linter is an important tool for any developer, as it simplifies their tasks and ensures the quality of the code they create. It achieves this by identifying and offering suggested resolutions to problems before they are pushed into production.

Modern linter's capabilities may extend beyond issue detection, contributing to enhancing code readability, maintainability, and overall consistency.

Linter's Working

A linter works through the analysis of a program's source code, where it directly compares the code to a predefined set of rules. Whenever the source code deviates from these rules, the linter notifies the user about the issue. A linter will often integrate with other developer tools as part of the development workflow.

These rules that linters use to analyze code can often be tailored, and depending upon the specific linter can range from broad and general checks to more specific and intricate evaluations of the code. Linters empower developers to uphold coding standards and enhance their code quality through systematic and dynamic checks.

The steps followed by linter :

1. **Parsing the Source Code**

   The linter is given source code to analyze which is then broken down into separate tokens that are the basic elements of programming languages (keywords, identifiers, operators, and so on). Linters excel at identifying syntax errors in interpreted languages such as JavaScript.

   These tokens are then utilized to build an Abstract Syntax Tree (AST), which is a tree-like model of the syntactic code structure. The AST shows the hierarchy and connections of the code's various parts.

   The linter then checks the analyzed code against a set of defined guidelines and standards. It may also search for specific code patterns that may be indicative of an issue. It will identify lengthy functions or complex code segments based on objective metrics such as cyclomatic complexity.

2. **Reporting Issues**

   Once a linter has identified a rule violation or suspect pattern this is flagged to the user.

   This usually takes the form of providing specific details to help the developer examine the issue such as line number, nature of the issue, and possible remediations.

Benefits of Linters

Linters play an important role in software development by analyzing code for possible issues and flagging these to the developer for potential remediation.

The result is code that is clean, meaning code that is easily understandable, portable, and capable of changing through structure and consistency but which remains maintainable, reliable, and secure for performance demands.

Recognized benefits of a linter include:

- **Improved Code Quality**

  Linters can assist developers in detecting and correcting issues in the code ensuring the overall improved quality of the source code.

  They can catch syntax errors early on in development to prevent bugs and other issues from making it into production plus enforce coding style requirements to enable adherence to consistent best practices.

  By establishing a common coding style and structure, linters can assist with Clean Code, that is, improving code readability and understandability.

  By utilizing certain constructs and patterns, linters can assist with the adoption of best practices in coding.

  A linter may also assist in the education of developers through the promotion of coding best practice, and by providing explanations of why a flagged issue is such. This can be particularly beneficial to less formally experienced team members.

- **Increase Developer Velocity and Productivity**

  Linters can speed up developer productivity by providing essential real-time feedback during the development process as issues arise. The early detection of issues prevents them from becoming a potentially more critical challenge later.

- **Enhancement of Collaboration and Teamwork**

  Common coding standards can be applied throughout the entire team or organization making cooperation and expectations more transparent and efficient.

  Linters can aid development teams in learning and grasping best practices and language complexities by explaining the concerns with the code.

  They can also help ensure team decisions that are taken regarding which issues are a priority and which should not be fixed are transparent to all team members.

- **Enhanced Security**

  Without question, this is a critical aspect of any modern application. If this becomes an issue, the implications can be disastrous in terms of finances, reputations, and international laws (GDPR, CCP).

  Linters can help detect and identify code patterns that could possibly lead to security vulnerabilities. They can be customized to specific security standards guaranteeing the source code meets industry or regulatory requirements and guidelines such as OWASP Top 10 and MISRA C++ 2023 to help protect applications from malicious attacks such as SQL injection or cross-site scripting, buffer overflows, and so on.

  By using secure coding guidelines, linters can flag the use of functions or methods that are known vulnerabilities or deprecated, driving developers to choose more secure alternatives.

  Security measures can be customized to specific programming languages or frameworks depending on the need.

- **Contribute to Reduced Costs**

  With the ability to detect and handle issues early before they become a problem, linters can positively impact the time and expense associated with debugging.

Conclusion

In this chapter, we learned about web frameworks in Deno and the classification of web framework architectures. We delved into the topic of stateless and stateful protocols as well as static and dynamic sites on Deno.

The difference between web frameworks for front-end development and back-end development was explained.

Then we learned about Deno deploy, API servers, and application playground. Linter developer tool is very important in improving coding.

Web frameworks provide a standard way to build and deploy web applications on the World Wide Web. A web development framework is a pre-established collection of software tools, libraries, and guidelines created to expedite and streamline the process of web application development.

In the next chapter, we shall learn more about Using React with Deno and Next.js.

References

1. **The State of Web Frameworks on Deno,September 18, 2023, by Kevin Whinnery**: https://deno.com/blog/web-frameworks-on-deno#fresh

2. **"CGI: Common Gateway Interface"**: Archived from the original on 2009-04-09.

3. **Thomson, Kris (2003-10-29). "Clarification on MVC= Pull and MVC Push"**: Retrieved 2007-07-29

4. **Fielding, Roy (2000). "3.4.3 Client-Stateless-Server (CSS)"**: Architectural Styles and the Design of Network-Based Software Architectures (Doctoral dissertation). University of California, Irvine. OCLC 45706361 page 7?

5. **Inter developer's guide**: https://www.sonarsource.com/learn/linter/

Chapter 8
React, HTML, and Next.js

Introduction

In this chapter, you will learn all the basic to advanced concepts of React such as React components, React props, React state, Functional components in React, React hooks, and so on.

Structure

In this chapter, we will cover the following topics:

React

- Introduction to React JavaScript Library
- API Reference: Create User Interfaces from Components
- Add React to Your Page: Go Full-Stack with a Framework
- Get Started with a Framework
- ECMAScript 6 (ES6)

HTML

- HTML
- HTML Attributes
- ISO Country Codes
- Comparing GET versus POST
- HTML Block and Inline Elements
- The Building Blocks of the Web: HTML and CSS
- Cascaded Style Sheet (CSS)
- Reason for Using CSS

- Prerequisites to Learn CSS
- Multiple Style Rules for Selectors
- CSS Universal Selector
- CSS - Color Picker
- Types of Primary Colors: Additive and Subtractive
- CSS Syntax
- Adding CSS to HTML
- Internal CSS
- Inline CSS
- External CSS File

Next.js

- Next.js
- Next.js Overview
- Building Blocks of a Web Application
- Rendering User Interfaces (UI)
- Document Object Mode (DOM)
- DOM and JavaScript
- Core Features of Next.js
- Comparing Next.js to Other Frameworks
- Most Common Use Cases for Next.js

Introduction to React JavaScript Library

React is a popular JavaScript library for building user interfaces. To use React with Deno, you can use the popular web framework Next.js.

React is a powerful JavaScript library used to build user interfaces for web and native applications.

React, often referred to as React.js or ReactJS, is a JavaScript library known for its flexibility and efficiency in creating interactive User Interfaces (UIs) for both web and native applications. With its component-based architecture, developers can create UI elements such as buttons or search bars, which can then be reused throughout an application. This not only streamlines the development process but also enhances maintainability. [1]

One of the distinguishing features of React is JavaScript XML (JSX). JSX looks similar to HTML and allows developers to write markup right inside their JavaScript code.

This unique capability simplifies coding by providing a more intuitive way to structure components.

React's influence does not end at the browser; it also plays a vital role in mobile app development with a variant called React Native.

It has strong ties with content platforms such as Sanity, where the Sanity Studio – a customizable content editing environment – is built using React. This allows for seamless integration between frontend UIs and backend content management workflows.

Above all else, one of the key attractions of using React is its declarative nature – it makes code easier to understand and debug because it describes what your application should look like in various states rather than detailing step-by-step instructions on achieving that look. This makes your code more predictable and easier for both you and others on your team to work with.

React is a JavaScript Library for frontend development. It is used to build user interfaces and UI components. It is developed by Facebook.

React is known for its component-based architecture which allows you to create reusable UI components, making complex web applications easier to manage and maintain. React is used to build single-page applications.

ReactJS is a very powerful frontend framework based on JavaScript. And, it is a wonderful creation by Facebook Inc. that solves many issues related to the frontend.

Firstly, it follows a component-based design, which allows developers to create resizable web applications or complex user interfaces by integrating small and isolated snippets of code. Then, the process may seem complicated but by gaining expertise in the right prerequisites for ReactJS, one can easily excel in it.

The most important thing to understand here is that many developers and experienced people commit the mistake of jumping straight into ReactJS without first understanding the prerequisites.

To use React in production, you need **npm which is included** to get an overview of what React is, you can write React code directly in HTML.

But in order to use React in production, you need npm and Node.js installed.

Start by including three scripts, the first two let us write React code in our JavaScripts, and the third, Babel, allows us to write JSX syntax and ES6 in older browsers.

Core Features of React

React is known for its component-based architecture. Components are independent, reusable pieces of code that function as building blocks of a React application. The combination of these components creates complex user interfaces. Moreover, each component can manage its own state, which means it can hold and manipulate data within itself.

Another significant feature is JavaScript XML (JSX), a syntax extension to JavaScript that allows developers to write HTML-like code within their JavaScript. This bridges the gap between JavaScript and HTML, making coding more intuitive and efficient.

React also utilizes a virtual Document Object Model (DOM), a programming concept where an ideal or "virtual" representation of UI is kept in memory and synced with the "real" DOM by React's reconciliation process. This feature brings about high efficiency in rendering web pages, making applications faster and more responsive.

State management in React is flexible; while there is built-in support through the 'state' in class components or the 'useState' hook in functional components, React also accommodates third-party libraries such as Redux for larger applications.

Finally, besides being excellent for building user interfaces on the web platform with its main library react-dom, it also supports mobile platform development using react-native. This makes it possible to create both web apps and native mobile apps using largely similar coding patterns.

Comparing React and Other Frameworks

When comparing React with other popular JavaScript frameworks or libraries such as Angular and Vue.js, one of the standout features is its flexibility. Unlike Angular and Vue, which are opinionated frameworks - meaning they dictate specific ways to solve problems - React is non-opinionated. This gives developers more freedom in choosing how to build and structure their applications.[1]

For example, while Angular uses NGXS or NGRX for state management and has its own router, Vue uses Vuex for state management; React does not enforce any specific solution. Developers have the liberty to choose different libraries according to their project's needs. For routing, you might use third-party packages such as 'React Router,' while for state management you could opt for Redux or even use the built-in context API.

When it comes to client-server communication, both Vue.js and React often use Axios while Angular provides its own HTTP Client module.

Another noteworthy comparison comes in terms of size when we consider lightweight counterparts such as Preact; a smaller alternative that offers similar functionality as React but with a significantly smaller footprint.

In summary, what makes React stand out among these options is not just its capabilities but also the flexibility it affords developers - whether they are building simple single-page applications or complex enterprise-grade solutions.

Most Common Use Cases for React

Because of its adaptability and durability, React can be used in a variety of applications. Single-Page Application (SPA) development is one of its main applications.

Similar to native desktop or mobile apps, SPAs offer a seamless user experience by loading a single HTML page and updating dynamically as users interact with the application. Another common use case is creating intricate user interfaces with numerous data-sharing and data-management components.

Developers can simplify complex user interfaces into manageable components thanks to React's component-based architecture, which increases development efficiency and maintainability. Rapid prototyping is made possible by React's capacity to produce reusable components. Designers do not need to write a lot of code to quickly create and test app layouts.

React is frequently used in scenarios where performance is crucial, like real-time data updates in applications such as stock trading platforms or live chat boxes, because of its effective rendering capabilities. Facebook created it, and along with a sizable community of companies and independent programmers, they still support it. Single-page applications are commonly programmed using React as their foundation. In terms of ratings, developer experience, and the most sought-after business tools, it currently holds a prominent position in many industry rankings. But how did React get started, and what led to its popularity and broad use?

In 2011, Facebook developers first ran into some maintenance issues. As the Facebook Ads app developed more features to ensure smooth operation, the team required additional staff. The growing number of employees and app features caused their business to lag. Over time, their software became increasingly difficult to manage due to the numerous escalating updates they had to deal with. Some of the noteworthy features that have contributed to React's popularity among developers are Components, DOM Virtualization, Lifecycle Methods, JSX, and React Hooks. The prerequisites for learning ReactJS will be covered in detail. On the surface, though, they all combine to provide React with three main advantages that have helped explain its extraordinary success. These three advantages are clean code, fast performance, and a strong community. Lastly, React gains even more strength when paired with content platforms such as Sanity. The deep integration capabilities of Sanity Studio are demonstrated by its React architecture, which enables developers to create rich digital experiences by fusing frontend user interfaces with backend content workflows.

API Reference: Create User Interfaces from Components

React lets you build user interfaces out of individual pieces called components. Create your own React components such as Thumbnail, LikeButton, and Video. Then combine them into entire screens, pages, and apps.

```
function Video({ video }) {
  return (
    <div>
      <Thumbnail video={video} />
      <a href={video.url}>
        <h3>{video.title}</h3>
        <p>{video.description}</p>
      </a>
      <LikeButton video={video} />
    </div>
  );
}
```

Whether you work on your own or with thousands of other developers, using React feels the same. It is designed to let you seamlessly combine components written by independent people, teams, and organizations.

Write Components with Code and Markup

React components are JavaScript functions. Want to show some content conditionally? Use an if statement, displaying a list. Try array **map()**. Learning React is learning programming.

```
function VideoList({ videos, emptyHeading }) {
  const count = videos.length;
  let heading = emptyHeading;
  if (count > 0) {
    const noun = count > 1 ? 'Videos' : 'Video';
    heading = count + ' ' + noun;
  }
  return (
    <section>
      <h2>{heading}</h2>
      {videos.map(video =>
        <Video key={video.id} video={video} />
      )}
    </section>
  );
}
```

This markup syntax is called JSX. It is a JavaScript syntax extension popularized by React. Putting JSX markup close to related rendering logic makes React components easy to create, maintain, and delete.

Add Interactivity Wherever You Need It

React components receive data and return what should appear on the screen. You can pass them new data in response to an interaction, like when the user types in an input. React will then update the screen to match the new data.

```
import { useState } from 'react';

function SearchableVideoList({ videos }) {
  const [searchText, setSearchText] = useState('');
  const foundVideos = filterVideos(videos, searchText);
  return (
    <>
      <SearchInput
        value={searchText}
        onChange={newText => setSearchText(newText)} />
      <VideoList
        videos={foundVideos}
        emptyHeading={`No matches for "${searchText}"`} />
    </>
  );
}
```

Introducing Server Components

You do not have to build your whole page in React. Add React to your existing HTML page, and render interactive React components anywhere on it.

Installation

React was intended to be adopted gradually from the beginning. React can be used in any amount you require. This section will help you get started, whether your goal is to sample React, add some interactivity to an HTML page, or create a sophisticated React-powered application. Nothing needs to be installed in order to use React. You should try editing this sandbox.

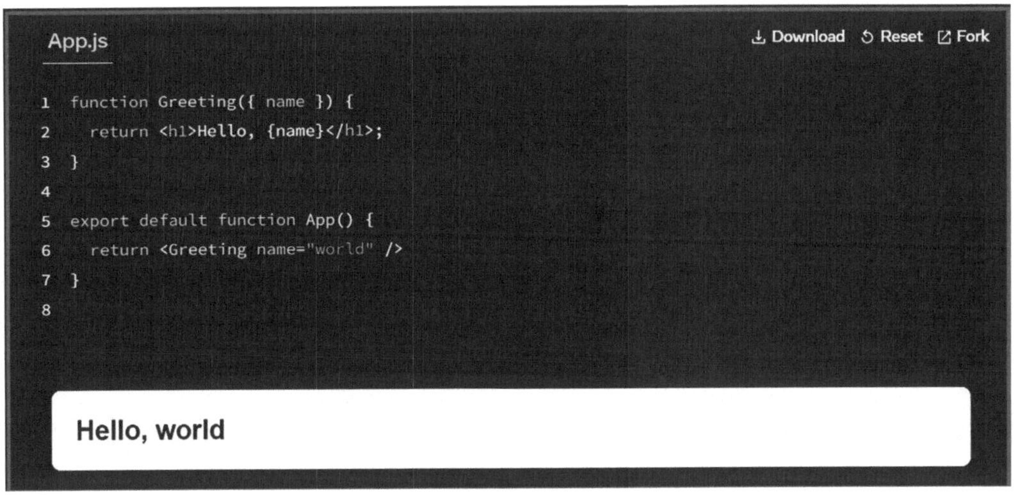

Figure 8.1: *Hello World Message*

You can edit it directly or open it in a new tab by pressing the "**Fork**" button in the upper right corner.

Most pages in the React documentation contain sandboxes like this. Outside of the React documentation, there are many online sandboxes that support React, for example, *CodeSandbox, StackBlitz, or CodePen.*

Add React to Your Page: Go Full-Stack with a Framework

React is a library. It lets you put components together, but it does not prescribe how to do routing and data fetching. To build an entire app with React, we recommend a full-stack React framework such as *Next.js or Remix.*

```
Import { db } from './database.js';
import { Suspense } from 'react';

async function ConferencePage({ slug }) {
  const conf = await db.Confs.find({ slug });
  return (
    <ConferenceLayout conf={conf}>
      <Suspense fallback={<TalksLoading />}>
        <Talks onfide={conf.id} />
      </Suspense>
    </ConferenceLayout>
  );
}
```

```
async function Talks({ onfide }) {
  const talks = await db.Talks.findAll({ onfide });
  const videos = talks.map(talk => talk.video);
  return <SearchableVideoList videos={videos} />;
}
```

Get Started with a Framework

React is also an architecture. Frameworks that implement it let you fetch data in asynchronous components that run on the server or even during the build. Read data from a file or a database, and pass it down to your interactive components.

React Directly in HTML

We will learn about HTML after this section.

The quickest way to start learning React is to write React directly in your HTML files.

```
<!DOCTYPE html>
<html>
  <head>
    <script src="https://unpkg.com/react@18/umd/react.development.
js" crossorigin></script>
    <script src="https://unpkg.com/react-dom@18/umd/react-dom.
development.js" crossorigin></script>
    <script src="https://unpkg.com/@babel/standalone/babel.min.
js"></script>
  </head>
  <body>

    <div id="mydiv"></div>

    <script type="text/babel">
      function Namaste() {
        return <h1>Namaste India!</h1>;
      }

      const container = document.getElementById('mydiv');
      const root = ReactDOM.createRoot(container);
      root.render(<Namste />)
    </script>

  </body>
</html>
```

Figure 8.2: *Displaying a Message by HTML "Namaste!"*

This way of using React can be OK for testing purposes, but for production, you will need to set up a **React environment**.

Setting Up a React Environment

If you have npx and Node.js installed, you can create a React application by using create-react-app.

If you have previously installed **`create-react-app`** globally, it is recommended that you uninstall the package to ensure npx always uses the latest version of **`create-react-app`**.

To uninstall, run this command: **`npm uninstall -g create-react-app`**.

Run this command to create a React application named my-react-app:

```
npx create-react-app my-react-app
```

The **`create-react-app`** will set up everything you need to run a React application.

Run the React Application

Now you are ready to run your first *real* React application!

Run this command to move to the my-react-app directory:

```
cd my-react-app
```

Run this command to run the React application my-react-app:

```
npm start
```

A new browser window will pop up with your newly created React App. If not, open your browser and type **`localhost:3000`** in the address bar.

The Result:

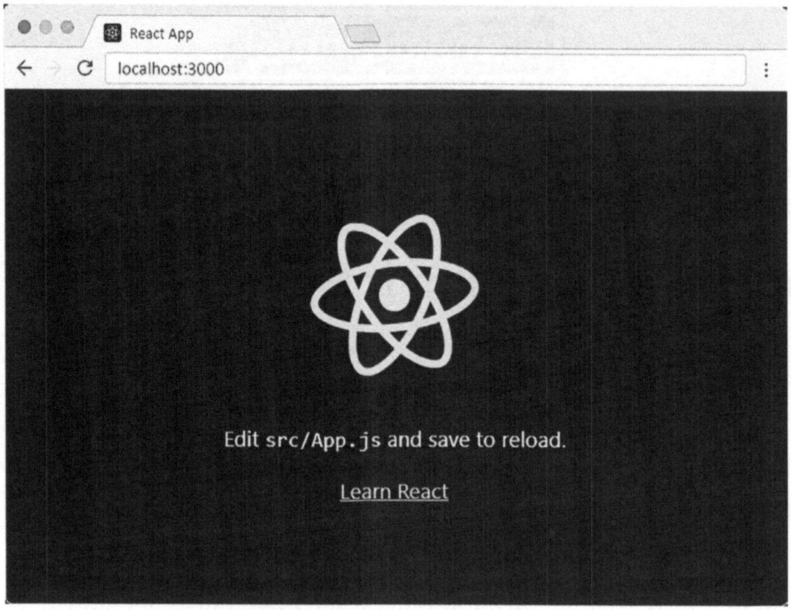

***Figure 8.3:** First Page of React App*

Modify the React Application

So far so good, but how do we change the content?

Look in the **my-react-app** directory, and you will find a **src** folder. Inside the **src** folder there is a file called **App.js**, open it and it will look like this:

```
/myReactApp/src/App.js:
import logo from './logo.svg';
import './App.css';

function App() {
  return (
    <div className="App">
      <header className="App-header">
        <img src={logo} className="App-logo" alt="logo" />
        <p>
          Edit <code>src/App.js</code> and save to reload.
        </p>
        <a
          className="App-link"
          href="https://reactjs.org"
          target="_blank"
          rel="noopener noreferrer"
        >
```

```
            Learn React
          </a>
        </header>
      </div>
    );
  }

export default App;
```

Try Changing the HTML Content and Save the File

Notice that the changes are visible immediately after you save the file, you do not have to reload the browser.

Example

Replace all the content inside the **`<div className="App">`** with a <h1> element.

See the changes in the browser when you click **`Save`**.

```
function App() {
  return (
    <div className="App">
      <h1>Hello World!</h1>
    </div>
  );
}

export default App;
```

Notice that we have removed the imports and do not need (**`logo.svg`** and **`App.css`**).

The Result:

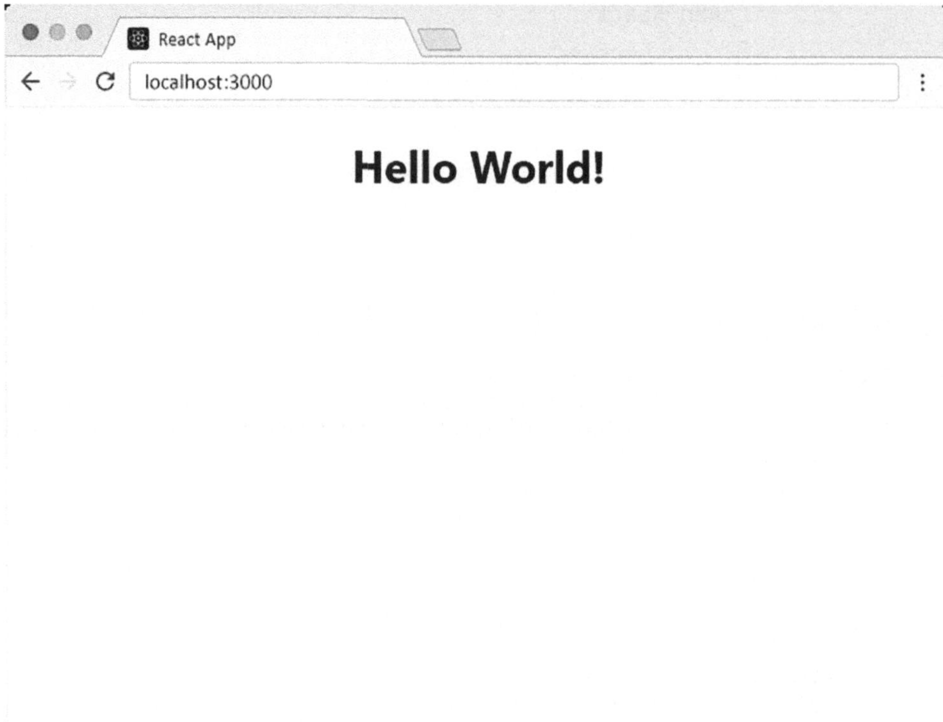

Figure 8.4: *Displaying Message "Hello World!" on Localhost*

Now that you have a React Environment on your computer, you are ready to learn more about React.

Prerequisites for Learning React

Before learning React, you must have the knowledge of the following:

- HTML
- CSS
- JavaScript

In the rest of this section, we will use our "**`Show React`**" tool to explain the various aspects of React, and how they are displayed in the browser.

If you want to follow the same steps on your computer, start by stripping down the src folder to only contain one file: index.js. You should also remove any unnecessary lines of code inside the index.js file to make them look like the example in the "**`Show React`**" tool as follows:

Example

Click the "`Run Example`" button to see the result.

```
index.js:
      import React from 'react';
      import ReactDOM from 'react-dom/client';

      const myFirstElement = <h1>Hello React!</h1>

      const root = ReactDOM.createRoot(document.getElementBy-
      Id('root'));
      root.render(myFirstElement);
```

When the aforementioned program snippet is run, we will get something as follows:

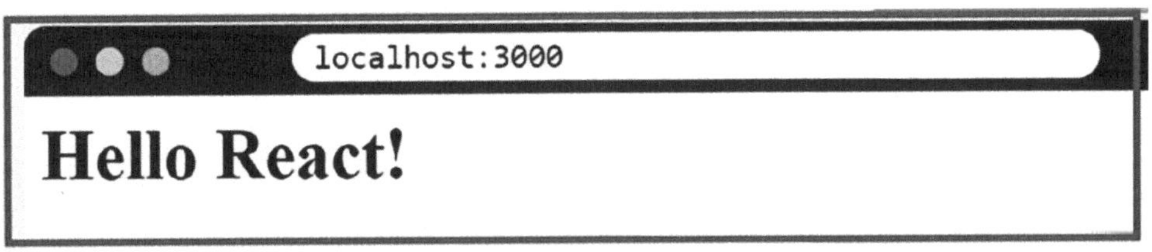

Figure 8.5: *Hello React Message Displayed on Localhost*

ECMAScript 6 (ES6)

ES6 stands for ECMAScript 6. It was created to standardize JavaScript, and ES6 is the 6th version of ECMAScript, it was published in 2015 and is also known as ECMAScript 2015.

Need for Learning ES6

React uses ES6, and you should be familiar with some of the new features, including:

- Classes
- Array Methods like **`.map()`**
- Class Inheritance
- Arrow Functions
- Variables (**`let`**, **`const`**, **`var`**)
- Destructuring
- Modules
- Ternary Operator
- Spread OperatorReact ES6 Classes

Classes

ES6 introduced classes.

A class is a type of function, but instead of using the keyword function to initiate it, we use the keyword class, and the properties are assigned inside a **`constructor()`** method.

A simple class constructor:

```
class Car {
  constructor(name) {
    this.brand = name;
  }
}
```

Notice the case of the class name. We have begun the name, "**`Car`**," with an uppercase character. This is a standard naming convention for classes.

Now you can create objects using the **`Car`** class.

Example

Create an object called "**`mycar`**" based on the Car class.

```
class Car {
  constructor(name) {
    this.brand = name;
  }
}

const mycar = new Car("Ciaz");
```

Note: *The constructor function is called automatically when the object is initialized.*

```
<!DOCTYPE html>
<html>

<body>

<script>
class Car {
  constructor(name) {
    this.brand = name;
  }
}

const mycar = new Car("Ciaz");

document.write(mycar.brand);
```

```
</script>

</body>
</html>
```

Ciaz

Method in Classes

You can add your own methods in a class.

Example

Create a method named "**present**".

```
class Car {
  constructor(name) {
    this.brand = name;
  }

  present() {
    return 'I have a ' + this.brand;
  }
}

const mycar = new Car("CIAZ");
mycar.present();
```

I have a CIAZ

Class Inheritance

To create a class inheritance, use the extends keyword.

A class created with a class inheritance inherits all the methods from another class.

Example

Create a class named "**Model**" which will inherit the methods from the "**Car**" class.

```
<!DOCTYPE html>
<html>

<body>

<script>
class Car {
  constructor(name) {
    this.brand = name;
```

```
  }

  present() {
    return 'I have a ' + this.brand;
  }
}

class Model extends Car {
  constructor(name, mod) {
    super(name);
    this.model = mod;
  }
  show() {
    return this.present() + ', it is a ' + this.model
  }
}

const mycar = new Model("CIAZ", "Maruti Suziki Brand");
document.write(mycar.show());
</script>

</body>
</html>
```

I have a CIAZ, it is a Maruti Suziki Brand

HTML

HTML is the language of the web, used by billions of websites to create the pages you see every day. Want to learn HTML from scratch and make your web pages? This tutorial is for you!

In this HTML section, you will learn how to use HTML to create and style web pages. You will start with HTML fundamentals, such as basic HTML tags and their attributes, classes, layout, and responsiveness. Then, you will move on to advanced HTML5 topics, such as HTML forms, media, APIs, and more. By the end of this tutorial, you will have a solid foundation in HTML.

HTML stands for HyperText Markup Language. It is the standard language used to create and design web pages on the internet. It was introduced by Tim Berners-Lee in 1991 at CERN as a simple markup language. Since then, it has evolved through versions from HTML 2.0 to HTML5 (the latest 2024 version).

HTML is a combination of Hypertext and Markup language. Hypertext defines the link between the web pages and Markup language defines the text document within the tag.

HTML is the standard markup language for Web pages.

With HTML you can create your own website.

HTML Attributes

- All HTML elements can have attributes.
- Attributes provide additional information about elements.
- Attributes are always specified in the start tag.
- Attributes usually come in name/value pairs like: name="value"
- Attributes are what makes HTML so powerful. Attributes are space-separated names and name/value pairs appearing in the opening tag, providing information about and functionality for the element.
- Attributes define the behavior, linkages, and functionality of elements. Some attributes are global, meaning they can appear within any element's opening tag. Other attributes apply to several elements but not all, while other attributes are element-specific and relevant only to a single element. In HTML, all attributes except boolean, and to some extent enumerated attributes, require a value.
- **The Title Attribute:**

  Example

```
<!DOCTYPE html>
<html>
<head>
<title>Page Title</title>
</head>
<body>

<h1>This is a Heading</h1>
<p>This is a paragraph.</p>

</body>
</html>
```

The following web will be generated:

```
<!DOCTYPE html>
<html>
<body>

<h2 title="I'm a header">The title Attribute</h2>

<p title="I'm a tooltip">Click with yor Mouse over this para-
graph, to display the title attribute as a tooltip.</p>

</body>
</html>
```

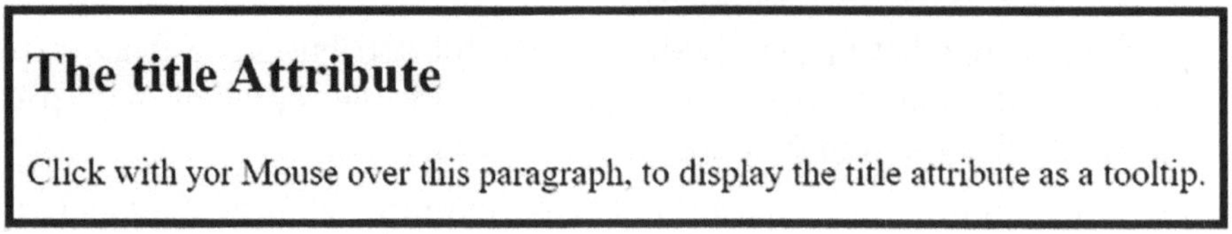

- **The href Attribute**

```
<!DOCTYPE html>
<html>
<body>

<h2>The href Attribute</h2>

<p>HTML links are defined with the a tag. The link address is
specified in the href attribute:</p>

<a href="https://www.w3schools.com">Visit VK Jain's Tutorial</a>

</body>
</html>
```

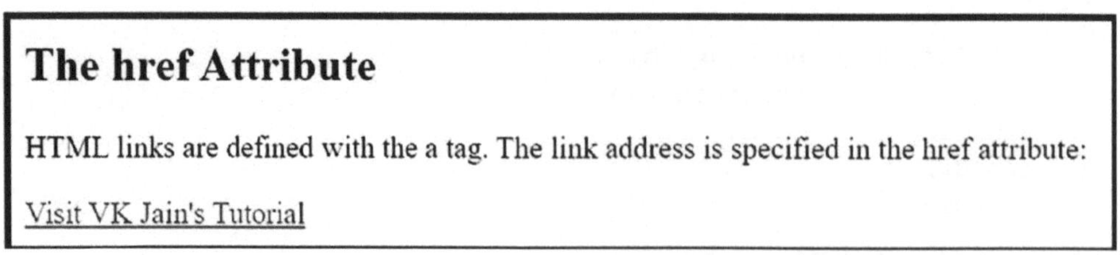

- **The src Attribute**

  The **<img>** tag is used to embed an image in an HTML page. The src attribute specifies the path to the image to be displayed:

```
<!DOCTYPE html>
<html>
<body>
```

```
<h2>The src Attribute</h2>
<p>HTML images are defined with the img tag, and the filename of
the image source is specified in the src attribute:</p>

<img src="img_girl.jpg" width="100" height="150">

</body>
</html>
```

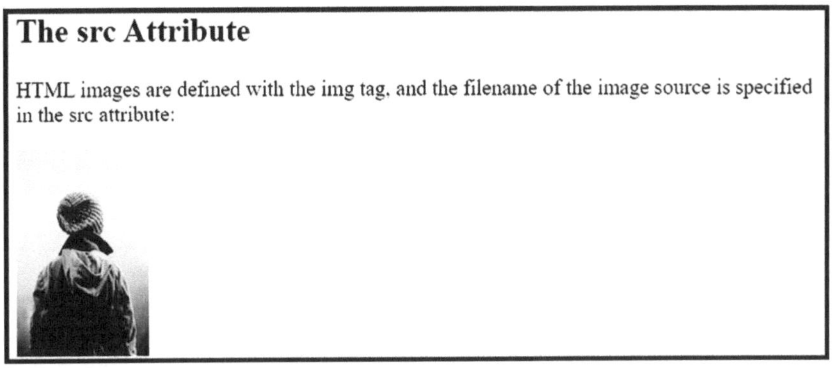

There are two ways to specify the URL in the src attribute:

- **Absolute URL:** Links to an external image that is hosted on another website. Example: src="https://www.w3schools.com/images/img_girl.jpg."

  Notes: *External images might be under copyright. If you do not get permission to use it, you may be in violation of copyright laws. In addition, you cannot control external images; they can suddenly be removed or changed.*

- **Relative URL:** Links to an image that is hosted within the website. Here, the URL does not include the domain name. If the URL begins without a slash, it will be relative to the current page. Example: src="img_girl.jpg." If the URL begins with a slash, it will be relative to the domain. Example: src="/images/img_girl.jpg."

  Tip: *It is almost always best to use relative URLs. They will not break if you change the domain.*

- **The Width and Height Attributes**

  The **<img>** tag should also contain the width and height attributes, which specify the width and height of the image (in pixels):

```
<!DOCTYPE html>
<html>
<body>

<h2>Width and Height Attributes</h2>
```

```
<p>The width and height attributes of the img tag, defines the
width and height of the image:</p>

<img src="img_girl.jpg" width="50" height="60">

</body>
</html>
```

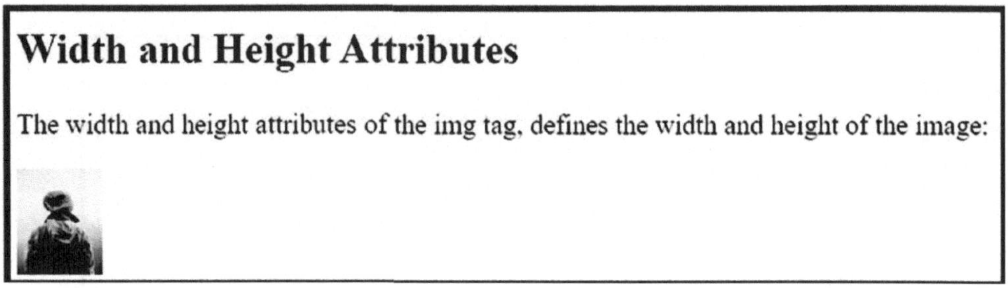

- **The alt Attribute**

  The required alt attribute for the **`<img>`** tag specifies an alternate text for an image if the image for some reason cannot be displayed. This can be due to a slow connection, an error in the src attribute, or if the user uses a screen reader.

```
<!DOCTYPE html>
<html>
<body>

<h2>The alt Attribute</h2>
<p>The alt attribute should reflect the image content, so users
who cannot see the image get an understanding of what the image
contains:</p>

<img src="img_girl.jpg" alt="Model Girl with a jacket" width="50"
height="60">

</body>
</html>
```

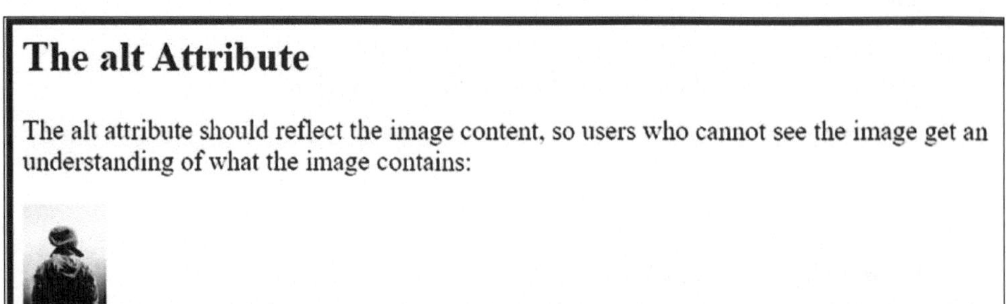

- **See What Happens if we Try to Display an Image that Does not Exist:**

```
<!DOCTYPE html>
<html>
<body>

<img src="img_typo.jpg" alt="Model Girl with a jacket">

<p>If we try to display an image that does not exist, the value
of the alt attribute will be displayed instead. </p>

</body>
</html>
```

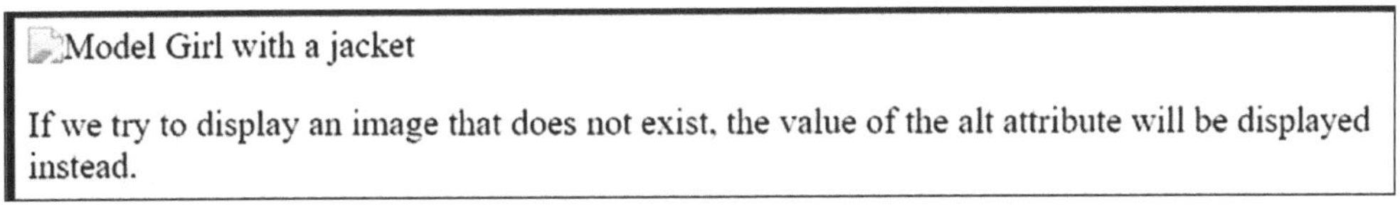

- **The style Attribute**

The style attribute is used to add styles to an element, such as color, font, size, and more.

```
<!DOCTYPE html>
<html>
<body>

<h2>The style Attribute</h2>
<p>The style attribute is used to add styles to an element, such
as color:</p>

<p style="color:red;">This is a Red paragraph.</p>

</body>
</html>
```

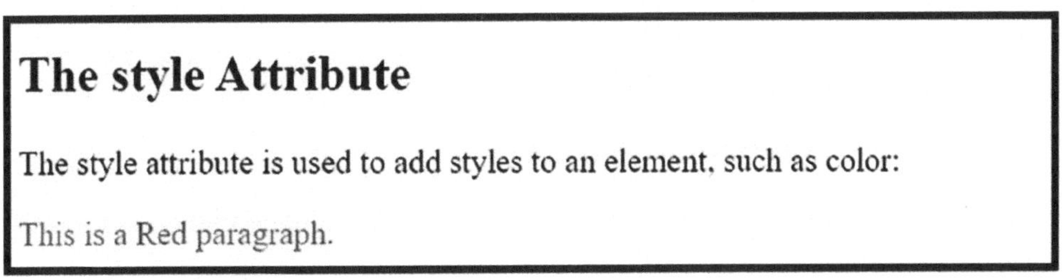

- **The lang Attribute**

You should always include the lang attribute inside the **`<html>`** tag, to declare the language of the web page. This is meant to assist search engines and browsers.

The following example specifies English as the language:

```
<!DOCTYPE html>
<html lang="en">
<body>
...
</body>
</html>
```

Country codes can also be added to the language code in the lang attribute. So, the first two characters define the language of the HTML page, and the last two characters define the country.

Language	ISO Code	Language	ISO Code	Language	ISO Code	Language	ISO Code	Language	ISO Code
Abkhazian	ab	Bambara	bm	Chichewa, Chewa, Nyanja	ny	English	en	Greek	el
Afar	aa	Bashkir	ba	Chinese	zh	Esperanto	eo	Greenlandic	kl
Afrikaans	af	Basque	eu	Chinese (Simplified)	zh-Hans	Estonian	et	Guarani	gn
Akan	ak	Belarusian	be	Chinese (Traditional)	zh-Hant	Ewe	ee	Gujarati	gu
Albanian	sq	Bengali (Bangla)	bn	Chuvash	cv	Faroese	fo	Haitian Creole	ht
Amharic	am	Bihari	bh	Cornish	kw	Fijian	fj	Hausa	ha
Arabic	ar	Bislama	bi	Corsican	co	Finnish	fi	Hebrew	he
Aragonese	an	Bosnian	bs	Cree	cr	French	fr	Herero	hz
Armenian	hy	Breton	br	Croatian	hr	Fula, Fulah, Pulaar, Pular	ff	Hindi	hi
Assamese	as	Bulgarian	bg	Czech	cs	Galician	gl		
Avaric	av	Burmese	my	Danish	da	Gaelic (Scottish)	gd		
Avestan	ae	Catalan	ca	Divehi, Dhivehi, Maldivian	dv	Gaelic (Manx)	gv		
Aymara	ay	Chamorro	ch	Dutch	nl	Georgian	ka		
Azerbaijani	az	Chechen	ce	Dzongkha	dz	German	de		

Table 8.1: *ISO Codes of Important Countries*

The following example specifies English as the language and United States as the country:

```
<!DOCTYPE html>
<html lang="en-US">
<body>
...
```

```
</body>
</html>
```

- **ISO 639-1 Language Codes**

  ISO 639-1 defines abbreviations for languages.

```
<!DOCTYPE html>
<html lang="hi">
<body>
आप हदिी देवनागरी में कुछ भी लखि सकते हैं

</body>
</html>
```

आप हिंदी देवनागरी में कुछ भी लिख सकते हैं

- **ISO Country Codes**

  In HTML, country codes can be used as an addition to the language code in the lang attribute.

  The first two characters of a language code define the language of the web page.

The last two characters define the country.

- **HTTP Request Methods**

  The Hypertext Transfer Protocol (HTTP) is designed to enable communications between clients and servers.

  HTTP works as a request-response protocol between a client and a server.

  Example: A client (browser) sends an HTTP request to the server; then the server returns a response to the client. The response contains status information about the request and may also contain the requested content.

  The two most common HTTP methods are: GET and POST.

  The GET Method

  GET is used to request data from a specified resource.

  Note that the query string (name/value pairs) is sent in the URL of a GET request.

```
/test/demo_form.php?name1=value1&name2=value2
```

  Some notes on GET requests:

  GET requests can be cached.

GET requests remain in the browser history.

GET requests can be bookmarked.

GET requests should never be used when dealing with sensitive data.

GET requests have length restrictions.

GET requests are only used to request data (not modify).

The POST Method

POST is used to send data to a server to create/update a resource.

The data sent to the server with POST is stored in the request body of the HTTP request.

```
POST /test/demo_form.php HTTP/1.1
Host: w3schools.com

name1=value1&name2=value2
```

Some notes on POST requests:

- POST requests are never cached.
- POST requests do not remain in the browser history.
- POST requests cannot be bookmarked.
- POST requests have no restrictions on data length.

Comparing GET versus POST

The following table compares the two HTTP methods: GET and POST.

Attribute	GET	POST
BACK Button/ Reload	Harmless.	Data will be re-submitted (the browser should alert the user that the data are about to be re-submitted).
Bookmarked	Can be bookmarked.	Cannot be bookmarked.
Cached	Can be cached.	Not cached.
Encoding Type	application/x-www-form-urlencoded.	application/x-www-form-urlencoded or multipart/ form-data. Use multipart encoding for binary data.
History	Parameters remain in browser history.	Parameters are not saved in browser history.

Restrictions on Data Length	Yes, when sending data, the GET method adds the data to the URL; and the length of a URL is limited (maximum URL length is 2048 characters).	No restrictions.
Restrictions on Data Type	Only ASCII characters are allowed.	No restrictions. Binary data is also allowed.
Security	GET is less secure compared to POST because the data sent is part of the URL.	POST is a little safer than GET because the parameters are not stored in browser history or web server logs.
	Never use GET when sending passwords or other sensitive information.	
Visibility	Data is visible to everyone in the URL.	Data is not displayed in the URL.

***Table 8.2:** Comparing GET versus POST*

- **The PUT Method**

  PUT is used to send data to a server to create/update a resource.

  The difference between POST and PUT is that PUT requests are idempotent. That is, calling the same PUT request multiple times will always produce the same result. In contrast, calling a POST request repeatedly has the side effect of creating the same resource multiple times.

- **The HEAD Method**

  HEAD is almost identical to GET but without the response body.

  In other words, if GET /users return a list of users, then HEAD /users will make the same request but will not return the list of users.

  A HEAD request is useful for checking what a GET request will return before actually making a GET request. A HEAD request can read the Content-Length header to check the size of the file, without actually downloading the file.

- **The DELETE Method**

  The DELETE method deletes the specified resource.

- **The PATCH Method**

  The PATCH method is used to apply partial modifications to a resource.

- **The OPTIONS Method**

  The OPTIONS method describes the communication options for the target resource.

- **The CONNECT Method**

  The CONNECT method is used to start a two-way communication (a tunnel) with the requested resource.

- **The TRACE Method**

  The TRACE method is used to perform a message loop-back test that tests the path for the target resource (useful for debugging purposes).

HTML Block and Inline Elements

Every HTML element has a default display value, depending on what type of element it is.

The two most common display values are block and inline.

- **Block-Level Elements**

  A block-level element always starts on a new line, and the browsers automatically add some space (a margin) before and after the element.

  A block-level element always takes up the full width available (stretches out to the left and right as far as it can).

  Two commonly used block elements are: **<p>** and **<div>.**

```
<!DOCTYPE html>
<html>
<body>

<p style="border: 1px solid black">Hello India in p style</p>
<div style="border: 1px solid black">Hello India div style</div>

<p>The P and the DIV elements are both block elements, and they
will always start on a new line and take up the full width avail-
able (stretches out to the left and right as far as it can).</p>

</body>
</html>
```

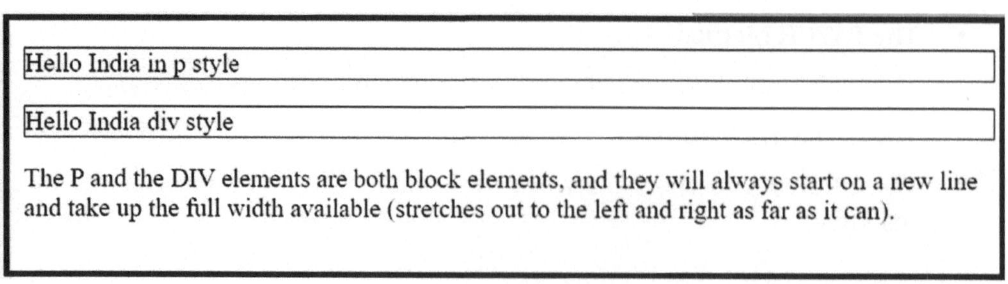

- **Positioning Blocks Defined by <div> Tag**

  HTML <div> Tag

  Example

```
A <div> section in a document that is styled with CSS:
<!DOCTYPE html>
<html>
<head>
<style>
.myDiv {
  border: 5px outset blue;
  background-color: red;
  text-align: center;
}
</style>
</head>
<body>

<h1>The div element</h1>

<div class="myDiv">
  <h2>This is a heading in a div element</h2>
  <p>This is some text in a div element.</p>
</div>

<p>This is some text outside the div element.</p>

</body>
</html>
```

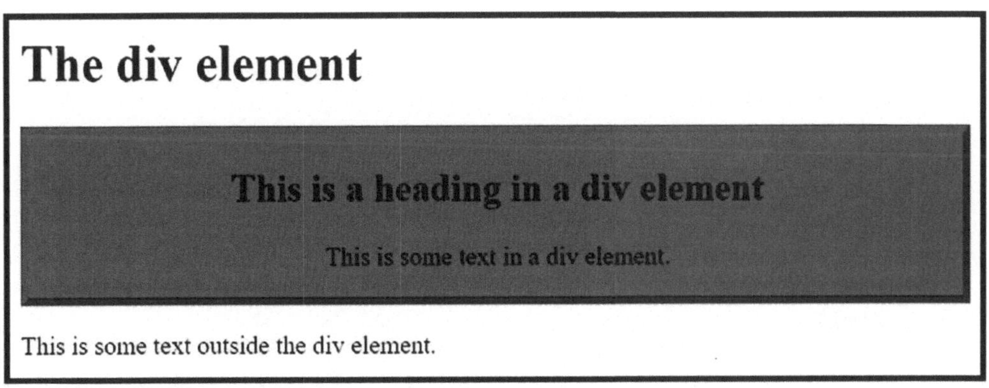

Since **<div>** is a block-level element, a line break is placed before and after it.

It is possible to place any HTML element within a **<div>** tag, including another **<div>.**

Syntax

The **<div>** tag comes in pairs. The content is written between the opening (**<div>**) and closing (**</div>**) tags.

```
<!DOCTYPE html>
<html>
<body>

<p>This is an inline span <span style="border: 1px solid
black">Hello World</span> element inside a paragraph.</p>

<p>The SPAN element is an inline element, and will not start on a
new line and only takes up as much width as necessary.</p>

</body>
</html>
```

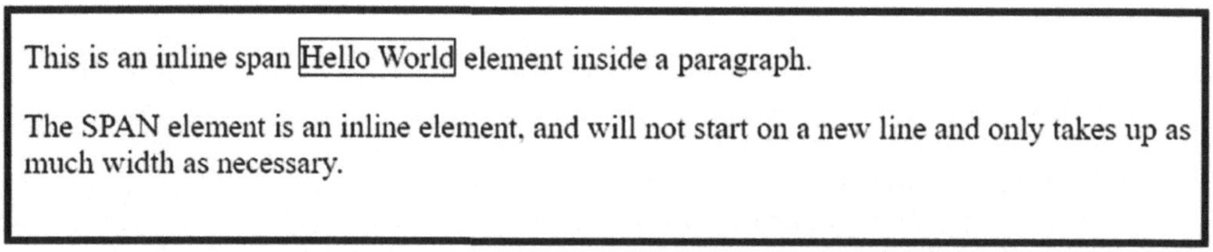

- **HTML <span> Tag**

  Example

  A **<span>** element which is used to color a part of a text:.

```
<!DOCTYPE html>
<html>
<body>

<h1>The span element</h1>

<p>My mother has <span style="color:blue;font-weight:bold">blue</
span> eyes and my father has <span style="color:darkolivegreen;-
font-weight:bold">dark green</span> eyes.</p>

</body>
</html>
```

The Building Blocks of the Web: HTML and CSS

HTML, or HyperText Markup Language, is the language in which all of a website's elements are described to your web browser. Thus, you can use HTML to specify headers, paragraphs, links, embeds, and more, which aids your browser in figuring out how to arrange the page you are viewing.

Web pages are created using a language called CSS, or Cascading Style Sheets, which determines how they look and feel. In other words, CSS is used to make visually appealing websites with sophisticated fonts, eye-catching backgrounds, vivid colors, and even sophisticated transitions and 3D effects.

Each and every frontend developer starts with HTML and CSS. Consequently, until you start learning how to use React, you should be good at coding in HTML and CSS.

To begin learning Reactjs, you must first begin learning HTML and CSS. You must be proficient in HTML and CSS for frontend and responsive web applications, as well as in creating semantic HTML tags, writing CSS selectors, using classes, implementing CSS resets, the box model, and resetting to flexbox and border-box.

Cascaded Style Sheet (CSS)

In order to style an HTML document, we utilize CSS. The way HTML elements are displayed is specified by CSS. Web pages are designed using CSS, which is a language that specifies how a document written in a markup language such as HTML should be presented. Controlling the layout and other visual elements of web pages is made easier for web developers by CSS.

"CSS stands for Cascading Style Sheets, it is a simple design language intended to simplify the process of making web pages presentable using CSS properties. CSS specifies how an HTML element should be displayed on the web page. If you think of the human body as a web page then CSS is styling part of the body. Like the color of the eyes, size of the nose, skin tone, and so on." [2]

CSS is a must for React learners, that is aspiring Web Designers and Developers from basics to advance. CSS knowledge is a must for whoever wants to be a web developer, there are a lot of CSS frameworks such as Bootstrap, Tailwind CSS, and so on.

Reason for Using CSS

- **Responsive Design:** CSS offers features such as media queries that enable developers to create responsive layouts that adapt to different screen sizes and devices, ensuring a consistent user experience.
- **Flexibility and Control**: CSS provides precise control over the presentation of HTML elements, allowing developers to customize layout, typography, colors, and other visual properties.
- **Consistency and Reusability**: Developers can ensure consistency across the

entire website, by defining styles in a central CSS file. Styles can be reused across multiple pages, reducing redundancy and making updates easier.

- **Search Engine Optimization (SEO):** CSS can be used to structure content in a way that improves search engine visibility.
- **Ease of Maintenance**: Centralized CSS files make it easier to maintain and update styles across a website. Changes can be applied globally, ensuring uniformity and reducing the risk of inconsistencies.
- **Faster Page Loading**: External CSS files can be cached by browsers, resulting in faster page loading times for subsequent visits to a website. This caching mechanism reduces server load and bandwidth consumption.

Prerequisites to Learn CSS

Before you start learning CSS, it is essential to have a basic understanding of HTML or any markup language, familiarity with computers, and basic working knowledge of files or directory.

CSS Syntax

Following is the syntax of styling using CSS.

```
selector {
    property: value;
}
```

Multiple Style Rules for Selectors

- **Selector:** CSS selectors are used to select the HTML element or groups of elements you want to style on a web page.
- **Property:** A CSS property is an aspect or characteristic of an HTML element that can be styled or modified using CSS, such as color, font size, or margin.
- **Value:** Values are assigned to properties. For example, color property can have values such as red, green, and so on.

For Example:

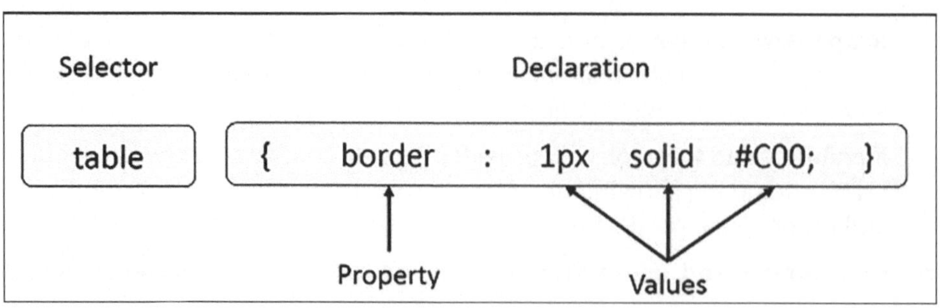

If you want to define multiple rules for a single selector, you can specify those in a single block separated by a semicolon (;).

Syntax

```
selector{
   property1: value1;
   property2: value2;
   property3: value3;
}
```

Now let us look at an example of styling using CSS.

Example

Open Compiler

```
<!DOCTYPE html>
<html>

<head>
    <style>
        /* Style all the paragraphs */
        p {
            background-color: yellow;
            color: red;
            padding: 7 px;
        }

        /* Style all elements with class 'special' */
        .special {
            color: black; /* Change text color */
        }
    </style>
</head>

<body>
    <p>
        "This a normal paragraph"
    </p>
    <br>

    <p class="special">
        "This is a paragraph with class special"
    </p>
    <br>

    <div class="special">
```

```
            "This is a div with class special"
        </div>
    </body>

    </html>
```

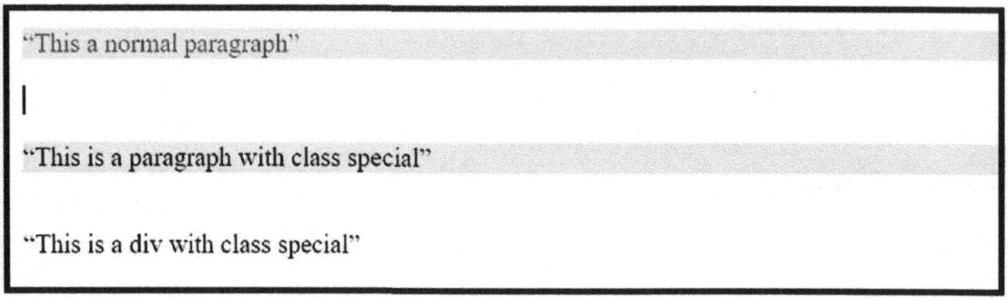

CSS Universal Selector

A universal selector, denoted by an asterisk mark (*), is a special selector that matches all elements in an HTML document. These are generally used to add the same length margin and padding to all the elements in a document.

Syntax

```
*{
  margin: 0;
  padding: 0;
}
```

As per the aforementioned syntax, the universal selector is used to apply a margin and padding of 0 to all HTML elements.

Example

The following example demonstrates the use of a universal selector (*):

Open Compiler

```
<html>
<head>
   <style>
      * {
         margin: 0;
         padding: 0;
         background-color: peachpuff;
         color: darkgreen;
         font-size: 25px;
      }
   </style>
</head>
```

```
<body>
   <h1>Universal selector (*)</h1>

   <div>
      Parent element
      <p>Child paragraph 1</p>
      <p>Child paragraph 2</p>
   </div>

   <p>Paragraph 3</p>
</body>
</html>
```

Explore our latest onl

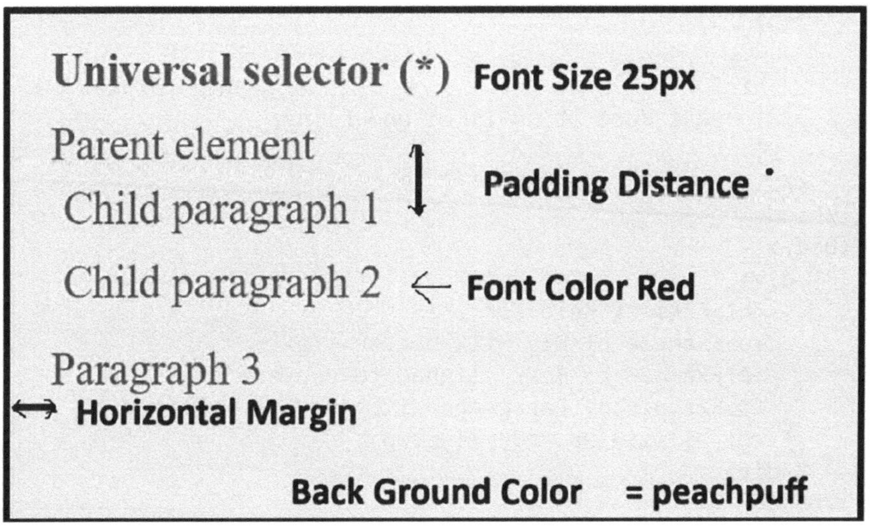

CSS Element Selector

An element selector targets an HTML element, such as **<h1>**, **<p>**, and so on. This is used when we want to apply a similar style to all the **<p>** tags or **<h1>** tags in the document.

Syntax

```
/* Sets text color of all p tags to green */
p{
  color: green;
}
/* Add underline to all h1 tags in document */
h1{
  text-decoration-line: underline;
}
```

Example

The following example demonstrates the use of an element selector:

```
<html>
<head>
   <style>
      div {
         border: 5px inset gold;
         width: 300px;
         text-align: center;
      }

      p {
         color: red;
      }

      h1 {
         text-decoration-line: underline;
      }
   </style>
</head>
<body>
   <div>
      <h1>Element selector</h1>
      <p>Example of Div with border </p>
      <p>Example of Text aligned to center</p>
      <p>Example of Paragraph with green color</p>
      <p> h1 with an underline</p>
   </div>
</body>
</html>
```

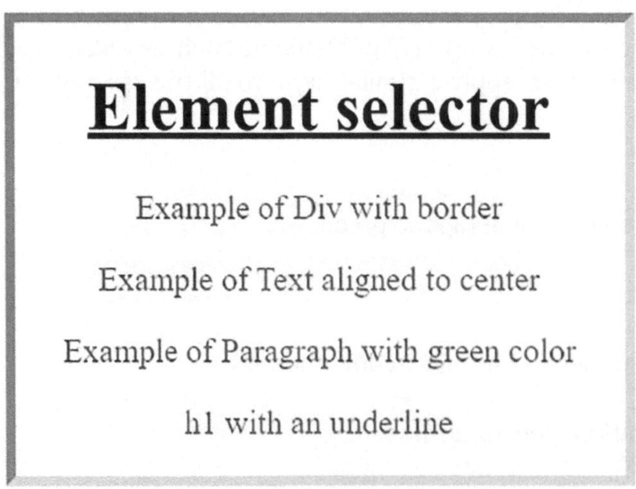

There are three ways to add styles to your HTML document using CSS. In this tutorial, we will learn the ways to add CSS to a webpage.

CSS - Color Picker

A user interface element called a CSS color picker is made to make it easier for users to choose colors for a website or application.

It offers a practical and simple approach for users to alter the appearance of items on a webpage by letting them visually select a color from a spectrum or palette.

The color values for a default white color are shown by the color picker as follows: Hexadecimal (#fff), RGB (255, 255, 255), RGBA (255, 255, 255, 1), and HSL (0, 0%, 100%).

The real-time changes dynamically reflect the selected color when users interact with the color picker by moving the graphical spectrum or inputting values in the input fields.

A smooth and interactive color customizing experience is offered by the color indicator, which modifies its backdrop color and instantaneously updates the appropriate color values (Hex, RGB, RGBA, and HSL) to reflect the newly selected color.

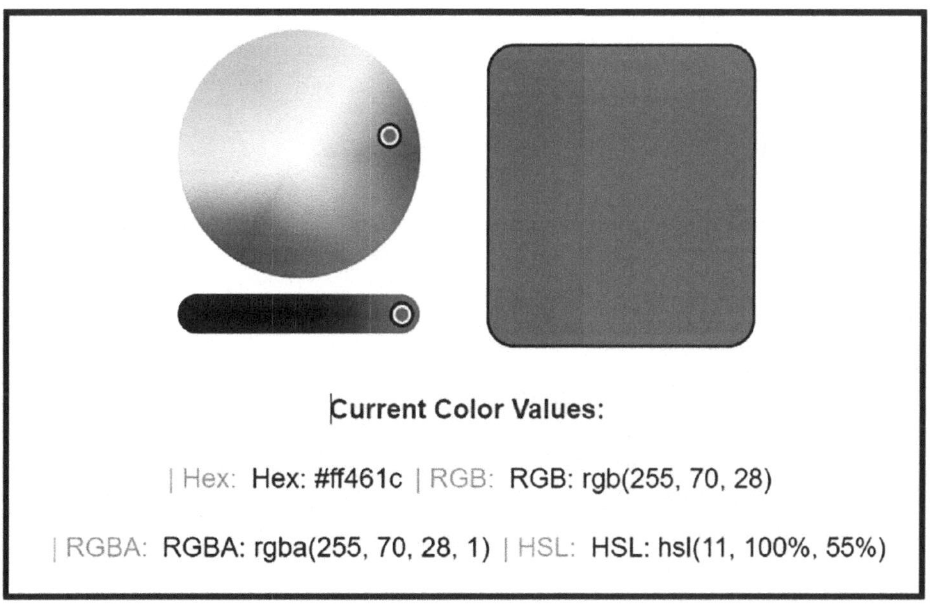

Colors were developed in three categories:

- Primary Colors System
- Secondary Colors System
- Tertiary Colors System

Primary Colors: Red, Yellow and Blue (RYB)

A *primary* color is a color that cannot be made from a combination of any other colors.

In traditional color theory (used in paint and pigments), primary colors are the 3 pigment colors that cannot be mixed or formed by any combination of other colors. All other colors are derived from these 3 hues.

Secondary Colors: Green, Orange and Purple

A *secondary* color is a color created from a combination of two primary colors.

These are the colors formed by mixing the primary colors.

Tertiary Colors: Yellow-orange, red-orange, red-purple, blue-purple, blue-green, and yellow-green.

Tertiary color is a combination of three colors (primary or secondary). These are the colors formed by mixing a primary and a secondary color. That is why the hue is a two-word name, such as blue-green, red-violet, and yellow-orange.

Complementary Colors: Those colors are located opposite each other on a color wheel.

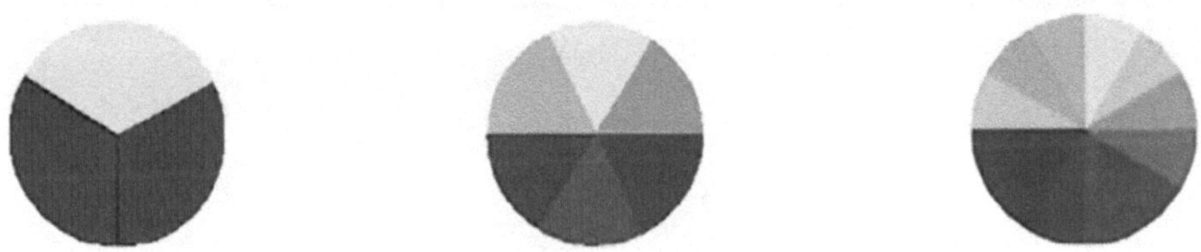

Primary Colors **Secondary Colors** **Tertiary Colors**

Types of Primary Colors: *Additive* and *Subtractive*

Artists and Scientists (computers) have different definitions for primary colors. The *traditional* primary colors that artists and painters have used are red, yellow, and blue (RYB). Television and Computer videos use Red, Green, and Blue (RGB). These two primary color systems obviously do not agree. Modern printing press uses secondary colors such as magenta, yellow, and cyan. *Additive* and *subtractive* are the two *modern* methods for reproducing a range of colors.

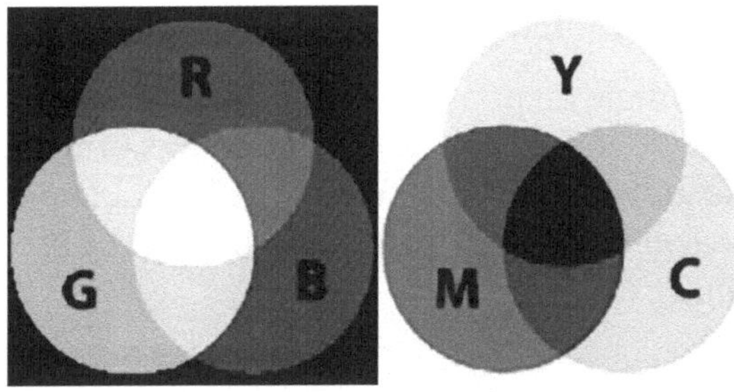

Additive Color **Subtractive Colors**

(**R**ed+**G**reen+**B**lue = **W**hite) (**C**yan+**M**agenta+**Y**ellow = Blac**K**)

The computer monitor uses RGB colors while painting and colorwash utilizes CMYK pattern.

- **Round Cornered Images**

  The following example demonstrates how to use the border-radius property to create a rounded border image.

  Example

  Open Compiler

```
    <!DOCTYPE html>
<html>

<head>
    <style>
        img {
            width: 100px;
            height: 100px;
            border-radius: 20px;
        }
    </style>
</head>

<body>
    <img src="/css/images/pink-flower.jpg" alt="pink-flower">
</body>

</html>
```

- **Circular And Elliptical Images**

  The following example demonstrates how to use **border-radius: 50%** (https://www.tutorialspoint.com/css/css_border-radius.htm) property to create images in circle and ellipse shape. When the height and width of the image are the same we will get a circular image and when they are not the same we will get elliptical images.

CSS Text Link

Text content when clicked will navigate to a different webpage or a section of the same page is called a text link. The following example shows how to make a text link:

Example

Open Compiler

```
<html>

<head>
    <style>
        body{
            padding: 10px;
        }
        a {
            color: blue;
            text-decoration: none;
        }
        a:hover {
            text-decoration: underline;
            transform: scale(1.1);
        }
    </style>
</head>

<body>
    <a href="/index.htm"> Click Me </a>
</body>

</html>
```

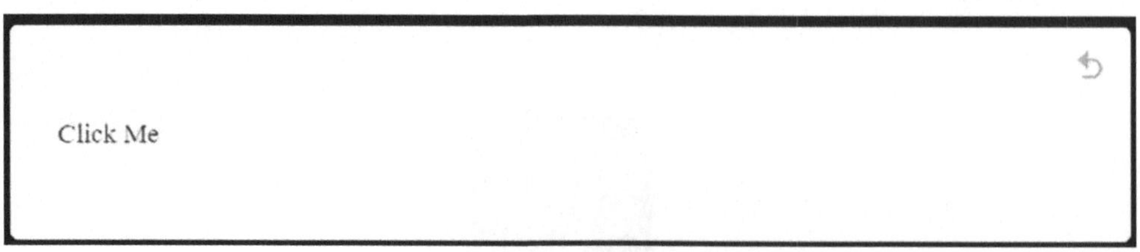

If you click over "**`Click Me`**," the following will be displayed:

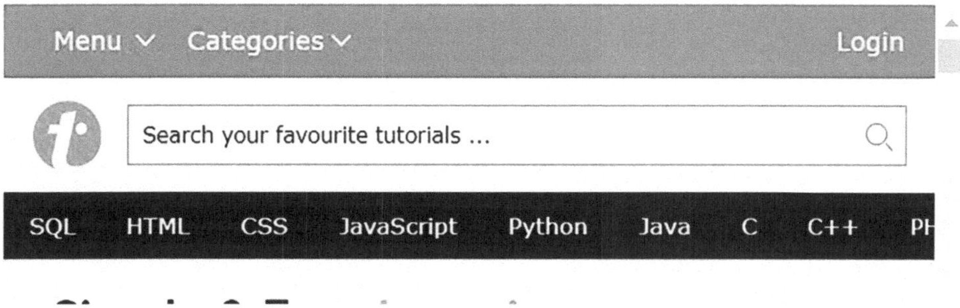

Name of colors, RGB, RGBA, HSL, HSLA, and Hexadecimal values. CSS allows us to change the background color, text color, border color, and caret color of any elements in HTML documents.

Colors are very important aspects of web design, as they not only enhance the visual appeal but also influence user behavior.

Background Color

- Red
- Green
- Blue
- Grey
- Pink

Text Color

- White
- Yellow
- Cyan
- Black
- Blue

CSS Background Color

In CSS, we can set the background color for elements such as div, span, body, paragraph, and so on using the background-color property.

Example

In this example, we set different background colors for body, div, and span elements in HTML.

CSS Example in Paragraph

```
<!DOCTYPE html>
<html>
<head>
<style>
body {
background-color: yellow;
}

h1 {
color: Red;
text-align: center;
}

p {
font-family: Times Roman;
font-size: 20px;
}
</style>
</head>
<body>

<h1>My First CSS Example</h1>
<p> Example of a paragraph.</p>

</body>
</html>
```

CSS Syntax

A CSS rule consists of a selector and a declaration block.

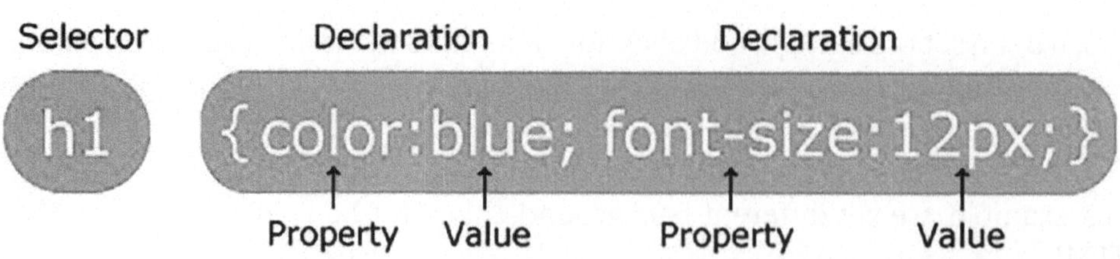

The selector points to the HTML element you want to style. The declaration block contains one or more declarations separated by semicolons. Each declaration includes a CSS property name and a value, separated by a colon. Multiple CSS declarations are separated with semicolons, and declaration blocks are surrounded by curly braces.

Example

In this example, all <p> elements will be center-aligned, with a red text color:

```
p {
  color: green;
  text-align: center;
}
```

Adding CSS to HTML

There are three ways to add CSS styles to an HTML webpage, including:

- **Internal CSS:** These are added inside the HTML files itself. Internal CSS is defined in the HTML head section inside of <style> tag to let the browser know where to look for the CSS.
- **External CSS:** A separate file is made for CSS and imported to an HTML file.

  External CSS is defined in a separate file that contains only CSS properties, this is the recommended way to use CSS when you are working on projects. It is easy to maintain and multiple CSS files can be created and you can use them by importing them into your HTML document using the HTML <link> tag.
- **Inline CSS**: Inline CSS is directly applied to the HTML elements and it is the most prioritized CSS among these three. This will override any external or internal CSS. Styles for each tag can be exclusively provided using the "style" attribute.

Internal CSS

You can include CSS styles in an HTML document using the `<style>` element. Rules defined using this syntax will be applied to all the elements available in the document.

```
<!DOCTYPE html>
<html>

<head>
    <style>
        body {
            background-color: yellow;
        }
        h1 {
            color: red;
            margin-left: 40px;
```

```
        }
    </style>
</head>

<body>
    <h1>This is a heading</h1>
    <p>This is a paragraph.</p>
</body>

</html>
```

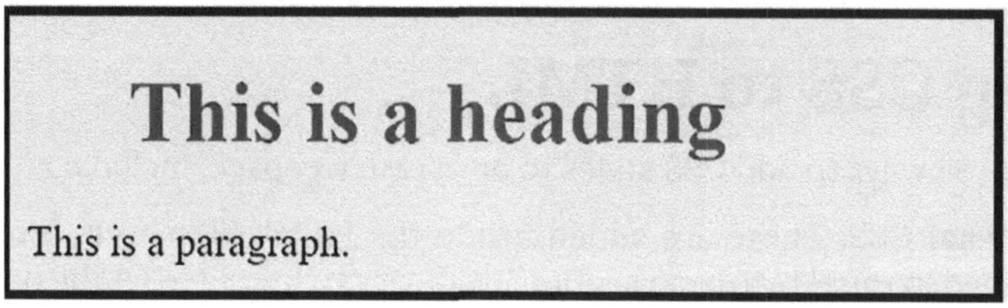

Inline CSS

You can use the style attribute of any HTML element to define style rules. These rules will be applied to that element only.

CSS Example

In this example, we will show you the aforementioned ways to use CSS on an HTML document.

```
<!DOCTYPE html>
<html>

<head>
   <title>CSS Tutorial</title>
   <!-- Internal CSS -->
   <style>
       span{
           color: blue;
       }
   </style>
   <!-- External CSS -->
   <link rel="stylesheet" href="/css/style.css">

</head>

<body>
   <h1><span>VK Jain'sTutorials</span> Example</h1>
```

```
    <!-- Inline CSS -->
    <p style="font-weight: bold;
            margin-top: -15px;
            padding-left: 5px">
        Learning in a Simple & Easy <span> Way </span>
    </p>
</body>

</html>
```

VK Jain'sTutorials Example

Learning in a Simple & Easy Way

External CSS File

We are importing this file into the aforementioned code through the <link> tag. And the file name is style.css. The aforementioned code will follow the style of this file on the portal you have to create files locally and try it on your system.

```
body {
    margin-left: 40%;
    margin-top: 40%;
}
```

Next.js

Next.js is a powerful web development framework that simplifies the process of building fast, interactive applications. Based on React, a popular JavaScript library, Next.js offers additional structure and features such as server-side rendering and static generation.

Next.js is a frontend framework that builds on the capabilities of React, a versatile JavaScript library used for crafting engaging user interfaces. What sets Next.js apart is its ability to simplify complex aspects of web development by providing a comprehensive suite of tools and features.

One key feature offered by Next.js is server-side rendering, which significantly improves the performance and Search Engine Optimization (SEO) attributes of web applications. This means websites built with Next.js load faster and rank better in search results.

Another distinguishing attribute of Next.js is static generation. This feature pre-generates files during build time, allowing them to be served ahead of time without needing to wait for data fetching.

To get started with Next.js in Deno, you can create a new next app and run it immediately with Deno:

```
deno run -A npm:create-next-app@latest my-next-app
cd my-next-app
deno task dev
```

This will create a new Next.js app with TypeScript and run it with Deno. You can then open your browser to http://localhost:3000 to see your new app and start editing **page.tsx** to see your changes live.

Next.js Overview

The files are then distributed globally ensuring even faster loading times.

Next.js also offers incremental static regeneration which blends static generation with dynamic updates for elements that have either not been generated statically or have changed since they were first generated.

Developers using Next.js often pair it with Sanity, a headless Content Management System (CMS), making it easier to manage content across their projects.

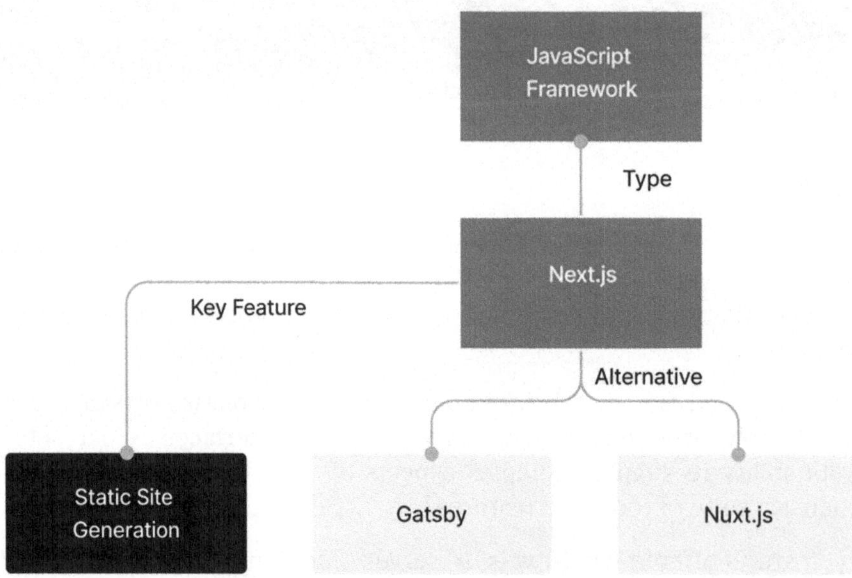

Figure 8.6: *A Diagram Showing a JavaScript Framework Next.js and Alternatives*

To put it briefly, this robust tool gives developers all they need to produce web applications that are highly dynamic, fully interactive, and performant. Following that, you can create quick, full-stack web applications with the help of the versatile React framework js. Let us take a moment to elaborate on what React and Next mean. Also, what do we mean by this Next.Js, and how it can be used to create web applications?

Building Blocks of a Web Application

There are a few things you need to consider when building modern applications, such as:

- **User Interface (UI):** How users will consume and interact with your application.
- **Routing:** How users navigate between different parts of your application.
- **Data Fetching:** Where your data lives and how to get it.
- **Rendering:** When and where you render static or dynamic content.
- **Integrations:** What third-party services do you use (for CMS, auth, payments, and so on), and how do you connect to them.
- **Infrastructure:** Where you deploy, store, and run your application code (serverless, CDN, edge, and so on).
- **Performance:** How to optimize your application for end-users.
- **Scalability:** How your application adapts as your team, data, and traffic grow.
- **Developer Experience:** Your team's experience building and maintaining your application.

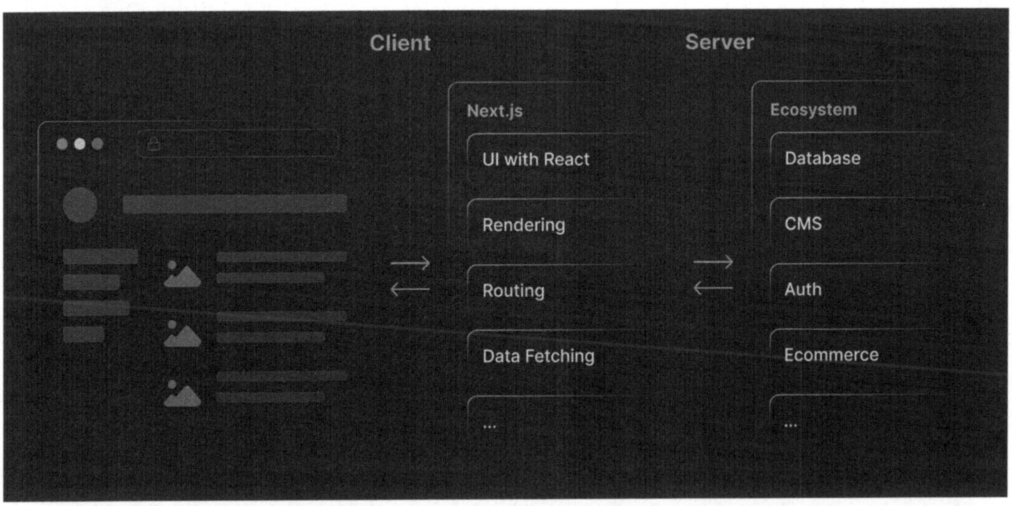

For each part of your application, you will need to decide whether you will build a solution yourself or use other tools, such as packages, libraries, and frameworks.

Next.js is a React framework that gives you building blocks to create web applications.

By framework, we mean Next.js handles the tooling and configuration needed for React and provides additional structure, features, and optimizations for your application.

Rendering User Interfaces (UI)

To understand how React works, we first need a basic understanding of how browsers interpret your code to create (or render) User Interfaces (UI).

When a user visits a web page, the server returns an HTML file to the browser that may look like this:

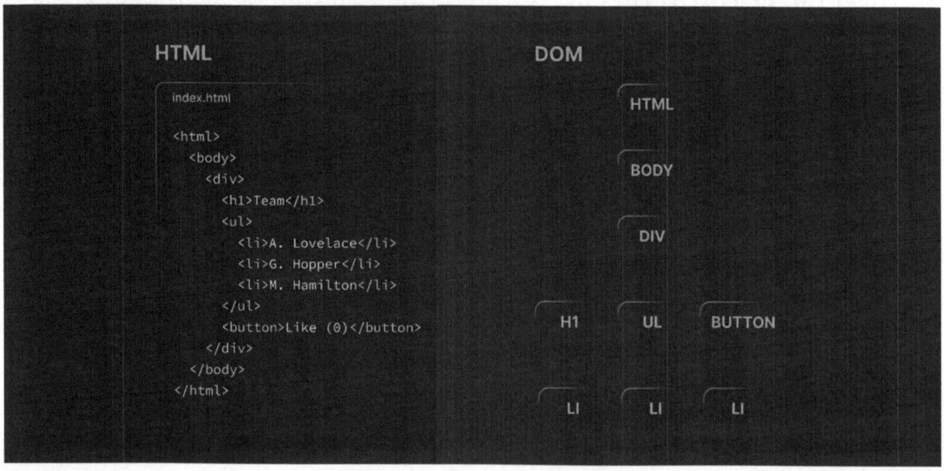

The browser then reads the HTML and constructs the Document Object Model (DOM).

Document Object Mode (DOM)

The DOM is an object representation of the HTML elements. It acts as a bridge between your code and the user interface and has a tree-like structure with parent and child relationships.

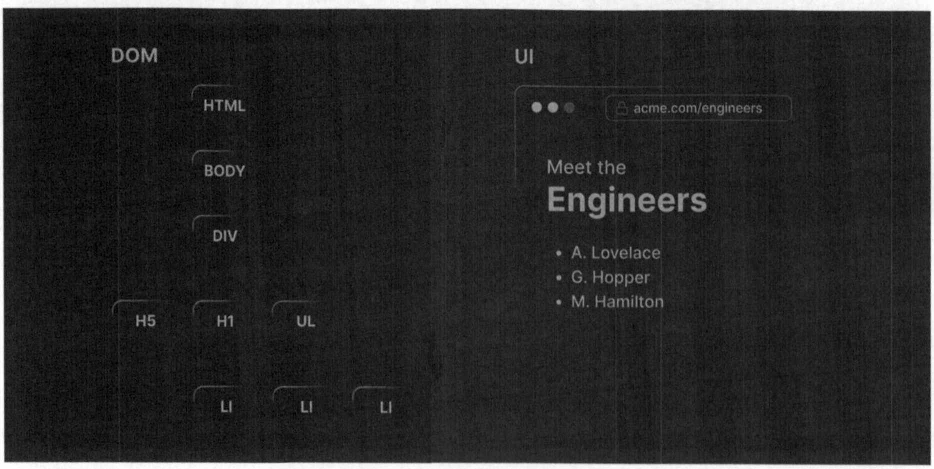

You can use DOM methods and JavaScript, to listen to user events and manipulate the DOM by selecting, adding, updating, and deleting specific elements in the user interface. DOM manipulation allows you to not only target specific elements but also change their style and content.

DOM is the data representation of the objects that comprise the structure and content of a document on the web. DOM represents an HTML document in memory and how to use APIs to create web content and applications. It is a programming interface for web documents. It represents the page so that programs can change the document structure, style, and content. The DOM represents the document as nodes and objects; that way, programming languages can interact with the page.

Needless to mention a web page is a document that can be either displayed in the browser window or as the HTML source. In both cases, it is the same document but the Document Object Model (DOM) representation allows it to be manipulated. As an object-oriented representation of the web page, it can be modified with a scripting language such as JavaScript.

For example, the DOM specifies that the querySelectorAll method in this code snippet must return a list of all the <p> elements in the document.

All of the properties, methods, and events available for manipulating and creating web pages are organized into objects. For example, the document object that represents the document itself, any table objects that implement the HTMLTableElement DOM interface for accessing HTML tables, and so forth, are all objects.

The DOM is built using multiple APIs that work together. The core DOM defines the entities describing any document and the objects within it. This is expanded upon as needed by other APIs that add new features and capabilities to the DOM. For example, the HTML DOM API adds support for representing HTML documents to the core DOM, and the SVG API adds support for representing SVG documents.

DOM and JavaScript

The previous short example, like nearly all examples, is JavaScript. That is to say, it is written in JavaScript but uses the DOM to access the document and its elements. The DOM is not a programming language, but without it, the JavaScript language would not have any model or notion of web pages, HTML documents, SVG documents, and their component parts. The document as a whole, the head, tables within the document, table headers, text within the table cells, and all other elements in a document are parts of the document object model for that document. They can all be accessed and manipulated using the DOM and a scripting language such as JavaScript.

The DOM is not part of the JavaScript language but is instead a Web API used to build websites. JavaScript can also be used in other contexts. For example, Node.js runs

JavaScript programs on a computer but provides a different set of APIs, and the DOM API is not a core part of the Node.js runtime.

Core Features of Next.js

At the heart of Next.js are several core features that set it apart from other web development frameworks. One such feature is its innovative approach to rendering, offering both server-side rendering and static site generation. Server-side rendering allows for data to be fetched at the request time, improving performance and SEO capabilities. On the other hand, static site generation enables files to be built at compile-time and served in advance, enhancing loading speeds.

Next.js also excels in code-splitting which ensures that only necessary code is loaded for each page, making the applications faster and more efficient. This feature significantly enhances response times leading to a better user experience.

Another notable aspect of Next.js is its tight integration with Sanity - a headless CMS service that provides an API for managing content updates effortlessly. The collaboration between Sanity and Next.js allows developers to build highly dynamic websites with ease.

Lastly, Next.js offers pre-configured JavaScript tooling based on Rust for faster builds while maintaining a high-quality developer experience. It is this combination of efficiency, speed, and flexibility- all backed by strong community support- that makes Next.js a preferred choice among many web developers today.

Comparing Next.js to Other Frameworks

Comparing Next.js to other frameworks, its unique value proposition becomes more clear. Unlike traditional React applications that require additional configurations for tooling and functionalities, Next.js comes out of the box with features such as server-side rendering and static site generation.

It is also important to note that while React is excellent for building user interfaces, it does not provide solutions for other aspects of application development. This means developers often have to spend considerable time configuring tools and solving common application requirements. With Next.js, these challenges are addressed head-on as it extends the capabilities of React by providing a structured framework with pre-configured functionalities.

Unlike many JavaScript frameworks which focus solely on client-side rendering - a method that can lead to performance issues and poor SEO outcomes - Next.js leverages server-side rendering as well as static site generation. These features make websites built with Next.js performant and SEO-friendly right from the get-go.

Most Common Use Cases for Next.js

Next.js is a versatile framework, capable of addressing diverse web development needs across multiple industries. One of its popular applications is in the realm of e-commerce. With its fast rendering and robust SEO capabilities, it offers an optimal solution for businesses looking to create high-performance online stores that rank well on search engines.

Blogs and marketing websites also often leverage the power of Next.js. Its server-side rendering and static site generation features allow for rapid content changes, making it ideal for publishing platforms that frequently update their content.

News apps and documentation websites benefit from Next.js's ability to handle real-time updates efficiently. Similarly, entertainment platforms and community-driven web apps can utilize its capabilities to offer interactive user experiences with high performance.

Booking apps, auction sites, information hubs – all these digital experiences can be enhanced using Next.js due to its speed, versatility, and scalability.

For many common use cases, when integrated with Sanity's modern headless CMS, managing content becomes effortless regardless of the website type or size.

Conclusion

This chapter concentrated on three main tools for the design of websites, React, HTML, and Next.js. React is a JavaScript library. We studied about setting up a React environment.

Next was the HTML components which bring everything for text manipulation. Text font, size, and color can be easily generated using HTML and cascaded style sheets.

After this, we learned another deno application, that is Next.js, and several Building blocks of a web application, rendering User Interfaces (UI), and Document Object Mode (DOM). Under this heading, we also tried to compare Next.js to other frameworks and the most common use cases for Next.js.

In the next chapter, we shall learn Microsoft Azure which is a cloud computing platform that offers a variety of services and products to help users build, run, and manage applications.

References

1. **React.js overview**: https://www.sanity.io/glossary/react-js
2. **CSS Tutorial**: https://www.tutorialspoint.com/css/index.html

Chapter 9
Using Microsoft Azure with Deno

Introduction

Microsoft Azure is a cloud computing platform that offers a variety of services and products to help users build, run, and manage applications. Azure offers a wide range of services, including compute, analytics, storage, and networking.

Azure offers four different cloud computing models: Infrastructure as a Service (IaaS), Platform as a Service (PaaS), Software as a Service (SaaS), and serverless functions. Azure offers multilayered security controls and threat intelligence to help protect against threats. Azure is compatible with open-source technologies, allowing users to use their preferred tools and technologies. Azure offers solutions for all industries, including retail, manufacturing, e-commerce, and finance.

After completely reading this chapter, the reader shall get acquainted with utilizing this application as a service portion of web design.

Structure

In this chapter, we shall learn about the following topics:

- Working of Azure
- Running the Azure CLI
- Location of Azure CLI on Device
- Deno for Azure Functions
- Deno REST API on Azure WebApp Service
- Installing the denofunc CLI
- Programming Model
- Visual Studio Codespaces

- Setting Up Deno Deploy
- Deploying a Hello World API

Working of Azure

To access Azure, users need an active internet connection and the ability to connect to the Azure portal. Users can start building on Azure for free.

The Azure Command-Line Interface (CLI)

The Azure Command-Line Interface (CLI) is a cross-platform command-line tool that can be installed locally on Windows computers. You can use the Azure CLI for Windows to connect to Azure and execute administrative commands on Azure resources. The Azure CLI for Windows can also be used from a browser through the Azure Cloud Shell or run from inside a Docker container. [1]

For Windows, the Azure CLI is installed via an MSI or a ZIP package, which gives you access to the CLI through the Windows Command Prompt (CMD) or PowerShell. When you perform an installation for Windows Subsystem for Linux (WSL), packages are available for your Linux distribution.

For a list of compatible package managers or instructions on how to install manually under WSL, visit the main install page.

There are four ways to install the Azure CLI in Windows:

- Microsoft Installer (MSI)
- Microsoft Installer (MSI) in PowerShell
- Windows package manager
- ZIP package

The current version of the Azure CLI is 2.65.0. For information about the latest release, see the release notes. To find your installed version and see if you need to update it, run the az version.

Install or Update

The MSI and ZIP distributable are used for installing or updating the Azure CLI on Windows. You do not need to uninstall current versions before using the MSI installer because the MSI updates any existing version.

Note: *To utilize the Azure CLI, you must shut and restart any open terminal window after opening the URL that appears on the screen. Install the most recent version of the Azure CLI after downloading it. Choose "**Yes**" when the installer asks if it has permission to alter your machine.*

For instance, you would use https://azcliprod.blob.core.windows.net/msi/azure-cli-2.51.0.msi to install the 32-bit MSI of Azure CLI version 2.51.0. https://azcliprod.blob.core.windows.net/msi/azure-cli-2.51.0-x64.msi is the 64-bit install for the relevant version.

Running the Azure CLI

You can now run the Azure CLI with the az command from either Windows Command Prompt or PowerShell. We shall go for PowerShell'.

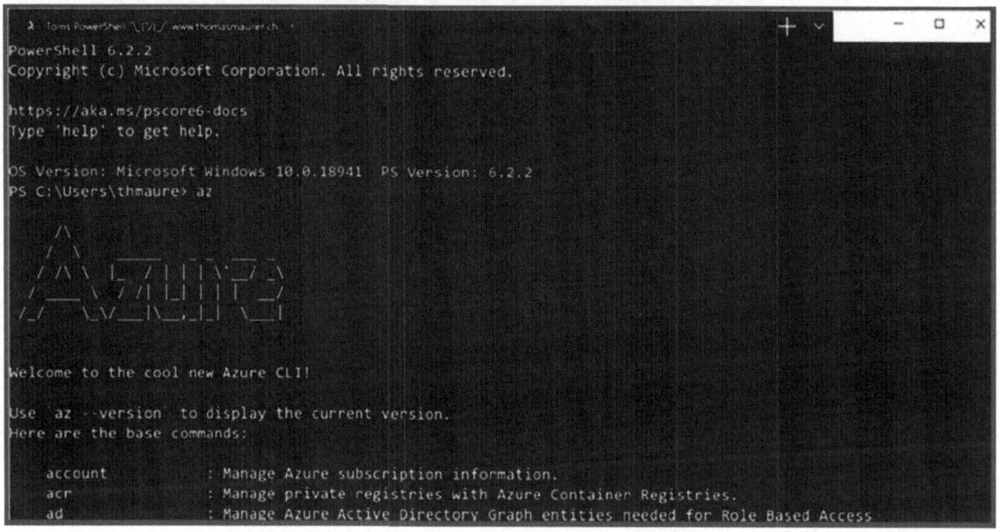

Figure 9.1: *Azure Command-Line Interface (CLI)*

Location of Azure CLI on the Device

When installing the Azure CLI, you cannot select an install location. In Windows, the 32-bit Azure CLI installs in **`C:\Program Files (x86)\Microsoft SDKs\Azure\CLI2`** and the 64-bit in **`C:\Program Files\Microsoft SDKs\Azure\CLI2`**. In Linux, the Azure CLI is installed in **`/opt/az/`** on Ubuntu and Debian, and in **`/lib64/az/`** on CentOS Stream, RHEL, and Azure Linux.

User-specific configuration files are located in **`$HOME/.azure`** on macOS and Linux, and **`%USERPROFILE%\.azure`** on Windows. These locations are known as the **`AZURE_CONFIG_DIR`**.

Knowing the Installed Version of the Azure CLI

Type the **az** version in a terminal window to know what version of the Azure CLI is installed. Your output looks as follows:

Figure 9.2: *Finding Azure Version Details by Windows Powershell*

Deno for Azure Functions

Deno is a secure runtime for JavaScript and TypeScript that can be used with Microsoft Azure. You can use the denofunc CLI to create, run, and deploy Deno for Azure Functions apps:

1. Install the denofunc CLI by running the command **deno install --allow-run --allow-read --allow-write --allow-net --unstable --force \ --name=denofunc**.
2. Create an empty folder and initialize the project with **denofunc init**.
3. Run the app locally with **denofunc start**.
4. Open the URL displayed on the screen to run the function.

Deno Deploy

Deno Deploy can scale and manage built-in APIs for a key/value database and job queue. You can deploy to a global network with a single command.

Deno REST API on Azure WebApp Service

You can create a REST API for Books Storage and deploy it to Azure WebApp service.

You may use this worker to run Deno on Azure Functions. It operates on the Azure Functions Consumption (serverless) plan and is built as an Azure Functions Custom Handler. To facilitate the creation, execution, and deployment of your Deno Azure Functions applications, the project comes with a CLI called denofunc.

Three commands to get started are as follows:

- `# initialize function app  : denofunc init`
- `# run function app locally : denofunc start`
- `# deploy the app`
  `denofunc publish $functionAppName [--slot $slotName] [--allow-run] [--allow-write]`

Installing the denofunc CLI

The denofunc CLI must be installed in order to assist with the creation, execution, and deployment of a Deno for Azure Functions application. The Azure Functions Core Tools (func) are wrapped in denofunc, which is used to create the artifacts needed to launch and deploy the application. Use the following Deno command to install the CLI:

```
deno install --allow-run --allow-read --allow-write --allow-net
--unstable --force \
    --name=denofunc https://raw.githubusercontent.com/anthonychu/
azure-functions-deno-worker/v0.8.0/denofunc.ts
```

Confirm it is installed correctly.

```
denofunc -help
```

Create and run an app locally.

Create and change into an empty folder.

Initialize the Project:

```
denofunc init
```

A few of the files that are important to know about:

`functions/hello_world.ts`: a basic HTTP triggered function

`worker.ts`: the Deno worker used by Azure Functions

`host.json`: configuration of the function host

Run the App Locally:

```
denofunc start
```

The Azure Functions Core Tools (**`func`**) is then called to run the function app.

Note: *The* ***`hello_world`*** *function automatically creates a subdirectory with a file called* ***`function.json`****, which the Azure Functions runtime uses to load the function (these are ignored in.gitnore).* To execute the function, open the URL that appears on the screen (**`http://localhost:7071/api/hello_world`**). To end the app, press *Ctrl-C*. Install the application on Azure. It is time to deploy the function application to Azure after running it locally!

Configure some variables (examples are in bash):

```
region=centralus # any region where Linux Azure Functions are
available
resourceGroupName=<resource_group_name>
functionAppName=<function_app_name>
storageName=<storage_name> # must be between 3 and 24 characters
in length and may contain numbers and lowercase letters only.
```

If you are not authenticated with the Azure CLI, log in.

```
# Log in to the Azure CLI
   az login
```

This might not work in some environments (for example, Codespaces). Try `az login --use-device-code` instead.

Run these Azure CLI commands to create and configure the function app:

```
# Create resource group
az group create -l $region -n $resourceGroupName

# Create storage account needed by function app
az storage account create -n $storageName -l $region -g
$resourceGroupName --sku
```

Standard_LRS

```
# Create function app (also works on Windows)
az functionapp create -n $functionAppName --storage-account $storageName \
    --consumption-plan-location $region -g $resourceGroupName \
    --functions-version 3 --runtime dotnet --os-type Linux
```

Deploy the App:

```
denofunc publish $functionAppName
```

Prior to deployment, **`denofunc`** tool will download the Deno Linux binary matching your locally installed version of deno that is included with the deployment package.

The deployment output will print out the URL of the deployed function. Open the URL to run your function.

🎉 Congratulations!

Programming Model

All Azure Functions triggers and bindings (including custom bindings) are supported.

In this simplified programming model, each function is a single file. Here are a couple of examples:

- HTTP trigger
- Queue trigger

Azure Functions Core Tools V3 - needed for running the app locally and deploying it

Azure CLI - needed to deploy the app

Codespaces

You can also get a preconfigured, cloud-based dev environment from Codespaces.

Visual Studio Codespaces

GitHub Codespaces (private preview) - go to the template repo and create a Codespace.

Install extensions automatically.

When you run an extension command that is not installed, the Azure CLI can recognize the command you run, and automatically install the extension for you starting from version 2.10.0. This feature, referred to as dynamic install is enabled by default since 2.12.0. You can also enable it through configuration for previously supported versions.

Pre-Requisites

If you are following along, you will need a few things to get started.

Setting Up Azure[2]

First, sign in to the Azure Portal and then click create a resource.

Pre-Requisites

If you are following along, you will need a few things to get started:

- An Azure account for spinning up Cosmos.
- An account with Deno Deploy.
- Deno installed locally. Instructions here are provided for a Windows machine, but you should be able to use any Linux or macOS machine to do this as well.
    1. For setting up Azure, sign in to the Azure Portal and then click "`Create a resource`".

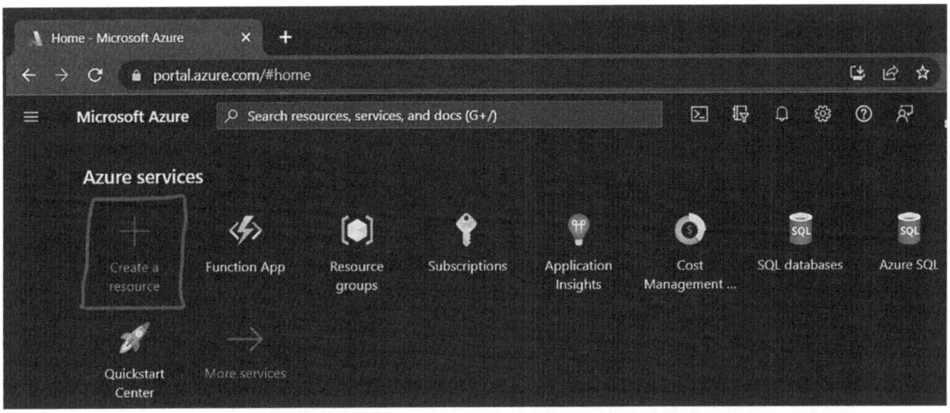

Figure 9.3: *Setting Up Azure - Creating a Resource*

2. Then, search for "**`cosmosdb`**" and select "**`Azure Cosmos DB`**" in the list.

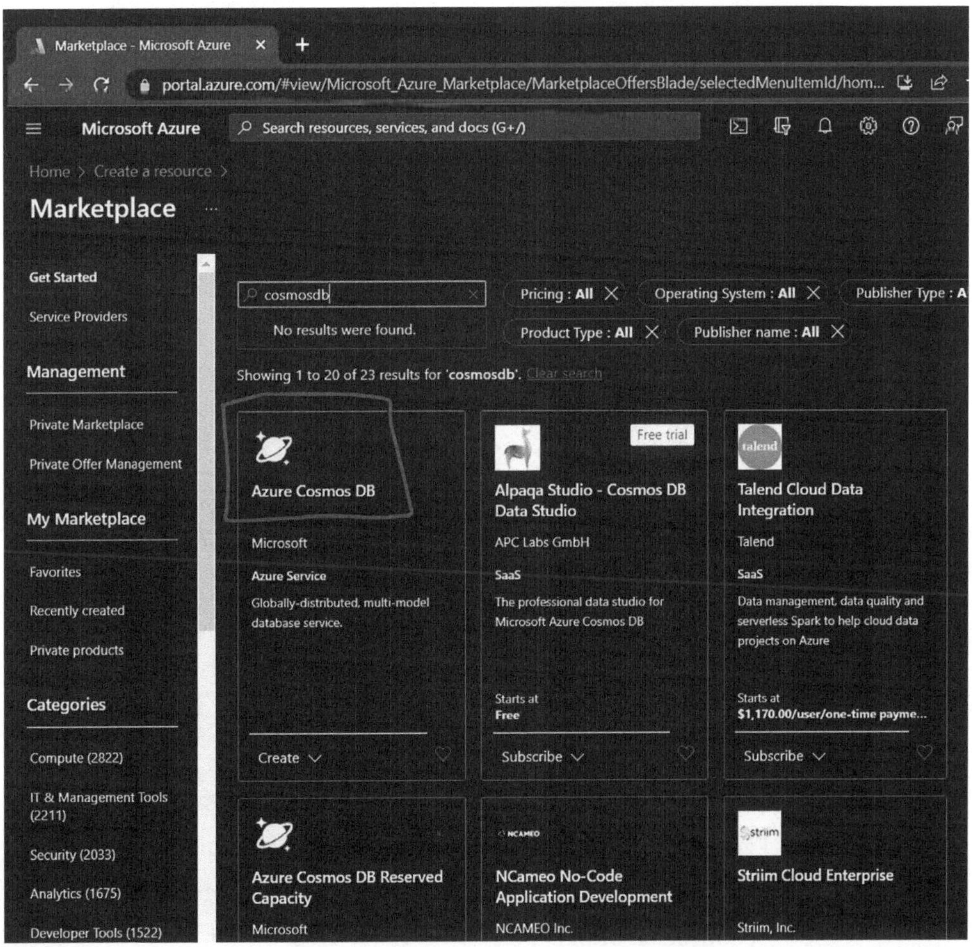

Figure 9.4: *Searching Azure Cosmos DB*

3. Then select "**Create**" on the next page.

Figure 9.5: *Creating Azure Cosmos DB Plan*

4. Then click "**Create**" on "**Azure Cosmos DB for NoSQL**".

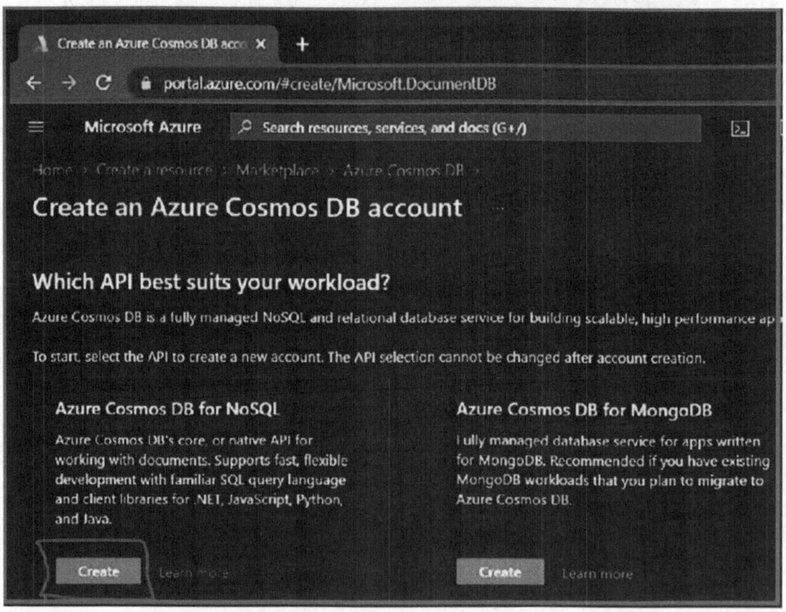

Figure 9.6: *The Create Button for Azure Cosmos NoSql*

5. At the bottom of the screen, click "**Review + create**" after establishing a new resource group called "**ThePizzaFarm**," which calls the account "**thepizzafarm-**." for deciding on the serverless capacity mode.

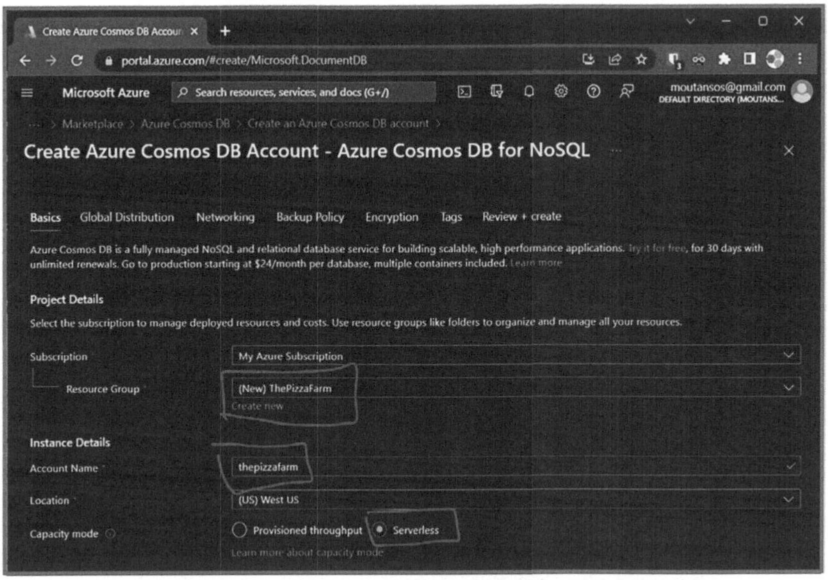

Figure 9.7: The Screen

Naming and Selecting Type of Database

1. Azure will then launch a new Cosmos instance and deploy the database. Usually, it takes a few minutes to finish. Once the deployment is complete, select "**`Go to resource`**."

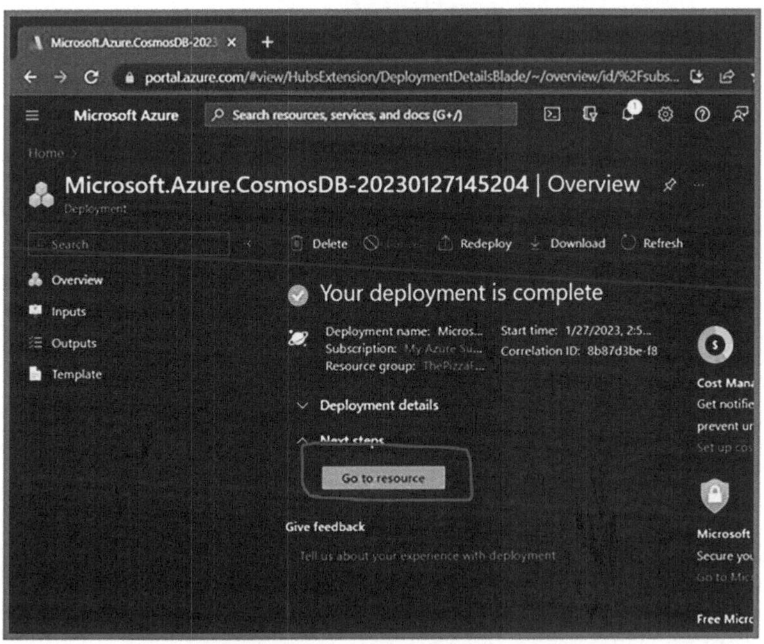

Figure 9.8: The Go to Resource Button

2. Next, select "**`Data Explorer`**" from the navigation column on the left.

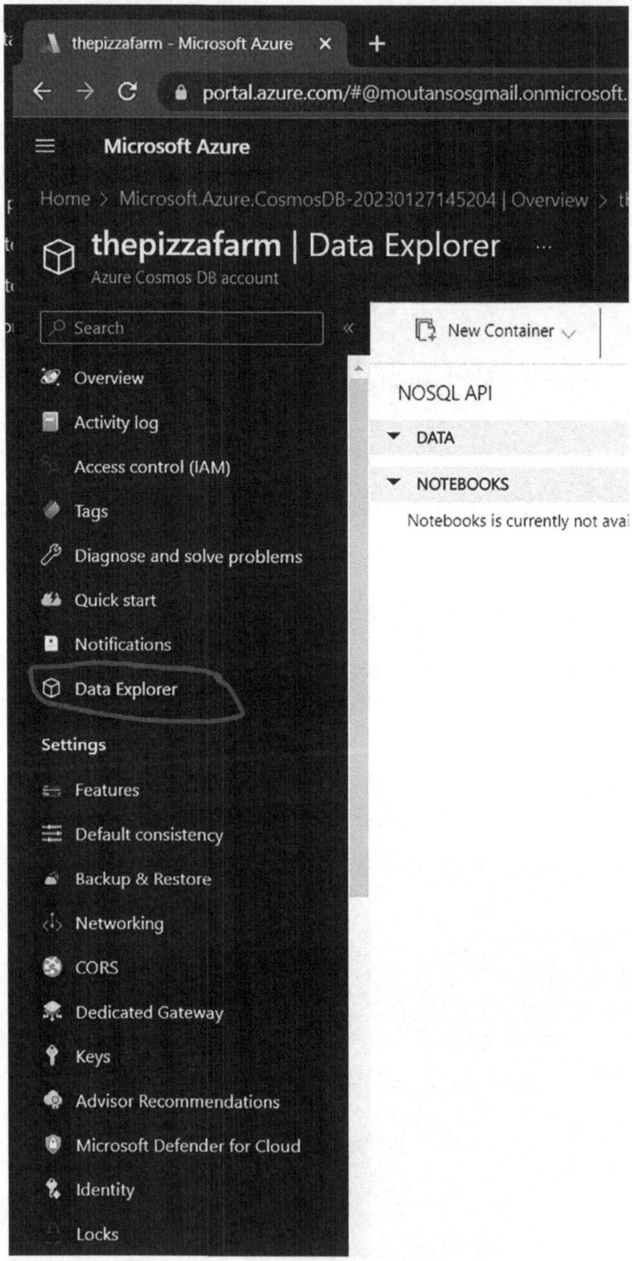

***Figure 9.9:** The Data Explorer Link in the Sidebar*

3. Click **`OK`** after choosing "**`New Container`**" and then "**`New Collection`**" on this page. Enter "**`ThePizzaFarm`**" for the database id and "**`Orders`**" for the container id.

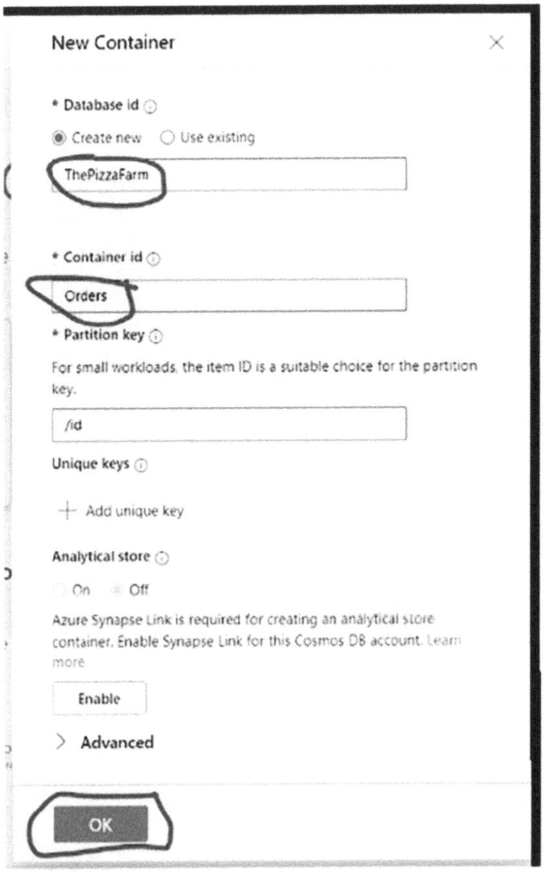

Figure 9.10: *Setting Up the Database id and Container id*

4. After selecting the "**Home**" tab, click the "**Connect**" option. Note the "**Primary Connection String**" on the following screen ought to begin with "**AccountEndpoint=**."

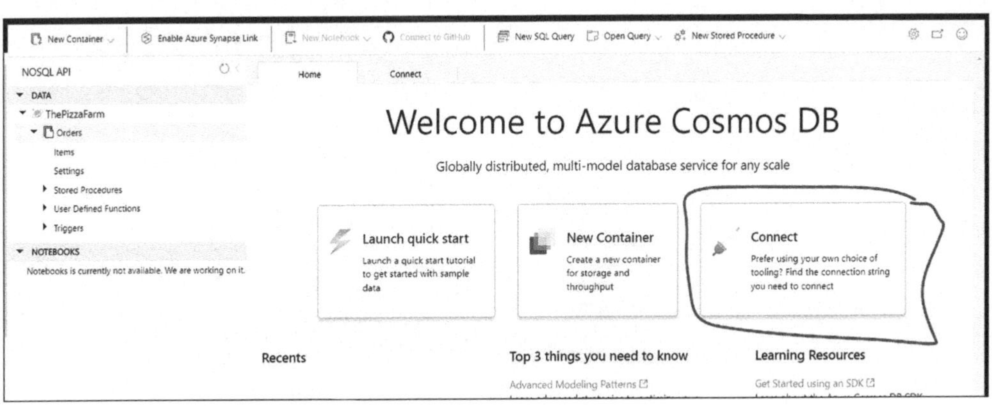

Figure 9.11: *Clicking the Connect Button in Data Explorer*

And with that, you have set up an Azure Cosmos database.

Setting Up Deno Deploy

Next, we will set up Deno Deploy and get a basic Hello World endpoint up and working.

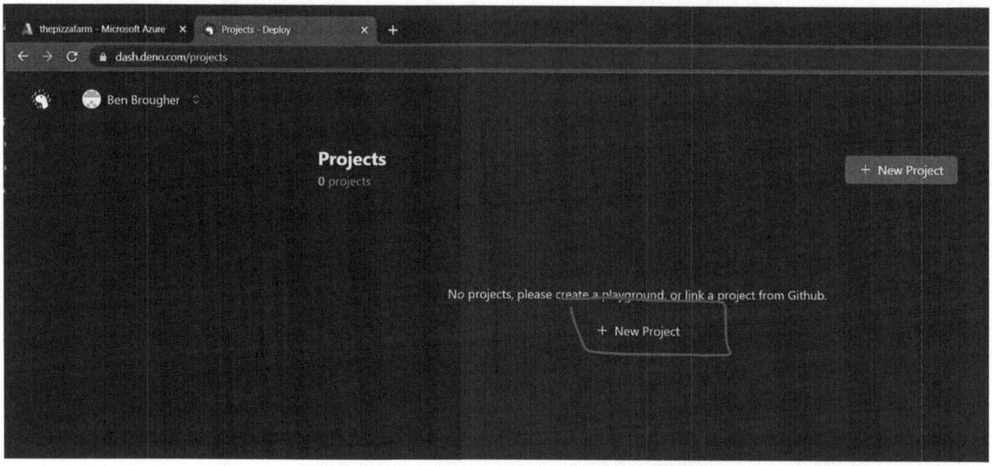

Figure 9.12: *Clicking the New Project Button*

1. Sign in to your Deno Deploy account, and then click "**`New Project`**."

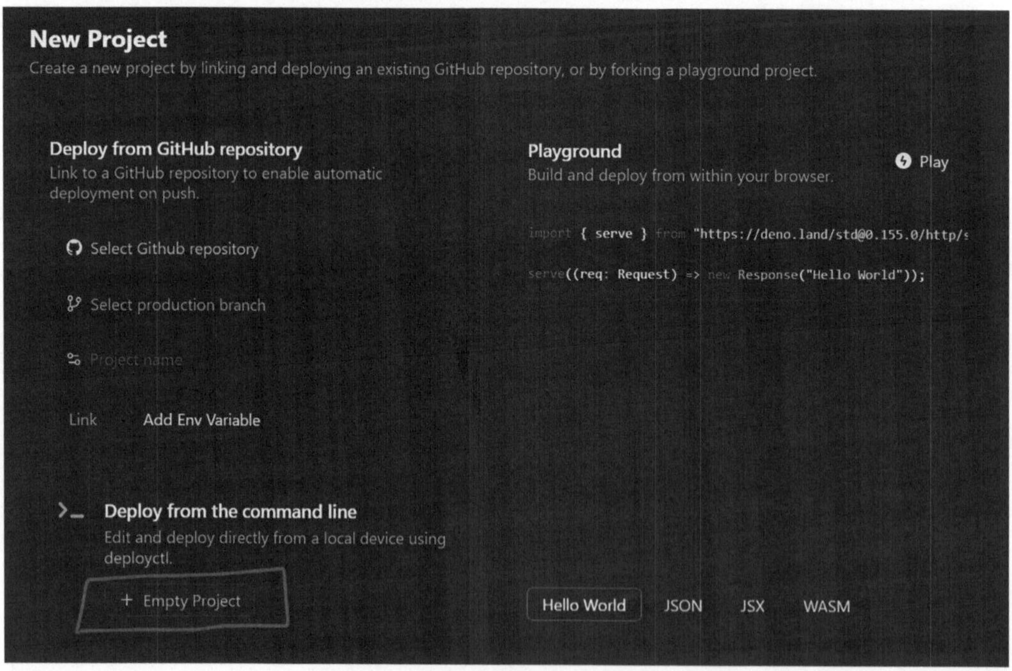

Figure 9.13: *Clicking the Empty Project Button*

2. Then click "**+ Empty Project**" in the "**Deploy from command line**" section.

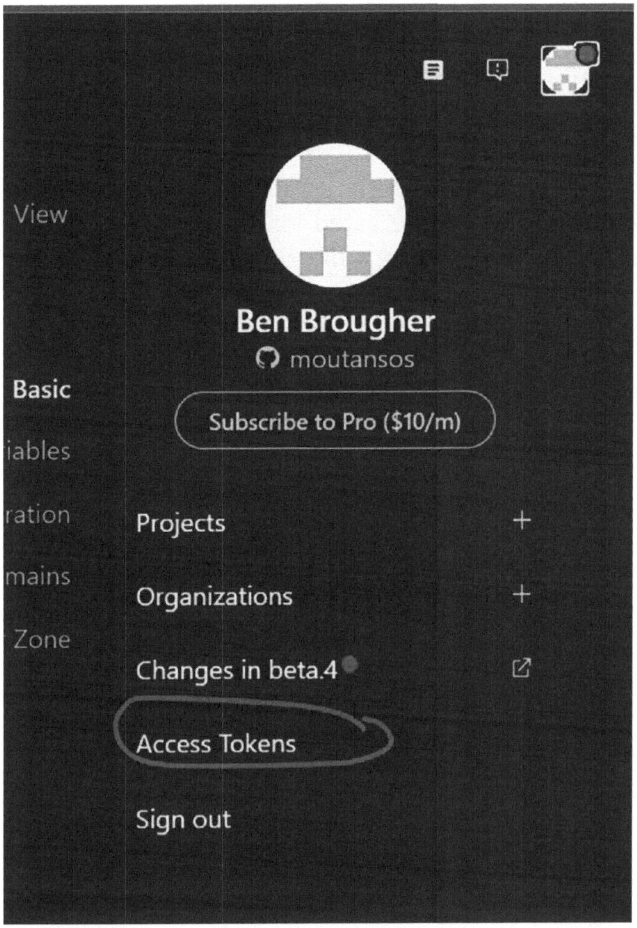

Figure 9.14: *Clicking the Access Tokens Button in the Profile Menu*

3. Open the profile menu by clicking its icon at the top right corner of the screen and click "**Access Tokens**" from the list.

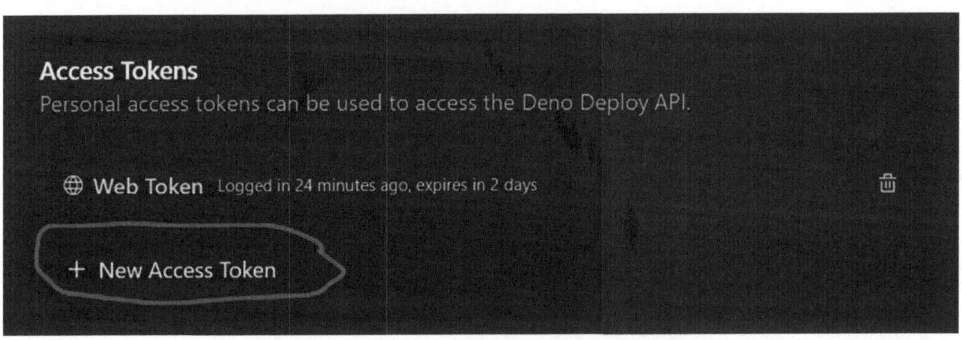

Figure 9.15: *Selecting New Access Token*

4. Then, in the "**Access Tokens**" section, click "**+ New Access Token**". For the description, call it "**Deployment**" and then take note of the key. Now, navigate back to the project that you created earlier.

Deploying a Hello World API

Installing the deployctl tool and launching a simple beginning app are the next steps. Open a terminal in the folder you created for your project on your local computer. We will require it shortly. Next, make a file named main.ts in that directory with the following information in it:

```
import { Application, Router } from "https://deno.land/x/oak/mod.ts";

  const router = new Router();
  router
    .get("/", (ctx): void => {
      ctx.response.body = "Hello World!";
    });

  const app = new Application();
  app.use(router.routes());

  app.addEventListener("listen", (e) =>
    console.log("Listening on http://localhost:8080");
  );

  await app.listen({ port: 8080 });
```

This code uses the Oak framework to develop a tiny web application. If you have ever used Node.js and Express.js, the development process is rather comparable. We can now test the functionality of this simple application locally. Within the terminal, type: **./main.ts deno run --allow-net**. The API should now be reachable at http://localhost:8080. Let us push it up and run it on Deno Deploy now that it is functioning. To install the deployctl utility, first execute the following command:

```
deno install --allow-read --allow-write --allow-env --allow-net
--allow-run --no-check -r -f https://deno.land/x/deploy/
deployctl.ts
```

After this, take the token you saved from the preceding, and set it to an environment variable on the command line:

```
# PowerShell
      $env:DENO_DEPLOY_TOKEN="<<token>>"
      # Linux/macOS
      export DENO_DEPLOY_TOKEN=<<token>>
```

Now run the following to deploy the app:

```
deployctl deploy --project=<<project name>> ./main.ts
```

You should now see a URL for your app in the terminal.

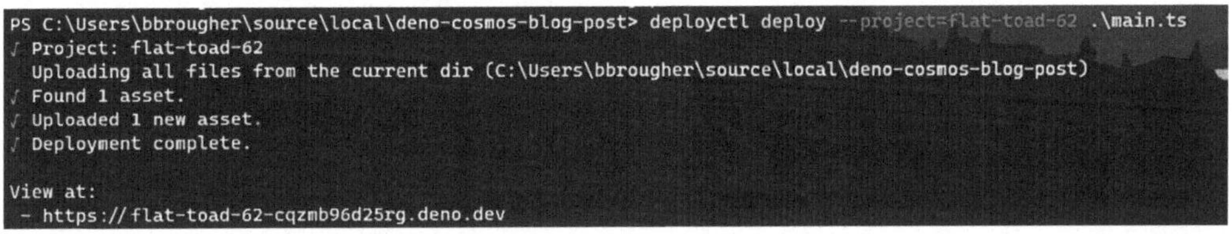

Figure 9.16: *Deploying Output*

This URL is not ready for production use. When you are ready to push out a production deploy, you may select "**`Promote to Production`**" to change the URL to match your project name. By default, Deno Deploy generates a new URL for each deployment. Check to see whether it works by using that URL. It should display "**`Hello World`**!" when you attempt to load it in Postman or a web browser.

Developing the Ordering API for Pizza Farm We may begin connecting Azure Cosmos and Deno Deploy now that they are both configured and operational. To store our Azure Cosmos connection string, we must set an environment variable on the server side. To accomplish this, go to "**`Settings`**" in Deno Deploy and click "**`+ Add Variable`**."

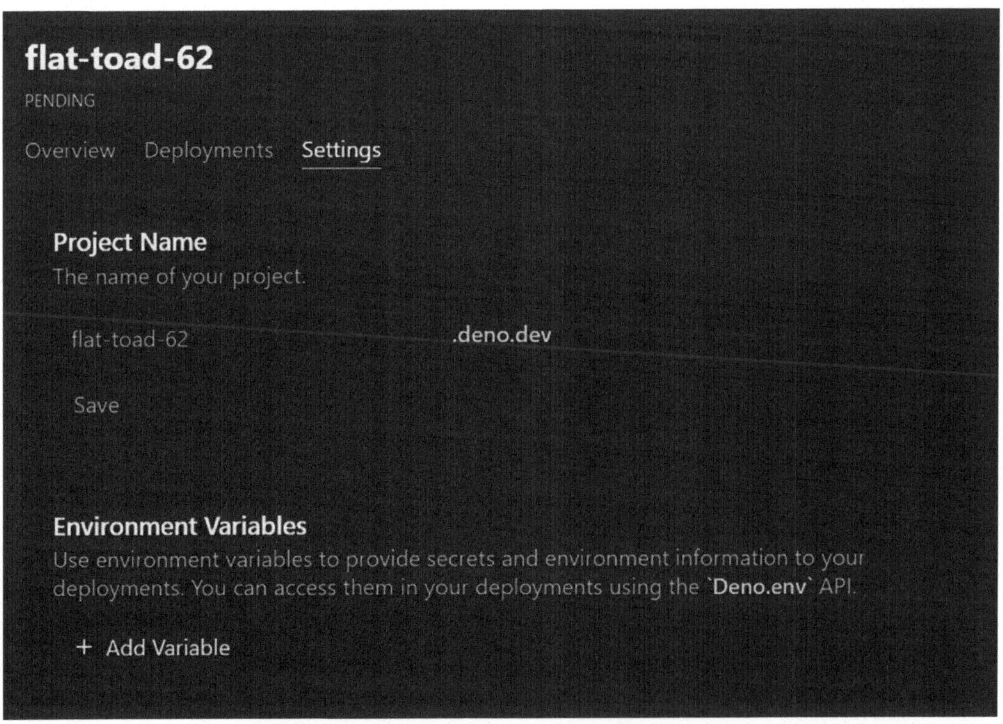

Figure 9.17: *The Add Variable Button in Settings*

Then input "**COSMOS_CON_STR**" as the key and then your connection string from the preceding for the value.

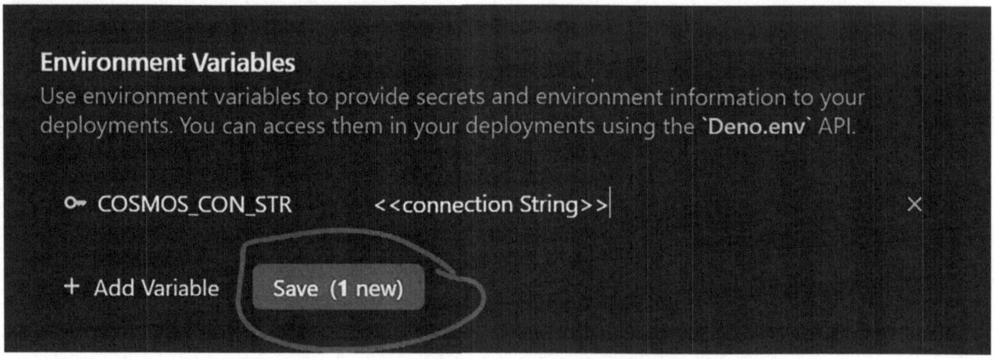

Figure 9.18: *Saving the Connection String to Variable*

Next, we need to start getting the model files that represent our data setup. Create a file called **models.ts** with the following contents:

```
export enum Size {
  Small = 'small',
  Medium = 'medium',
  Large = 'large',
}

export enum PizzaType {
  Cheese = 'cheese',
  Pepperoni = 'pepperoni',
  Sausage = 'sausage',
  Hawaiian = 'hawaiian',
}

export enum OrderStatus {
  Placed = 'placed',
  InProgress = 'inProgress',
  OutForDelivery = 'outForDelivery',
  Delivered = 'delivered',
}

export interface PizzaItem {
  size: Size;
  type: PizzaType;
}

export interface Order {
  id?: string;
  customerName: string;
```

```
  items: PizzaItem[];
  status: OrderStatus;
}

export function cleanOrder(order: Order): Order {
  return {
    id: order.id,
    customerName: order.customerName,
    items: order.items,
    status: order.status,
  };
}
```

There are a few types of things in here. Our **Order** and **PizzaItems** objects represent what a customer ordered, and then a few enums to define what size the pizza is, what type of pizza it is, and what the status of the order is currently. Also, we have a basic function at the end that cleans up the order and removes extraneous fields that may be present when pulling in the data from the request. Ideally, that would be more robust and it would validate all the input in a production application, but we are keeping it simple here.

Next, we need to update the main file to appear as follows:

```
import { Application, Router } from 'https://deno.land/x/oak@
v11.1.0/mod.ts';
import {
  CosmosClient,
  PatchOperation,
} from 'https://cdn.skypack.dev/@azure/cosmos?dts';
import { cleanOrder, Order, OrderStatus } from './models.ts';
import { Status } from 'https://deno.land/std@0.152.0/http/http_
status.ts';

//Added the cosmos client here and grab our connection string
const cosmosClient = new CosmosClient(Deno.env.get('COSMOS_CON_
STR') ?? '');
const cosmosDatabase = cosmosClient.database('ThePizzaFarm');
const cosmosContainer = cosmosDatabase.container('Orders');

const router = new Router();
router.get('/', (ctx): void => {
  ctx.response.body = 'Hello world! Anyone hungry for pizza?';
});

// Added an endpoint for creating an order
router.post('/orders', async (ctx) => {
  const { value } = ctx.request.body({ type: 'json' });
```

```
  const orderBody: Order = cleanOrder(await value);
  const response = await cosmosContainer.items.create(orderBody);
  ctx.response.body = { status: 'Added', recordId: response.item.
id };
});

// Added a general orders endpoint for getting all the orders in
the system
router.get('/orders', async (ctx) => {
  const response = await cosmosContainer.items.readAll();
  const queryResponse = await response.fetchAll();
  const rawItems: Order[] = <Order[]>queryResponse.resources;
  ctx.response.body = rawItems;
});

// Added an endpoint for updating the orders status as the pizza
goes from just
// being placed to in progress, to out for delivery and finally
delivered
router.patch('/orders/status', async (ctx) => {
  const { value } = ctx.request.body({ type: 'json' });
  const statusUpdateBody: { status: OrderStatus; id: string } =
await value;
  const item = cosmosContainer.item(statusUpdateBody.id, statu-
sUpdateBody.id);
  const updateTransaction: PatchOperation[] = [
    {
      op: 'replace',
      path: '/status',
      value: statusUpdateBody.status,
    },
  ];
  await item.patch(updateTransaction);
  const { resource: updatedItem } = await item.read();
  ctx.response.body = cleanOrder(updatedItem);
});

// Added the delete endpoint for deleting the order from the
system when it is no
// longer needed.
router.delete('/orders', async (ctx) => {
  const id = ctx.request.url.searchParams.get('id');
  if (!id) {
    ctx.response.body = {
      status: 'Id not specified in the search params!',
    };
    ctx.response.status = Status.BadRequest;
```

```
    return;
  }
  await cosmosContainer.item(id, id).delete();
  ctx.response.body = {
    status: 'Deleted',
  };
});

const app = new Application();
app.use(router.routes());

app.addEventListener('listen', (e) =>
  console.log('Listening on http://localhost:8080')
);

await app.listen({ port: 8080 });
```

There seem to be a lot of changes! Like we did before, let us deploy this to deno deploy before testing it out!

Testing

Grab your URL from your deploy and get your favorite way to make API calls ready. (Postman is a popular choice.)

Create an Order

First, we will create an order. In the real world, this would likely be called by a web app after the user submits an order.

URL: `https://<<my deployed function>>.deno.dev/orders`

Method: `POST`

Request Body

```
{
    "customerName": "Elroy Jetson",
    "items": [
        {
            "size": "medium",
            "type": "pepperoni"
        }
    ],
    "status": "placed"
}
Expected Response:
```

```
{
    "status": "Added",
    "recordId": "<<record id will be here>>"
}
```

List the Orders

The orders can then be listed. To display the staff what orders are coming in and their status, you can see a screen at the store pulling in this info.

URL: `https://<<my deployed function>>.deno.dev/orders`

Method: `POST`

Expected Response:

```
[
    {
        "id": "<< same record id from above will be here >>",
        "customerName": "Elroy Jetson",
        "items": [
            {
                "size": "medium",
                "type": "pepperoni"
            }
        ],
        "status": "placed",
        .... azure cosmos fields ....
    }
]
```

Update the Order's Status

Employees at the business must be able to update the order status both when they begin cooking the pizza and when they send it out for delivery. The delivery driver may make this request on their phone, computer, or tablet at the business.

URL: `https://<<my deployed function>>.deno.dev/orders`

Method: `PATCH`

Request Body

```
{
    "id": "<< record id from above >>",
    "status": "inProgress"
}
Expected Response:

{
    "id": "<< record id >>",
```

```
        "customerName": "Elroy Jetson",
        "items": [
            {
                "size": "medium",
                "type": "pepperoni"
            }
        ],
        "status": "inProgress"
    }
```

Delete the Order

Employees would likely prefer that the order be removed from their displays after it has been delivered. Let us request that the order be deleted.

URL: https://<<my deployed function>>.deno.dev/orders?id=<< record id >>

Method: PATCH

Expected Response:

```
{
    "status": "Deleted"
}
```

Conclusion

In this chapter, we learned about Microsoft's production Azure that is not exclusively for Deno but provides facilities through certain features. To achieving this, we learned to install and run the Azure CLI and set up Azure. Moreover, we learned the programming model and then about Deno Deploy.

In the next chapter, we shall work on creating a practical example of Deno in Web Development Using Chocolatey.

Reference

1. **Install Azure CLI on Windows Article 08/19/2024**: https://learn.microsoft.com/en-us/cli/azure/install-azure-cli-windows?tabs=azure-cli
2. **How to Use Deno Deploy with Azure Cosmos DB**: https://benbrougher.tech/posts/deno-deploy-with-azure-cosmos/

CHAPTER 10 Deno Web Development Using Chocolatey

Introduction

Chocolatey is a software management solution that allows you to use any of your usual configuration or system management tools to create a basic software package and then deploy it any place Windows is installed. Chocolatey has an incredibly business-friendly FOSS Apache 2.0 license. Chocolatey and the majority of its infrastructure are free to use. Additionally, Chocolatey offers a corporate edition with features that businesses require for improved software administration. Npm is a package manager for JavaScript, and Chocolatey is a package manager for Windows. Chocolatey makes it simple to automate software installs by concentrating on installing and maintaining Windows software packages.

Structure

In this chapter, we will study about Chocolatey, a Windows Software Management under the following topics:

- Chocolatey for Business
- Setup/Install Chocolatey CLI (Choco)
- Extend Chocolatey with PowerShell Modules (Extensions)
- An Elevated Command Prompt

Chocolatey for Business

Chocolatey for Business (C4B) has helped hundreds of system admins save time, reduce downtime, and accelerate deployment.

Chocolatey is a software management tool that automates the process of installing and updating software on Windows machines:

- **Simplifies Software Management:** Chocolatey can be used to create a software deployment package and then deploy it to multiple Windows machines.
- **Automate Repetitive Tasks:** Chocolatey can be used to automate tasks such as downloading, unblocking, and installing software.
- **Works with Familiar Technologies:** Chocolatey uses PowerShell and the NuGet packaging infrastructure.
- **Manages a Variety of Files and Configurations**: Chocolatey can manage files, configurations, registry settings, and more.
- **Free to Use:** Chocolatey is free to use, even for internal use within an organization.
- **Software Deployment with Chocolatey:** Chocolatey can be used to deploy software packages, applications, zips, binaries, scripts, and installers.

Chocolatey versus npm

Package managers npm and chocolatey are made for distinct environments. Let us examine their main distinctions.

- **Installation Procedure**: Npm is a package manager for JavaScript, and Chocolatey is a package manager for Windows. Chocolatey makes it simple to automate software installs by concentrating on installing and maintaining Windows software packages. However, npm is mainly used for Node.js projects to install and manage JavaScript packages and dependencies.
- **Package Management:** By using the Chocolatey community package repository, users can find and install a variety of software packages, including both commercial and open-source programs.

  It also offers the capability of developing, overseeing, and distributing personalized packages. In contrast, npm offers a vast collection of JavaScript packages and modules that are simple to install and maintain in Node.js projects.
- **Dependency Management:** By enabling packages to designate other packages as dependencies, Chocolatey offers fundamental dependency management. Chocolatey will install any necessary dependencies automatically when you install a package. In contrast, npm is excellent at managing dependencies, enabling packages to define exact versions of dependencies and handling intricate dependency trees.
- **Command-Line Interface:** Chocolatey offers a robust Command-Line

Interface (CLI) that enables users to carry out a variety of tasks, including package searches, installations, upgrades, and uninstallations.

It is appropriate for a range of use cases because it also offers automation and scripting. Although it is mainly used for managing JavaScript packages in Node.js projects, npm also offers a CLI with comparable features.

- **Community Assistance:** The vibrant Chocolatey community offers a large collection of software packages, documentation, and assistance.

  A pro edition with more features and support choices is also available. A vital tool for JavaScript development, npm boasts a sizable and active community with a wealth of tutorials, documentation, and help channels.

- **Platform Compatibility:** Chocolatey is compatible with multiple Windows operating system versions and was created especially for Windows. It can be incorporated into the current Windows management procedures and tools. Conversely, npm is platform-neutral and may be used on any operating system that supports Node.js.

Chocolatey is software management automation. Chocolatey works with over 20+ installer technologies for Windows, but it can manage things you would normally xcopy deploy (such as runtime binaries and zip files). You can also work with registry settings managing files and configurations, or any combination.

Extend Chocolatey with PowerShell Modules (Extensions)

You have been able to add your own PowerShell modules and features to Chocolatey for years. We call these extensions. With extensions, you may bundle PowerShell functions that you might use in different packages into a package that other products can rely on. This enables you to utilize those same features just like you would if they were built into Chocolatey. These PowerShell modules are loaded by Chocolatey as part of the standard module import load for pre-installed PowerShell modules. [1]

The Necessity of Establishing an Extension

To make your Chocolatey automation scripts have less code. It is quite powerful to package logic as functions inside a PowerShell module that you can version separately, improve, and correct without affecting your already-existing packages.

Making a Chocolatey Add-On

Chocolatey has a traditional strategy when it comes to extensions. At least one PowerShell module must be present in the extensions folder, and a package with the ending "`.extension`" must be created.

The name of this package is "**extensionname.extension**". The name of the installed extension will be the package name less "**.extension**."

1. **Run** choco new name.extension to build an extension package, then remove anything but the nuspec.
2. Next, make an extensions folder in the package's root.
3. Make your PowerShell module in the extensions folder.
4. A PowerShell Module (PSM1) file that loads and verifies that functionalities are present is the crucial file you will require. Examine the chocolatey-core. extensions module and the profile module.

Chocolatey will load those functions, so when your scripts run, they will already be accessible, saving you the trouble of loading the files in your install scripts later.

Here is an illustration:

> This is the extension for **https://community.chocolatey.org/packages/chocolatey-core.** **https://github.com/chocolatey-community/chocolatey-packages/tree/master/extensions** is the location of the source.

Choosing a Name for Your Extension

Do not include "Chocolatey" in the name. Yes, that is the name of the example; however, since the Core Chocolatey team owns this extension, it makes logical for that to be the name.

Modules for PowerShell

Generally speaking, an extension should have as few PowerShell modules as possible–just enough to demonstrate its functionality. While it might not be feasible, aim for one module per extension package.

The functions, aliases, and cmdlets that are intended to be utilized in Chocolatey automation scripts should be expressly exported by the module.

Using an Extension Package as a Dependency It is advised to use a minimum version dependency when relying on an extension package. You should update the dependent version if the extension has improved functionality.

Minimum Requirements for Versions

Here is how one defines a minimum version dependency:

```
<dependencies>
  <dependency id="chocolatey-core.extension" version="1.1.0" />
</dependencies>
```

Avoid Version Ranges for Extensions

Avoid version ranges when it comes to extensions as it can lock out fixes and enhancements in the future.

```
<dependencies>
  <!-- This means at least 1.0.0, and anything less than 2 -->
  <dependency id="chocolatey-core.extension" version="[1.0.0, 2)"
/>
  <!-- This means anything between 1.0.0 and 2.0.1 (including
2.0.1) is good to go -->
  <dependency id="another.extension" version="[1.0.0, 2.0.1]" />
</dependencies>
```

Avoid Exact Version Dependencies for Extensions at All Costs

Try to never lock into an exact version dependency.

```
<!-- DO NOT DO THIS -->
<dependencies>
  <dependency id="chocolatey-core.extension" version="[1.1.0]" />
</dependencies>
```

This locks every other package into that singular version and does not allow for upgrades and fixes.

Version-Less Dependencies

There is also the concept of version-less dependencies.

```
<dependencies>
  <dependency id="chocolatey-core.extension" />
</dependencies>
```

Folks typically have used these in the past. They are less bad, but it just means that any version will do.

Routing and Rendering

There are numerous methods for using Deno to create a website or application. Building a site with a router and components is the simplest method because Deno natively supports JSX and TSX. An incredibly basic example of a website with Home and About pages is provided here:

```
import { router } from "https://crux.land/router@0.0.11";
import { h, ssr } from "https://crux.land/nanossr@0.0.4";

const render = (component) => ssr(() => <App>{component}</App>);

Deno.serve(router(
  {
```

```
    "/": () => render(<Home />),
    "/about": () => render(<About />),
  },
));

function App({ children }) {
  return (
    <div>
      <NavBar />
      {children}
    </div>
  );
}

function NavBar() {
  return (
    <nav>
      <div>
        <a href="/">
          Home
        </a>
      </div>
      <div>
        <a href="/about">
          About
        </a>
      </div>
    </nav>
  );
}

function Home() {
  return (
    <div>
      <span>Home</span>
    </div>
  );
}

function About() {
  return (
    <div>
      <span>About</span>
    </div>
  );
}
```

This example comes from a blog article about a straightforward portfolio website that only requires one JavaScript file. A web form that is likewise included in a single JavaScript file is part of this more interactive version. The state is added using Deno KV. What about a logical web application? Here is an example of a web application that uses Deno KV for storing just 23 lines of code to reduce links:

```
const kv = await Deno.openKv();

Deno.serve(async (request: Request) => {
  // Create short links
  if (request.method == "POST") {
    const body = await request.text();
    const { slug, url } = JSON.parse(body);
    const result = await kv.set(["links", slug], url);
    return new Response(JSON.stringify(result));
  }

  // Redirect short links
  const slug = request.url.split("/").pop() || "";
  const url = (await kv.get(["links", slug])).value as string;
  if (url) {
    return Response.redirect(url, 301);
  } else {
    const m = !slug ? "Please provide a slug." : `Slug "${slug}"
not found`;
    return new Response(m, {
      status: 404,
    });
  }
});
```

Setup/Install Chocolatey CLI (Choco)

Chocolatey is a package manager for Windows that gives you a command-line approach to install, update, and remove software. It makes managing software on a Windows PC easy and saves you time and effort.

This section demonstrates the process of installing Chocolatey.

Requirements

- A supported version of Windows.
- A supported version of PowerShell.

Chocolatey CLI v2.0+

.NET Framework 4.8

The installation script will attempt to install .NET 4.8 if it is not installed.

Chocolatey CLI v1.x

.NET Framework 4+

The installation will attempt to install .NET 4.0 if you do not have it installed.

NET Framework 4.5+ is required for installation directly from the Chocolatey Community Repository, due to the TLS 1.2 requirement.

Installing Chocolatey CLI

First, ensure that you are using an administrative shell.

1. Refer to Non-Administrative Installation for information on installing without administrative rights.
2. Copy the text specific to your command shell **- `cmd.exe`** or **`powershell.exe`**.
3. Paste the copied text into your shell and press Enter.
4. Wait a few seconds for the command to complete.
5. If you do not see any errors, you are ready to use Chocolatey CLI.
6. Type choco or choco -? now, or refer to Getting Started for usage instructions.

Install with PowerShell.exe

With PowerShell, there is an additional step. You must ensure that **`Get-ExecutionPolicy`** is not Restricted. We suggest using Bypass to bypass the policy to get things installed or All Signed for quite a bit more security.

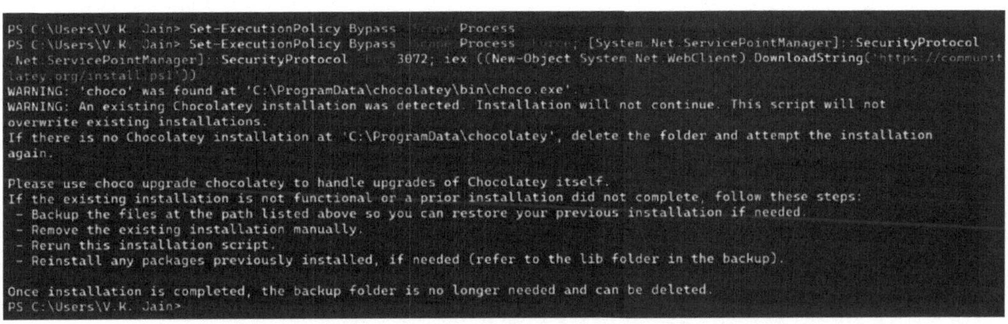

Figure 10.1: *Message that First Appears During Installation Process*

Run **`Get-ExecutionPolicy`**. If it returns **`Restricted`**, run **`Set-ExecutionPolicy AllSigned`** or **`Set-ExecutionPolicy Bypass -Scope Process`**.

Now run the following command:

```
Set-ExecutionPolicy Bypass -Scope Process -Force; [System.Net.
ServicePointManager]::SecurityProtocol = [System.Net.Service-
PointManager]::SecurityProtocol -bor 3072; iex ((New-Object Sys-
```

```
tem.Net.WebClient).DownloadString('https://community.chocolatey.
org/install.ps1'))
```

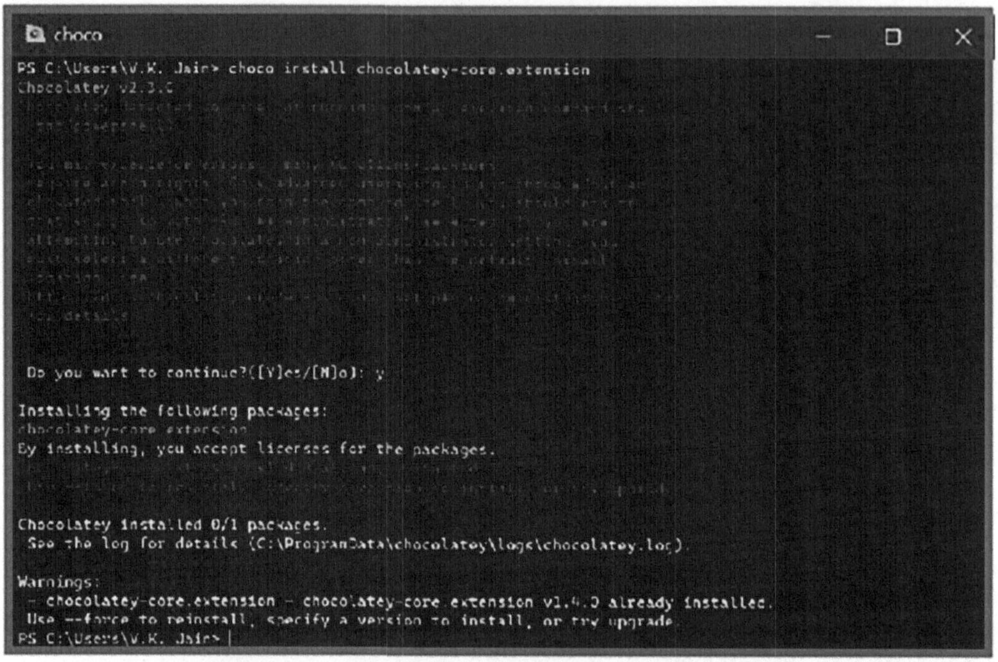

Figure 10.2: *Next Message Received During Installation Process*

Extend Chocolatey with PowerShell Modules (Extensions)

For years Chocolatey has allowed you to extend Chocolatey with your own PowerShell modules and functions. These are known as extensions.

Overview

Extensions allow you to package up PowerShell functions that you may reuse across packages as a package that other packages can use and depend on. This allows you to use those same functions as if they were part of Chocolatey itself. Chocolatey loads these PowerShell modules up as part of the regular module import load as it does for built-in PowerShell modules.

Need for Creating an Extension Chocolatey

To reduce code in your Chocolatey automation scripts. Packaging up logic as functions into a PowerShell module that you can version independently, fix issues in, and enhance without needing to touch existing packages that you have is pretty powerful.

Creating a Chocolatey Extension

When it comes to extensions, Chocolatey takes a conventional approach. You must create a package with the suffix "`.extension`" and have an extensions folder with at least one PowerShell module in it.

The name of the package should be "`extensionname.extension`". The name of the package minus "`.extension`" will be the name of the extension that is installed.

1. To create an extension package, run `choco new name.extension` and then delete everything but the nuspec.
2. Then create an extensions folder in the root of the package.
3. In the extensions folder, create your PowerShell module.
4. The important file you will need is a PowerShell Module (PSM1) file that loads up and ensures functions are available. Have a look at the profile module and `chocolatey-core.extensions` module.
5. When those functions are loaded by Chocolatey, they will already be available when your scripts run so you will not need to load up the files again in your install scripts - the functions will already be available!

Here is an example: `https://community.chocolatey.org/packages/chocolatey-core.extension`. The source is at `https://github.com/chocolatey-community/chocolatey-packages/tree/master/extensions`.

Naming Your Extension

Avoid "Chocolatey" as part of the name. Yes, the example is named that, but this extension is owned by the Core Chocolatey team, so it makes sense for that to be the name.

PowerShell Modules

The recommendation is typically as few PowerShell modules as possible in an extension, just enough to represent what that extension does. Strive for one module per extension package, although that may not be realistic.

The module should explicitly export the functions, aliases, and cmdlets that are wanted to be used in Chocolatey automation scripts.

Taking a Dependency on an Extension Package

When taking a dependency on an extension package, it is recommended to take a minimum version dependency. If there is functionality that is enhanced in that extension, you should bump that dependency version.

Minimum Version Dependencies

This is what a minimum version dependency looks like:

```
<dependencies>
  <dependency id="chocolatey-core.extension" version="1.1.0" />
</dependencies>
```

Avoid Version Ranges for Extensions

Avoid version ranges when it comes to extensions as it can lock out fixes and enhancements in the future.

```
<dependencies>
  <!-- This means at least 1.0.0, and anything less than 2 -->
  <dependency id="chocolatey-core.extension" version="[1.0.0, 2)" />
  <!-- This means anything between 1.0.0 and 2.0.1 (including 2.0.1) is
good to go -->
  <dependency id="another.extension" version="[1.0.0, 2.0.1]" />
</dependencies>
```

Avoid Exact Version Dependencies for Extensions at All Costs

Try to never lock into an exact version dependency.

```
<!-- DO NOT DO THIS -->
<dependencies>
  <dependency id="chocolatey-core.extension" version="[1.1.0]" />
</dependencies>
```

This locks every other package into that singular version and does not allow for upgrades and fixes.

Version-Less Dependencies

There is also the concept of version-less dependencies.

```
<dependencies>
  <dependency id="chocolatey-core.extension" />
</dependencies>
```

Folks typically have used these in the past. They are less bad, but it just means that any version will do.

An Elevated Command Prompt

An elevated command prompt, also known as an administrator command prompt, is a command line interface in Windows that allows you to execute commands with administrative privileges. When you run the command prompt as an administrator, you gain elevated rights and can perform tasks that require higher permission levels, such as modifying system files or settings.

Need of Using an Elevated Command Prompt

You might need to use an elevated command prompt when you want to perform administrative tasks that are not possible with regular user privileges. Some examples include installing or uninstalling software, modifying system configurations, managing user accounts, or troubleshooting issues that require administrative access.

Opening an Elevated Command Prompt

To open an elevated command prompt, you can follow these steps:

1. Press the Windows key on your keyboard or click on the Windows icon in the taskbar to open the `Start` menu.
2. Type "`cmd`" in the search bar.
3. Right-click "`command prompt`" or "`command prompt (Admin)`" in the search results.
4. Select "`Run as administrator`."

Alternatively, you can open the Run dialog box by pressing the Windows key + *R*, type "`cmd`," and then press *Ctrl* + *Shift* + *Enter* to run it as an administrator.

Running the Command Prompt as an Administrator

Running command prompt as an administrator is necessary to perform certain administrative tasks that require elevated privileges. It ensures that you have the necessary permissions to execute commands that can modify system settings, access protected files, or make changes that affect other users on the computer.

Effects of Running Command Prompt as an Administrator

When you run the command prompt as an administrator, you will notice that the title of the window changes to "Administrator: command prompt." This indicates that you have elevated privileges, and any commands you execute will have administrative rights. You may see a User Account Control (UAC) prompt asking for confirmation before allowing administrative access.

Installation of Chocolatey GUI

The easiest way to install Chocolatey GUI is to use Chocolatey. Use the following command to install the latest version of Chocolatey GUI:

```
choco install chocolateygui
```

But this command will work on an elevated command prompt, the method for which has been described previously.

Figure 10.3: *Using Windows for Installing Command Line*

During the installation process, the version number shall be displayed.

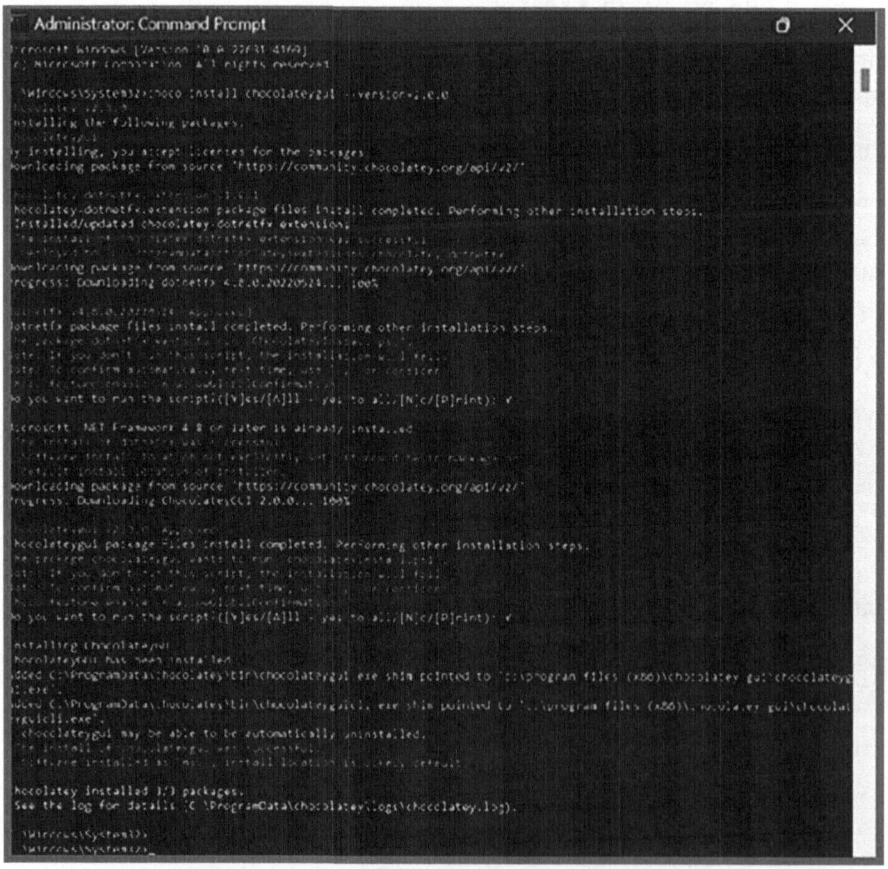

Figure 10.4: *Messages Received on Completion of Installation Process*

Chocolatey Client

With the Chocolatey (choco) client itself, these are the important things to know:

- Chocolatey is open-source.
- On release, everything is authenticode signed. Binaries and PowerShell scripts.
- Chocolatey is also verified against VirusTotal (60-70 ramped up anti-virus scanners).
- **Completely Offline:** By default choco is installed with the community package repository as a source, but that is easily adjusted to internal repositories.
- **No Data Collection/Telemetry: Chocolatey Client**
- **With the Chocolatey (choco) client itself, these are the important things to know:**
    - **Chocolatey is open-source.**
    - **On release, everything is authenticode signed. Binaries and PowerShell scripts.**
    - **Chocolatey is also verified against VirusTotal (60-70 ramped up anti-virus scanners).**
    - **Completely Offline: By default choco is installed with the community package repository as a source, but that is easily adjusted to internal repositories.**
    - **No Data Collection/Telemetry: No call home, not even in the commercial options (license tracking is honor-based) and there are organizations (or internal processes) that verify/validate (and karma) that will adjust any abuses of licensing.**

  Honor-based license means that the provider of license is not enforcing the terms and conditions by disabling the feature in the abseence of a valid license file. The license agreement is based on the maximum allowed concurrent user sessions by user type.

  Chocolatey itself is licensed under the Apache License, Version 2.0. This is an open-source license that allows you to use Chocolatey for commercial and non-commercial purposes; you can even redistribute Chocolatey's components as you wish, so long as you include the appropriate copyright notice and disclaimers.
- **No Third-Party Advertising:** We do feel that our commercial options make sense for anyone that can afford them, so you will see we lean folks to that.
- Commercial code is not open source and it will not be open sourced. There is no need for discussion, as there are many reasons we do not need to get into. Primarily, it protects our ability to ensure all infrastructure costs can be paid for.

Chocolatey Community Package Repository

Use of the community package repository is optional. The community package repository is the same thing as community.chocolatey.org packages and represents less than 5% of the existing packages in existence (nearly all are internal). Most organizations using Chocolatey do NOT use the community repository, and Chocolatey Software also DOES NOT RECOMMEND using the community repository for organizational deployments for a variety of reasons.

Here are some other important things to understand:

- Every version of every package submitted must pass through a rigorous moderation review process before it becomes publicly available (includes checks for quality, consistency, installation, and validations against VirusTotal).

  NOTE: *Only en-US installers are tested by default via Chocolatey's Package Scanner.*

- **Data Collection/Telemetry:** IP address, package, and a timestamp - this provides statistics for install counts for community folks. Google analytics for site usage: For more information on what is automatically collected for the Community Repository, see our Privacy Policy.
- **No Third-Party Advertising:** "That is right, we do not have any advertising on the site. We do not agree with the ideas behind ad-based income (but others might and that is fine). People should never be the product and we do not want to waste your time. If you see any of the tools we use (such as Disqus) put up advertisements on our pages, please notify us immediately as we might have missed a policy change with them and will need to seek alternatives."

Conclusion

In this chapter, we studied Chocolatey, a Windows software management. We also learned to set up and install Chocolatey CLI (also with the nickname choco) and then learned to extend the Chocolatey facility with PowerShell Modules (extensions).

In the next chapter, we shall learn about adding users via migrating to Oak, another deno application package.

References

1. **Extend Chocolatey With PowerShell Modules (extensions)**: https://docs.chocolatey.org/en-us/features/extensions/ Extend Chocolatey With PowerShell Modules (extensions)
2. **Security**: https://docs.chocolatey.org/en-us/information/security/

Chapter 11
Adding Users and Migrating to Oak

Introduction

At this point in the book, we have laid the foundations for a web application with a structure that will enable us to add more functionalities as we proceed. As you might have guessed by the name of this chapter, we will start by adding the middleware framework of our choice to the current web application, Oak.

At the end of this chapter, the programmer shall be conversant in using Oak, a middleware framework that uses Deno to handle HTTP.

Structure

In this chapter, we will cover the following topics:

- Introduction to Oak, a Middleware
- Static Content
- Migration of `Deno.serve()` and Fetch API

Introduction to Oak, a Middleware

A framework for middleware that uses Deno CLI, Deno Deploy, Cloudflare Workers, Node.js, and Bun to handle HTTP. Koa is the inspiration for Oak. Your frontend application and a possible database or other data sources (such as REST APIs or GraphQL APIs) are connected by Oak.

Bun, Cloudflare Workers, Node.js 16.5, and later, Deno Deploy, and a middleware framework for Deno's native HTTP server. It comes with a middleware router as well. Koa and @koa/router served as the inspiration for this middleware framework and middleware router, respectively.

Oak is a middleware framework that uses Deno to handle HTTP. Your frontend application and a possible database or other data sources (such as REST APIs or GraphQL APIs) are connected by Oak. In comparison to the native Deno HTTP server, Oak provides extra features such as JSON parser, middlewares, plugins, and a simple router.

Create a file named **server.ts** and add the following to get Oak started.

The following command may be used to Run the server:

```
import { Application } from "jsr:@oak/oak/application";
import { Router } from "jsr:@oak/oak/router";
const router = new Router();
router.get("/", (ctx) => {
  ctx.response.body = `<!DOCTYPE html>
    <html>
      <head><title>Hello oak!</title><head>
      <body>
        <h1>Hello oak!</h1>
      </body>
    </html>
  `;
});

const app = new Application();
const port = 8080;

app.use(router.routes());
app.use(router.allowedMethods());
console.log(`Server running on http://localhost:${port}`);

app.listen({ port: port });
```

```
deno run --allow-net server.ts
```

Here is some information about adding users to Deno and migrating to oak:

Oak: A framework for middleware that manages HTTP requests between Node.js and Deno. Inspired by Koa, it may be found on JSR and **deno.land/x**.

A middleware framework for Deno's built-in HTTP server is called Deno Deploy.

Making use of oak from **deno.land/x** can be done as follows:

It can be imported into a module.

Code

```
import { Application } from "https://deno.land/x/oak/mod.ts";
```

Opening and Closing the Server:

To open the server, you can use the application method **`.listen()`**. This method will start listening for requests and process the registered middleware for each request. To close the application, you can use the abort signal.

Error Handling:

You can use middleware to handle other errors.

Session ID:

A session ID is required to be saved in a cookie so incoming requests can be identified. You can modify the options used when setting or deleting the session ID in the cookie.

You can learn how to build and deploy a simple application to Deno Deploy in the Prisma documentation.

Both **`deno.land/x`** and JSR offer the Deno CLI and Deno Deploy Oak. Use **`deno.land/x`** by importing it into a module:

```
from "https://deno.land/x/oak/mod.ts" import { Application };
```

Use JSR by Importing it into a Module:

`import { Application } from "jsr:@oak/oak@14"`; Node.js oak is compatible with both JSR and npm versions of Node.js. Install the following package to use from npm:

```
@oakserver/oak@14 npm i
```

And import into a module after that:

```
import "@oakserver/oak" { Application };
```

Install the package in order to utilize it from JSR:

```
JSR I @oak/oak@14 npx
```

And import into a module after that:

```
import { Application } from "@oak/oak/application";
```

Note:

Currently, there is no support for send, websocket upgrades, or serving over TLS/HTTPS.

Furthermore, middleware does not presently have access to the Cloudflare Worker environment or execution context.

On JSR, Cloudflare Workers have access to Cloudflare Workers Oak. Add the package to your Cloudflare Worker project in order to use it:

Add **@oak/oak@14** to **npx jsr** and import into a module after that:

```
import "@oak/oak/application" from "{ Application}";
```

The Oak application manages worker fetch requests rather than listening for incoming requests like other runtimes do. A basic illustration of a server might be:

```
import { Application } from "@oak/oak/application";
const app = new Application();
app.use((ctx) => {
  ctx.response.body = "Hello CFW!";
});
export default { fetch: app.fetch };
```

Note:

Upgrades for send and websocket are not supported at this time.

Bun on JSR has access to Bun oak. Install the package to get started.

JSR I Bunx @oak/oak@14 And import into a module after that.

```
import "@oak/oak/application" from "{ Application}";
```

Context, Middleware, and Application

Managing the HTTP server, executing middleware, and resolving request processing issues are all coordinated by the Application class. **.use()** and **.listen()** are two of the most frequently utilized methods. The **.use()** function adds middleware, and the **.listen()** method launches the server and begins using the registered middleware to process requests.

Using **Hello World!** to answer each request is a simple usage.

```
import { Application } from "jsr:@oak/oak/application";
const app = new Application();
app.use((ctx) => {
  ctx.response.body = "Hello World!";
});

await app.listen({ port: 8000 });
```

After that, you would execute this script in Deno as follows:

```
> run deno with allow-net HiWorld.ts
```

Refer to the Deno handbook for additional details on installing the Deno CLI or running code under Deno.

Each middleware function has the ability to regulate the response's flow when the middleware is executed as a stack. A context and a reference to the stack's "next" method are supplied to the middleware when it is invoked.

An example that is more intricate:

```
import { Application } from "jsr:@oak/oak/application";

const app = new Application();

// Logger
app.use(async (ctx, next) => {
  await next();
  const rt = ctx.response.headers.get("X-Response-Time");
  console.log(`${ctx.request.method} ${ctx.request.url} -
${rt}`);
});

// Timing
app.use(async (ctx, next) => {
  const start = Date.now();
  await next();
  const ms = Date.now() - start;
  ctx.response.headers.set("X-Response-Time", `${ms}ms`);
});

// Hello World!
app.use((ctx) => {
  ctx.response.body = "Hello World!";
});

await app.listen({ port: 8000 });
```

To provide an HTTPS server, then the **app.listen()** options need to **include.secure** option set to true and supply a **.certFile** and a **.keyFile** options as well.

.handle() Method

The **.handle()** method is used to process requests and receive responses without having the application manage the server aspect. This is advanced usage and most users will want to use **.listen()**.

The **.handle()** method accepts up to three arguments. The first is a Request argument, and the second is a **Deno.Conn** argument. The third optional argument is a flag to indicate if the request was "secure" in the sense it originated from a TLS connection to the remote client. The method is resolved with a Response object or undefined if the **ctx.respond === true**.

An Example:

```
import { Application } from "jsr:@oak/oak/application";

const app = new Application();

app.use((ctx) => {
  ctx.response.body = "Hello World!";
});

const listener = Deno.listen({ hostname: "localhost", port: 8000
});

for await (const conn of listener) {
  (async () => {
    const requests = Deno.serveHttp(conn);
    for await (const { request, respondWith } of requests) {
      const response = await app.handle(request, conn);
      if (response) {
        respondWith(response);
      }
    }
  });
}
```

Additionally, an instance of an application includes the following properties:

`contextState:`

Specifies how a new context's state is created. If "clone" is selected, the state will be a copy of the app state. A value of "prototype" indicates that the state of the application will serve as the model for the state of the context. When "alias" is set, the state of the application and the context will both refer to the same object. When "empty" is entered, an empty object will be used to initialize the context's state.

When creating a response, the optional replacer **`function.jsonBodyReplacer`** will be used for JSON bodies.

When reading JSON bodies in a request, the optional reviver **`function.jsonBodyReviver`** will be used.

`.keys:`

Keys to be used for cookie verification and signing. An array of keys, an instance of KeyStack, or an object that has the same interface as KeyStack (such as an instance of Keygrip) can be used as the value. If only the keys are supplied, Oak will handle them using KeyStack, making key rotation simple and eliminating the need to re-sign data values.

.proxy:

This can be changed using the Application constructor options, although it defaults to false. This is meant to show that the application is using a proxy and will handle the request using X-Forwarded-Proto, X-Forwarded-Host, and X-Forwarded-For, which should give more precise details about the request.

.app:

The application that is using this middleware is referenced.

Cookies:

You can read and set cookies using this context's Cookies instance.

Request:

The Request object holds the request's specifics.

React:

It decides whether the application should send the response to the client after the middleware has finished processing. The response will be sent if it is true, and it will not be sent if it is false. Certain methods, such as. **`upgrade()`** and **`.sendEvents()`**, will set this to false, even though the default is true.

.response:

An application state record can be inferred by supplying a state object (for example, `Application({ state })`) or tightly typed by passing a generic argument when creating an **`Application()`**.

Background:

There are various characteristics of the context that is sent to middleware.

The response that is sent back to the requestor will be formed using the Response object.

The socket:

If the connection has not been changed to a web socket, this will be undefined. The **`.socket`** interface will be set if the connection has been improved.

.state:

An application state record can be inferred by supplying a state object (for example, **`Application({ state })`**) or tightly typed by passing a generic argument when creating an **`Application()`**.

There are several methods in the context that are provided to middleware:

.assert():

Makes a claim that, if untrue, raises an HTTPError. The message is the third argument, and the second argument indicates which subclass it is.

`.send()`:

Sends a file to the customer who has made the request.

`.sendEvents()`:

Provide a ServerSentEventTarget where events and messages can be broadcast to the client after converting the current connection into a server-sent event response. This is going to set .Answer "false."

`.throw()`:

Throws an HTTPError, with the message being passed as the second parameter and the subclass specified by the first.

`Upgrade()`:

A WebSocket interface should be returned after attempting to upgrade the connection to a web socket connection. This would be a Promise resolving with a std/ws web connection in an earlier version of Oak.

There are not many aliases in context, in contrast to other middleware frameworks. Only the **`.request`** extension contains the request's information, while the response's information is only located in **`.request`** and the information about the response is only located in **`.response`**.

`Request`

Details about the request are contained in the **`context.request`**. It has a number of attributes, including:

`.body`: An object that grants access to the request's body. Details on the request body API are provided in the next section.

`HasBody`: If the request has a body, set it to true; if not, set it to false. However, it does not verify whether the body is supported by the built-in body parser.

Caution: This API is not trustworthy. Because HTTP/2 is streaming, it is frequently impossible to tell whether a request has a body until you try to read the body. That behavior is likewise reflected in Deno as of Deno 1.16.1 for HTTP/1.1.

The only trustworthy method for figuring out whether a request has a body or not is to attempt to read the body.

If a body is significant in a particular context, it is advisable to try to read and digest it after determining whether it might be meaningful to you using a particular way. For instance, methods such as DELETE and OPTIONS may have a body and should be conditionally evaluated if it is relevant to your application, but GET and HEAD should never have a body.

`.headers`: An instance of Headers that contains the request's headers.

`.method`: A string that indicates the request's HTTP method.

`.originalRequest`: DEPRECATED: This will be eliminated in an upcoming Oak version.

The DOM Request instance that is being handled is the "raw" NativeServer request, which is an abstraction over the DOM Request **`object.instance`** that is being processed. Users should generally avoid using these.

`.url`: A URL instance that is derived from the request's complete URL. Instead of exposing portions of the URL on the remainder of the request object, this is used.

And a few techniques, including:

`(...types: string[]) accepts:`

It negotiates the kind of material that the answer request supports. The method returns a prioritized array of acceptable content types if no content types are supplied. The best negotiated content type is returned if content types are passed. Undefined is returned if there is no content type match.

`...encodings: string[]).acceptsEncodings:`

It negotiates the content encoding that the response request supports. The method returns a prioritized array of approved encodings if no encodings are given. The best negotiated encoding is returned if encodings are passed.

If no encodings match, undefined is returned.

`.acceptsLanguages(...languages: string[]):`

It negotiates the language that the client can comprehend where preference is given to a locale variant. The method returns a prioritized array of languages understood if no encodings are supplied. The best negotiated language is returned if languages are passed. Undefined is returned if there are no languages that match.

Request Body: Crucial

With Oak v13 and beyond, this API underwent considerable changes. Since Oak was established in 2018, the prior API had developed naturally and did not correspond to any other widely used API. Developers who are new to Oak should be more accustomed to the API introduced in version 13, which is more in line with the Fetch API's Request method of handling the body.

The API for the oak **`request .body`** is inspired by the Fetch API's Request but with some added functionality. The context's **`request.body`** is an instance of an object which provides several properties, such as:

- `.has`
- `.stream`

The body can be read in Uint8Array chunks using a ReadableStream<Uint8Array>. This is comparable to a Fetch API Request's.body property.

`Utilized`

If the body has been used, set it to true; if not, put it to false.

It also employs a number of techniques:

> **`arrayBuffer()`:** Resolves using an ArrayBuffer containing the body's contents, if any. It is appropriate for managing and reading binary data.
>
> **`Blob()`:** Resolves with a blob containing the body's contents. It is appropriate for managing and reading binary data.
>
> **`form()`:** Resolves with a **`URLSearchParams`** which has been decoded from the contents of a body. This is appropriate for a body with a content type of application/x-www-form-urlencoded.
>
> **`formData()`:** Resolves with a FormData instance that has been decoded from the contents of a body. This is appropriate for a body with a content type of multipart/form-data.
>
> **`json()`:** Resolves with the data from the body parsed as JSON. If a jsonBodyReviver has been specified in the application, it will be used when parsing the JSON.
>
> **`text()`:** Resolves with a string that represents the contents of the body.
>
> **`type()`:** Attempts to provide guidance on how the body is encoded which can be used to determine what method to use to decode the body. The method returns a string that represents the interpreted body type:

`Reaction`

Information about the response that will be returned to the requestor is contained in the **`context.response`**. It has a number of attributes:

> **`.body`:** The response's body, which is frequently managed by the automated response body processing is described in the following section.

Headers

The response's headers are contained in a Headers instance.

`.status`: The response will be returned with an HTTP Status code. Oak will default to 200 OK if there is a .body and 404 Not Found otherwise if this is not specified before replying.

.type: An extension or media type to set the response's Content-Type header. To describe the body, for instance, you can use text/plain or txt.

And a few techniques, including:

.redirect(alt?: string | URL, url?: string | URL | REDIRECT_BACK):

A way to make rerouting the response to a different URL easier. Unless the status is already 3XX, it will set the location header to the provided URL and the status to 302 Found.

When the url has the symbol **REDIRECT_BACK**, it means that the request's Referer header should be used as the direction; if the Referer is not set, the alt is the alternate location. The redirect will go to/if neither the alt nor the Referer are set. If the requestor supports it, a basic HTML or a text body will be set explaining they are being redirected.

with(response: Response) and .with(body?: BodyInit, init?: ResponseInit):

This sets the response to a web standard Response. Note that this will ignore/override any other information set on the response by other middleware including things such as headers or cookies to be set.

Automatic Response Body Handling

When the response Content-Type is not set in the headers of the .response, oak will automatically try to determine the appropriate Content-Type. First, it will look at **.response.type**. If assigned, it will try to resolve the appropriate media type based on treating the value of .type as either the media type or resolving the media type based on an extension. For example, if .type was set to "html," then the Content-Type will be set to "text/html."

If .type is not set with a value, then oak will inspect the value of **.response.body**.

Oak will determine whether the value is a string or not, and if it appears to be HTML, it will set the Content-Type to text/html; if not, it will set it to text/plain. The value will be given to **JSON.stringify()** with the Content-Type set to **application/json** if it is an object other than a Uint8Array, a Deno.Reader, or null.

It will be forced to a string and handled as text if the body type is a number, bigint, or symbol.

The function will be called without any arguments if the value of the body is a function. The resolved result will be treated as described previously if the function's return value is promise-like. If the value of the body is a function, the function will be called with no arguments.

If the return value of the function is promise like, that will be await, and the resolved value will be processed as above. If the value is not promise like, it will be processed as above.

Turning On the Server

The Way in Which it is Applied

The server is opened using **listen()**, which also begins listening for requests and executing the registered middleware for each one. When the server closes, this method gives back a promise.

The.**addEventListener()** method can be used to listen for the "listen" event that the application will fire once the server is open, prior to it beginning to handle requests. For instance:

```
import { Application } from "jsr:@oak/oak/application";

const app = new Application();

app.addEventListener("listen", ({ hostname, port, secure }) => {
  console.log(
    `Listening on: ${secure ? "https://" : "http://"}${
      hostname ?? "localhost"
    }:${port}`,
  );
});

// register some middleware

await app.listen({ port: 80 });
```

Shutting Down the Server

The application has the ability to send an abort signal if you wish to end it. Here is an illustration of how to use the signal:

```
import { Application } from "jsr:@oak/oak/application";

const app = new Application();

const controller = new AbortController();
const { signal } = controller;

// Add some middleware using `app.use()`

const listenPromise = app.listen({ port: 8000, signal });
```

```
// In order to close the server...
controller.abort();

// Listen will stop listening for requests and the promise will
resolve...
await listenPromise;
// and you can do something after the close to shutdown
```

Error Handling

More faults that can be handled by middleware. While capturing failures, other middleware is being executed. Thus, the operation of an error-handling middleware that offers a controlled reaction to mistakes would be as follows:

```
import { Application } from "jsr:@oak/oak/application";
import { isHttpError } from "jsr:@oak/commons/http_errors";
import { Status } from "jsr:@oak/commons/status";

const app = new Application();

app.use(async (ctx, next) => {
  try {
    await next();
  } catch (err) {
    if (isHttpError(err)) {
      switch (err.status) {
        case Status.NotFound:
          // handle NotFound
          break;
        default:
          // handle other statuses
      }
    } else {
      // rethrow if you can't handle the error
      throw err;
    }
  }
});
```

The application will catch uncaught middleware exceptions. The application extends Deno's global EventTarget, and it will receive an EventError if there are uncaught failures in the middleware or response sending. You would add an event handler to the application instance in order to listen for these errors.

```
import { Application } from "jsr:@oak/oak/application";

const app = new Application();
```

```
app.addEventListener("error", (evt) => {
  // Will log the thrown error to the console.
  console.log(evt.error);
});

app.use((ctx) => {
  // Will throw a 500 on every request.
  ctx.throw(500);
});

await app.listen({ port: 80 });
```

The Router class creates middleware that an application can utilize to enable routing according to the request's pathname.

Simple Use

The example that follows provides a RESTful service of a book map, where the book with ID "**1**" is returned by **http://localhost:8000/book/1** and an array of books is returned by **http://localhost:8000/book/**.

```
import { Application } from "jsr:@oak/oak/application";
import { Router } from "jsr:@oak/oak/router";

const books = new Map<string, any>();
books.set("1", {
  id: "1",
  title: "The Hound of the Baskervilles",
  author: "Conan Doyle, Arthur",
});

const router = new Router();
router
  .get("/", (context) => {
    context.response.body = "Hello world!";
  })
  .get("/book", (context) => {
    context.response.body = Array.from(books.values());
  })
  .get("/book/:id", (context) => {
    if (books.has(context?.params?.id)) {
      context.response.body = books.get(context.params.id);
    }
  });

const app = new Application();
```

```
app.use(router.routes());
app.use(router.allowedMethods());

await app.listen({ port: 8000 });
```

Path-to-regexp is used to transform a route passed to a regular expression, meaning that parameters expressed in the pattern will be changed. With its sophisticated usage, path-to-regexp can produce intricate patterns that can be utilized for matching. If you have sophisticated use cases, read through that library's documentation.

Most of the time, typescript magic automatically determines the type of **context.params** from the path template string. However, this could not produce the right outcome in more complicated situations. If so, you can use the router to alter the **type.get<RouteParams>**, where the explicit type for **context.params** is **RouteParams.**

Stacking Routers

It supports nesting routers. Both **http://localhost:8000/forums/oak/posts** and **http://localhost:8000/forums/oak/posts/nested-routers** are addressed in the example as follows:

```
import { Application } from "jsr:@oak/oak/application";
import { Router } from "jsr:@oak/oak/router";

const posts = new Router()
  .get("/", (ctx) => {
    ctx.response.body = `Forum: ${ctx.params.forumId}`;
  })
  .get("/:postId", (ctx) => {
    ctx.response.body =
      `Forum: ${ctx.params.forumId}, Post: ${ctx.params.postId}`;
  });

const forums = new Router().use(
  "/forums/:forumId/posts",
  posts.routes(),
  posts.allowedMethods(),
);

await new Application().use(forums.routes()).listen({ port: 8000
});
```

Static Content

The function **send()** is designed to serve static content as part of a middleware function. In the most straightforward usage, a root and requests provided to the function are fulfilled with files from the local file system relative to the root from the requested path.

A basic usage would look something like this:

```
import { Application } from "jsr:@oak/oak/application";

const app = new Application();

app.use(async (context, next) => {
  try {
    await context.send({
      root: `${Deno.cwd()}/examples/static`,
      index: "index.html",
    });
  } catch {
    await next();
  }
});

await app.listen({ port: 8000 });
```

send() automatically supports features such as providing ETag and Last-Modified headers in the response as well as processing If-None-Match and If-Modified-Since headers in the request. This means when serving up static content, clients will be able to rely upon their cached versions of assets instead of re-downloading them.

ETag Support

The **send()** method automatically supports generating an ETag header for static assets. The header allows the client to determine if it needs to re-download an asset or not, but it can be useful to calculate ETags for other scenarios.

There is a middleware function that assesses the **context.reponse.body** and determines if it can create an ETag header for that body type, and if so, sets the ETag header on the response. Basic usage would look something like this:

```
import { Application } from "jsr:@oak/oak/application";
import { factory } from "jsr:@oak/oak/etag";

const app = new Application();

app.use(factory());

// ... other middleware for the application
```

There is also a function which retrieves an entity for a given context based on what is logical to read into memory which can be passed to the etag calculate that is part of the Deno std library:

```
import { Application } from "jsr:@oak/oak/application";
import { getEntity } from "jsr:@oak/oak/etag";
import { calculate } from "jsr:@std/http/etag";

const app = new Application();

// The context.response.body has already been set...

app.use(async (ctx) => {
  const entity = await getEntity(ctx);
  if (entity) {
    const etag = await calculate(entity);
  }
});
```

Migration of `Deno.serve()` and Fetch API

There are a few characteristics of Oak that can help if you are switching from **`Deno.serve()`** or modifying code made for the web standard Fetch API Request and Response **`ctx.request.source`**. This will be configured as a Fetch API Request when running under Deno, providing direct access to the initial request **`ctx.response.with()`**. Using the supplied BodyInit and ResponseInit, this method will either generate a new response or accept a Fetch API response. Additionally, this will complete the response and disregard any settings that might have been made on the Oak response. You can use both **`middelware/serve#route()`** and **`middleware/serve#serve()`** middleware generators to modify code that functions more similarly to **`Deno.serve()`**, which offers a Fetch API Request and anticipates the handler to resolve with a Fetch API Response.

An Example of Using `serve()` with `Application.prototype.use()`:

```
import { Application } from "jsr:@oak/oak/application";
import { serve } from "jsr:@oak/oak/serve";

const app = new Application();

app.use(serve((req, ctx) => {
  console.log(req.url);
  return new Response("Hello world!");
}));

app.listen();
```

A similar solution works with **`route()`** where the context contains the information about the router, like the params:

```
import { Application } from "jsr:@oak/oak/application";
import { Router } from "jsr:@oak/oak/router";
import { route } from "jsr:@oak/oak/serve";

const app = new Application;

const router = new Router();

router.get("/books/:id", route((req, ctx) => {
  console.log(ctx.params.id);
  return Response.json({ title: "hello world", id: ctx.params.id
});
}));

app.use(router.routes());

app.listen();
```

Examining

An object called testing, which contains some tools for testing any Oak middleware you might write, is exported by the mod.ts. For more details, see Testing with Oak.

A few of the modules are straight adaptations of other modules. Their separate copyrights and permissions have been maintained. The MIT License governs all of the modules, including those that have been directly modified.

Conclusion

In this chapter, we have been introduced to Oak, a middleware, and further learned about its static content. At last, we learned how to migrate between **`Deno.serve()`** and Fetch API.

In the next chapter, we are going to learn about testing deno codes. Deno provides a built-in test runner for writing and running tests in both JavaScript and TypeScript.

CHAPTER 12
Testing in Deno

Introduction

An essential component of the software lifecycle is **testing**. It can be used to express needs clearly, save time, or just give us confidence when we rewrite and refactor later. Whatever the reason, one thing is for sure: tests will be written. We firmly think that software design heavily relies on testing. Easy-to-test code is probably easy-to-maintain.

We really believe that testing is essential, so we could not claim that this is a comprehensive guide to Deno without knowing about it.

Structure

We are going to learn about the following topics in this chapter:

- Topics in Testing Procedure
- Writing Tests
- Running Tests
- Procedures for Testing
- To Run Specific Tests or Groups of Tests
- Reporters to Format Test Output
- Time-Faking, Stubbing, Mocking, and Spying (Test Doubles)
- Coverage Flag
- Documentation Tests
- Sanitizers
- Writing an Integration Test
- Web Server Testing
- How to Test the Client for the API
- Composing our Initial Exam in Deno
- Learn How to Use a Deno

Topics in Testing Procedure

A few factors should be kept in mind before we begin writing our test. The most important of them is, why are we testing?

Specifying a Test

To create a test, Deno.test needs to be called with a test name and a test function (at minimum).

A few factors should be kept in mind before we begin writing our test. The most important of them is, why are we testing?

While there may be more than one response to this inquiry, the majority will indicate that the code is functioning. We can agree with both of these viewpoints. We could also argue that using them offers flexibility in terms of refactoring or that it is very advantageous to value brief feedback cycles throughout development. The latter does not really apply to us because we did not develop a test before putting these features into use.

Throughout this chapter, we will maintain these goals in mind. We will write our first test in this class. We will add tests to the application we created in the earlier chapters. Both integration and unit tests will be written.

Integration tests will evaluate the interactions between the application's various components. The unit tests test layers in isolation.

On a scale, integration tests are closer to the user, whereas unit tests are closer to the code. Additionally, there are end-to-end tests on the user side. These tests, which we will not discuss in this chapter, simulate user behavior to test the program.

Testing benefits greatly from several of the principles we employed in the actual application development, such as dependency injection and inversion of control. All we need to do now is mimic those dependencies in tests because we built our code by injecting all of its dependencies. Keep in mind that code that is simple to test is typically simple to maintain.

Writing tests for the business logic will be our first task. Our API currently lacks a lot of business logic because it is so basic. Due to the simplicity of MuseumController, the majority of it runs on UserController. The latter will be our first focus.

We will need to utilize the following in order to write tests in Deno:

1. The test runner for Deno
2. The Deno namespace's test function
3. The Deno standard library's assertion methods

The core team distributes and maintains all of these as part of Deno. There are other additional libraries available in the community that can be utilized in tests. Since it works perfectly and enables us to write clearly, we will use what Deno provides by default.

Writing Tests

The **`Deno.test()`** function is used to define a test in Deno. Here are a few instances:

```
my_test.ts
import { assertEquals } from "jsr:@std/assert";

Deno.test("simple test", () => {
  const x = 1 + 2;
  assertEquals(x, 3);
});

import { delay } from "jsr:@std/async";

Deno.test("async test", async () => {
  const x = 1 + 2;
  await delay(100);
  assertEquals(x, 3);
});

Deno.test({
  name: "read file test",
  permissions: { read: true },
  fn: () => {
    const data = Deno.readTextFileSync("./somefile.txt");
    assertEquals(data, "expected content");
  },
});
```

The Deno standard library offers an expect method that can be used in place of assertEquals if you would rather utilize assertions in a "jest-like" fashion:

```
my_test.ts
import { expect } from "jsr:@std/expect";
import { add } from "./add.js";

Deno.test("add function adds two numbers correctly", () => {
  const result = add(2, 3);
  expect(result).toBe(5);
});
```

Running Tests

Use the deno test subcommand to execute your tests. [1]

This subcommand will automatically locate and run all tests in the current directory (recursively) that match the glob `{*_,*.,}test` if it is run without a file or directory name `.{ts, tsx, mts, js, mjs, jsx}`.

```
# Execute every test in every subdirectory and the current
directory.

# Execute my_test.ts alone and deno test my_test.ts.
```

Use the deno test subcommand to execute your tests. [1]

This subcommand will automatically locate and run all tests in the current directory (recursively) that match the glob `{*_,*.,}test` if it is run without a file or directory name `.{ts, tsx, mts, js, mjs, jsx}`.

```
# Execute test modules concurrently using deno test --parallel

# Add more arguments that are visible in `Deno.args` to the test
file.
My_test.ts deno test -- -e --foo --bar

# To ensure that the last test above passes, provide deno access
to read from the filesystem. # allow-read my_test.ts
```

Procedures for Testing

Additionally, Deno provides test phases, which let you divide tests into more manageable chunks. This is helpful for test setup and takedown procedures:

```
Async (t) => { Deno.test("database operations")
  using db = await openDatabase();
  await t.step("insert user", async () => {
    // Insert user logic
  });
  await t.step("insert book", async () => {
    // Insert book logic
  });
});
```

To Run Specific Tests or Groups of Tests

Deno allows you to run specific tests or groups of tests using the --filter option on the command line. This option accepts either a string or a pattern to match test names.

Filtering does not affect steps; if a test name matches the filter, all of its steps are executed.

- **Filtering by Command Line**

  With Deno, you may use the **`--filter`** option on the command line to execute particular tests or sets of tests. To match test names, this option takes a pattern or a string. Filtering has no effect on steps; all of a test's steps are carried out if its name matches the filter.

  Examine the following tests:

  `"my-test"; "test-1"; "test-2"; "test-1", () => {}; Deno.test ("my-test", () => {});`

  String-based filtering Go to heading#

  Use the following to execute any tests whose names include the term "my":

  `filter "my" tests with deno test --filter`

  Due to the term **`"my"`** being present, this command will run **`my-test`**.

- **Pattern-Based Filtering**

  To execute tests that adhere to a particular pattern, use:

  `tests/deno test --filter "/test-*\d/"`

  Because **`test-1`** and **`test-2`** fit the pattern **`test-*`** followed by a digit, this command will execute them.

  Similar to JavaScript's regular expression syntax, wrap your filter value in forward slashes / to show that you are using a pattern (regular expression).

  The configuration file's inclusion and exclusion of test files go to heading#.

  By defining which paths to include or exclude in the Deno configuration file, you can additionally filter tests.

  For instance, if you wish to exclude everything in out/: and only test `src/fetch_test.ts and src/signal_test.ts.`

```
{
  "test": {
    "include": [
      "src/fetch_test.ts",
      "src/signal_test.ts"
    ]
  }
}
```

Or more likely:

```
{
  "test": {
    "exclude": ["out/"]
  }
}
```

- **Test Definition Selection**

  Within the test criteria itself, Deno offers two choices for test selection: disregarding tests and concentrating on particular tests.

- **Disregarding or Avoiding** The ignore boolean in the test specification allows you to disregard specific tests under particular circumstances. The test will not be run if ignore is set to true. For instance, this is helpful if you want a test to only run on a particular operating system.

  ```
  Deno.test({
    name: "do macOS feature",
    ignore: Deno.build.os !== "darwin", // This test will be
  ignored if not running on macOS
    fn() {
      // do MacOS feature here
    },
  });
  ```

If you want to ignore a test without passing any conditions, you can use the ignore() function from the **`Deno.test`** object.

```
Deno.test.ignore("my test", () => {
  // your test code
});
```

- **Only Run Specific Tests**

  You can use the only option if you wish to concentrate on one test and disregard the others. This instructs the test runner to execute the tests with only the true option selected. This option can be set for more than one test. However, as this is meant to be a temporary debugging solution, if any test is tagged with only, the entire test run would always fail.

  ```
  Deno.test.only("my test", () => {
    // some test code
  });
  ```

  or

  ```
  Deno.test({
    name: "Focus on this test only",
    only: true, // Only this test will run
  ```

```
    fn() {
      // test complicated stuff here
    },
  });
```

Failing Fast

You can use the **--fail-fast** flag when running a lengthy test suite if you want it to terminate on the first failure.

```
deno test—fail-quick
```

As a result, following the initial test failure, the test runner will terminate.

Reporters to Format Test Output

- Deno comes with three built-in reporters: **beautiful (default):** Offers an output that is readable and comprehensive.
- **dot:** Provides a succinct output that is helpful for viewing test findings rapidly.
- **JUnit:** When integrating with CI/CD technologies, junit's output in JUnit XML format is helpful. The **-- reporter** flag allows you to choose which reporter to use.

1. **Use the Default Pretty Reporter**

   ```
   deno test
   ```

2. **Use the Dot Reporter for Concise Output**

   ```
   deno test --reporter=dot
   ```

3. **Use the JUnit Reporter**

   ```
   deno test --reporter=junit
   ```

Additionally, you can use the **--junit-**path flag to send the JUnit report to a file while still receiving output in the terminal that is accessible by humans: **--junit-path=./report.xml deno test**

Time-mocking, Stubbing, Mocking, and Spying (Test Doubles)

A collection of functions from the Deno Standard Library can assist you in creating tests that use mocking, stubbing, and spying.

Spying, mocking, stubbing, and faking are all types of test doubles used in software testing to simulate the behavior of real objects.

- **Spies**: Wrap around the real object and observe its behavior. Spies record information based on how they were called. For example, an email service spy might record how many messages it was sent.
- **Mocks**: Similar to stubs, but mocks are more interaction-based. Mocks allow you to verify that a method was called, and you can change the behavior of the mocked interface based on scenarios.
- **Stubs:** Return predetermined responses to calls made during the test. Stubs are used when you do not want to involve objects that would answer with real data or have undesirable side effects.
- **Fakes:** Have a complete working implementation, but the implementation is a shortcut that makes them incapable of production.

Test doubles are used to isolate the component under test and ensure that the tests are not affected by external dependencies. Understanding the differences between these types of test doubles can help you improve the effectiveness of your unit tests.

Coverage Flag

If you start the deno test with the coverage flag, Deno will gather test coverage into a directory for your code. High accuracy is ensured because this coverage data is obtained straight from the V8 JavaScript engine. The deno coverage tool can then be used to further transform this from the internal format into popular formats such as lcov.

Development Driven by Behavior You can combine tests and add setup/teardown hooks that are used by other JavaScript testing frameworks, such as Jasmine, Jest, and Mocha, by using the **`@std/testing/bdd`** module. Several similar tests are grouped together in a block created by the describe function. An individual test case is registered by the it function. For instance:

```
import { describe, it } from "jsr:@std/testing/bdd";
import { expect } from "jsr:@std/expect";
import { add } from "./add.js";

describe("add function", () => {
  it("adds two numbers correctly", () => {
    const result = add(2, 3);
    expect(result).toBe(5);
  });

  it("handles negative numbers", () => {
    const result = add(-2, -3);
    expect(result).toBe(-5);
  });
});
```

Documentation Tests

Deno supports both type-checking and evaluating your documentation examples. This makes sure that examples within your documentation are up-to-date and working.

The basic idea is this:

```
/**
 * # Examples
 *
 * ```ts
 * import { assertEquals } from "jsr:@std/assert/equals";
 *
 * const sum = add(1, 2);
 * assertEquals(sum, 3);
 * ```
 */
export function add(a: number, b: number): number {
  return a + b;
}
```

Code blocks are denoted by triple backticks, and the language is identified by the language identification attribute, which could be any of the following:

- js
- JavaScript
- ts;
- cjs;
- jsx;
- mjs
- Typescript
- tsx
- cts
- mts

The media type of the source document from which the code block is retrieved is used to determine the language if no language identifier is provided.

```
--doc example.ts deno test
```

This example will be extracted by the aforementioned command, which will then transform it into a mock test case that looks like this:

```
example.ts$4-10.ts
      import { assertEquals } from "jsr:@std/assert/equals";
      import { add } from "file:///path/to/example.ts";
```

```
Deno.test("example.ts$4-10.ts", async () => {
  const sum = add(1, 2);
  assertEquals(sum, 3);
});
```

Then run it as a standalone module living in the same directory as the module being documented.

If You Want to Type-Check Only

If you want to type-check your code snippets in JSDoc and markdown files without actually running them, you can use deno check command with **--doc** option (for JSDoc) or with **--doc-only** option (for markdown) instead.

Exported Items are Automatically Imported

Looking at the generated test code previously, you will notice that it includes the import statement to import the add function even though the original code block does not have it. When documenting a module, any items exported from the module are automatically included in the generated test code using the same name.

Let us say we have the following module:

```
example.ts
      /**
       * # Examples
       *
       * ```ts
       * import { assertEquals } from "jsr:@std/assert/equals";
       *
       * const sum = add(ONE, getTwo());
       * assertEquals(sum, 3);
       * ```
       */
      export function add(a: number, b: number): number {
        return a + b;
      }

      export const ONE = 1;
      export default function getTwo() {
        return 2;
      }
```

This will be converted to the following test case:

```
example.ts$4-10.ts
import { assertEquals } from "jsr:@std/assert/equals";
import { add, ONE }, getTwo from "file:///path/to/example.ts";
```

```
Deno.test("example.ts$4-10.ts", async () => {
  const sum = add(ONE, getTwo());
  assertEquals(sum, 3);
});
```

Skipping Code Blocks

You can skip the evaluation of code blocks by adding the ignore attribute.

````
/**
 * This code block will not be run.
 *
 * ```ts ignore
 * await sendEmail("deno@example.com");
 * ```
 */
export async function sendEmail(to: string) {
  // send an email to the given address...
}
````

Sanitizers

The test runner offers several sanitizers to ensure that the test behaves in a reasonable and expected way.

- **Resource Sanitizer**

  The resource sanitizer ensures that all I/O resources created during a test are closed, to prevent leaks.

  I/O resources are things such as Deno.FsFile handles, network connections, fetch bodies, timers, and other resources that are not automatically garbage collected.

  You should always close resources when you are done with them. For example,

To Close a File:

```
const file = await Deno.open("hello.txt");

// Do something with the file
file.close(); // <- Always close the file when you are done with it
```

To Close a Network Connection:

```
const conn = await Deno.connect({ hostname: "example.com", port: 80 });
// Do something with the connection
conn.close(); // <- Always close the connection when you are done with it
```

To Close a Fetch Body:

```
const response = await fetch("https://example.com");
// Do something with the response
await response.body?.cancel(); // <- Always cancel the body when
you are done with it, if you didn't consume it otherwise
```

This sanitizer is enabled by default, but can be disabled in this test with sanitizeResources: false:

```
Deno.test({
  name: "leaky resource test",
  async fn() {
    await Deno.open("hello.txt");
  },
  sanitizeResources: false,
});
```

- **Async Operation Sanitizer**

  The async operation sanitizer ensures that all async operations started in a test are completed before the test ends. This is important because if an async operation is not awaited, the test will end before the operation is completed, and the test will be marked as successful even if the operation may have actually failed.

  You should always await all async operations in your tests. For example:

```
Deno.test({
  name: "async operation test",
  async fn() {
    await new Promise((resolve) => setTimeout(resolve, 1000));
  },
});
```

  This sanitizer is enabled by default, but can be disabled with `sanitizeOps: false`:

```
Deno.test({
  name: "leaky operation test",
  fn() {
    crypto.subtle.digest(
      "SHA-256",
      new TextEncoder().encode("a".repeat(100000000)),
    );
  },
  sanitizeOps: false,
});
```

- **Exit Sanitizer**

  In order to prevent a false test success, the exit sanitizer makes sure that the code being tested does not call **`Deno.exit()`**. sanitizeExit: false can be used to disable this sanitizer, which is enabled by default.

```
Deno.test({
  name: "false success",
  fn() {
    Deno.exit(0);
  },
  sanitizeExit: false,
});

// This test never runs, because the process exits during "false
success" test
Deno.test({
  name: "failing test",
  fn() {
    throw new Error("this test fails");
  },
});
```

- **Snapshot Testing**

  A snapshot module in the Deno Standard Library enables programmers to create tests by contrasting values with reference snapshots. These snapshots, which are kept with the test files, are serialized versions of the original data.

  With just a small amount of code, snapshot testing makes it possible to find a variety of flaws. It is especially useful when the assertions a test makes are likely to vary frequently or when it is challenging to exactly explain what should be claimed without needing an excessive amount of code.

Writing an Integration Test

To ensure that our controller was functioning, we used a mocked instance of the repository in our first unit test, which we had previously developed.

That test is quite helpful in identifying MuseumController errors, but it does not provide any insight into how effectively the controller integrates with the repository.

Testing how various components integrate with one another is the goal of integration tests.

MuseumController and MuseumRepository Integration Tests

The integration test that evaluates MuseumController and MuseumRepository will be written by us. These tests will aid us later on in identifying any issues between these two classes because they closely resemble what occurs when the application runs.

Let us begin:

The first test case should be added to the **museums.test.ts** file, which should be created under **src/museums** for this module's integration tests.

This time, it should utilize an instance of the repository rather than a fake one to verify if it is feasible to obtain all the museums.

Web Server Testing

Discover how to build a web module and check to see if it is able to connect to the web server.

We have already built an integration test and a unit test, but we have not yet written any tests for the web portion of our program, which uses HTTP. Now, we will discover how to test the web layer's logic independently, without the need for any other modules.

Thus far, we have learned how to test various application components. The web layer still lacks tests, so we began with the business logic, which examines how it interacted with the modules that dealt with persistence (the repository).

It is true that those tests are crucial, but we can also agree that the user will not have access to any of that reasoning if the web layer fails.

In this lesson, we will do just that. To make sure that the web unit is functioning, we will launch our web server, simulate its dependencies, and send it a few queries.

Writing a Unit Test for a Web Module

First, let us create the unit test for the web module by doing the following:

Visit **src/web** and make a file named **web.test.ts**.

We must now return to the **createServer** function in **src/web/index.ts** and export the Application object it generates in **src/web/index.ts** in order to test the web server:

Using the API Client to Test the Application

Discover how to test any program that has a client API embedded into it.

How to Test the Client for the API

When we first developed our JavaScript client, we noted that one benefit of having it in the API code base was that it made it simple to write tests to ensure the client and API functioned properly together. We will show you how to achieve this in this lesson. We will utilize the API client we made for these tests rather than fetch and raw requests.

- Production traffic replication
- Postman

When we give our users an API client, it is our duty to ensure that it integrates perfectly with our application. Having a comprehensive test suite that tests the client's integration with the API in addition to its functionality is one way to ensure this. We will address the latter in the next section.

How to Test the Client for the API

We will use one of the API client's features and write a test to ensure it functions. There will be some parallels between these and the tests we previously wrote, to reiterate. We will duplicate the reasoning in the PR.

API Testing Methodologies

In this section, you will be presented with five testing methodologies that can be combined to create the most efficient pipeline, in order to ensure comprehensive coverage of your entire API.

- **Testing for Functionality**

  Functional testing is essential to confirming the functionality of APIs. Unit tests and integration tests are two examples of this, where the capabilities of the code execution are prioritized over efficiency.

  Because functional tests are the fastest and most effective, they are frequently the first kind of testing you use. Functional testing has the disadvantage of providing little to no information about how code changes really perform; for this reason, non-functional testing is also necessary.

- **Non-Functional Examination**

  You can begin investigating the features' performance and stability after making sure they all function as intended. Non-functional testing can confirm your application's capabilities and responses in a variety of scenarios.

  The ability of your application to manage a specific load can be confirmed with the use of API load testing. Its ability to manage traffic spikes can be confirmed by stress testing. Before releasing any modifications to production, performance testing as a whole offers valuable and significant insights into the operation of your application, such as assessing response times, throughput, and resource utilization.

- **Examining Security**

  Perhaps the most crucial elements of an application to test are its functionality and performance, but security should not be disregarded. Pen testing, another name for penetration testing, is a type of testing that mimics assaults on a system to evaluate its security. These days, automated solutions such as Snyk can help you get by. By examining the code and its dependencies, Snyk is a tool that assists in identifying vulnerabilities and automatically fixing them.

- **Examining Regression**

  Testing new features is vital, but it is possibly even more critical to make sure that regression—the term for declining performance—is not affecting already-existing features.

  Regression testing is the process of rerunning previously completed tests in your pipeline to make sure that new features are not being adversely affected by modifications. It may also entail comparing performance measurements gathered during a stress test with those recorded in production, such as Transactions-Per-Second (TPS).

  Regression testing is a crucial component of preserving good quality and dependability as your API develops, regardless of how you choose to implement it.

- **Replication of Production Traffic**

  Production traffic replication, a quicker option than traffic mirroring, is one of the most effective ways to use all of the aforementioned approaches. Using this method, real-world traffic from your production system is captured and then replayed in your testing environment.

  Since you will always be using the most recent test data, this is the only reliable method of testing your API in real-world scenarios. Additionally, since traffic is taken straight from production, you can be certain that you are testing every aspect of the API that is currently in use.

  For creating and executing tests in TypeScript and JavaScript, Deno offers an integrated test runner. This eliminates the need to install extra dependencies or tools and makes it simple to make sure your code is dependable and performs as intended. By giving you fine-grained control over permissions for every test, the deno test runner makes sure that the code does not do anything unexpected.

You can utilize alternative test runners from the JS ecosystem, such as Jest, Mocha, or AVA, with Deno in addition to the built-in one. However, we shall not discuss this in this document.

Advantages of Testing APIs

The advantages of API testing are indisputable, and it is an essential component of contemporary software development processes. Among these advantages are:

- **Quality Assurance**: By allowing teams to consistently make sure their API operates as intended, API testing helps maintain customer trust and safeguard the company's brand.
- **Early Problem Identification and Fixing**: Teams can find flaws as soon as they are introduced by using a shift-left approach to API testing. This helps teams stay on schedule and increases the predictability of the development process.
- **Conserving Resources**: An increasing number of teams are automating their approach to API testing, which frees up team members' time to concentrate on creativity.
- **Quick Iteration**: A lot of teams use CI/CD pipelines to run their API tests, allowing them to automatically verify each code change before it is put into production. This method lowers the chance of issues while supporting more frequent releases.

The Top Five Greatest Tools for Testing APIs [3]

We have listed some of the most well-liked API testing tools as follows, along with information on their advantages and best applications.

The Postman

Postman is one of the most popular API testing tools–and for good reason. Its collaboration platform has gathered more than 20 million developers working across 500,000 companies across the world, allowing them to streamline collaboration and simplify every step of API building.

Postman's user-friendliness is one of its key benefits. It is easy to set up and cheaply priced, with the basic bundle costing only $12. Postman makes it simple to test method calls and distribute APIs in a timely manner. Indeed, users have the ability to store collections and distribute them among their peers. Because of its main capabilities, many web developers consider it to be an indispensable tool.

The User Interface of Postman

Postman is more helpful for promptly initiating local requests or maintaining a systematic collection of the requests connected to your application, while some users have found the reporting features to be a little lacking. Using Postman may become time-consuming as you start automated API testing, particularly continuous testing.

While tools such as Apache JMeter might be more appropriate for performance testing, Postman is better suited for functional testing.

When it comes to sharing with people who are not in the workspace, there is a lot of room for improvement, even though the sharing features within a single team are excellent. Because of the platform's complexity, some of its more sophisticated functions are essentially "hidden" until you progress far enough down the learning curve.

Taking everything into account, Postman is a good option for an API testing tool. Although the platform's getting started guide is not as comprehensive as you might want, there is a wealth of knowledge available online to assist you become proficient with the tool.

Using the platform's mock servers, Postman is a great method to quickly put up mock APIs, enabling developers to design and test as they go. Since it is simple to build mock servers using API schemas, you can submit requests in Postman even if you do not have a production API ready to use. However, there is no built-in method for seeding data according to production traffic.

The platform's primary attraction is unquestionably its cooperation features, which include the capacity to swiftly develop and implement API requests. If you need an easy way to share API requests or an easy alternative to running curl commands, Postman is likely to be a good choice. But in terms of API test automation, you may find another tool more suitable.

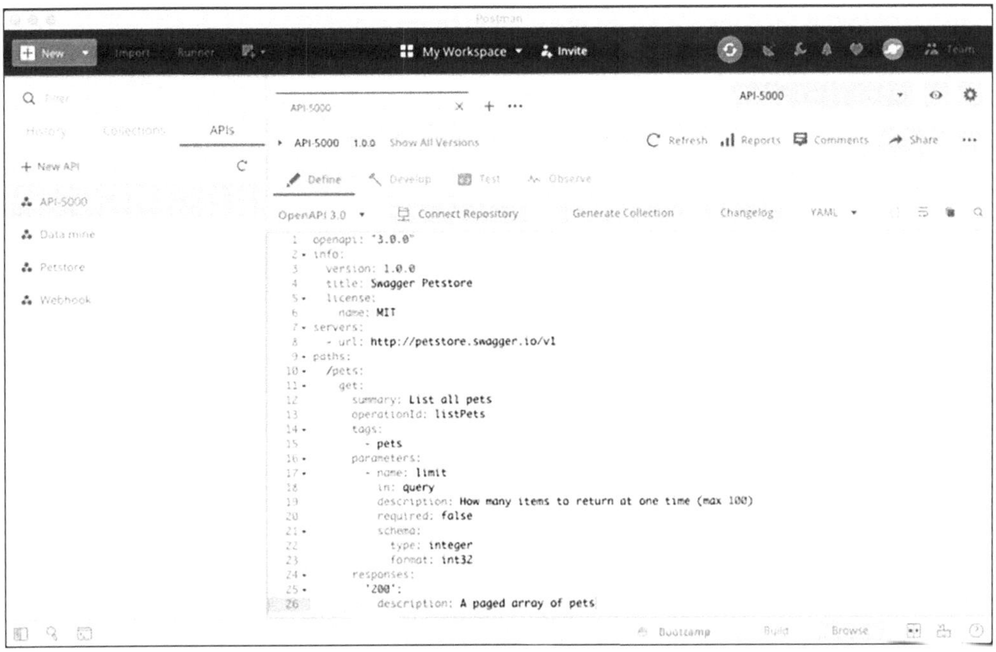

Figure 12.1: API 5000

Postman allows you to:

- **Use Pre-Configured Code Snippets to Test any API**: Postman comes with a library of code snippets based on JavaScript that lets teams quickly create tests that verify the functionality, dependability, and performance of their API. A range of API designs, such as REST, GraphQL, SOAP, and gRPC, can be used with these snippets.
- **Verify Intricate, End-to-End Processes:** Teams can link requests together, carry them out in particular order, and record test results using Postman's Collection Runner. Teams may now develop test suites that verify the most complex, crucial business user experiences.
- **Automate Test Executions Using Postman Cloud**: Postman allows customers to plan test executions at specific times and frequencies, as well as get alerts when tests are unsuccessful. Because Postman's infrastructure will be used for these executions, teams will not have to be concerned about failures brought on by a lack of local resources.
- **Run API Tests Inside CI/CD Pipelines**: Teams may run collections and tests inside their CI/CD pipelines using Newman or the Postman CLI. Preventing changes from disrupting the production environment helps guarantee backward compatibility.
- **Track Test Results and Troubleshoot Bugs:** Postman users may examine all network calls, including headers, certificates, requests, and responses, using

the Postman Console to analyze test failures. Additionally, they may track the outcomes of both automated and manual runs–and access reports to identify testing trends.

- **Establish a Specific Testing Environment:** Postman enables users to save values in environment-level variables that may be utilized in the URL, headers, and body of any request. Before putting code into production, this enables users to execute automated API tests in a specialized testing environment.
- **Include Postman API Tests in Issue Response Processes**: Teams may add Postman test data to their incident response processes by integrating Postman with a number of third-party monitoring and incident response technologies, including Datadog, New Relic, and Opsgenie.

Insomnia

A contemporary, easy-to-use API testing tool, Insomnia is primarily positioned as a rival to Postman, which means that it has many of the same advantages as Postman but also many of the same drawbacks.

The primary distinction with Insomnia is its approach to the user interface and user experience, emphasizing a more simplified and effective experience. Insomnia is more straightforward and frequently easier to use than Postman, which users frequently find to be too bloated. This proves to be quite helpful in a number of ways.

However, this does put some restrictions on insomnia. For instance, both tools support request chaining; however, Postman enables you to execute a series of requests simultaneously, whereas Insomnia requires you to execute one request at a time.

When it comes to the fundamentals of API testing, Insomnia excels at offering a straightforward and uncomplicated user interface that most developers will discover improves workflow efficiency. However, it has the same limitations as Postman, as creating automated and continuous tests is limited. Overall, Insomnia is a great tool depending on your use case.

The Speed Scale

With the straightforward aim of creating a solution that can guarantee API upgrades will not disrupt services or apps, Speedscale is one of the most innovative and recent entries to the market for automated API testing tools.

It is nearly impossible to ensure quality without a lot of manual labor when there are so many connections across various applications. Test automation with actual traffic should allow developers to expedite their release timetables.

Best practices for API testing were taken into consideration when developing Speedscale. The main feature of Speedscale is its ability to use realistic data in a strong and effective manner, enabling teams to identify and address problems prior to release.

The platform conducts traffic-based API tests for performance, integration, chaos testing, and other purposes, and it creates QA automation without the need for scripting. With Speedscale, developers can quickly see how their app will work under production demand, whereas other solutions take scripting and observation. This enables you to run isolated performance testing and make quick adjustments. Furthermore, without depending on users, Speedscale provides developers with accurate insight into how applications behave. The program automatically creates mocks from API traffic and simulates faults, arbitrary latencies, and non-responsiveness to demonstrate how the application functions in real-world scenarios.

Speedscale employs characteristics unique to Kubernetes and concentrates only on Kubernetes. For instance, installing an Operator into your cluster is necessary to set up the tool.

SoapUI

All web service providers can benefit from SoapUI's features, and its own development staff provides great assistance and is quick to address any issues that users may report.

SoapUI comes in two versions: *a premium, paid version, and a free, open-source version.* Nevertheless, since you only need to point to the WSDL file, even the open-source version might be helpful for producing effective web service mocks without writing any code. The majority of apps nowadays are supported by RESTful web services rather than SOAP, which means they are not described with a WSDL, therefore this will still be of limited use without the premium version.

Aside from that, it is very effective with both basic mocks and intricate test suites. Additionally, you may create Java-like code and modify requests and answers for your web services using the Groovy script. An extremely useful tool for testing and developing web services is the ability to directly access a database and verify whether the content has been altered by a web service.

But there are drawbacks to it as well. Although there are still many sophisticated capabilities available in the free version, the API documentation is appalling. To learn how to use the more potent options offered by the Groovy script capabilities, you will essentially need to read through a number of forum postings. Most likely, you will have to use trial and experience a lot of it together yourself.

Additionally, there appear to be some problems with SoapUI's memory utilization, which can escalate to the point that the program crashes. This is still a major stability problem; however, it can be slightly mitigated by giving the program more RAM at startup and adjusting the logging levels.

Ultimately, if you are willing to invest time and effort into a simple fake service–or a more complicated one that is difficult to use–SoapUI is an excellent option. But as an API testing tool, SoapUI has a lot of strength and functionality if you understand how to use it.

Paw

Although it is only compatible with Mac devices, Paw's free tier offers more sophisticated features than most of its competitors and works incredibly well with GraphQL. With an incredibly effective UI that makes exporting API definitions, creating client code, examining server answers, and creating requests simple, it is a complete HTTP client for testing your APIs.

For macOS users, Paw is far superior to programs such as Postman or Insomnia, particularly when it comes to GUI design and usability. The crowded user interface (or absence thereof in the case of REST Assured) of the majority of other API testing solutions is one of their main problems. Paw, on the other hand, avoids this issue by offering a visually appealing and user-friendly interface.

However, Paw manages to sidestep this problem by providing an aesthetically pleasing and intuitive UI. Its variable system was made with great care, as was the JS-based plugin system that is incredibly easy to use.

Paw enables you to rapidly combine requests, arrange them according to certain criteria, and more. Along with having excellent support for S3, Basic Auth, and OAuth 1 and 2, it also generates JWT tokens with ease. Many developers value how simple it is to create useable client code with Paw–all you have to do is import a cURL and change the request, and PAW will assist you in creating code for Python, Java, and other languages.

As we have already discussed, it is very user-friendly, particularly with the abundance of clever keyboard and mouse shortcuts. Though it is more focused and concisely built due to its exclusive support for Mac devices, this is also one of Paw's main drawbacks.

Many developers who prefer Windows and Linux devices will not be able to use Paw because of its lack of support for these operating systems. Another major disappointment is the absence of mock API functionality, which means you will need to use another program from our list to accomplish that. Lastly, it is not the most economical option for larger teams due to its astronomically high per-user cost.

Conclusion

In this chapter, we learned most of the things about writing, running, and procedure testing in Deno. This involved running specific tests or groups of tests. Reporters are used to format test output. Then we learned about time-faking, stubbing, mocking, spying (test doubles), and coverage flags. Also, about documentation tests and sanitizers. Further, we were provided with the method of writing an integration test. In the end, we learned about web server testing and testing the client for the API.

In the next chapter, we shall learn about configuring Hypertext Transfer Protocol Server (HTTPS) and using Deno in the browser.

References

1. **Testing**: https://docs.deno.com/runtime/fundamentals/testing/
2. **What are the four methods of API testing?**: https://www.google.com/search?q=Steps+to+test+the+API+client
3. **Top 5 API Testing Tools & Methodologies, Nate Lee,12.2023**: https://speedscale.com/blog/api-testing-tools/

Chapter 13
Web (HTTP) Server

Introduction

A web server is a computer system (including hardware and software) that stores and delivers web content to users over the internet.

Hardware: A computer that stores the website's files and web server software.

Software: Includes an HTTP server that understands URLs and HTTP, the protocol browsers as clients to view web pages.

The HTTP protocol is used to encode and transfer data between a web server and a client like a web browser. The main protocol used to transfer data over the internet is HTTP. HTTP gets its name from the hypertext documents that are used to transmit information between clients and servers.

Hypertext documents on the internet are documents that use hyperlinks to link related information together. Hypertext is a key concept of the World Wide Web (WWW), which is based on HyperText Markup Language (HTML).

Function: When a user (that is client) visits a website, their browser sends a request to the web server, which then processes the request and sends back the requested web pages.

Web servers use a variety of protocols to communicate with browsers, including Hypertext Transfer Protocol (HTTP) that is used to communicate with a web browser. They also support Simple Mail Transfer Protocol (SMTP) which is exclusively used for email. Web servers previously also deployed File Transfer Protocol (FTP) for file transfer and storage.

Structure

In this chapter, we shall study the following topics:

- Types of Webservers
- A Local Host Server
- Serving JSON

- Providing CSV
- Serving HTML

Types of Webservers

There are mainly four types of web servers: Apache, IIS, Nginx, and LiteSpeed.

- Apache web server is one of the most popular web servers developed by the Apache Software Foundation.
- Nginx is an open-source web server that is known for its high performance, stability, and low resource usage.
- LiteSpeed Web Server is an Apache alternative that conserves resources without sacrificing performance, security, or convenience.
- Internet Information Services (IIS) is a web server from Microsoft that runs on Windows and is used to host, deploy, and manage web content. IIS can be used to share information with users on the internet, an intranet, or an extranet.

Hypertext Transfer Protocol Secure (HTTPS) is the secure version of HTTP, which is the primary protocol used to send data between a web browser and a website. HTTPS is encrypted in order to increase the security of data transfer.

But in this chapter, we are trying to make our own server.

A Local Host Server

A local host server also known as a localhost, is a loopback network interface on a computer that allows users to test and access websites and web applications locally.

A localhost is a closed development environment that allows users to run a web server on their own computer, without the need for an internet connection. This allows users to develop and test their projects without having to connect to a remote server.

Some applications of a localhost include:

- **Web Development**: Users can test and develop web applications.
- **Mobile App Development**: Users can test how their app interacts with the server without having to deploy it to a remote server.
- **Secure Applications**: Users can test and develop secure applications locally.

The default internal loop IP for a localhost is usually 127.0.0.1 in Internet Protocol Version 4, or ::1 in Internet Protocol Version 6.

To set up a local testing server, users can:

1. Check if Python or C++ is installed.
2. Navigate to the directory that contains the website code to be tested.
3. Enter the command to start up the server in that directory.
4. Go to the URL localhost:8000 in a web browser.

A Uniform Resource Locator (URL) is the address of a unique resource on the internet. It is one of the key mechanisms used by browsers to retrieve published resources, such as HTML pages, CSS documents, images, and so on. In theory, each valid URL points to a unique resource.

Web servers are vulnerable to security threats, such as online attacks, application attacks, and site authentication vulnerabilities. To protect servers, administrators can use Web Application Firewalls (WAFs) and vulnerability scanners (WVSC).

You are sending a request to another computer on the internet when you view a webpage on your browser, and that machine responds by sending you the webpage. A web server is the computer you are communicating with online. When a client, such as your browser, sends an HTTP request, a web server responds with an HTTP response, such as an HTML page or JSON from an API. [1]

For a server to return a webpage, a lot of software is needed. Frontend and backend are the two general categories into which this software falls. The presentation of the material, including text styling and navigation bar color, is handled by frontend code. Data processing, storage, and interchange are all handled by backend code.

The code that handles network requests from your browser or communicates with the database is primarily managed by backend code.

Although JavaScript has always been used in browsers to write frontend code, Node.js enables developers to use it to write backend code. One of the main reasons Node.js is a popular choice for building backend code is that it makes creating a web server easier when the frontend and backend are combined in this way.

This tutorial will teach you how to use the http module that comes with Node.js to create web servers. You will construct web servers that are capable of returning HTML web pages, CSV files, and JSON data.

Use the DigitalOcean App Platform to streamline the deployment of Node.js applications. Install Node straight from GitHub in a matter of minutes.

Conditions for Deploying Node.js for Establishing HTTP Server

- Verify that the development machine has Node.js installed. Version 10.19.0 of Node.js is used in this part. In *Chapter* 4 of the book, we previously learned about Node.js. Installing using a PPA portion of how to install Node.js on Ubuntu 18.04 or how to install Node.js and create a local development environment on macOS instructions to install this on macOS or Ubuntu 18.04.
- Web servers can be created using the Node.js technology right out of the box. Make sure you know the fundamentals of Node.js before you begin. Take a look at our how to write and run your first program in order to get started.

Step 1: Establishing a Simple HTTP Server

First, let us build a server that gives the user plain text. The fundamental ideas needed to build up a server will be covered in this, giving you the groundwork to return more complicated data formats like JSON.

In order to complete our activities and the others in the article, we must first set up an accessible coding environment. Make a folder named first-servers in the terminal.

```
mkdir first-servers
```

Then enter that folder.

```
cd first-servers
```

Create the file that contains the code now.

```
Touch hello.js
```

Launch a text editor and open the file. Since nano is available at the terminal, we shall use it.

```
hello.js nano
```

The http module comes with every Node.js.

The host and port that our server will be bound to are the two constants that we will declare next:

```
Hello.js/first-servers...
var port = 8000; const host = 'localhost';
```

As previously stated, browsers and other clients send requests to web servers. By entering a domain name, which a DNS server converts to an IP address, we can communicate with a web server. A machine on a network, such as the internet, is uniquely identified by its IP address, which is a string of numbers.

The worth Computers utilize the unique private address localhost to identify themselves. It is usually the same as the internal IP address 127.0.0.1 and is only accessible by the local computer; neither the internet nor any local networks we have joined can access it.

Servers utilize the port as an endpoint, or "door," to our IP address. We will use port 8000 for our web server in this example. Most of the time, developers will choose ports 8080 and 8000 instead of other ports for HTTP servers because these are the default ports in development.

We can access our server by going to http://localhost:8000 in a local browser after binding it to this host and port.

Let us include a unique function that we refer to as a request listener in Node.js. The purpose of this function is to process an incoming HTTP request and provide an HTTP response. Two arguments are required for this function: a request object and a response object. All of the information in the incoming HTTP request is captured by the request object. The server receives HTTP responses from the response object.

The message **"My first server!"** should be returned by our first server anytime someone tries to access it.

Next, let us include that function:

```
first-servers/hello.js
      const requestListener = function (req, res) {
          res.writeHead(200);
          res.end("My first server!");
      };
```

Typically, the function's name is determined by its function. For instance, we would probably call a request listener function **listBooks()** if we wanted it to return a list of books. We will use the generic name **requestListener** because this is a sample case.

Two arguments are accepted by all Node.js request listener functions: req and res (we can call them something else if we would like). The first argument, req, represents the Request object that contains the user's HTTP request. We work with the Response object in the second argument, res, to create the HTTP response that we send back to the user.

The response's HTTP status code is specified in the first line, **res.writeHead(200)**. HTTP status codes show how successfully the server processed an HTTP request. "OK" is represented by the status code 200 in this instance. Our post on how to troubleshoot common HTTP error codes is a wonderful place to start if you want to learn about the different HTTP codes that your web servers can return along with the meaning they represent.

The function's subsequent line, **`res.end("My first server!");`** returns the HTTP response to the client that made the request. Any data that the server has to return is returned by this function. It is returning text data in this instance.

At last, we can build our server and utilize our request listener:

`first-servers/hello.js`

```
const server = http.createServer(requestListener);
server.listen(port, host, () => {
    console.log(`Server is running on http://${host}:${port}`);
});
```

Use CTRL+X to save and exit Nano.

The **`createServer()`** function of the http module is used in the first line to create a new server object. HTTP requests are received by this server and forwarded to our **`requestListener()`** function.

Our server has to be bound to a network address after it has been created. We use the **`listen()`** method for that. Three parameters are required: host, port, and a callback function that is triggered when the server starts listening.

Although each of these options is optional, it is a good idea to specify the host and port that we would want a web server to utilize. Understanding the port and host that a web server is running on is necessary when deploying it to various contexts in order to set up load balancing or a DNS alias.

To let us know when the server starts listening to connections, the callback method broadcasts a message to our console.

Note: *The req object must be the function's first argument even though* ***`requestListener()`*** *does not use it.*

We now have a web server with less than fifteen lines of code. Let us execute the program to observe it in operation and test it from beginning to end:

```
Hello.js in node
```

This output will appear in the console:

Figure 13.1: *Message for Existence of HTTP Server on a Device*

Observe how the prompt vanishes. This is due to the lengthy nature of a Node.js server. Only when an error occurs that causes it to crash and quit, or when we terminate the Node.js process that is operating the server, does it exit.

We will use curL, a CLI utility for transferring data to and from a network, to interact with the server in a different terminal window. To send an HTTP GET request to our active server, type the following command:

```
curl http://8000.localhost
```

The following output will appear on our terminal when we hit ENTER:

Figure 13.2: *Declaration of Installing the Server First Time*

After setting up a server, we received our first response.

Let us examine what transpired throughout our server test. We made a GET request to the server located at http://localhost:8000 using cURL. Connections from that address were listened to by our Node.js server. The **`requestListener()`** method received that request from the server. Text data with the status code 200 was returned by the function. After receiving the answer from the server, cURL showed the message in our terminal.

Let us hit CTRL+C to end our running server before we proceed. This returns us to the command line prompt by stopping the execution of our server.

The server answers are rarely in plain text on the majority of websites we visit or APIs we use. Common response formats that we receive are HTML pages and JSON data. We shall discover how to return HTTP answers in typical web data forms in the following phase.

Step 2: Returning Various Content Types

A web server may return a response in a number of different formats. As was previously indicated, we can return various text forms such as XML and CSV in addition to JSON and HTML. Lastly, non-text data such as PDFs, compressed files, audio, and video can be returned by web servers.

This part will teach you how to return the following kinds of data in addition to the plain text that we just returned:

- JSON
- CSV
- HTML

All three of the data types are text-based and are widely used formats for online content delivery. Returning these various data kinds is supported by a wide range of server-side developer languages and tools. Two things must be done in the Node.js context:

- Provide the correct value in the Content-Type header of our HTTP responses.

  Make sure that the data is received in the correct format using **`res.end()`**.

  Let us look at some examples to demonstrate this. There are numerous parallels between the code we wrote earlier and the code we will write in this part and others. The **`requestListener()`** function contains the majority of the modifications. To make the following sections easier to follow, let us build files using this "template code."

- Produce a fresh file named **`html.js`**. This file will be utilized later to return HTML text in an HTTP response. We will put the template code here and copy it to the other servers that return various types.

In the terminal, enter the following:

```
touch html.js
```

Now open this file in a text editor:

```
nano html.js
```

Let us copy the "template code." Enter this in nano:

```
first-servers/html.js
const http = require("http");

const host = 'localhost';
const port = 8000;

const requestListener = function (req, res) {};

const server = http.createServer(requestListener);
server.listen(port, host, () => {
    console.log(`Server is running on http://${host}:${port}`);
});
```

Use CTRL+X to save and quit html.js, then go back to the console.

Let us now make two copies of this file. The first file in the HTTP response will be used to return CSV data:

```
cp html.js CSV.js
```

The server will receive a JSON response from the second file:

```
cp html.js JSON.js
```

Later exercises will use the remaining files:

```
cp html.js routes.js cp html.js htmlFile.js
```

We are now prepared to carry on with our exercises. Let us start with the JSON return.

Serving JSON

JSON, or JavaScript Object Notation, is a text-based data interchange format. Although it is derived from JavaScript objects, as its name implies, it is language independent, therefore any programming language that can parse its syntax can use it.

APIs frequently take and return data in JSON format. Because of its smaller data transfer size compared to earlier data interchange standards like XML and the available tools that make it easy for programs to parse them, it has become very popular. You can read our guide on how to work with JSON in JavaScript to gain more knowledge about JSON.

Use nano to open the json.js file:

```
nano  JSON.js
```

We would like a JSON response back. By altering the highlighted lines as follows, we can change the **`requestListener()`** function to deliver the correct header that all JSON responses contain:

first-servers/json.js

```
const requestListener = function (req, res) {
    res.setHeader("Content-Type", "application/json");
};
```

An HTTP header is added to the response using the **`res.setHeader()`** method. Additional data that might be included with a request or response are known as HTTP headers. The name and value of the header are the two arguments that the **`res.setHeader()`** function accepts.

The format of the data, commonly referred to as the media type, that is being sent with the request or response is indicated by the Content-Type header. Our Content-Type in this instance is **`application/json`**.

Let us now provide the user with their JSON content back. Change **`json.js`** to appear as follows:

first-servers/json.js

```
const requestListener = function (req, res) {
    res.setHeader("Content-Type", "application/json");
    res.writeHead(200);
    res.end(`{"message": "This is a JSON response"}`);
};
```

As previously, we deliver a status code of 200 to the user to indicate that their request was successful. This time, there is a valid JSON in our string argument in the **`response.end()`** method.

Use the keyboard shortcut CTRL+X to save and exit **`json.js`**. Let us now use the node command to launch the server:

```
Node.json.js
```

Let us use cURL to access the server in a different terminal:

```
curl http://8000.localhost
```

When we hit ENTER, the following outcome will appear:

The output on the console will look like this:

```
Output
{"message": "This is a JSON response"}
```

Figure 13.3: *Utilizing JSON to Access the Server in a Different Terminal*

Similar to many of the well-known APIs we use to build apps, we have now successfully delivered a JSON answer. To return to the usual terminal prompt, make sure you use CTRL+C to quit the running server. Let us now examine CSV, another widely used data return type.

Providing CSV

A popular text standard for supplying tabular data, such as in Excel or other spreadsheets, is the Comma Separated Values (CSV) file format. Typically, a comma is used to divide each item in a row, and a newline is used to separate each row.

Use a text editor to access the csv.js file in our workspace:

```
CSV.js nano
```

Let us update our **`requestListener()`** function with the following lines:

```
csv.js/first-servers
    const requestListener = function (req, res) {
        res.setHeader("Content-Type", "text/csv");
        res.setHeader("Content-Disposition", "attachment;filename=-
    oceanpals.csv");
    };
```

Since the result is **`text/csv`** this time, our Content-Type indicates that a CSV file is being delivered. We add the Content-Disposition header as the second one. This header instructs the browser on how to provide the data, specifically as a separate file or within the browser. Even if the Content-Disposition header is not set, the majority of contemporary browsers will download the file automatically when we return CSV replies. This header should still be included when returning a CSV file, though, since it lets us specify the file's name. The browser is informed that this CSV file is an attachment in this instance and needs to be downloaded. The browser is subsequently informed that the file is called oceanpals.csv. Let us upload the CSV file to the HTTP.

first-servers/csv.js

```
const requestListener = function (req, res) {
    res.setHeader("Content-Type", "text/csv");
    res.setHeader("Content-Disposition", "attachment;filename=-
oceanpals.csv");
    res.writeHead(200);
    res.end(`id,name,email\n1,Sammy Shark,shark@ocean.com`);
};
```

As before, our answer returns a 200/OK status. This time, a valid CSV string is returned by our call to **res.end()**. Each column's value is separated by a comma, while the rows are separated by the new line character (\n). One row contains the data, and the other has the table header.

We will use the browser to test this server. Save csv.js, then press CTRL+X to close the editor.

Use the Node.js command to launch the server.

```
CSV.js node
```

Let us use cURL to access the server in a different terminal.

```
curl http://8000.localhost
```

This will appear as output in the console:

```
Output
id,name,email
1,Sammy Shark,shark@ocean.com
```

Figure 13.4: *Finding a Node Containing CSV*

If we go to http://localhost:8000 in our browser, a CSV file will be downloaded. Its file name will be oceanpals.csv.

Exit the running server with CTRL+C to return to the standard terminal prompt.

Having returned JSON and CSV, we have covered two cases that are popular for APIs. Let us move on to how we return data for websites people view in a browser.

Serving HTML

HTML, HyperText Markup Language, is the most common format to use when we want users to interact with our server via a web browser. It was created to structure web content. We have already learned about HTML in *Chapter 8* of this book. Web browsers are built to display HTML content, as well as any styles we add with CSS, another frontend web technology that allows us to change the aesthetics of our websites.

Let us use our text editor to reopen html.js.

```
HTML.js nano
```

To return the proper Content-Type header for an HTML response, modify the **requestListener()** method as follows:

first-servers/html.js

```
const requestListener = function (req, res) {
    res.setHeader("Content-Type", "text/html");
};
```

Now, let us return HTML content to the user. Add the highlighted lines to html.js so it looks like this:

first-servers/html.js

```
const requestListener = function (req, res) {
    res.setHeader("Content-Type", "text/html");
    res.writeHead(200);
    res.end(`<html><body><h1>This is HTML</h1></body></html>`);
};
```

The HTTP status code is added first. Next, we pass a string parameter containing valid HTML to **response.end()**. An HTML page with a single header tag that reads "This is HTML" will appear when we access our server in a browser.

Let us hit CTRL+X to save and exit. Let us now use the node command to launch the server.

HTML.js and Node.js

When our software has launched, we will see that the server is running at http://localhost:8000.

Go to http://localhost:8000 in the browser now. This is how our page will appear:

Figure 13.5: *Image of HTML Response Returned from Node.js Server*

Let us use CTRL+C to end the operating server and go back to the usual terminal prompt.

HTML is frequently written in a file, distinct from the server-side code, as is the case with our Node.js applications. Let us now examine how to retrieve HTML responses from files.

Step 3: Using a File to Serve an HTML Page

It is better to load HTML files and serve their content to the user, however, we can deliver HTML as strings with Node.js. This keeps our Node.js code shorter and enables us to work on each component of our website separately as the HTML file expands by removing the need to retain lengthy strings in it. Since many web development settings use this "separation of concerns," it is wise to know how to load HTML files to support it in Node.js.

We utilize the fs module to load the HTML file and use its contents while composing our HTTP response in order to deliver HTML files.

Initially, we will generate an HTML file that will be returned by the web server. Make a fresh HTML document:

Go to **`index.html`**

Now, launch a text editor and open **`index.html`**:

nano index.html

We will have a simple website. It will display some greeting words in the center and have an orange background. Include this code in the document:

index.html/first-servers.html

```
<!DOCTYPE html>

<head>
    <title>My Website</title>
    <style>
        *,
        html {
            margin: 0;
            padding: 0;
            border: 0;
        }

        html {
            width: 100%;
            height: 100%;
        }

        body {
            width: 100%;
            height: 100%;
            position: relative;
            background-color: rgb(236, 152, 42);
        }

        .center {
            width: 100%;
            height: 50%;
            margin: 0;
            position: absolute;
            top: 50%;
            left: 50%;
            transform: translate(-50%, -50%);
            color: white;
            font-family: "Trebuchet MS", Helvetica, sans-serif;
            text-align: center;
        }

        h1 {
```

```
            font-size: 144px;
        }

        p {
            font-size: 64px;
        }
    </style>
</head>

<body>
    <div class="center">
        <h1>Hello Again!</h1>
        <p>This is served from a file</p>
    </div>
</body>

</html>
```

Two lines of text are displayed on this single webpage: **"Hello Again!"** and **"This is served from a file."** The lines are positioned one above the other in the middle of the page. The first line of text would be huge because it is placed in a header. It will look like the second line of text is a little bit smaller. The webpage will have an orange background and all of the text will be white.

Although it is outside the purview of this article or series, Mozilla's Getting Started with the Web tutorial is a good place to start if you want to learn more about HTML, CSS, and other frontend web technologies.

That is all we need for the HTML, so use *CTRL+X* to save and close the file. We can now proceed to the server code.

For this exercise, we will work on **htmlFile.js**. Open it with the text editor.

nano htmlFile.js

As we have to read a file, let us begin by importing the fs module:

```
first-servers/htmlFile.js
const http = require("http");
const fs = require('fs').promises;
...
```

This module contains a **readFile()** function that we will use to load the HTML file in place. We import the promise variant in keeping with modern JavaScript best practices. We use promises as it is syntactically more succinct than callbacks, which we would have to use if we assigned fs to just require('fs').

We want our HTML file to be read when a user requests our system. Let us begin by modifying **requestListener()** to read the file:

first-servers/htmlFile.js

```
const requestListener = function (req, res) {
    fs.readFile(__dirname + "/index.html")
};
```

The file is loaded using the **fs.readFile()** function. **__dirname + "/index.html"** is its argument. The absolute path to the location where the Node.js code is being executed is stored in the special variable **__dirname**. In order to load the HTML file we previously produced, we then append /index.html.

After the HTML page loads, let us return it:

first-servers/htmlFile.js

```
const requestListener = function (req, res) {
    fs.readFile(__dirname + "/index.html")
        .then(contents => {
            res.setHeader("Content-Type", "text/html");
            res.writeHead(200);
            res.end(contents);
        })
};
```

The data will be returned if the **fs.readFile()** promise is fulfilled. To deal with this situation, we employ the **then()** technique. The HTML file's data is contained in the contents parameter.

To inform the client that we are providing HTML data, we first set the Content-Type header to **text/html**. After that, we write the status code to show that the request was fulfilled. After loading the HTML page, we transmit it to the client with the contents variable containing the data.

We should handle this situation when we receive an error because the **fs.readFile()** method can occasionally fail. Include this in the function **requestListener():**

first-servers/htmlFile.js

```
const requestListener = function (req, res) {
    fs.readFile(__dirname + "/index.html")
        .then(contents => {
            res.setHeader("Content-Type", "text/html");
            res.writeHead(200);
            res.end(contents);
        })
```

```
                .catch(err => {
                    res.writeHead(500);
                    res.end(err);
                    return;
                });
        };
```

Use CTRL+X to exit Nano and save the file.

A promise is denied if it contains a mistake. We use the **`catch()`** method to deal with that situation. It accepts the error returned by **`fs.readFile()`**, returns the error to the user, and sets the status code to 500, which indicates that an internal issue occurred.

Use the following node command to launch our server:

HTMLFile.js node

Go to http://localhost:8000 in the browser. You will see this page on the sole:

Figure 13.6: *Image of HTML Page Loaded from a File in Node.js*

The user has now received an HTML page back from the server. Use CTRL+C to end the active server. When you do, the terminal prompt will appear again.

You might not want to load an HTML page each time you receive an HTTP request when writing code like this in production. More complicated websites can be megabytes in size, whereas this HTML page is about 800 bytes. It may take some time for large files to load. It could be beneficial to load HTML files at launch and store their contents if your website is likely to receive a lot of traffic. You can configure the server to listen to requests on an address once they have been loaded.

To illustrate this method, let us see how we can rework our server to be more efficient and scalable.

Reopen the Node.js script in the terminal using a text editor.

```
htmlFile.js nano
```

Before we write the **requestListener()** function, let us add a new variable.

first-servers/htmlFile.js

```
let indexFile;

const requestListener = function (req, res) {
```

When we run this program, this variable will hold the HTML file's contents.

Let us now modify the **requestListener()** code once more. It will now return the contents of **indexFile** rather than loading the file.

```
HTML and first-serversFile.js... const requestListener = function (req,
res) { res.setHeader("Content-Type", "text/html"); ~;
...
```

We then move the **requestListener()** function's file reading logic to our server initialization. As the server is being created, make the following adjustments:

HTMLFile.js/first-servers

```
const server = http.createServer(requestListener);

fs.readFile(__dirname + "/index.html")
    .then(contents => {
        indexFile = contents;
        server.listen(port, host, () => {
            console.log(`Server is running on
http://${host}:${port}`);
        });
    })
    .catch(err => {
        console.error(`Could not read index.html file: ${err}`);
        process.exit(1);
    });
```

Save the file and exit nano with CTRL+X.

The code that reads the file is similar to what we wrote in our first attempt. However, when we successfully read the file, we save its contents to our global **indexFile** variable. We then start the server with the **listen()** method. The key thing is that the file is loaded before the server is run. This way, the **requestListener()** function will be sure to return an HTML page, as **indexFile** is no longer an empty variable.

Our error handler has changed as well. If the file cannot be loaded, we capture the error and print it to our console. We then exit the Node.js program with the exit() function without starting the server. This way we can see why the file reading failed, address the problem, and then start the server again.

We have now created different web servers that return various types of data to a user. So far, we have not used any request data to determine what should be returned. We will need to use request data when setting up different routes or paths in a Node.js server, so let us see how they work together.

Step 4: Managing Routes Using an HTTP Request Object

Most websites we visit or APIs we use usually have more than one endpoint so we can access various resources. A good example would be a book management system, one that might be used in a library. It would not only need to manage book data, but it would also manage author data for cataloging and searching convenience.

Even though the data for books and authors are related, they are two different objects. In these cases, software developers usually code each object on different endpoints as a way to indicate to the API user what kind of data they are interacting with.

Let us create a new server for a small library, which will return two different types of data. If the user goes to our server's address at **`/books`**, they will receive a list of books in JSON. If they go to **`/authors`**, they will receive a list of author information in JSON.

So far, we have been returning the same response to every request we get. Let us illustrate this quickly.

Re-run our JSON response example:

```
node json.js
In another terminal, let us do a cURL request like before.

curl http://localhost:8000
```

You will see:

Output

```
{"message": "This is a JSON response"}
```

Now let us try another curl command.

```
curl http://localhost:8000/todos
```

After pressing Enter, you will see the same result on the console as the output.

Figure 13.7: *JSON Response*

We have not built any special logic in our **requestListener()** function to handle a request whose URL contains **/todos**, so Node.js returns the same JSON message by default.

As we want to build a miniature library management server, we will now separate the kind of data that is returned based on the endpoint the user accesses.

First, exit the running server with CTRL+C.

Now open routes.js in your text editor.

nano routes.js

Let us begin by storing our JSON data in variables before the **requestListener()** function.

first-servers/routes.js

```
const books = JSON.stringify([
    { title: "The Alchemist", author: "Paulo Coelho", year: 1988 },
    { title: "The Prophet", author: "Kahlil Gibran", year: 1923 }
]);

const authors = JSON.stringify([
    { name: "Paulo Coelho", countryOfBirth: "Brazil", yearOf-
Birth: 1947 },
    { name: "Kahlil Gibran", countryOfBirth: "Lebanon", yearOf-
Birth: 1883 }
]);
```

The **books** variable is a string that contains JSON for an array of book objects. Each book has a title or name, an author, and the year it was published.

The **authors** variable is a string that contains the JSON for an array of author objects. Each author has a name, a country of birth, and their year of birth.

Now that we have the data, our responses will return. Let us start modifying the **requestListener()** function to return them to the correct routes.

First, we will ensure that every response from our server has the correct Content-Type header.

first-servers/routes.js

```
const requestListener = function (req, res) {
    res.setHeader("Content-Type", "application/json");
}
```

Now, we want to return the right JSON depending on the URL path the user visits. Let us create a switch statement on the request's URL.

first-servers/routes.js

```
const requestListener = function (req, res) {
    res.setHeader("Content-Type", "application/json");
    switch (req.url) {}
}
```

To get the URL path from a request object, we need to access its url property. We can now add cases to the switch statement to return the appropriate JSON.

JavaScript's switch statement provides a way to control what code is run depending on the value of an object or JavaScript expression (for example, the result of mathematical operations). If you need a lesson or reminder on how to use them, take a look at our guide on how to use the switch statement in JavaScript.

Let us continue by adding a case for when the user wants to get our list of books.

first-servers/routes.js

```
const requestListener = function (req, res) {
    res.setHeader("Content-Type", "application/json");
    switch (req.url) {
        case "/books":
            res.writeHead(200);
            res.end(books);
            break
    }
}
```

To show that the request is okay, we set our status code to 200 and send back the JSON file with our book list. Let us give our writers one more example now.

first-servers/routes.js

```
const requestListener = function (req, res) {
    res.setHeader("Content-Type", "application/json");
    switch (req.url) {
        case "/books":
            res.writeHead(200);
            res.end(books);
            break
        case "/authors":
            res.writeHead(200);
            res.end(authors);
            break
    }
}
```

Since the request is acceptable, the status code will remain at 200. This time, we provide back the JSON file with our authors' list.

If the user attempts to navigate to any other path, we want to return an error. To accomplish this, let us include the default case.

routes.js

```
const requestListener = function (req, res) {
    res.setHeader("Content-Type", "application/json");
    switch (req.url) {
        case "/books":
            res.writeHead(200);
            res.end(books);
            break
        case "/authors":
            res.writeHead(200);
            res.end(authors);
            break
        default:
            res.writeHead(404);
            res.end(JSON.stringify({error:"Resource not found"}));
    }
}
```

To catch all other circumstances that were not covered by our earlier examples, we utilize the default keyword in a switch statement. To let them know that the URL they were looking for could not be located, we set the status code to 404. Next, we set a JSON object with an error message in it.

To check if our server performs as we anticipate, let us test it. Let us first execute a command in a different terminal to check if our list of books is returned:

```
curl 8000/books at http://localhost
```

To view the following output on the console, press *Enter*:

Figure 13.8: *A Case of the User Wanting to Get Books on a Particular Website*

Everything is going OK so far. Let us give **/authors** a shot. In the terminal, type the following command:

```
curl http://8000/authors on localhost
```

When the command is finished, the console will display the following output:

```
Output
[{"name":"Paulo Coelho","countryOfBirth":"Brazil","yearOfBirth":1947},{"name":"Kahlil Gibran",'
```

Figure 13.9: *Finding Book by Author's Name*

Finally, to make sure **`requestListener()`** receives the error response, let us attempt an incorrect URL:

```
curl http://8000/notreal/localhost
```

When you enter that command, the following output will appear on the console:

You can use CTRL+C to end the running server.

We have now established various channels for people to obtain various types of data. Additionally, we included a default response that, in the event that a user submits a URL that we do not support, returns an HTTP error.

Conclusion

In this chapter, we first studied the types of webservers and how to set up a local host server. Then, we learned about serving JSON, providing CSV, and servicing HTML.

The next chapter will provide methods for deploying deno applications, websites, and projects.

Reference

1. **How To Create a Web Server in Node.js with the HTTP Module,Published on April 11, 2020**: https://www.digitalocean.com/community/tutorials/how-to-create-a-web-server-in-node-js-with-the-http-module

Chapter 14
Deploying Deno Applications, Websites and Projects

Introduction

Deno offers a range of built-in tools that enhance the development process, from formatters and linters to task automation. These tools reduce the reliance on third-party dependencies and promote a consistent development environment. Despite its limitations, due to its security model, Deno can be ideal for building very secure and sensitive applications. Additionally, its native TypeScript support takes away the troubles of setting up TypeScript in your project. There are many approaches to building a website or app with Deno. Since Deno natively supports JSX and TSX, the simplest approach to building a site is with a router and components.

Deploying applications built with Deno is straightforward, with several platforms supporting Deno deployments. While Deno Deploy is optimized for Deno code, other platforms such as AWS, GCP, and Azure offer flexibility through Docker containers and runtimes.

You can be productive immediately with Deno when you start building your website or application.

No configuring your toolchain, project, and TypeScript, since Deno ships with a modern development toolchain with native TypeScript suppor.

Structure

In this chapter, we are going to learn about Deno applications, websites, and projects under the following headings:

- Making a Deno Project
- Run Your Project
- Running Your Tests
- JetBrains IDEs
- Setting up Your Editor/IDE
- Command Line Interface
- Passing Script Arguments
- React/Next
- Fresh
- Astro
- Vite
- Lume
- Docusaurus
- Hono
- Oak

Making a Deno Project

To make your development experience as seamless as possible, Deno comes with a number of built-in tools. The project initializer, which generates a new Deno project with a simple file structure and setup, is one of these tools. Although you are free to utilize JavaScript, we will be utilizing TypeScript in this article because Deno has built-in support for TypeScript. You can delete the type annotations and rename the files to.js if you would rather utilize JavaScript.

Launch a New Project

To initialize a new Deno project, run the following command in your terminal:

```
deno init my_project
```

This will create a new directory called **my_project** with the following structure:

```
my_project
├── deno.json
├── main_test.ts
└── main.ts
```

Two TypeScript files are created: **`main.ts`** and **`main_test.ts`**, along with a **`deno.json`** file for project configuration. Your application code will be written in the **`main.ts`** file, which initially has a basic program that adds two numbers together. You can write tests in the **`main_test.ts`** file; at first, it will have a test for your addition program.

Complete Your Project

You can use the following command to launch this program:

```
$ deno main.ts
```

Add 2 + 3 = 5

Running Your Tests

Deno has a built-in test runner. You can write tests for your code and run them with the deno test command. Run the tests in your new project with:

```
$ deno test
running 1 test from ./main_test.ts
addTest ... ok (1ms)
```

Output

```
ok | 1 passed | 0 failed (3ms)
```

Now that you have a basic project set up, you can start building your application. Check out our examples and tutorials for more ideas on what to build with Deno.

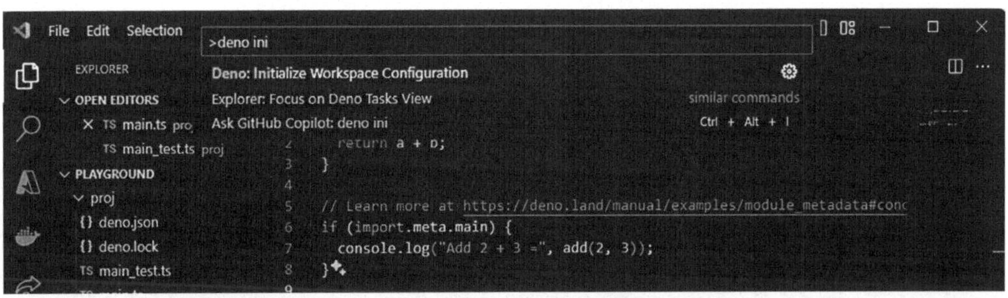

Figure 14.1: *Initialisation of Workspace Configuration in Deno*

Setting up Your Editor/IDE

Look up "**Deno**" under the **Extensions** tab, then install the Denoland extension.

Next, press *Ctrl+Shift+P* to access the Command Palette, then type **Deno**: Initialize Workspace Configuration. In order to set up Deno for your workstation, choose this option.

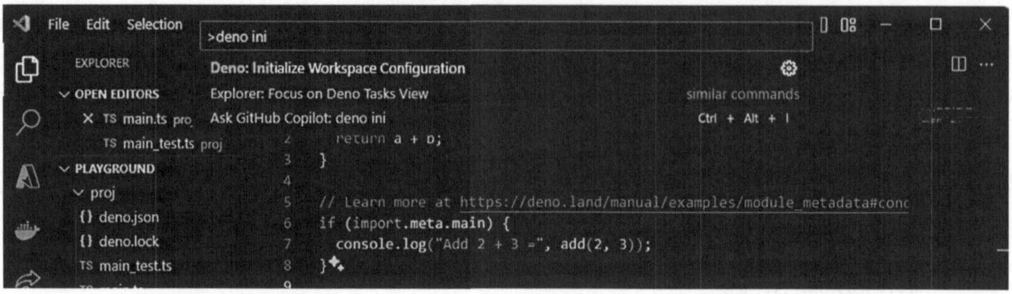

Figure 14.2: *Selecting this Option to Configure Deno for Your Workspace*

A file called **`.vscode/settings.json`** will be created in your workspace with the following configuration:

```
{
  "deno.enable": true
}
```

That is it!

You have used VSCode to successfully set up your Deno development environment. All of Deno's LSP features, such as IntelliSense, code formatting, linting, and more, are now available to you.

IDEs from JetBrains

- Open your IDE and select **`File > Settings`** to install the Deno Plugin.
- Go to **`Plugins`**, then look for **`Deno`**. Get the official Deno plugin installed.

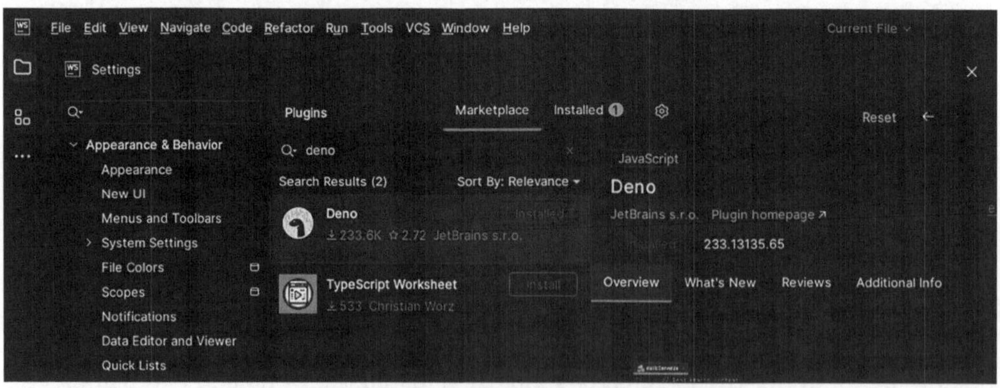

Figure 14.3: *Install the Official Deno Plugin*

- Return to **`File > Settings`** to configure the plugin. Go to Deno under Languages and Frameworks. Verify that Deno is enabled for your project and, if it has not been automatically detected, provide the path of the Deno executable.

Configuring the Editor

Look up "**Deno**" under the Extensions tab, then install the Denoland extension.

Next, press *Ctrl+Shift+P* to access the **Command Palette**, then type **Deno**: Initialize Workspace Configuration. In order to set up Deno for your workstation, choose this option.

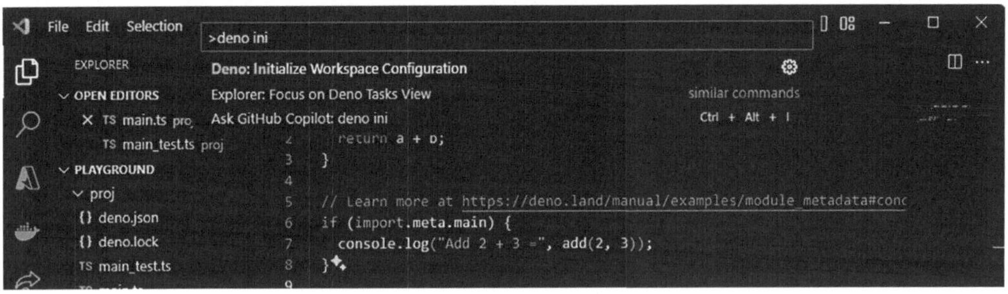

Figure 14.4: *Configuring Deno for Your Workspace*

A file called **.vscode/settings.json** will be created in your workspace with the following configuration:

```
{
  "deno.enable": true
}
```

That is it!

You have used VSCode to successfully set up your Deno development environment. All of Deno's LSP features, such as IntelliSense, code formatting, linting, and more, are now available to you.

Deno Command Line Interface (CLI)

You may manage dependencies, run scripts, and even compile your code into independent executables using the Deno Command Line Interface (CLI). Having studied the examples up to this point, you could be familiar with some basic commands. A more thorough description of the Deno CLI will be given in this section. There are several subcommands in the Deno CLI, including run, init, and test. They are employed in the Deno runtime environment to carry out various tasks. Every subcommand has a unique collection of options and flags (for example, -version) that can be used to customize its behavior.

Using the **-h** or **--help** flags, or the deno help subcommand in your terminal, you may see all of the commands and flags that are available.

For further information on all of the various subcommands and flags, consult the CLI reference handbook. In the next section, we will examine a few commands in greater detail to discover how to use and configure them.

Deno run is an example of a subcommand.

By providing its path in relation to the current working directory, you can launch a local TypeScript or JavaScript file.

```
deno run main.ts
```

Deno supports running scripts directly from URLs. This is particularly useful for quickly testing or running code without downloading it first.

```
deno run https://docs.deno.com/examples/hello-world.ts
```

Another way to execute a script is to pipe it through regular input. This is helpful for dynamically producing scripts or integrating with other command-line tools.

```
run deno | cat main.ts -
```

Script Arguments

Additional parameters you can supply to your script when executing it from the command line are known as script arguments. With the use of these parameters, you may alter how your program behaves depending on the runtime input you supply. After the script name, arguments must be given.

We can create a script that logs the arguments sent to it in order to test this.

```
main.ts
console.log(Deno.args);
```

When we run that script and pass it some arguments, it will log them to the console.

```
$ deno run main.ts arg1 arg2 arg3
[ "arg1", "arg2", "arg3" ]
```

React/Next: A Well-Liked JavaScript User Interface Development Library

A well-liked JavaScript package for creating user interfaces is called React. You can utilize the well-known web framework Next.js to integrate React with Deno.

You may start using Next.js in Deno by making a new Next app and launching it right away.

```
Deno task dev deno run -A npm:create-next-app@latest my-next-app
cd my-next-app
```

This will use TypeScript to construct a new Next.js application and use Deno to run it. After that, you can view your new application by opening your browser to http://

localhost:3000. You can then begin editing **page.tsx** to observe your changes as they happen.

Fresh: Deno's Most Widely Used Web Framework

The most often used web framework for Deno is called Fresh. It employs a methodology in which clients are not automatically sent any JavaScript.

You can create your app by using the following command and following the cli instructions to get started with a fresh app:

```
deno run -A -r https://fresh.deno.dev
cd my-fresh-app
deno task start
```

By doing this, a brand-new app will be created and run with Deno. After that, you may view your new app by opening your browser to http://localhost:8000. To view your modifications in real time, **edit /routes/index.tsx**.

The client is only in charge of re-rendering little islands of interaction; Fresh handles the rest of its rendering on the server. This indicates that the developer specifically chooses to use client-side rendering for particular components.

Astro: Generator of Static Sites

Developers may quickly and easily construct websites with Astro, a static site generator.

You can establish a new Astro site to get started with Astro by using the following command:

```
deno run -A npm:create-astro my-astro-site
cd my-astro-site
deno task dev
```

By doing this, a new Astro website will be created and operated with Deno. After that, you can view your new website by opening your browser at http://localhost:4321. To view your changes instantly, **edit /src/pages/index.astro**.

.Vite: A Build Tool for Web Developers

Vite is a web developer build tool that allows you to run your code directly in the browser by using native ES modules. When using Deno to create contemporary web applications, Vite is a fantastic option.

You can start using Vite by creating a new Vite app using the following command:

```
npm:create-vite@latest deno run -A
cd my-vite-app
deno install
deno task dev
```

.Lume: Deno's Static Site Generator

Inspired by existing static site generators such as Jekyll or Eleventy, Lume is a static site generator for Deno.

You can start using Lume by creating a new Lume site with the following command:

```
My-lume-site CD mkdir run-A my-lume-site deno Deno task serve
https://lume.land/init.ts
```

Docusaurus: Generator of Static Sites

A static site generator designed specifically for websites with technical documentation is called Docusaurus.

You can start Docusaurus by creating a new Docusaurus site with the following command:

```
deno run -A npm:create-docusaurus@latest my-website classic
cd my-website
deno task start
```

Hono: A Lightweight Framework for Web Applications

Following in the footsteps of Sinatra and Express, Hono is a lightweight web application framework.

You can create a new Hono app with the following command to get started with Hono:

```
npm:create-hono@latest cd deno run -A My-Hono-App
```

Deno Task Commencement:

By doing this, a new Hono app will be created and run alongside Deno. After that, you may view your new app by opening your browser to http://localhost:8000.

Oak: A Middleware Framework that Uses Deno to Handle HTTP

Oak is a middleware framework that uses Deno to handle HTTP. Your frontend application and a possible database or other data sources (such as REST APIs or GraphQL APIs) are connected by Oak.

In comparison to the native Deno HTTP server, Oak provides extra features such as JSON parser, middlewares, plugins, and a simple router.

Create a file named **`server.ts`** and add the following to get Oak started:

```
import { Application } from "jsr:@oak/oak/application";
import { Router } from "jsr:@oak/oak/router";

const router = new Router();
router.get("/", (ctx) => {
  ctx.response.body = `<!DOCTYPE html>
    <html>
      <head><title>Hello oak!</title><head>
      <body>
        <h1>Hello oak!</h1>
      </body>
    </html>
  `;
});

const app = new Application();
const port = 8080;

app.use(router.routes());
app.use(router.allowedMethods());
console.log(`Server running on http://localhost:${port}`);

app.listen({ port: port });
```

Run the server with the following command:

```
deno run --allow-net server.ts
```

Advantages of Using Deno for Web Development

The following are the advantages of using Deno for web development:

- Deno makes becoming a web developer enjoyable by providing a safe and developer-friendly environment for creating web apps.
- Deno has secure defaults, which lowers the possibility of security flaws by requiring express consent for file, network, and environment access.
- Deno comes with built-in TypeScript support, so you do not need any extra setup or tools to write TypeScript code.
- A standard library for common activities, such as file system operations and HTTP servers, is included with Deno.
- If you are developing a more intricate application, you will probably use a web framework to communicate with Deno.

Conclusion

In this chapter, we learned about various topics regarding making, testing, and running a Deno project.

Apart from that we learned about JetBrains integrated development environment and setting up your editor/IDE. Then we learned the command line interface and passing script arguments. Later on, we moved on to working on

React/Next, a well-liked JavaScript user interface development library,

We also learned about Fresh, Deno's most widely used web framework and Astro which is a generator of static sites. Vite is a build tool for web developers. Further, we learned in brief about two static site builder applications, Lume and Docusaurus. At last, in short, we learned about Hono, a lightweight framework for web applications, and Oak, a middleware framework that uses Deno to handle HTTP.

That is the end of this book. Goodbye!

Index

Symbols

A

B

C

D

E